Jean-Paul Sartre: Basic Writings

'This immensely useful volume makes it possible for readers to get a substantial and comprehensive knowledge of Sartrean philosophy. It is a remarkable achievement.'

Hazel E. Barnes, *University of Colorado at Boulder*

'. . . this is a worthwhile and illuminating book.'

Baroness Mary Warnock

'. . . brings together just the right texts, ordered in the right way, to draw the student into Sartre.'

John J. Compton, *Emeritus Professor of Philosophy, Vanderbilt University*

'Stephen Priest's succinct, analytical introductions are invaluable . . . a wide-ranging collection of extracts.'

Christina Howells, *Wadham College, Oxford*

Jean-Paul Sartre is one of the most famous philosophers of the twentieth century. The principal founder of existentialism, a political thinker and famous novelist and dramatist, his work has exerted enormous influence in philosophy, literature, politics and cultural studies. *Jean-Paul Sartre: Basic Writings* is the first collection of Sartre's key philosophical writings and provides an indispensable resource for all students and readers of his work. Stephen Priest's clear and helpful introductions set each reading in context, making the volume an ideal companion for those coming to Sartre's writings for the first time.

A key feature of the anthology is that it includes the full text of Sartre's famous *Existentialism and Humanism*.

The selections are from:
Existentialism and Humanism
Being and Nothingness
Transcendence of the Ego
The Psychology of Imagination
What is Literature?
Search for a Method
Notebooks for an Ethics
The Family Idiot
Critique of Dialectical Reason

D0162423

Stephen Priest is Reader in Philosophy at the University of Edinburgh and a Visiting Scholar of Wolfson College, Oxford. He is the author of *The British Empiricists*, *Theories of the Mind*, *Merleau-Ponty* and *The Subject in Question* and also editor of *Hegel's Critique of Kant*.

Jean-Paul Sartre: Basic Writings

Edited by
Stephen Priest

Routledge
Taylor & Francis Group

LONDON AND NEW YORK

First published 2001
by Routledge
2 Park Square, Milton Park, Abingdon, Oxon, OX14 4RN

Simultaneously published in the USA and Canada
by Routledge
711 Third Avenue, New York, NY 10017

Routledge is an imprint of the Taylor & Francis Group, an informa business

© 2001 Stephen Priest

Typeset in Times by
BOOK NOW Ltd

British Library Cataloguing in Publication Data
A catalogue record for this book is available
from the British Library

Library of Congress Cataloging in Publication Data
Sartre, Jean-Paul, 1905–80
   [Selections. English, 2000]
   Jean-Paul Sartre : basic writings / [edited by] Stephen Priest.
     p.   cm.
   Includes bibliographical references.
   1. Existentialism. I. Priest, Stephen. II. Title.
   B2430.S31 P75 2000
   194–dc21   00–056017

ISBN 978-0-415-21367-7 (hbk)
ISBN 978-0-415-21368-4 (pbk)

Contents

Acknowledgements

The editor and the publishers wish to thank the following for permission to use copyright material:

Jean-Paul Sartre, *Existentialism and Humanism*; translation and introduction by Philip Mairet. First published in Great Britain in 1948 by Methuen, now Methuen Publishing Limited, 215 Vauxhall Bridge Road, London SW1V 1EJ. All rights reserved.

Jean-Paul Sartre, *Esquisse d'une théorie des émotions* (*Sketch for a theory of the emotions*). Copyright © 1939. Paris, Hermann.

Jean-Paul Sartre, *Being and Nothingness*; translated and with an introduction by Hazel E. Barnes, 1956. Used by permission of the Philosophical Library, New York and International Thomson Publishing Services.

"The *Cogito* As Reflective Consciousness" from "the I and the Me" from *Transcendence of the Ego: an Existentialist Theory of Consciousness* by Jean-Paul Sartre, translated and annotated with an introduction by Forrest Williams and Robert Kirkpatrick. Copyright © 1960, The Noonday Press, Inc., New York. Reprinted by permission of Farrar, Straus and Giroux, LLC.

Jean-Paul Sartre, *The Psychology of Imagination*. Copyright © 1948. Reprinted by permission of Philosophical Library Inc. and International Thomson Publishing Services.

Jean-Paul Sartre, *What is Literature?*; translated from French by Bernard Frechtman. Copyright © 1950, Methuen. Used by permission of the Philosophical Library, New York and International Thomson Publishing Services.

Jean-Paul Sartre, *Search for a Method* (New York: Vintage Books, 1963). Originally published in French as "Questions de Méthode" in *Critique de la Raison Dialectique, Vol. 1*. Copyright © 1960 by Editions Gallimard. Reprinted by permission of Georges Borchardt, Inc. and by permission of Alfred A. Knopf, a Division of Random House, Inc.

Jean-Paul Sartre, *Notebooks for an Ethics*; translated by David Pellauer. Reprinted by permission of The University of Chicago Press.

Gustave Flaubert, *The Family Idiot*. Reprinted by permission of The University of Chicago Press.

Jean-Paul Sartre, *Critique of Dialectical Reason, Vol. 1: Theory of Practical Ensembles,* translated by Alan Sheridan Smith. London: Verso, 1991.

Every effort has been made to trace all the copyright holders, but if any have been inadvertently overlooked the publishers will be pleased to make the necessary arrangement at the first opportunity.

1 Sartre in the world

Stephen Priest

Liberty, Equality, Fraternity

Jean-Paul Sartre (1905–80) is one of the greatest French thinkers. A polemical and witty essayist, a metaphysician of subjectivity, a political activist, a revolutionary political theorist, a humanistic novelist, a didactic playwright, his genius lies in his powers of philosophical synthesis and the genre-breaching breadth of his imagination.

In the 1970s, the French journalist Michel Rybalka delivered a lecture on Sartre which divided his intellectual development into three stages: *liberty, equality* and *fraternity*. The three concepts of the slogan of the French revolutionaries of 1789 were used to denote three kinds of philosophy which Sartre endorsed: existentialism, from the mid-1930s, Marxism, increasingly from the Second World War, and anarchism, in the last few years before he died in 1980.

Rybalka's threefold taxonomy is too neat, too clean and, however appealing, it is an over simplification. The adult Sartre was always an existentialist, a practitioner of that style of philosophising which addresses the fundamental problems of human existence: death, anxiety, political, religious and sexual commitment, freedom and responsibility, the meaning of existence itself. It follows that Sartre remained an existentialist during his long Marxist phase and during his final overtly anarchist phase.

Sartre's existentialism was never a pure existentialism. One of his outstanding philosophical syntheses is the fusing of existentialism with phenomenology. The Moravian, German-speaking philosopher Edmund Husserl (1859–1938) and his Austrian teacher, the psychologist and philosopher Franz Brentano (1838–1917), are the founders of phenomenology. Phenomenology is the attempt to explain the possibility of all knowledge, including philosophy, by describing the content and structure of consciousness. It was Husserl's hope that this partly Cartesian and partly Kantian project would place all knowledge on indubitable and incorrigible foundations. Husserlian phenomenology is Cartesian because

it shares with Descartes the ambition of methodically exposing pre-
conceptions and grounding knowledge in certainty. It is Kantian because it
shares with the German idealist philosopher Immanuel Kant (1724–1804)
the 'transcendental' ambition of showing how all knowledge is possible
(notably in his *Critique of Pure Reason*, 1781 and 1787).

The Danish protestant theologian Søren Kierkegaard (1813–59) and
the German atheistic nihilist Friedrich Nietzsche (1844–1900) are
considered the initiators of existentialism. Profound dilemmas of human
existence are explored in the works of the Russian novelist Fydor
Dostoievski (1821–81). His *Notes From the Underground* (1864) particularly anticipates Sartrean themes.

Sartre was not alone or wholly original in marrying phenomenology and
existentialism into a single philosophy. Phenomenology had already
undergone the profound transformation into 'fundamental ontology' at the
hands of the German philosopher Martin Heidegger in his large, if
incomplete, 1927 masterwork, *Being and Time* (*Sein und Zeit*). The
book is an examination of what it means to *be*, especially as this is
disclosed through one's own existence (*Dasein*). The 1945 synthesis of
phenomenology and existentialism in *Phenomenology of Perception*
(*Phénoménologie de la Perception*) by Maurice Merleau-Ponty, Sartre's
philosophical friend and political antagonist, follows hard on the heels of
Sartre's own 1943 synthesis, *Being and Nothingness* (*l'Etre et le Néant*),
with which it is partly inconsistent. Sartre's existentialism, like that of
Merleau-Ponty, is 'existential phenomenology'. Maurice Merleau-Ponty
(1908–61) offers a phenomenology of the body which eschews mind–body
dualism, reductivist materialism and idealism. He influenced Sartre
politically and collaborated in editing *Les Temps Modernes* but broke with
Sartre over what he saw as the latter's 'ultrabolshevism'.[1]

Sartre's Marxism was never a pure Marxism. Not only did he never join
the PCF (Parti Communiste Français), the second massive synthesis of his
philosophical career was the fusion of Marxism with existentialism. The
large 1960 first volume of *Critique of Dialectical Reason* (*Critique de la
Raison Dialectique I*) is an attempt to exhibit existentialist philosophy and
Marxist political theory as not only mutually consistent but as mutually
dependent: as dialectically requiring one another for an adequate
understanding of human reality. This neo-Hegelian 'totalising' philosophy
promises us all the intellectual apparatus we need to understand the
direction of history and the unique human individual in their complex
mutual constitution. The German idealist philosopher G. W. F. Hegel
(1770–1831) thought that philosophical problems could be exhibited as
apparent contradictions that could be relieved, overcome or 'synthesised'
(*aufgehoben*). Hence, for example, human beings are both free and

causally determined, both mental and physical, social and individual, subjective and objective, and so on; not one to the exclusion of the other. 'Synthetic' or 'totalising' philosophy shows seemingly mutually exclusive views to be not only compatible but mutually necessary.[2]

Sartre's Marxism is a 'humanistic' Marxism. His faith in Marxism as the most advanced philosophy of human liberation is tempered by his awareness of the crushing of the aspirations of the human individual by actual Marxism in, for example, the Soviet collectivisation of the farms and purges of the 1930s and 1940s, the supression of the Hungarian uprising of 1956, the decades of atrocities in the Soviet Gulag, the ending of the Prague Spring in 1968. Like the Austrian philosopher Karl Popper, Sartre does not think the oppression of the individual by communism is only a problem of political *practice*.[3] He thinks Marxist political *theory* is flawed. Unlike Popper however, he seeks to humanise Marxist theory rather than reject it utterly. Also unlike Popper, he thinks the neglected resources for a theory of the freedom of the individual can be found within the early writings of Marx himself. The young Marx is to be construed as a kind of proto-existentialist.

The putative synthesis of existentialism and Marxism is extraordinarily ambitious. Some of the most fundamental and intractable problems of metaphysics and the philosophy of mind are obstacles to that synthesis. Classical Marxism is determinist and materialist. Sartre's existentialism is libertarian and phenomenological. Marxism includes a theory of history with prescriptive prognoses for the future. Existentialism explores agency in a spontaneous present which bestows only a derivative existence on past and future. Marxism is a social theory in which the class is the subject and object of change. In existentialism individuals do things and things are done to individuals. Marxism has pretensions to be a science. Existentialism regards science as part of the very problem of dehumanisation and alienation.

Despite the fact that Sartre's overt anarchism emerges only at the end of his life – it is mainly professed in a series of interviews with his then secretary Benny Lévy for the magazine *Le Nouvel Observateur* – Sartre also claimed in the 1970s that he had always been an anarchist.

Anarchism is the theory that the abolition of the state is both possible and desirable. It is true that Sartre was a figure who increasingly challenged authority, especially the authority of the state; from the mocking of bourgeois values in the 1938 novel *Nausea (La Nausée)*, through the support for the Algerian and Cuban rebels in the 1950s and early 1960s, and a host of other left-wing or anti-colonial causes, to his hawking of Maoist newsheets on the streets of Paris in the early 1970s. Sartre never wrote a philosophical synthesis of anarchism and the other philosophies he espoused. Rather, his anarchism is in his behaviour.

Sartre lost patience with communism after the failure of the May 1968 riots to develop into a revolutionary overthrow of French capitalism. He penned the tract *Les Communistes ont peur de la révolution* (*The Communists are Afraid of Revolution*) to condemn what he saw as the betrayal of the revolution by the PCF. His acceptance of the editorship of *La Cause du Peuple* (*The People's Cause*) and other Maoist papers was his last significant Marxist gesture. In the 1970s he struggled to learn the political stance of his young revolutionary colleagues who sometimes viewed the ageing writer with mirth or contempt.

Despite these complexities, there is something profoundly apposite about Rybalka's use of *liberty, equality, fraternity* to denote Sartre's existentialism, Marxism and anarchism. The doctrine that human beings have an ineliminable freedom to choose, no matter how constrained they may be, is essential to Sartre's existentialism. We are the beings who choose what we are. In Marxism, equality is not only a value, it is the core political value: the value upon which other values depend. In anarchism, fraternity makes social harmony in the absence of the power of the state possible. Ordinary human friendships do not need to be sustained by police, army, courts or taxation and this is a clue to the fact that society without the state is possible.

It could be that existentialism, Marxism and anarchism are not mutually consistent. If philosophical problems need to be solved to show their compatibility, then this applies equally to the slogan of the French revolution of 1789. Arguably the history of the Westernised world since the 1790s has conspicuously included the attempt to reconcile the competing claims of liberty, equality and fraternity. If that is right, the avid reception of Sartre's works worldwide becomes more comprehensible.

Sartre, then, is a synthesiser. It is not unusual for the greatness of a philosopher to consist in being a synthesiser. Plato reconciled the static, rationalist, monist world-picture of Parmenides with the pluralistic, empirical, process ontology of Heraclitus. Descartes, wrote his dualist philosophy to reconcile the medieval theological world picture he had inherited, with the findings of the new physical science.[4] Kant, consciously if messily, synthesised the continental rationalism of Descartes, Leibniz and Spinoza with the British empiricism of Hobbes, Locke, Berkeley and Hume. Marxism, as Lenin pointed out, is a meeting of French socialism, British economics, and German philosophy. Sartre's syntheses of phenomenology and existentialism in the 1940s and existentialism with Marxism from the late 1950s take their place with these others in the history of philosophy. They are at least as philosophically significant as the synthesis of psychoanalysis and Marxism of his German-American contemporary, the Frankfurt School radical Herbert Marcuse, who was so much more influential than Sartre in the *événements* of May '68.[5]

Who was Sartre?

He was born Jean-Paul Charles Aymard Sartre on 21st June 1905, in Paris. His naval officer father died of a tropical disease the following year and so Sartre was brought up by his doting mother and rather austere maternal grandparents. His grandfather, Charles Schweitzer (who was the uncle of Albert Schweitzer the famous Protestant theologian) dominated the household. Paradoxically, he treated Sartre as an adult and Sartre's mother as a child.

Sartre was allowed no friends of his own age so he sought the companionship of the books in his grandfather's large library. Educated at home by Charles until he was eleven, Sartre attended a string of Lycées until intellectual and personal liberation came in the form of admittance to the École Normale Supérieure in 1924.

It was at the École Normale that Sartre met his lifelong companion and lover Simone de Beauvoir (1908–86). She was to become the brilliant feminist existentialist author of *Le Deuxième Sexe* (*The Second Sex*), (1948) many philosophical novels, and the most significant work of existentialist ethics: *Pour Une Morale de L'Ambiguité* (*For a Morality of Ambiguity*) (1944). The mutual influence of de Beauvoir and Sartre is immense. They tested their ideas against each other. Their relationship seems to have allowed of a frankness extremely rare between two human beings.[6]

It was usually in the company of de Beauvoir that Sartre travelled abroad. At first just for holidays, later at the invitation of political leaders, Sartre visited between the 1930s and 1980s Spain, England, Germany, Austria, Czechoslovakia, Swizterland, Greece, Morocco, Algeria, Norway, Iceland, Scotland, Ireland, China, Italy, Yugoslavia, Cuba, the USA, Russia, Brazil and Japan. Some countries he visited more than once. He met Tito in Yugoslavia, Breznef in Russia and Castro in Cuba, as well as the Chinese communist leadership.

Sartre's literary and philosophical output is immense. What enabled him to write so much was a combination of a naturally strong physical constitution, high motivation, an extremely efficient writing routine, and the intermittent abuse of amphetamine tablets which increased his production, if not his coherence.

Sartre suffered problems with his eyes. In 1909 he caught a cold which led to a leucoma in his right eye and strabism. Henceforth, he had hardly any vision left in that eye and was left with the distinctive squint which would be exploited with ruthless hilarity by political cartoonists when he became a world figure. In the 1970s he went blind. Fortunately, by 1975 (when he was seventy) he felt able to claim in an interview 'I have said everything I had to say' (*Life/Situations*, p. 20). Although Sartre sometimes suffered from the symptoms of stress he was blessed with great physical and intellectual stamina.

Many conjectures could be made about his motivation to write. Perhaps in his solitary childhood his early reading and writing was a substitute for the human conversation and playful childhood interchanges that were denied him. Certainly, the release from his grandfather's orderly study into the comparative chaos of the world fascinated him. The contrast motivates his existentialism and perhaps his later socialism. Perhaps he wrote because of the excitement of realising he could write. It is certain that he hated his childhood and much of his writing is writing against it.

Sartre's writing routine was as follows: at 8.30 am he got up. From 9.30 am to 1.30 pm he would write. (Four hours in the morning and four hours in the evening, that was his only rule.) From 2.00–4.00 pm he would lunch in a café such as Les Deux Magots or Café Flore on Boulevard Saint Germaine, La Coupoule in Montparnasse or Les Trois Mousquetaires on the Avenue de Maine, perhaps work there on some writing but certainly meet friends for conversation. Before 5.00 pm he would walk home and the second four-hour stretch of writing would be from 5.00–9.00 pm. At 9.00 pm he would typically walk to Simone de Beauvoir's flat and they would talk and listen to music. Sartre would be asleep by 12.30 am and, in the morning, would breakfast in a local café, between 8.30 and 9.30 am. The apropriately named La Liberté on the corner of rue de la Gaité and Boulevard Edgar Quinet was his favourite for breakfast. He would not overeat. Although he drank plenty of black coffee and smoked excessively, he drank very little alcohol. His social life took place in the afternoons. Three o'clock in the afternoon, he thought, was too late to finish anything and too late to start anything. The first volume of the *Critique of Dialectical Reason* was written at three times the normal speed because Sartre took twenty amphetamine tablets per day to finish it. Although he was physically strong, or perhaps partly because of it, Sartre took little care of his body. Sport bored him. He was happy to abuse his body to accelerate his written output.

Sartre never owned a house or an apartment. For long stretches he would rent rooms in hotels. Indeed, his personal possessions were few: modest clothes, cigarettes, writing materials. When money came, say from Gallimard, he would carry all of it as a wad of banknotes in his wallet donating it copiously to friends or worthy causes. Michel Rybalka reports that on arriving to interview Sartre about *Critique of Dialectical Reason* they had to walk to a local bookshop to buy a copy. The interview was hard to conduct. Sartre wanted to know all about the role of the committed journalist.

The Second World War is the most decisive turning point of Sartre's intellectual career. Before the war, Sartre was an individualist in theory and practice. His philosophy and literature treated human subjects as atomic agents. Although he spent 1933–4 in Germany studying phenomenology, he seems to have been oblivious to the Nazi rise to power, with the exception of noting that the communists had gone underground in Berlin. Despite the anti-Fascist sentiments of 'The Wall' and 'Childhood of a Leader', and despite his mocking cynicism towards the middle classes in *Nausea*, his own life remained that of an essentially apolitical writer of growing reputation. Some of his friends joined the Popular Front but he did not. Nor did he show any of the overt political commitment to the republicans in the Spanish Civil War (1936–9) that motivated so many left-wing intellectuals in Europe and the USA, if not to fight, then at least to write. During the 1938 Munich crisis he was a pacifist. When war comes in September 1939 he is anti-Nazi but for the nationalist reason that France could be invaded; a reason he would later regard as embarrassingly inadequate. The Sartre of the 1930s had no developed political consciousness. Sartre's immediate impact in the post-war period was still not as a Marxist but as the world leader of the philosophical vogue called 'Existentialism'.

On Monday 29th October 1945 in Le Club Maintenant ('The Now Club') at 8 rue Jean Goujon, Sartre delivered his lecture *L'Existentialisme est un Humanisme*. This title is usually translated into English as 'Existentialism and Humanism' but the literal rendering is 'Existentialism is a Humanism', meaning that Existentialism is a kind of humanist philosophy. Sartre expressed regret that this short text, delivered without notes, came to be taken as an authoritive guide to his thought. He also felt uncomfortable with the label 'Existentialist'. Even as Existentialism flourished in the cafés, theatres and bars in a way that exceeded the popularity of Henri Bergson's philosophy after the First World War, Sartre's serious commitment was to revolutionary Marxism.

What was it about the Second World War which turned Sartre the naive individualist into Sartre the political figure? In an interview late in his life he says of being called up for military service in September 1939 that this was what made him suddenly realise that he was a *social being*. He spent the 'phoney war', September 1939–May 1940, in the meterological corps of the French army, on the militarily ineffectual Maginot Line, taking the opportunity to make copious notes that would much later be *Les Carnets de la Drôle de Guerre* (*War Diaries*) (1983). The diaries anticipate themes in *Being and Nothingness*. It was his capture by the Wehrmacht on 21st June 1940, along with thousands of other French soldiers, and his incarceration in a prisoner-of-war camp in Triers that made Sartre realise that he was subject to political forces and needed to take political action. On his escape in March 1941 he helped found the resistance group *Socialisme et Liberté*.

It could be that the experience of the 1939–45 war left Sartre with two enduring models or attitudes for his politics in the period 1945–80. The Nazi occupation of France provided him with a stark contrast between oppressor and oppressed. It seemed so obviously right to side with democracy, socialism and France against the violent totalitarianism of the invader (even if, for many of Sartre's contemporaries, collaboration or passive acquiescence was a more prudent strategy). This clean distinction between the rights of the oppressed and the wrongs of the oppressors is a moral distinction that informs nearly all his post-war political commitments. The French state and the Algerian people, the Batista regime and the Cuban rebels, the USA and the Vietnamese communists, the Franco regime in Madrid and the ETA separatists, German business and government and the Baader Meinhof gang, the Renault management and the striking car workers: in each case Sartre unquestioningly divides political antagonists into oppressor and oppressed, immoral and moral. The Nazi occupying forces and the French resistance are the prototype for these clashes of Good and Evil.

The other enduring political attitude bequeathed to Sartre by the Second World War was an immense sympathy for the Soviet Union. In their café arguments in the 1950s Sartre would allow himself to criticise Soviet policy, but if Albert Camus or Maurice Merleau-Ponty joined him he would spring to the Soviet Union's defence. It was not just the fact that the Soviet Union was the most effective antidote to Nazism in the period 1941–5, it was also that, in Sartre's eyes, the communist French resistance seemed so much more effective than the Gaullist, pro-Western, French resistance in killing Germans and sabotaging the Nazi military economy. His admiration for the communist resistance fighters was immense. In himself he felt ashamed and inadequate: ashamed of his bourgeois upbringing, ashamed of his privileged education and lifestyle, ashamed of his political and military ineffectiveness as an intellectual rather than a fighter.

Indeed, it was mainly by writing that he resisted. In January 1943 he joined the *Comité National des Ecrivains* and in 1944 started writing for the resistance paper *Combat*. He staged the politically didactic *Bariona* in the Stalag and *Les Mouches* (*The Flies*) in Paris in 1943, the descent of the flies onto Argos being a barely concealed allegory for the Nazi occupation of France. In September 1944 Sartre formed the editorial committee for the socialist literary, political and philosophical review *Les Temps Modernes*. In 1945 he declined the Légion d'honneur.

Sartre entered the Second World War young but emerged middle aged. He was thirty-four when it began in 1939 and forty when it ended in 1945, so it was the mature Sartre who was the socialist Sartre.

The Sartre that emerged from the 1945 conflict was increasingly a Marxist, an eloquent and committed revolutionary who felt a duty to speak out for the dispossessed of the world, a mass media critic of French colonialism in Indo-China and Algeria, the Batista regime in Cuba, the treatment of the Basques in Spain, and the American involvement in Vietnam. His serious theoretical works were increasingly political works, from the June 1946 essay 'Materialism and Revolution' (*Materialisme et Révolution* in *Les Temps Modernes*) through the massive first volume of *Critique of Dialectical Reason* (1960) and its prefatory *Questions of Method* (*Questions de Méthode*) until his final loss of patience with Marxism in the aftermath of '68. In October 1948 his works were placed on the prohibited list of the Catholic church. A perennial irritant to the Gaullist government and a communist 'fellow traveller', Sartre always eschewed formal membership of the Parti Communiste Français, which he criticised as doctrinally fixed, inauthentic and too far to the right. In February 1948 Sartre joined in the attempt to form a coalition of left-wing political parties, the Rassemblement Démocratique Révolutionaire (RDR) but this proved a failure when the PCF left. In January 1950 Sartre and Merleau-Ponty jointly condemned the Soviet Gulag system. Nevertheless, Sartre worked closely with the PCF, for example over the Henri Martin affair, until the Soviet crushing of the Hungarian uprising of 1956 which he condemned in the November of that year. In the same month he condemned the Anglo–French invasion of Egypt in the Suez Crisis.

The post-war Sartre was willing to take risks. From January 1955 *Les Temps Modernes* officially condemned French rule in Algeria and Sartre spoke out at press conferences and at demonstrations. On 19th July 1961 Sartre's rented accommodation at 42 rue Bonaparte was bombed, probably by *pieds noirs* appalled by his urging the French to withdraw from Algeria. On 7th January of the following year it was bombed again, so he moved to an appartment on Quai Blériot. That was bombed too so he had to move to 222 boulevard Raspail. During the Cuban missile crisis of 1963 Sartre pleaded with the Soviet government not to give in to American pressure to withdraw their weapons from Cuban soil. Regarded by many as irresponsible behaviour in a world on the brink of nuclear holocaust, this for Sartre was an authentic political act.

In 1964 Sartre was offered the Nobel Prize for Literature but refused it, adding that he would also have declined the Lenin Prize had it been offered him. Authentic writing is not subject to an authority with the power to grant or withhold prizes.

From July 1966 Sartre sat on the International Wars Crimes Tribunal formed by Bertrand Russell to investigate US military actions in Vietnam. He condemned US involvement in south east Asia at the tribunal's press conferences in 1967, taking the chair at the Stockholm session of 2nd–10th May. On 19th December 1969 he condemned the My Lai killings, on French television.

In the *événements* of May 1968 Sartre's aim, like that of the Marxists, situationists and anarchists, was to turn the demonstrations and strikes of the trades union and student movements into the revolutionary overthrow of French capitalism. Taking to the streets with the students and workers amidst tear-gas, flying paving-stone fragments and CRS baton charges, he urged them to revolutionary violence. He was interviewed by Daniel Cohn-Bendit on Radio Luxembourg on 11th May and addressed the crowd at the Sorbonne on the 20th. One of the slogans daubed on walls was 'Pouvoir à l'Imagination', 'Power to the Imagination'. When capitalism was not overthrown and the Gaullist government did not fall, he publicly held the PCF responsible in a July interview in the German magazine *Der Spiegel*, and despaired of it as a genuinely revolutionary movement.

In April 1970, when the two young editors of the Maoist paper *La Cause du Peuple* were arrested, Sartre took over their editorial role and spoke in their defence at their trial on 27th May. Distributing the paper in the street he was bundled into a police van and arrested. However, De Gaulle soon had him released, explaining that one does not imprison Voltaire. From October 1970 to the following April he actively supported the long strike by Renault car workers, being finally ejected from the Renault factory by police on 14th April 1972 and being present at the burial of the Renault worker Pierre Overney on 14th March.

From 1972 Sartre's sympathies were increasingly anarchist. This emerges in the series of interviews conducted by Benny Lévy and Philippe Gavi, which began in the November. Nineteen seventy-two also saw the height of the Baader Meinhof gang's violent attempts to destroy capitalist hegenomy over the Third World. When its leading members were caught, tried and imprisoned by the West German government Sartre gave an interview to *Der Spiegel* urging their release, and visited Andreas Baader in Stammheim jail on 4th December 1974. When Baader and other gang members died in prison, Sartre insisted that they had been murdered by the authorities. In 1976 he led the campaign to release Mikhail Stern from political imprisonment in the Soviet Union.

In 1978–9 Sartre devoted his remaining political energies to speaking out on behalf of Vietnamese refugees and to trying to further the Arab–Israeli peace process. He had, he said, many good friends on both sides of that conflict.

Sartre fell into unconsciousness on 13th April 1980 and died at 9.00 pm on the 15th in Broussais hospital. He had arterial blockages which affected the functioning of his lungs and kidneys. Tens of thousands filled the streets, following the funeral cortege to Montparnasse cemetery on the 19th.

Sartre's works

Sartre's oeuvre oscillates between fact and fiction and ends as a synthesis of the two. His juvenalia are literary; already at thirteen years of age he was penning a novel about Goetz von Berlichingen. Five years later his 'L'Ange du Morbide' and 'Jesus la Chouette' appear in *La Revue Sans Titre* in 1923. It is just over a decade later, on his return from a formative visit to the French Institute at Berlin, that he began work on the novel that would be *La Nausée* (*Nausea*). The 1933–4 period in Germany was spent learning phenomenology, and in Sartre's first serious publications we can see him situating himself partly within and partly outside that philosophy.

La Transcendance de l'Ego (*The Transcendence of the Ego*) appeared in 1937 as a long paper in the 1936/7 volume of *Recherches Philosophiques*, a distinguished journal of academic philosophy. Sartre attacks Husserl's thesis that there exists an irreducibly subjective source of one's own consciousness called the 'transcendental ego': an inner self that is a condition for the possibility of a person's experience. Sartre argues that the postulation of the transcendental ego is phenomenologically illegitimate. Phenomenology describes only what appears to consciousness. No transcendental ego appears to consciousness, so no consistent phenomenologist can maintain the existence of the transcendental ego. (The difference between Sartre and Husserl here is in some ways analogous to that between Hume and Descartes on the self.)

When Sartre was a philosophy undergraduate at the École Normale Supérieure he wrote his final year dissertation on the philosophy and psychology of the imagination: 'L'Image dans la vie psychologique' ('The Image in Psychological Life'). On his return from Berlin he rewrote this as the 1936 book *L'Imagination*. It reads mainly as a survey of metaphysical and psychological theories, though its final chapter entails a partial break with Husserl on the *epoché*, or methodological reduction of the world to its appearance, on intentionality, or the 'aboutness' of all consciousness, and on the mental image, which Sartre treats as an act not a psychic entity. Sartre's other book on the imagination, *L'Imaginaire: Psychologie Phénoménologique de l'Imagination* (*The Imaginary*) (1940), takes up this theme. Rather like Wittgenstein and Ryle, Sartre argues that a mental image is not a private picture, a non-physical psychological item that may be scrutinised by introspection.[7] Mental images are mental acts directed to objects in the world that may or may not exist. We see here already a departure from the phenomenological description of the interiority of consciousness and an endorsement of the neo-Heideggerian existentialist thesis that our being, including our psychological being, is 'being-in-the world'.

Like the early philosophical writings, the novel *Nausea* published in April 1938 is a work of both existentialism and phenomenology. The central character, Antoine Roquentin, confronts the brute contingency and meaninglessness of his own existence in a way that produces existential angst and the nausea of the novel's title. The thesis that existence, including one's own existence, is contingent rather than necessary is essential to existentialism. There are also many passages in *Nausea* when Roquentin confronts the world as it would appear if it were subjected to neo-Husserlian phenomenological description. On the bus, on the sea shore, looking at a chesnut tree, objects are reduced to phenomena. What is is what appears to be.

Nausea is an overtly philosophical novel. To the extent that Sartre's portrayals of Roquentin's experiences are internally consistent, credibility is lent to existential phenomenology. Roquentin confronts philosophical problems as problems in life. The problems of induction, universals and particulars, how language refers to the world, objective truth, and what it is for something to *be* are all sources of profound anxiety and discomfort to him.

Although *Nausea* is a strongly didactic novel, it has one strength lacking in, say, Albert Camus' *The Plague* (*La Peste*, 1948) or Tolstoy's *War and Peace* (1868–9). Although Tolstoy is a stronger artist than Sartre, he paints in more detail, he constructs mentality with at once a greater economy and a greater plausibility, his grasp of history is less naive, Tolstoy can only include philosophy in *War and Peace* by addressing the reader directly. Tolstoy has to lecture us for many pages to convince us of his atomistic historical determinism. With slightly more subtlety, Camus in *The Plague* philosophises about the confrontation with death and meaninglessness through conversations between Dr. Rieux (who turns out to be the narrator) and his humanistic neighbour, Tarrou. The reader is allowed to eavesdrop on their profoundity. Sartre has the better of both these writers in weaving existentialism and phenomenology into the experience of his character. Although the experience is necessarily thereby unusual, Sartre himself does not have to intervene to tell us about philosophy, nor does Roquentin.

Sartre's second significant work of fiction is the collection of short stories *Le Mur (The Wall)*, published in 1939. In each story at least one central existential problem is lived *from the inside* by a fictional character. Notably, the condemned Republican volunteer Pablo Ibieta contemplates being shot at dawn by a Fascist firing squad in the Spanish Civil War story 'Le Mur' which gives the collection its title. Two very different kinds of bad faith, or refusal to recognise one's own freedom and its consequent responsibility, are exhibited by Lulu in 'Intimité' ('Intimacy') and by the young Lucien Fleurier in 'L'Enfance d'un Chef' ('Childhood of a Leader'). Lulu feels unable to quite leave her husband, Henri, or quite commit herself to the new lover, Pierre, and by choosing neither allows herself to be manipulated by her friend Rirette. Lucien becomes an anti-semite and a fascist French nationalist leader, thus committing that double act of bad faith that Sartre calls 'being a swine' (*salaud*): not only denying one's own freedom by the adoption of a ready-made ideology, but denying others their own freedom.

In *The Wall* Sartre experiments stylistically, for example by unexpectedly changing tenses or changing grammatical person, sometimes within a single sentence. He is unable to do this with the confidence and lack of artificiality that one finds in Dos Passos or Joyce who are Sartre's influences.[8] It is, however, the beginning of that disavowal of the mastery of the author over the authored that will be essential to the mature literary theory of *Qu'est que la Littérature?* (*What is Literature?*) (1948).

In *Esquisse d'une théorie des émotions* (*Sketch For a Theory of Emotions*) (1938) Sartre criticises the scientific or pseudo-scientific psychology of his time, including psycho-analysis, introduces us to phenomenological psychology and advances the provocative thesis that we *choose* our emotions. Rather than my being involuntarily subject to a wave of emotion, I choose, say, to be sad and to cry at a strategic moment, to control another's behaviour or evade the other's control of myself.

The culmination of Sartre's fusion of existentialism and phenomenology is the massive and complex philosophical treatise *L'Etre et le Néant* (*Being and Nothingness*) (1943). The book can be read in many ways: as a reconciliation of Heidegger's thought with much of what Heidegger rejected in Husserl, as an antidote to the positivism and pseudo-science that dominates twentieth-century philosophy, as the imposition of the ontological constraints of 'existentialism' on phenomenological 'essentialism', as an atheistic metaphysics, as a series of profound psychological and sociological observations.

The 'being' of the book's title is divided by Sartre into two types, roughly speaking subjective being and objective being, which he labels 'l'être-pour-soi' ('being-for-itself') and 'l'être-en-soi' ('being-in-itself'). This neo-Hegelian distinction is between the active existing of a free conscious human individual, and the passive being of inert non-human reality. The 'nothingness' of the book's title is introduced into the world by human reality. Only human beings have the power to imaginatively negate their surroundings. I am myself a kind of nothingness at the heart of being.

In chapters on freedom, bad faith, temporality, transcendence, and social relations Sartre describes the existential structures of human reality. The complexity of insight, the richness of description, exceed Heidegger's *Being and Time* and Merleau-Ponty's *Phenomenology of Perception*. What is perhaps most striking about the book is that where a scientific treatise would seek mechanisms 'behind the scenes', or a law-like physical reality beyond appearance, Sartre treats everything as 'surface'. Appearance is reality. It is science that fabricates a world of abstractions and our daily world of choice and consciousness is concrete reality.

Sartre left *Being and Nothingness* unfinished. A large impression of the moral philosophy promised in its closing pages appeared posthumously as *Cahiers pour une morale* (*Notebooks for an Ethics*) (1983). There is however something in principle incompletable about Sartrean existential phenomenology. If the distinction between being-for-itself and being-in-itself is Hegelian in origin, it resists any Hegelian overcoming or synthesis in absolute knowing. Although human reality is the desire to be God, this desire is forever frustrated. In this incompleteness, this perpetual deferral, lies our capacity for self-definition, our freedom. We make ourselves what we are by our choices and this process of self-definition is only complete at the moment of death.

What is Literature? (1948) is an attempt to answer the questions: What is writing?, Why write? and For whom does one write?, and ends with a meditation on the situation of the writer in the post-liberation France of 1947. Sartre insists that one should write for one's own age, not for posterity, not to restore the past, not to gain status or money. Literature must be committed literature or engaged literature (*la littérature engagée*). The literature of a given age is alienated and inauthentic when it does not recognise within itself its own freedom but subjects itself to a prevailing ideology or ruling interest. The writer should write to express their own freedom and liberate the reader. Committed literature is committed to freedom.

A paradigm case of Sartrean committed literature is the *Roads to Freedom* (*Les Chemins de la liberté*) trilogy: *The Age of Reason* (*L'Age de Raison*, 1945), *The Reprieve* (*Le Sursis*, 1945), and *Iron in the Soul* (*La Mort dans l'Âme* , 1949). Parts of a fourth volume *The Last Chance* (*La Dernière Chance*) were serialised in the November and December 1949 issues of *Les Temps Modernes*. In a famous passage, which concludes the first part of the last complete volume of the trilogy, *Iron in the Soul*, Mathieu Delarue, the previously ineffectual schoolteacher, acts meaningfully and decisively for the first time in his life. Deserted by their bourgeois officers during the May–June 1940 Nazi invasion of France he and his comrades choose to resist to the death the oncoming Wehrmacht from the cover of a village clock tower:

> Mathieu was in no hurry. He kept his eye on this man; he had plenty of time. The German army is vulnerable. He fired. The man gave a funny little jerk and fell on his stomach, throwing his arms forward like somebody learning to swim.
>
> (*Iron in the Soul*, Penguin, Harmondsworth, 1963, p. 216)

In the narrative, Mathieu's shooting of the German infantryman is a freely chosen and deliberate act for which he alone is responsible. It is a deeply significant act metaphysically, personally, and politically. Metaphysically it is the termination of a life. Personally it is Mathieu's recognition of his own freedom; 'For years he had tried, in vain, to act' (p. 217) Sartre reminds us. Politically it is the commitment to resist the forces of right-wing totalitarianism.

The Germans shell the clock tower and one by one Mathieu's comrades are killed. Mathieu is alone and becomes infused with the feeling that he is going to die. Facing death alone, as in a profound sense we all must, he realises his own freedom:

> Just time enough to fire at that smart officer, at all the Beauty of the Earth, at the street, at the flowers, at the gardens, at everything he had loved. Beauty dived downwards, like some obscene bird. But Mathieu went on firing. He fired. He was cleansed. He was all powerful. He was free.
>
> (ibid., p. 225)

In the play *Men Without Shadows* (*Morts sans Sépulture*, 1946), one of Sartre's most poignant pieces, captured French resistance fighters are being tortured and interrogated by Nazi collaborators. Even under torture, Sartre has his characters choose whether to talk, scream or remain silent. Sorbier deliberately throws himself through the window to his death rather than disclose the location of the group's leader. Canoris chooses to talk. Even under the most extreme duress we still have a choice according to Sartre. Indeed, under duress, the agonising reality of our freedom of choice is inescapable. Bad faith or the *denial* of freedom is then impossible.

Our freedom is a burden that confronts us. It is a source of profound anxiety because it carries with it a terrible responsibility. I and I alone can make my choices and I and I alone am accountable to the rest of humanity for my actions. Sartre illustrates this with an episode from his own life experience in a passage in *Existentialism and Humanism*. During the Second World War one of his pupils approached him with this dilemma: His elder brother had been killed by the Germans in 1940 and the young man burned to avenge his brother's death and fight in the struggle against Nazism. On the other hand, the young man's mother was sick with grief at his brother's death, lived alone, and needed her remaining son to care for her. If he joins the Free French he deserts his mother. If he stays with his mother he does nothing to avenge his brother or fight the Nazis. Sartre's advice to his tormented pupil was this: 'You are free, therefore choose' (p. 38).

Sartre cannot make his choice for him. To choose an adviser is to make a choice. It is also to choose the kind of advice one would like to hear. In this example Sartre turns the tables on the determinist. It is the lived confrontation with freedom that is concrete and real. Determinism is a scientific abstraction. Even if determinism *were* true it would not be of the least help to the young man in resolving his dilemma. Nothing can lift from us the burden of our freedom.

Sartre says we are *condemned* to be free. We did not choose to be free; indeed, we did not choose to exist. In the Heideggerian idiom, Sartre says we are *thrown* into the world. We have no pre-determined essence. First of all we exist, then we face the lifelong burden of creating ourselves, generating our essence by free choices. We are nothing other than what we do and the only constraint on our freedom is this: we are are not free not to be free.

The recognition of our own freedom causes such anxiety that we pretend to ourselves that we are not free. The multitude of behavioural strategies which make up this pretence Sartre calls *bad faith*. He thinks most of us are in bad faith most of the time. It is usually only *in extremis,* like Mathieu in the clock tower, that we are confronted with the reality of our own freedom. The *locus classicus* of bad faith is in *Being and Nothingness*:

> Let us consider the waiter in the café. His movement is quick and forward, a little too precise, a little too rapid. He comes toward the patrons with a step a little too quick. He bends forwards a little too eagerly; his voice, his eyes express an interest a little too solicitous for the order of the customer [. . .] He is playing, he is amusing himself. But what is he playing? We need not watch long before we can explain it: he is playing *at being* a café waiter.
>
> (p. 59)

Committed literature combats bad faith.

Questions of Method prefaces the first volume of *Critique of Dialectical Reason* (1960). (It had appeared in an earlier version in a Polish magazine in 1958.) Sartre argues that existentialism and Marxism are mutually necessary in the explanation of human reality. Henceforth, the lived present of the choosing existential individual is located in history. Sartre says 'philosophy' does not exist, there are only philosophies. Any philosophy is an expression of a rising social class, and in modern history there have been three: the bourgeois individualism of Descartes and Locke, the idealist philosophy of Kant and Hegel and now Marxism. It is not possible to think 'beyond' a philosophy unless the historical conditions of its genesis are replaced. Hence, any putative anti-Marxist philosophy can only be a return to pre-Marxist ideas according to Sartre. In *Questions of Method* Sartre allocates only a modest place for existentialism, calling it an 'ideology', not in the Marxist sense, but in the sense of a parasitical system living in the margin of knowledge. Existentialism is prima facie opposed to Marxism but needs to be dialectically incorporated into a wider Marxism, rather as Kierkegaard's existentialist individualism is puportedly opposed to Hegel's 'totalising' philosophy but ultimately subsumable by it.

In the final section of *Questions of Method* Sartre outlines the Progressive–Regressive Method. The aim is nothing less than the total explanation of the human. We have to understand, according to Sartre, that humanity makes history and history makes humanity. Humanity fashions the world in accordance with human ends and projects. The human-manipulated world of history constitutes humanity in turn. It follows that the human–history relation is dialectical, or reciprocal. In this framework Sartre seeks to overcome the 'contradictions' between existentialism and Marxism: the individual and the social, the free and the determined, the conscious and the material, the subjective and the objective, the actual and the historical.

These problems are addressed in the complex Marxist and Hegelian vocabulary of *Critique of Dialectical Reason*. Sartre of course envisages this book as a synthesis of Marxism and existentialism. In it existentialism is allocated a more salient role than the modest remarks in *Questions of Method* would suggest.

Sartre is also a biographer, but not a conventional biographer. Aside from the autobiography *Les Mots* (*Words*) (1963), there exist *Baudelaire* (1947), *Saint Genet, comédien et martyr* (1952) and the massive three volume study of Flaubert: *L'Idiot de la Famille* (*The Family Idiot*) (1971). His aim, especially in the *Flaubert*, is nothing less than the total explanation of one human being by another. Sartre's method is the Progressive–Regressive Method. Why Flaubert? Because Gustave Flaubert (1821–80), realist and objectivist author of *Madame Bovary* (1857) and perfecter of the short story in *Trois Contes* (1877) is the inauthentic antithesis of Sartre. By repressing his own passions and by writing with an almost scientific detachment Flaubert writes uncommitted literature.

Sartre intends the *Flaubert* as a 'true novel' that overcomes the 'contradiction' between fact and fiction. The Progressive–Regressive Method of *Questions of Method* and the *Critique* is deployed alongside the existential psychoanalysis of *Being and Nothingness* and Sartre's fictional imagination to understand the total Flaubert: psychological interiority and social exteriority, Flaubert in the world, history's constitution of Flaubert and Flaubert's reciprocal effect on history. Although Sartre's Maoist friends around *La Cause du Peuple* had no patience with what they saw as the indulgent bourgeois individualism of the *Flaubert* project, it may in fact be read as the synthesis of Sartrean syntheses: Marxism and existentialism, existential phenomenology and psychoanalysis, and fact and fiction.

Since Sartre's death in 1980 a number of significant works have been published: *War Diaries* (*Les Carnets de la Drôle de Guerre*, 1983) composed on the Maginot Line during the 'phoney war' period September 1939–May 1940, *Notebooks for an Ethics* (*Cahiers pour une morale*, 1983) which provides some of the moral philosophy promised at the end of *Being and Nothingness*, two volumes of correspondence with Simone de Beauvoir and others: *Lettres au Castor et à Quelques Autres, I 1926–39, II 1940–63* (1983), the screenplay for a film about Freud, *Le Scenario Freud* (1984), the second volume of *Critique of Dialectical Reason* (*Critique de la Raison Dialectique, Tome II: L'intelligibilité de l'Histoire*, 1986) and the metaphysically trenchant *Truth and Existence* (*Vérité et Existence*, 1989). The thesis that self-definition ceases at the moment of death clearly needs to be treated with some caution.[9]

Notes

1 See Maurice Merleau-Ponty, *Phenomenology of Perception* (London, 1962), *The Visible and the Invisible* (Evanston, 1968), *Adventures of the Dialectic* (Evanston, 1973) and Stephen Priest *Merleau-Ponty* (London, 1998)

2 The form of this kind of philosophical problem solving, dialectic, is presented by Hegel in his Science of Logic (*Wissenshaft der Logic*, Nuremberg 1812–16). It is given content in The *Phenomenology of Spirit* (*Phänomenolgie des Geistes*, Jena 1807), The *Philosophy of Right* (*Grundlinien der Philosophie des Rechts*, Berlin 1821) the volumes of the *Encyclopaedia of the Philosophical Sciences* (Heidelberg, 1815–30) and posthumously published series of lectures. See Michael Inwood (ed.), *Hegel: Selections* (London and New York, 1989).

3 Karl Popper (1902–94) attacks the philosophical foundations of right-wing

totalitarianism in the first volume of *The Open Society and Its Enemies* (London, 1945) (subtitled 'Plato') and left wing totalitarianism in the second volume (subtitled 'Hegel and Marx'). The assumption that what happens in the present is historically inevitable is criticised in *The Poverty of Historicism* (London, 1957). See also Anthony O'Hear, *Karl Popper* (London, 1980) and Bryan Magee, *Popper* (London 1973).

4 The philosopher and mathematician René Descartes (1596–1650) attempted to reconcile the theocentric world picture of the middle ages with the emerging modern science of the seventeenth century. Although Sartre rejected Descartes' substantial distinction between mind and matter, he inherited his profound concern with human subjectivity. See René Descartes, *Discourse on Method and the Meditations* (Harmondsworth, 1974), Stephen Priest, *Theories of the Mind* (London, 1991) and Anthony Kenny, *Descartes: A Study of His Philosophy* (New York, 1968).

5 The critical theorist Herbert Marcuse synthesises Freudianism and Marxism in *Eros and Civilisation* (Boston, 1955). In *One Dimensional Man* (Boston, 1964) and *Negations* (Harmondsworth, 1968), he argues that the capitalist system defuses the opposition of those it exploits, by a combination of liberal 'repressive tolerance', the construal of everything as a commodity and the ideological production of consumerist appetite. See Alasdair MacIntyre, *Marcuse* (London, 1970). On the May 1968 *événements* see Charles Posner (ed.), *Reflections on the Revolution in France: 1968* (Harmondsworth, 1970).

6 On de Beauvoir see T. Keefe, *Simone de Beauvoir: A Study of Her Writings* (London, 1984), M. Evans, *Simone de Beauvoir: A Feminist Mandarin* (London, 1985) and Judith Okely, *Simone de Beauvoir: A Re-Reading* (London, 1986). On the relationship between de Beauvoir and Sartre see Alex Madsen, *Hearts and Minds: The Common Journey of Simone de Beauvoir and Jean-Paul Sartre* (New York, 1977) and Kate Fullbrook and Edward Fullbrook, *Simone de Beauvoir and Jean-Paul Sartre: the Remaking of a Twentieth-Century Legend* (New York, 1994).

7 The Austrian philosopher Ludwig Wittgenstein and the English philosopher Gilbert Ryle attack the Cartesian idea that psychological concepts take on meaning only by reference to inner and private mental states and argue that there have to be third person criteria for psychological ascriptions. See Gilbert Ryle, *The Concept of Mind* (London, 1949), Ludwig Wittgenstein, *Philosophical Investigations* (Oxford, 1952) and Stephen Priest, *Theories of the Mind* (London, 1991).

8 The American modernist novelist John dos Passos deployed the radical technique of 'montage' in his *U.S.A.* trilogy (New York, 1930, 1933, 1936). The literary inventiveness and authentic concern with human reality shown by the Irish novelist James Joyce (1882–1941) in his *Ulysses* (Paris, 1922) possibly makes it the most significant work of fiction of the twentieth century.

9 Sartre speaks frankly about his life and work in 'Simone de Beauvoir interviews Sartre' in Jean-Paul Sartre, *Life/Situations: Essays Written and Spoken*, trans. Paul Auster and Lydia Davies (New York, 1977) and Simone de Beauvoir, *Adieux: A Farewell to Sartre* (Harmondsworth and New York, 1985). Two thoroughly researched and informative biographies of Sartre are Ronald Hayman, *Writing Against: A Biography of Sartre* (London, 1986) and Annie Cohen-Solal, *Sartre: A Life* (London, 1987).

2 Existentialism

Existentialism is the movement in nineteenth- and twentieth-century philosophy that addresses fundamental problems of human existence. The existentialists are not a self-consciously defined homogeneous school. They include: the Danish protestant theologian and philosopher Søren Kierkegaard (1813–55), the iconoclastic German atheist Friedrich Nietzsche (1844–1900), the German fundamental ontologist Martin Heidegger (1889–1976), the French Catholic philosopher, critic and playwright Gabriel Marcel (1889–1973), the German psychiatrist and philosopher Karl Jaspers (1883–1969), the French feminist philosopher and novelist Simone de Beauvoir (1908–86), and the French phenomenologist and critic of 'objective thought' Maurice Merleau-Ponty (1908–61). Existentialist themes are salient in the literature of Mikhail Lermontov (1814–41), Fydor Dostoyevsky (1821–81), André Malraux (1901–75), Antoine de Saint-Exupéry (1900–44), Samuel Beckett (1906–89), Albert Camus (1913–60) and Jean Genet (1910–86), and discernible in more.

There is no set of problems addressed by all and only those thinkers labelled 'existentialist'. However, most of them are interested in some of: What is it to exist? Does existence have a purpose? Is there an objective difference between right and wrong? Are we free? Are we responsible for our actions? What is the right sort of religious, political or sexual commitment? How should we face death?

The term 'existentialism' only gained currency after the Second World War, so it is applied retrospectively (but not therefore falsely) to earlier thinkers. Heidegger refused to accept the label. At first Sartre himself was extremely uncomfortable to be called an existentialist, by the 1970s less so. The word features in the title of the famous October 1945 lecture *Existentialism and Humanism* (*L'Existentialisme est un Humanisme*) which Sartre regarded as an inadequate substitute for reading his denser works. The text nevertheless remains an excellent introduction to Sartrean themes so is reprinted below in full.

What does the term 'existentialism' mean in its application to Sartre's philosophy? To say that something *exists* is to say *that* it is. To state something's *essence* is to state *what* it is. Understanding Sartre's existentialism requires understanding his thoughts on the relation between existence and essence and these are most clearly presented in the 1938 novel *Nausea*. I shall discuss the existentialism that emerges from *Nausea* and then make some remarks about *Existentialism and Humanism*.

In *Nausea*, Antoine Roquentin, the existentialist anti-hero and voice-piece for Sartre's own philosophy, makes a series of profound and traumatic philosophical discoveries. Each discovery is a thesis canvassed intermittently in Western philosophy.

Roquentin notices a change. He is not sure whether the change is in the things around him or in his consciousness of them but it amounts to this: he discovers that the things he perceives *exist*. More specifically, he realises that the bare existence of things can not be captured by our ways of describing them. When for example he acts on an urge to join some children throwing pebbles into the sea he suddenly has to drop his pebble in disgust: it exists. Staring closely at his beer glass in a bar he notes its shape, the name of the brewery written on it and further properties. Even so, something about the glass eludes all these perceptible qualities: the existence of the glass.

Roquentin has discovered that existence cannot be reduced to essence. From no description of a putative object, no matter how complete, can we logically derive the claim that that object exists. As Roquentin puts it: 'To exist is simply to be there; what exists appears, lets itself be encountered, but you can never deduce it.' (*Nausea*, trans. Robert Baldick, Penguin, Harmondsworth, 1966, p. 188)

Sartre presents Roquentin's discovery as an empirical one. Roquentin sees existence and sees that existence is distinct from essence. The experience oppresses Roquentin emotionally and gives him the physical nausea of the novel's title. Those passages in which Roquentin nauseously discovers existence are masterpieces of phenomenological description and exemplary philosophical fiction. Roquentin is riding on a tram in Bouville ('Mudtown'):

I murmur: 'It's a seat,' rather like an exorcism. But the word remains on my lips, it refuses to settle on the thing. It stays what it is, with its red plush, thousands of little red paws in the air, all stiff, little dead paws. This huge belly turns upwards, bleeding, puffed up – bloated with all its dead paws, this belly floating in this box, in this grey sky, is not a seat.

(*ibid.*, p. 180)

Our customary, taken-for-granted, means-to-end thinking fails to find its application. Typically our idea of what an artefact is is whatever that object is for. Indeed, we usually only notice the aspects of objects necessary for us to use them as means to our ends. We take objects to be their functions and for this reason barely attend to them. In Roquentin's case these habitual preconceptions are stripped away and instead he sees just what is directly given in perception: the empirical content of the present. In the tram seat example Roquentin interprets what he experiences under grotesque surrealistic descriptions but there is typically a further phase to a bad attack of nausea; the disclosure of existence becomes overwhelming:

> I'm suffocating: existence is penetrating me all over, through the eyes, through the nose, through the mouth . . .. And suddenly, all at once, the veil is torn away, I have understood, I have *seen*.
>
> (ibid., p. 181)

The veil is essence. What is seen is existence.

Most shattering of all, Roquentin realises that he himself exists. He contemplates his own hand:

> I see my hand spread out on the table. It is alive – it is me. It opens, the fingers unfold and point. It is lying on its back. It shows me its fat under-belly. It looks like an animal upside down.
>
> (ibid., pp. 143–4)

and a little later says, 'I am. I am, I exist' (ibid., p. 146).

What disgusts Roquentin most about existence is its *contingency*. In philosophy contingency is contrasted with necessity. If something exists contingently then it exists but it is possible that it should not have existed: It is but it might not have been. If something exists necessarily then it exists and it is not possible that it should not have existed: It is and it could not fail to be. Roquentin sees that existence is contingent. Although what is is, there is no reason for it to be: 'The essential thing is contingency. I mean that, by definition, existence is not necessity' (ibid., p. 188). From the fact that something is it does not logically follow that it necessarily is. However, conversely, it does not logically follow that what exists exists contingently either. Nobody from Parmenides to Heidegger has managed to provide 'existence' with an adequate definition. What is existence? is an unsolved philosophical problem. So is whether what is has to be or could have not been.

If everything that exists exists contingently and if Roquentin exists then it follows that Roquentin exists contingently. It strikes Roquentin with the force of a revelation 'I too was superfluous' (ibid., p. 184). The realisation that there is no necessity for his own existence produces in him a profound anxiety: 'I hadn't any right to exist. I had appeared by chance, I existed like a stone, a plant, a microbe' (ibid., p. 124). The expression translated as 'superfluous' here is 'de trop'. 'De trop' also means 'too much' and 'être de trop' has the sense of 'to be in the way' or 'unwelcome'. Roquentin is at once fascinated and disgusted by there being no reason, no justification, for his own existence.

Not only is existence contingent for Roquentin but essence is contingent also. It is a contingent fact about the things that are that they are what they are. Everything could be other than what it is. Indeed, this is the force of Roquentin's surrealistic interpretations of his experiences. The tram seat and his own hand are seen as animals. Anything, including himself, can be other than what it is.

Once essence is seen as illusion Roquentin realises that only particular things exist, in all their uniqueness and individuality. In other words, Roquentin suddenly sees the world as if *conceptualism* or *nominalism* were true. Conceptualism and nominalism are both solutions to the problem of universals which is that of stating what generality consists in, or what it is for there to be types or sorts of things. According to nominalism, generality only belongs to language. According to conceptualism, generality belongs only to our conceptual scheme, to our modes of classification. On both theories there are not kinds or sorts of things outside language or concepts. The world is not already objectively divided up. We divide it up linguist- ically or conceptually by imposing an organising framework upon it. In Roquentin's experiences the classificatory framework is peeled off the world and objects are revealed in their particularity. This produces in him feelings of both freedom and terror. Sartre has Roquentin discover the contingency of essences in two ways; by depicting him as feeling the force of the problem of induction and by having him realise that classification is largely linguistic. The problem of induction is that of justifying putative inferences from 'Some A's are B's' to 'This A is a B' or from 'Some A's are B's' to 'All A's are B's' given that they are logically fallacious. The problem of induction arises *inter alia* for non- deductive reasoning from self to others, others to self, from one of past, present and future to one or both of the other two. For example, Roquentin says:

It is out of laziness, I suppose, that the world looks the same day after day. Today it seemed to want to change. And in that case anything, anything could happen.

(ibid., n114)

The past course of experience is consistent with *any* present or future course of experience. From the fact that the world has always looked one way it does not follow that it will not look radically otherwise. Roquentin reports the nauseous contemplation of a chestnut tree root in the park in Bouville; 'I no longer remembered that it was a root' (ibid., p. 182). In *Nausea* what something is depends closely on what it is called, and the linguistic taxonomy depends in turn upon human pragmatic interests. Roquentin says of the chestnut root, 'The function explained nothing' (ibid., p. 186) and in the tram 'Things have broken free from their names' (ibid., p. 180).

In *Nausea*, then, Sartre introduces some of the central themes of Existentialism. Existence is inherently meaningless and pointless but brutally and oppressively present. Existence is contingent. There might as easily have been nothing as something and, in particular, one's own existence is inherently meaningless and contingent. Only particulars exist and things being what they are depends on the fragile contingencies of human language and faces the unsolved problem of induction. The effect of this Existentialist vision on those who experience it is a most profound sickness and anxiety.

It could be objected that Sartre's presentation of the existentialist theses as discoveries is rather tendentious. The fictional format allows him to dispense with arguing for existentialism and in the absence of argument we might as well believe the opposite of Existentialism. For example, someone could write a philosophical novel, call it *Ecstasy*, or *Exuberance*, in which the central character discovers that existence, including his own existence, is necessary and inherently meaningful. Not only do particular things exist but they really are objectively divided into sorts where this division depends neither on our language nor our pragmatic interests. The problem of induction emerges as a pseudo-problem which need cause no-one any psychological, still less physical, discomfort. Not only is everything as it is, it could not be other than as it is. The staggering realisation of this *Essentialism* is accompanied by profound sensations of well-being and harmony called 'ecstasies' or 'exuberances'. The existentialist solutions to philosophical problems in *Nausea* are as plausible as their experience by Roquentin is credible.

In *Existentialism and Humanism* Sartre clarifies and partly revises his view of existence and essence. He divides the things that exist into three kinds: human beings, artefacts, and naturally occurring objects. In the case of human beings *existence precedes essence*. In the case of artefacts *essence precedes existence* and in the case of naturally occurring objects *existence and essence coincide*.

We need to understand the relation *precedes*. 'Precedes' admits of both a chronological and a logical reading, both of which Sartre intends. Chronologically, 'precedes' means 'predates' or 'occurs before'. Logically, 'precedes' means 'is a necessary condition for' or 'is a prerequisite for'.

Take the case of artefacts first. If a person makes a paper-knife the idea of the paper-knife in the mind of the manufacturer predates the existence of the paper-knife itself. The idea of the object is also necessary for the object to exist. Essence precedes existence in this case because there is an answer to the question *What is it?* before, and independently of, a correct affirmative answer to the question *Is it?* The essence of the paper-knife predates and is required by its existence. The 'what' precedes the 'is'.

In the case of naturally occurring objects, such as stones and trees, their being what they are does not predate their being and their being does not predate their being what they are. They are and they are what they are simultaneously. Their being and their being what they are are mutually dependent. In this sense the existence and essence of natural things coincide.

In the case of human beings, in contrast with both of these, existence comes before essence. Sartre means there is no predetermined human essence and there is no human nature fixed in advance of human existence. Human beings first of all exist and subsequently make themselves what they are by their own actions. When we are born we have no essence as human beings. Only the totality of choices we make in life makes us the people who we are. In this sense, we are profoundly free.

Sartre's anti-essentialist view of humanity is incompatible with a certain theological view. If we were God's creation then we would stand in a relation to God rather like that of the paper-knife to the manufacturer. Our essence would precede our existence because the idea of what we are would exist in the mind of God and predate our existence. If Sartre is right then this theological view must be false. We may turn now to the text of the October 1945 lecture at the Club Maintenant.

EXISTENTIALISM AND HUMANISM

My purpose here is to offer a defence of existentialism against several reproaches that have been laid against it.

First, it has been reproached as an invitation to people to dwell in quietism of despair. For if every way to a solution is barred, one would have to regard any action in this world as entirely ineffective, and one would arrive finally at a contemplative philosophy. Moreover, since contemplation is a luxury, this would be only another bourgeois philosophy. This is, especially, the reproach made by the Communists.

From another quarter we are reproached for having underlined all that is ignominious in the human situation, for depicting what is mean, sordid or base to the neglect of certain things that possess charm and beauty and belong to the brighter side of human nature: for example, according to the Catholic critic, Mlle. Mercier, we forget how an infant smiles. Both from this side and from the other we are also reproached for leaving out of account the solidarity of mankind and considering man in isolation. And this, say the Communists, is because we base our doctrine upon pure subjectivity—upon the Cartesian "I think": which is the moment in which solitary man attains to himself; a position from which it is impossible to regain solidarity with other men who exist outside of the self. The *ego* cannot reach them through the *cogito*.

From the Christian side, we are reproached as people who deny the reality and seriousness of human affairs. For since we ignore the commandments of God and all values prescribed as eternal, nothing remains but what is strictly voluntary. Everyone can do what he likes, and will be incapable, from such a point of view, of condemning either the point of view or the action of anyone else.

It is to these various reproaches that I shall endeavour to reply to-day; that is why I have entitled this brief exposition "Existentialism and Humanism." Many may be surprised at the mention of humanism in this connection, but we shall try to see in what sense we understand it. In any case, we can begin by saying that existentialism, in our sense of the word, is a doctrine that does render human life possible: a doctrine, also, which affirms that every truth and every action imply both an environment and a human subjectivity. The essential charge laid against us is, of course, that of over-emphasis upon the evil side of human life. I have lately been told of a lady who, whenever she lets slip a vulgar expression in a moment of nervousness, excuses herself by exclaiming, "I believe I am becoming an existentialist." So it appears that ugliness is being identified with existentialism. That is why some people say we are "naturalistic," and if we are, it is strange to see how much we scandalise and horrify them, for no one seems to be much frightened or humiliated nowadays by what is properly called naturalism. Those who can quite well keep down a novel by Zola such as *La Terre* are sickened as soon as they read an existentialist novel. Those who appeal to the wisdom of the people—which is a sad wisdom—find ours sadder still. And yet, what could be more disillusioned than such sayings as "Charity begins at home" or "Promote a rogue and he'll sue you for damage, knock him down and he'll do you homage"?[1] We all know how many common sayings can be quoted to this effect, and they all mean much the same—that you must not oppose the powers-that-be; that you must not fight against superior force; must not meddle in matters that are above your station. Or that any action not in accordance with some tradition is mere romanticism; or that any undertaking which has not the support of proven experience is foredoomed to frustration; and that since experience has shown men to be invariably inclined to evil, there must be firm rules to restrain them, otherwise we shall have anarchy. It is, however, the people who are forever mouthing these dismal proverbs and, whenever they are told of some more or less repulsive action, say "How like human nature!"—it is these very people, always harping upon realism, who complain that existentialism is too gloomy a view of things. Indeed their excessive protests make me suspect that what is annoying them is not so much our pessimism, but, much more likely, our optimism. For at bottom, what is alarming in the doctrine that I am about to try to explain to you is—is it not?—that it confronts man with a possibility of choice. To verily this, let us review the whole question upon the strictly philosophic level. What, then, is this that we call existentialism?

Most of those who are making use of this word would be highly confused if required to explain its meaning. For since it has become fashionable, people cheerfully declare that this musician or that painter is "existentialist." A columnist in *Clartés* signs himself "The Existentialist," and, indeed, the word is now so loosely applied to so many things that it no longer means anything at all. It would appear that, for the lack of any novel doctrine such as that of surrealism, all those who are eager to join in the latest scandal or movement now seize upon this philosophy in which, however, they can find nothing to their purpose. For in truth this is of all teachings the least scandalous and the most austere: it is intended strictly for technicians and philosophers. All the same, it can easily be defined.

The question is only complicated because there are two kinds of existentialists. There are, on the one hand, the Christians, amongst whom I shall name Jaspers and Gabriel Marcel, both professed Catholics; and on the other the existential atheists, amongst whom we must place Heidegger as well as the French existentialists and myself. What they have in common is simply the fact that they believe that *existence* comes before *essence*—or, if you will, that we must begin from the subjective. 'What exactly do we mean by that?

If one considers an article of manufacture—as, for example, a book or a paper-knife—one sees that it has been made by an artisan who had a conception of it; and he has paid attention, equally, to the conception of a paper-knife and to the pre-existent technique of production which is a part of that conception and is, at bottom, a formula. Thus the paper-knife is at the same time an article producible in a certain manner and one which, on the other hand, serves a definite purpose, for one cannot suppose that a man would produce a paper-knife without knowing what it was for. Let us say, then, of the paper-knife that its essence—that is to say the sum of the formulae and the qualities which made its production and its definition possible—precedes its existence. The presence of such-and-such a paper-knife or book is thus determined before my eyes. Here, then, we are viewing the world from a technical standpoint, and we can say that production precedes existence.

When we think of God as the creator, we are thinking of him, most of the time, as a supernal artisan. Whatever doctrine we may be considering, whether it be a doctrine like that of Descartes, or of Leibnitz himself, we always imply that the will follows, more or less, from the understanding or at least accompanies it, so that when God creates he knows precisely what he is creating. Thus, the conception of man in the mind of God is comparable to that of the paper-knife in the mind of the artisan: God makes man according to a procedure and a conception, exactly as the artisan manufactures a paper-knife, following a definition and a formula. Thus each individual man is the realisation of a certain conception which dwells in the divine understanding. In the philosophic atheism of the eighteenth century, the notion of God is suppressed, but not, for all that, the idea that essence is prior to existence; something of that idea we still find everywhere, in Diderot, in Voltaire and even in Kant. Man possesses a human nature; that "human nature," which is the conception of human being, is found in every man; which means that each man is a particular example of an universal conception, the conception of Man. In Kant, this universality goes so far that the wild man of the woods, man in the state of nature and the bourgeois are all contained in the same definition and have the same fundamental qualities. Here again, the essence of man precedes that historic existence which we confront in experience.

Atheistic existentialism, of which I am a representative, declares with greater consistency that if God does not exist there is at least one being whose existence comes before its essence, a being which exists before it can be defined by any conception of it. That being is man or, as Heidegger has it, the human reality. What do we mean by saying that existence precedes essence? We mean that man first of all exists, encounters himself, surges up in the world—and defines himself afterwards. If man as the existentialist sees him is not definable, it is because to begin with he is nothing. He will not be anything until later, and then he will be what he makes of himself. Thus, there is no human nature, because there is no God to have a conception of it. Man simply is. Not that he is simply what he conceives himself to be, but he is what he wills, and as he conceives himself after already existing—as he wills to be after that leap towards existence. Man is nothing else but that which he makes of himself. That is the first principle of existentialism. And this is what people call its "subjectivity," using the word as a reproach against us. But what do we mean to say by this, but that man is of a greater dignity than a stone or a table? For we mean to say that man primarily exists—that man is, before all else, something which propels itself towards a future and is aware that it is doing so. Man is, indeed, a project which possesses a subjective life, instead of being a kind of moss, or a fungus or a cauliflower. Before that projection of the self nothing exists; not even in the heaven of intelligence: man will only attain existence when he is what he purposes to be. Not, however, what he may wish to be. For what we usually understand by wishing or willing is a conscious decision taken— much more often than not—after we have made ourselves what we are. I may wish to join a party, to write a book or to marry—but in such a case what is usually called my will is probably a manifestation of a prior and more spontaneous decision. If, however, it is true that existence is prior to essence, man is responsible for what he is. Thus, the first effect of existentialism is that it puts every man in possession of himself as he is, and places the entire responsibility for his existence squarely upon his own shoulders. And, when we say that man is responsible for himself, we do not mean that he is responsible only for his own individuality, but that he is responsible for all men. The word "subjectivism" is to be understood in two senses, and our adversaries play upon only one of them. Subjectivism means, on the one hand, the freedom of the individual subject and, on the other, that man cannot pass beyond human subjectivity. It is the latter which is the deeper meaning of existentialism. When we say that man chooses himself, we do mean that every one of us must choose himself; but by that we also mean that in choosing for himself he chooses for all men. For in effect, of all the actions a man may take in order to create himself as he wills to be, there is not one which is not creative, at the same time, of an image of man such as he believes he ought to be. To choose between this or that is at the same time to affirm the value of that which is chosen; for we are unable ever to choose the worse. What we choose is always the better; and nothing can be better for us unless it is better for all. If, moreover, existence precedes essence and we will to exist at the same time as we fashion our image, that image is valid for all and for the entire epoch in which we find ourselves. Our responsibility is thus much greater than we had supposed, for it concerns mankind as a whole. If I am a worker, for instance, I may choose to join a Christian rather than a Communist trade union. And if, by that membership, I choose to signify that resignation is, after all, the attitude that best becomes a man, that man's kingdom is not upon this earth, I do not commit myself alone to that view. Resignation is my will for everyone, and my action is, in consequence, a commitment on behalf of all mankind. Or if, to take a more personal case, I decide to marry and to have children, even though this decision proceeds simply from my situation, from my passion or my desire, I am thereby committing not only myself, but humanity as a whole, to the practice of monogamy. I am thus responsible for myself and for all men, and I am creating a certain image of man as I would have him to be. In fashioning myself I fashion man.

This may enable us to understand what is meant by such terms—perhaps a little grandiloquent—as anguish, abandonment and despair. As you will soon see, it is very simple. First, what do we mean by anguish? The existentialist frankly states that man is in anguish. His meaning is as follows—When a man commits himself to anything, fully realising that he is not only choosing what he will be, but is thereby at the same time a legislator deciding for the whole of mankind—in such a moment a man cannot escape from the sense of complete and profound responsibility. There are many, indeed, who show no such anxiety. But we affirm that they are merely disguising their anguish or are in flight from it. Certainly, many people think that in what they are doing they commit no one but themselves to anything: and if you ask them, "What would happen if everyone did so?" they shrug their shoulders and reply, "Everyone does not do so." But in truth, one ought always to ask oneself what would happen if everyone did as one is doing; nor can one escape from that disturbing thought except by a kind of self-deception. The man who lies in self-excuse, by saying "Everyone will not do it" must be ill at ease in his conscience, for the act of lying implies the universal value which it denies. By its very disguise his anguish reveals itself. This is the anguish that Kierkegaard called "the anguish of Abraham." You know the story: An angel commanded Abraham to sacrifice his son: and obedience was obligatory, if it really was an angel who had appeared and said, "Thou, Abraham, shalt sacrifice thy son." But anyone in such a case would wonder, first, whether it was indeed an angel and secondly, whether I am really Abraham. Where are the proofs? A certain mad woman who suffered from hallucinations said that people were telephoning to her, and giving her orders. The doctor asked, "But who is it that speaks to you?" She replied: "He says it is God." And what, indeed, could prove to her that it was God? If an angel appears to me, what is the proof that it is an angel; or, if I hear voices, who can prove that they proceed from heaven and not from hell, or from my own subconsciousness or some pathological condition? Who can prove that they are really addressed to me?

Who, then, can prove that I am the proper person to impose, by my own choice, my conception of man upon mankind? I shall never find any proof whatever; there will be no sign to convince me of it. If a voice speaks to me, it is still I myself who must decide whether the voice is or is not that of an angel. If I regard a certain course of action as good, it is only I who choose to say that it is good and not bad. There is nothing to show that I am Abraham: nevertheless I also am obliged at every instant to perform actions which are examples. Everything happens to every man as though the whole human race had its eyes fixed upon what he is doing and regulated its conduct accordingly. So every man ought to say, "Am I really a man who has the right to act in such a manner that humanity regulates itself by what I do." If a man does not say that, he is dissembling his anguish. Clearly, the anguish with which we are concerned here is not one that could lead to quietism or inaction. It is anguish pure and simple, of the kind well known to all those who have borne responsibilities. When, for instance, a military leader takes upon himself the responsibility for an attack and sends a number of men to their death, he chooses to do it and at bottom he alone chooses. No doubt he acts under a higher command, but its orders, which are more general, require interpretation by him and upon that interpretation depends the life of ten, fourteen or twenty men. In making the decision, he cannot but feel a certain anguish. All leaders know that anguish. It does not prevent their acting, on the contrary it is the very condition of their action, for the action presupposes that there is a plurality of possibilities, and in choosing one of these, they realise that it has value only because it is chosen. Now it is anguish of that kind which existentialism describes, and moreover, as we shall see, makes explicit through direct responsibility towards other men who are concerned. Far from being a screen which could separate us from action, it is a condition of action itself.

And when we speak of "abandonment"—a favourite word of Heidegger—we only mean to say that God does not exist, and that it is necessary to draw the consequences of his absence right to the end. The existentialist is strongly opposed to a certain type of secular moralism which seeks to suppress God at the least possible expense. Towards 1880, when the French professors endeavoured to formulate a secular morality, they said something like this:—God is a useless and costly hypothesis, so we will do without it. However, if we are to have morality, a society and a law-abiding world, it is essential that certain values should be taken seriously; they must have an *a priori* existence ascribed to them. It must be considered obligatory *a priori* to be honest, not to lie, not to beat one's wife, to bring up children and so forth; so we are going to do a little work on this subject, which will enable us to show that these values exist all the same, inscribed in an intelligible heaven although, of course, there is no God. In other words—and this is, I believe, the purport of all that we in France call radicalism—nothing will be changed if God does not exist; we shall re-discover the same norms of honesty, progress and humanity, and we shall have disposed of God as an out-of-date hypothesis which will die away quietly of itself. The existentialist, on the contrary, finds it extremely embarrassing that God does not exist, for there disappears with Him all possibility of finding values in an intelligible heaven. There can no longer be any good *a priori*, since there is no infinite and perfect consciousness to think it. It is nowhere written that "the good" exists, that one must be honest or must not lie, since we are now upon the plane where there are only men. Dostoievsky once wrote "If God did not exist, everything would be permitted"; and that, for existentialism, is the starting point. Everything is indeed permitted if God does not exist, and man is in consequence forlorn. For he cannot find anything to depend upon either within or outside himself. He discovers forthwith, that he is without excuse. For if indeed existence precedes essence, one will never be able to explain one's action by reference to a given and specific human nature; in other words, there is no determinism—man is free, man *is* freedom. Nor, on the other hand, if God does not exist, are we provided with any values or commands that could legitimise our behaviour. Thus we have neither behind us, nor before us in a luminous realm of values, any means of justification or excuse. We are left alone, without excuse. That is what I mean when I say that man is condemned to be free. Condemned, because he did not create himself, yet is nevertheless at liberty, and from the moment that he is thrown into this world he is responsible for everything he does. The existentialist does not believe in the power of passion. He will never regard a grand passion as a destructive torrent upon which a man is swept into certain actions as by fate, and which, therefore, is an excuse for them. He thinks that man is responsible for his passion. Neither will an existentialist think that a man can find help through some sign being vouchsafed upon earth for his orientation: for he thinks that the man himself interprets the sign as he chooses. He thinks that every man, without any support or help whatever, is condemned at every instant to invent man. As Ponge has written in a very fine article, "Man is the future of man." That is exactly true. Only, if one took this to mean that the future is laid up in Heaven, that God knows what it is, it would be false, for then it would no longer even be a future. If, however, it means that, whatever man may now appear to be, there is a future to be fashioned, a virgin future that awaits him—then it is a true saying. But in the present one is forsaken.

As an example by which you may the better understand this state of abandonment, I will refer to the case of a pupil of mine, who sought me out in the following circumstances. His father was quarrelling with his mother and was also inclined to be a "collaborator"; his elder brother had been killed in the German offensive of 1940 and this young man, with a sentiment somewhat primitive but generous, burned to avenge him. His mother was living alone with him, deeply afflicted by the semi-treason of his father and by the death of her eldest son, and her one consolation was in this young man. But he, at this moment, had the choice between going to England to join the Free French Forces or of staying near his mother and helping her to live. He fully realised that this woman lived only for him and that his disappearance—or perhaps his death—would plunge her into despair. He also realised that, concretely and in fact, every action he performed on his mother's behalf would be sure of effect in the sense of aiding her to live, where as anything he did in order to go and fight would be an ambiguous action which might vanish like water into sand and serve no purpose. For instance, to set out for England he would have to wait indefinitely in a Spanish camp on the way through Spain; or, on arriving in England or in Algiers he might be put into an office to fill up forms. Consequently, he found himself confronted by two very different modes of action; the one concrete, immediate, but directed towards only one individual; and the other an action addressed to an end infinitely greater, a national collectivity, but for that very reason ambiguous—and it might be frustrated on the way. At the same time, he was hesitating between two kinds of morality; on the one side the morality of sympathy, of personal devotion and, on the other side, a morality of wider scope but of more debatable validity. He had to choose between those two. What could help him to choose? Could the Christian doctrine? No. Christian doctrine says: Act with charity, love your neighbour, deny yourself for others, choose the way which is hardest, and so forth. But which is the harder road? To whom does one owe the more brotherly love, the patriot or the mother? Which is the more useful aim, the general one of fighting in and for the whole community, or the precise aim of helping one particular person to live? Who can give an answer to that *a priori*? No one. Nor is it given in any ethical scripture. The Kantian ethic says, Never regard another as a means, but always as an end. Very well; if I remain with my mother, I shall be regarding her as the end and not as a means: but by the same token I am in danger of treating as means those who are fighting on my behalf; and the converse is also true, that if I go to the aid of the combatants I shall be treating them as the end at the risk of treating my mother as a means.

If values are uncertain, if they are still too abstract to determine the particular, concrete case under consideration, nothing remains but to trust in our instincts. That is what this young man tried to do; and when I saw him he said, "In the end, it is feeling that counts; the direction in which it is really pushing me is the one I ought to choose. If I feel that I love my mother enough to sacrifice everything else for her—my will to be avenged, all my longings for action and adventure—then I stay with her. If, on the contrary, I feel that my love for her is not enough, I go." But how does one estimate the strength of a feeling? The value of his feeling for his mother was determined precisely by the fact that he was standing by her. I may say that I love a certain friend enough to sacrifice such or such a sum of money for him, but I cannot prove that unless I have done it. I may say, "I love my mother enough to remain with her," if actually I have remained with her. I can only estimate the strength of this affection if I have performed an action by which it is defined and ratified. But if I then appeal to this affection to justify my action, I find myself drawn into a vicious circle.

Moreover, as Gide has very well said, a sentiment which is play-acting and one which is vital are two things that are hardly distinguishable one from another. To decide that I love my mother by staying beside her, and to play a comedy the upshot of which is that I do so—these are nearly the same thing. In other words, feeling is formed by the deeds that one does; therefore I cannot consult it as a guide to action. And that is to say that I can neither seek within myself for an authentic impulse to action, nor can I expect, from some ethic, formulae that will enable me to act. You may say that the youth did, at least, go to a professor to ask for advice. But if you seek counsel—from a priest, for example—you have selected that priest; and at bottom you already knew, more or less, what he would advise. In other words, to choose an adviser is nevertheless to commit oneself by that choice. If you are a Christian, you will say, Consult a priest; but there are collaborationists, priests who are resisters and priests who wait for the tide to turn: which will you choose? Had this young man chosen a priest of the resistance, or one of the collaboration, he would have decided beforehand the kind of advice he was to receive. Similarly, in coming to me, he knew what advice I should give him, and I had but one reply to make. You are free, therefore choose—that is to say, invent. No rule of general morality can show you what you ought to do: no signs are vouchsafed in this world. The Catholics will reply, "Oh, but they are!" Very well; still, it is I myself, in every case, who have to interpret the signs. Whilst I was imprisoned, I made the acquaintance of a somewhat remarkable man, a Jesuit, who had become a member of that order in the following manner. In his life he had suffered a succession of rather severe setbacks. His father had died when he was a child, leaving him in poverty, and he had been awarded a free scholarship in a religious institution, where he had been made continually to feel that he was accepted for charity's sake, and, in consequence, he had been denied several of those distinctions and honours which gratify children. Later, about the age of eighteen, he came to grief in a sentimental affair; and finally, at twenty-two—this was a trifle in itself, but it was the last drop that overflowed his cup—he failed in his military examination. This young man, then, could regard himself as a total failure: it was a sign— but a sign of what? He might have taken refuge in bitterness or despair. But he took it—very cleverly for him—as a sign that he was not intended for secular successes, and that only the attainments of religion, those of sanctity and of faith, were accessible to him. He interpreted his record as a message from God, and became a member of the Order. Who can doubt but that this decision as to the meaning of the sign was his, and his alone? One could have drawn quite different conclusions from such a series of reverses—as, for example, that he had better become a carpenter or a revolutionary. For the decipherment of the sign, however, he bears the entire responsibility. That is what "abandonment" implies, that we ourselves decide our being. And with this abandonment goes anguish.

As for "despair," the meaning of this expression is extremely simple. It merely means that we limit ourselves to a reliance upon that which is within our wills, or within the sum of the probabilities which render our action feasible. Whenever one wills anything, there are always these elements of probability. If I am counting upon a visit from a friend, who may be coming by train or by tram, I presuppose that the train will arrive at the appointed time, or that the tram will not be derailed. I remain in the realm of possibilities; but one does not rely upon any possibilities beyond those that are strictly concerned in one's action. Beyond the point at which the possibilities under consideration cease to affect my action, I ought to disinterest myself. For there is no God and no pre- venient design, which can adapt the world and all its possibilities to my will. When Descartes said, "Conquer yourself rather than the world," what he meant was, at bottom, the same—that we should act without hope.

Marxists, to whom I have said this, have answered: "Your action is limited, obviously, by your death; but you can rely upon the help of others. That is, you can count both upon what the others are doing to help you elsewhere, as in China and in Russia, and upon what they will do later, after your death, to take up your action and carry it forward to its final accomplishment which will be the revolution. Moreover you must rely upon this; not to do so is immoral." To this I rejoin, first, that I shall always count upon my comrades-in-arms in the struggle, in so far as they are committed, as I am, to a definite, common cause; and in the unity of a party or a group which I can more or less control—that is, in which I am enrolled as a militant and whose movements at every moment are known to me. In that respect, to rely upon the unity and the will of the party is exactly like my reckoning that the train will run to time or that the tram will not be derailed. But I cannot count upon men whom I do not know, I cannot base my confidence upon human goodness or upon man's interest in the good of society, seeing that man is free and that there is no human nature which I can take as foundational. I do not know whither the Russian revolution will lead. I can admire it and take it as an example in so far as it is evident, to-day, that the proletariat plays a part in Russia which it has attained in no other nation. But I cannot affirm that this will necessarily lead to the triumph of the proletariat: I must confine myself to what I can see. Nor can I be sure that comrades-in-arms will take up my work after my death and carry it to the maximum perfection, seeing that those men are free agents and will freely decide, to-morrow, what man is then to be. To-morrow, after my death, some men may decide to establish Fascism, and the others may be so cowardly or so slack as to let them do so. If so, Fascism will then be the truth of man, and so much the worse for us. In reality, things will be such as men have decided they shall be. Does that mean that I should abandon myself to quietism? No. First I ought to commit myself and then act my commitment, according to the time-honoured formula that "one need not hope in order to undertake one's work." Nor does this mean that I should not belong to a party, but only that I should be without illusion and that I should do what I can. For instance, if I ask myself "Will the social ideal, as such, ever become a reality?" I cannot tell, I only know that whatever may be in my power to make it so, I shall do; beyond that, I can count upon nothing. Quietism is the attitude of people who say, "let others do what I cannot do." The doctrine I am presenting before you is precisely the opposite of this, since it declares that there is no reality except in action. It goes further, indeed, and adds, "Man is nothing else but what he purposes, he exists only in so far as he realises himself, he is therefore nothing else but the sum of his actions, nothing else but what his life is." Hence we can well understand why some people are horrified by our teaching. For many have but one resource to sustain them in their misery, and that is to think, "Circumstances have been against me, I was worthy to be something much better than I have been. I admit I have never had a great love or a great friendship; but that is because I never met a man or a woman who were worthy of it; if I have not written any very good books, it is because I had not the leisure to do so; or, if I have had no children to whom I could devote myself it is because I did not find the man I could have lived with. So there remains within me a wide range of abilities, inclinations and potentialities, unused but perfectly viable, which endow me with a worthiness that could never be inferred from the mere history of my actions." But in reality and for the existentialist, there is no love apart from the deeds of love; no potentiality of love other than that which is manifested in loving; there is no genius other than that which is expressed in works of art. The genius of Proust is the totality of the works of Proust; the genius of Racine is the series of his tragedies, outside of which there is nothing. Why should we attribute to Racine the capacity to write yet another tragedy when that is precisely what he did not write? In life, a man commits himself, draws his own portrait and there is nothing but that portrait. No doubt this thought may seem comfortless to one who has not made a success of his life. On the other hand, it puts everyone in a position to understand that reality alone is reliable; that dreams, expectations and hopes serve to define a man only as deceptive dreams, abortive hopes, expectations unfulfilled; that is to say, they define him negatively, not positively. Nevertheless, when one says, "You are nothing else but what you live," it does not imply that an artist is to be judged solely by his works of art, for a thousand other things contribute no less to his definition as a man. What we mean to say is that a man is no other than a series of undertakings, that he is the sum, the organisation, the set of relations that constitute these undertakings.

In the light of all this, what people reproach us with is not, after all, our pessimism, but the sternness of our optimism. If people condemn our works of fiction, in which we describe characters that are base, weak, cowardly and sometimes even frankly evil, it is not only because those characters are base, weak, cowardly or evil. For suppose that, like Zola, we showed that the behaviour of these characters was caused by their heredity, or by the action of their environment upon them, or by determining factors, psychic or organic. People would be reassured, they would say, "You see, that is what we are like, no one can do anything about it." But the existentialist, when he portrays a coward, shows him as responsible for his cowardice. He is not like that on account of a cowardly heart or lungs or cerebrum, he has not become like that through his physiological organism; he is like that because he has made himself into a coward by his actions. There is no such thing as a cowardly temperament. There are nervous temperaments; there is what is called impoverished blood, and there are also rich temperaments. But the man whose blood is poor is not a coward for all that, for what produces cowardice is the act of giving up or giving way; and a temperament is not an action. A coward is defined by the deed that he his done. What people feel obscurely, and with horror, is that the coward as we present him is guilty of being a coward. What people would prefer would be to be born either a coward or a hero. One of the charges most often laid against the *Chemins de la Liberté* is something like this—"But, after all, these people being so base, how can you make them into heroes?" That objection is really rather comic, for it implies that people are born heroes: and that is, at bottom, what such people would like to think. If you are born cowards, you can be quite content, you can do nothing about it and you will be cowards all your lives whatever you do; and if you are born heroes you can again be quite content; you will be heroes all your lives, eating and drinking heroically. Whereas the existentialist says that the coward makes himself cowardly, the hero makes himself heroic; and that there is always a possibility for the coward to give up cowardice and for the hero to stop being a hero. What counts is the total commitment, and it is not by a particular case or particular action that you are committed altogether.

We have now, I think, dealt with a certain number of the reproaches against existentialism. You have seen that it cannot be regarded as a philosophy of quietism since it defines man by his action; nor as a pessimistic description of man, for no doctrine is more optimistic, the destiny of man is placed within himself. Nor is it an attempt to discourage man from action since it tells him that there is no hope except in his action, and that the one thing which permits him to have life is the deed. Upon this level therefore, what we are considering is an ethic of action and self-commitment. However, we are still reproached, upon these few data, for confirming man within his individual subjectivity. There again people badly misunderstand us.

Our point of departure is, indeed, the subjectivity of the individual; and that for strictly philosophic reasons. It is not because we are bourgeois, but because we seek to base our teaching upon the truth, and not upon a collection of fine theories, full of hope but lacking real foundations. And at the point of departure there cannot be any other truth than this, *I think, therefore I am*, which is the absolute truth of consciousness as it attains to itself. Every theory which begins with man, outside of this moment of self-attainment, is a theory which thereby suppresses the truth, for outside of the Cartesian *cogito*, all objects are no more than probable, and any doctrine of probabilities which is not attached to a truth will crumble into nothing. In order to define the probable one must possess the true. Before there can be any truth whatever, then, there must be an absolute truth, and there is such a truth which is simple, easily attained and within the reach of everybody; it consists in one's immediate sense of one's self.

In the second place, this theory alone is compatible with the dignity of man, it is the only one which does not make man into an object. All kinds of materialism lead one to treat every man including oneself as an object—that is, as a set of pre-determined reactions, in no way different from the patterns of qualities and phenomena which constitute a table, or a chair or a stone. Our aim is precisely to establish the human kingdom as a pattern of values in distinction from the material world. But the subjectivity which we thus postulate as the standard of truth is no narrowly individual subjectivism, for as we have demonstrated, it is not only one's own self that one discovers in the *cogito*, but those of others too. Contrary to the philosophy of Descartes, contrary to that of Kant, when we say "I think" we are attaining to ourselves in the presence of the other, and we are just as certain of the other as we are of ourselves. Thus the man who discovers himself directly in the *cogito* also discovers all the others, and discovers them as the condition of his own existence. He recognises that he cannot be anything (in the sense in which one says one is spiritual, or that one is wicked or jealous) unless others recognise him as such. I cannot obtain any truth whatsoever about myself, except through the mediation of another. The other is indispensable to my existence, and equally so to any knowledge I can have of myself. Under these conditions, the intimate discovery of myself is at the same time the revelation of the other as a freedom which confronts mine, and which cannot think or will without doing so either for or against me. Thus, at once, we find ourselves in a world which is, let us say, that of "inter-subjectivity." It is in this world that man his to decide what he is and what others are.

Furthermore, although it is impossible to find in each and every man a universal essence that can be called human nature, there is nevertheless a human universality of *condition*. It is not by chance that the thinkers of to-day are so much more ready to speak of the condition than of the nature of man. By his condition they understand, with more or less clarity, all the *limitations* which *a priori* define man's fundamental situation in the universe. His historical situations are variable: man may be born a slave in a pagan society, or may be a feudal baron, or a proletarian. But what never vary are the necessities of being in the world, of having to labour and to die there. These limitations are neither subjective nor objective, or rather there is both a subjective and an objective aspect of them. Objective, because we meet with them every-where and they are everywhere recognisable: and subjective because they are *lived* and are nothing if man does not live them—if, that is to say, he does not freely determine himself and his existence in relation to them. And, diverse though man's purposes may be, at least none of them is wholly foreign to me, since every human purpose presents itself as an attempt either to surpass these limitations, or to widen them, or else to deny or to accommodate oneself to them. Consequently every purpose, however individual it may be, is of universal value. Every purpose, even that of a Chinese, an Indian or a Negro, can be understood by a European. To say it can be understood, means that the European of 1945 may be striving out of a certain situation towards the same limitations in the same way, and that he may reconceive in himself the purpose of the Chinese, of the Indian or the African. In every purpose there is universality, in this sense that every purpose is comprehensible to every man. Not that this or that purpose defines man for ever, but that it may be entertained again and again. There is always some way of understanding an idiot, a child, a primitive man or a foreigner if one has sufficient information. In this sense we may say that there is a human universality, but it is not something given; it is being perpetually made. I make this universality in choosing myself; I also make it by understanding the purpose of any other man, of whatever epoch. This absoluteness of the act of choice does not alter the relativity of each epoch.

What is at the very heart and centre of existentialism, is the absolute character of the free commitment, by which every man realises himself in realising a type of humanity—a commitment always understandable, to no matter whom in no matter what epoch—and its bearing upon the relativity of the cultural pattern which may result from such absolute commitment. One must observe equally the relativity of Cartesianism and the absolute character of the Cartesian commitment, in this sense you may say, if you like, that every one of us makes the absolute by breathing, by eating, by sleeping or by behaving in any fashion whatsoever. There is no difference between free being—being as self-committal, as existence choosing its essence—and absolute being. And there is no difference whatever between being as an absolute, temporarily localised—that is, localised in history—and universally intelligible being.

This does not completely refute the charge of subjectivism. Indeed that objection appears in several other forms, of which the first is as follows. People say to us, "Then it does not matter what you do," and they say this in various ways. First they tax us with anarchy; then they say, "You cannot judge others, for there is no reason for preferring one purpose to another"; finally, they may say, "Everything being merely voluntary in this choice of yours, you give away with one hand what you pretend to gain with the other." These three are not very serious objections. As to the first, to say that it matters not what you choose is not correct. In one sense choice is possible, but what is not possible is not to choose. I can always choose, but I must know that if I do not choose, that is still a choice. This, although it may appear merely formal, is of great importance as a limit to fantasy and caprice. For, when I confront a real situation—for example, that I am a sexual being, able to have relations with a being of the other sex and able to have children—I am obliged to choose my attitude to it, and in every respect I bear the responsibility of the choice which, in committing myself, also commits the whole of humanity. Even if my choice is determined by no *a priori* value whatever, it can have nothing to do with caprice: and if anyone thinks that this is only Gide's theory of the *acte gratuit* over again, he has failed to see the enormous difference between this theory and that of Gide. Gide does not know what a situation is, his "act" is one of pure caprice. In our view, on the contrary, man finds himself in an organised situation in which he is himself involved: his choice involves mankind in its entirety, and he cannot avoid choosing. Either he must remain single, or he must marry without having children, or he must marry and have children. In any case, and whichever he may choose, it is impossible for him, in respect of this situation, not to take complete responsibility. Doubtless he chooses without reference to any pre-established values, but it is unjust to tax him with caprice. Rather let us say that the moral choice is comparable to the construction of a work of art.

But here I must at once digress to make it quite clear that we are not propounding an aesthetic morality, for our adversaries are disingenuous enough to reproach us even with that. I mention the work of art only by way of comparison. That being understood, does anyone reproach an artist when he paints a picture for not following rules established *a priori?* Does one ever ask what is the picture that he ought to paint? As everyone knows, there is no pre-defined picture for him to make; the artist applies himself to the composition of a picture, and the picture that ought to be made is precisely that which he will have made. As everyone knows, there are no aesthetic values *a priori*, but there are values which will appear in due course in the coherence of the picture, in the relation between the will to create and the finished work. No one can tell what the painting of to-morrow will be like; one cannot judge a painting until it is done. What has that to do with morality? We are in the same creative situation. We never speak of a work of art as irresponsible; when we are discussing a canvas by Picasso, we understand very well that the composition became what it is at the time when he was painting it, and that his works are part and parcel of his entire life.

It is the same upon the plane of morality. There is this in common between art and morality, that in both we have to do with creation and invention. We cannot decide *a priori* what it is that should be done. I think it was made sufficiently clear to you in the case of that student who came to see me, that to whatever ethical system he might appeal, the Kantian or any other, he could find no sort of guidance whatever; he was obliged to invent the law for himself. Certainly we cannot say that this man, in choosing to remain with his mother—that is, in taking sentiment, personal devotion and concrete charity as his moral foundations— would be making an irresponsible choice, nor could we do so if he preferred the sacrifice of going away to England. Man makes himself; he is not found ready-made: he makes himself by the choice of his morality, and he cannot but choose a morality, such is the pressure of circumstances upon him. We define man only in relation to his commitments; it is therefore absurd to reproach us for irresponsibility in our choice.

In the second place, people say to us, "You are unable to judge others." This is true in one sense and false in another. It is true in this sense, that whenever a man chooses his purpose and his commitment in all clearness and in all sincerity, whatever that purpose may be it is impossible to prefer another for him. It is true in the sense that we do not believe in progress. Progress implies amelioration; but man is always the same, facing a situation which is always changing, and choice remains always a choice in the situation. The moral problem has not changed since the time when it was a choice between slavery and anti-slavery— from the time of the war of Secession, for example, until the present moment when one chooses between the M.R.P.[2] and the Communists.

We can judge, nevertheless, for, as I have said, one chooses in view of others, and in view of others one chooses himself. One can judge, first— and perhaps this is not a judgment of value, but it is a logical judgment— that in certain cases choice is founded upon an error, and in others upon the truth. One can judge a man by saying that he deceives himself. Since we have defined the situation of man as one of free choice, without excuse and without help, any man who takes refuge behind the excuse of his passions, or by inventing some deterministic doctrine, is a self-deceiver. One may object: "But why should he not choose to deceive himself?" I reply that it is not for me to judge him morally, but I define his self-deception as an error. Here one cannot avoid pronouncing a judgment of truth. The self-deception is evidently a falsehood, because it is a dissimulation of man's complete liberty of commitment. Upon this same level, I say that it is also a self-deception if I choose to declare that certain values are incumbent upon me; I am in contradiction with myself if I will these values and at the same time say that they impose themselves upon me. If anyone says to me, "And what if I wish to deceive myself?" I answer, "There is no reason why you should not, but I declare that you are doing so, and that the attitude of strict consistency alone is that of good faith. Furthermore, I can pronounce a moral judgment. For I declare that freedom, in respect of concrete circumstances, can have no other end and aim but itself; and when once a man has seen that values depend upon himself, in that state of forsakenness he can will only one thing, and that is freedom as the foundation of all values. That does not mean that he wills it in the abstract: it simply means that the actions of men of good faith have, as their ultimate significance, the quest of freedom itself as such. A man who belongs to some communist or revolutionary society wills certain concrete ends, which imply the will to freedom, but that freedom is willed in community. We will freedom for freedom's sake, and in and through particular circumstances. And in thus willing freedom we discover that it depends entirely upon the freedom of others and that the freedom of others depends upon our own. Obviously, freedom as the definition of a man does not depend upon others, but as soon as there is a commitment, I am obliged to will the liberty of others at the same time as mine. I cannot make liberty my aim unless I make that of others equally my aim. Consequently, when I recognise, as entirely authentic, that man is a being whose existence precedes his essence, and that he is a free being who cannot, in any circumstances, but will his freedom, at the same time I realise that I cannot not will the freedom of others. Thus, in the name of that will to freedom which is implied in freedom itself I can form judgments upon those who seek to hide from themselves the wholly voluntary nature of their existence and its complete freedom. Those who hide from this total freedom, in a guise of solemnity or with deterministic excuses, I shall call cowards. Others, who try to show that their existence is necessary, when it is merely an accident of the appearance of the human race on earth,— I shall call scum. But neither cowards nor scum can be identified except upon the plane of strict authenticity. Thus, although the content of morality is variable, a certain form of this morality is universal. Kant declared that freedom is a will both to itself and to the freedom of others. Agreed: but he thinks that the formal and the universal suffice for the constitution of a morality. We think, on the contrary, that principles that are too abstract break down when we come to defining action. To take once again the case of that student; by what authority, in the name of what golden rule of morality, do you think he could have decided, in perfect peace of mind, either to abandon his mother or to remain with her? There are no means of judging. The content is always concrete and therefore unpredictable; it has always to be invented. The one thing that counts, is to know whether the invention is made in the name of freedom.

Let us, for example, examine the two following cases, and you will see how far they are similar in spite of their difference. Let us take *The Mill on the Floss*. We find here a certain young woman, Maggie Tulliver, who is an incarnation of the value of passion and is aware of it. She is in love with a young man, Stephen, who is engaged to another, an insignificant young woman. This Maggie Tulliver, instead of heedlessly seeking her own happiness, chooses in the name of human solidarity to sacrifice herself and to give up the man she loves. On the other hand, La Sanseverina in Stendhal's *Chartreuse de Parme*, believing that it is passion which endows man with his real value, would have declared that a grand passion justifies its sacrifices, and must be preferred to the banality of such conjugal love as would unite Stephen to the little goose he was engaged to marry. It is the latter that she would have chosen to sacrifice in realising her own happiness, and, as Stendhal shows, she would also sacrifice herself upon the plane of passion if life made that demand upon her. Here we are facing two clearly opposed moralities; but I claim that they are equivalent, seeing that in both cases the overruling aim is freedom. You can imagine two attitudes exactly similar in effect, in that one girl might prefer, in resignation, to give up her lover whilst the other preferred, in fulfilment of sexual desire, to ignore the prior engagement of the man she loved; and, externally, these two cases might appear the same as the two we have just cited, while being in fact entirely different. The attitude of La Sanseverina is much nearer to that of Maggie Tulliver than to one of careless greed. Thus, you see, the second objection is at once true and false. One can choose anything, but only if it is upon the plane of free commitment.

The third objection, stated by saying, "You take with one hand what you give with the other," means, at bottom, "your values are not serious, since you choose them yourselves." To that I can only say that I am very sorry that it should be so; but if I have excluded God the Father, there must be somebody to invent values. We have to take things as they are. And moreover, to say that we invent values means neither more nor less than this; that there is no sense in life *a priori*. Life is nothing until it is lived; but it is yours to make sense of, and the value of it is nothing else but the sense that you choose. Therefore, you can see that there is a possibility of creating a human community. I have been reproached for suggesting that existentialism is a form of humanism: people have said to me, "But you have written in your *Nauseé* that the humanists are wrong, you have even ridiculed a certain type of humanism, why do you now go back upon that?" In reality, the word humanism has two very different meanings. One may understand by humanism a theory which upholds man as the end-in-itself and as the supreme value. Humanism in this sense appears, for instance, in Cocteau's story *Round the World in 80*

Hours, in which one of the characters declares, because he is flying over mountains in an aeroplane, "Man is magnificent!" This signifies that although I, personally, have not built aeroplanes I have the benefit of those particular inventions and that I personally, being a man, can consider myself responsible for, and honoured by, achievements that are peculiar to some men. It is to assume that we can ascribe value to man according to the most distinguished deeds of certain men. That kind of humanism is absurd, for only the dog or the horse would be in a position to pronounce a general judgment upon man and declare that he is magnificent, which they have never been such fools as to do—at least, not as far as I know. But neither is it admissible that a man should pronounce judgment upon Man. Existentialism dispenses with any judgment of this sort: an existentialist will never take man as the end, since man is still to be determined. And we have no right to believe that humanity is something to which we could set up a cult, after the manner of Auguste Comte. The cult of humanity ends in Comtian humanism, shut-in upon itself, and—this must be said—in Fascism. We do not want a humanism like that.

But there is another sense of the word, of which the fundamental meaning is this: Man is all the time outside of himself: it is in projecting and losing himself beyond himself that he makes man to exist: and, on the other hand, it is by pursuing transcendent aims that he himself is able to exist. Since man is thus self-surpassing, and can grasp objects only in relation to his self-surpassing, he is himself the heart and centre of his transcendence. There is no other universe except the human universe, the universe of human subjectivity. This relation of transcendence as constitutive of man (not in the sense that God is transcendent, but in the sense of self-surpassing) with subjectivity (in such a sense that man is not shut up in himself but forever present in a human universe)—it is this that we call existential humanism. This is humanism, because we remind man that there is no legislator but himself; that he himself, thus abandoned, must decide for himself; also because we show that it is not by turning back upon himself, but always by seeking, beyond himself, an aim which is one of liberation or of some particular realisation, that man can realise himself as truly human.

You can see from these few reflections that nothing could be more unjust than the objections people raise against us. Existentialism is nothing else but an attempt to draw the full conclusions from a consistently atheistic position. Its intention is not in the least that of plunging men into despair. And if by despair one means—as the Christians do—any attitude of unbelief, the despair of the existentialists is something different. Existentialism is not atheist in the sense that it would exhaust itself in demonstrations of the non-existence of God. It declares, rather, that even if God existed that would make no difference from its point of view. Not that we believe God does exist, but we think that the real problem is not that of His existence; what man needs is to find himself again and to understand that nothing can save him from himself, not even a valid proof of the existence of God. In this sense existentialism is optimistic. It is a doctrine of action, and it is only by self-deception, by confusing their own despair with ours that Christians can describe us as without hope.

Discussion

Questioner

I do not know whether this attempt to make yourself understood will make you better understood, or less so; but I think that the explanation in *Action* will only make people misunderstand you more. The words "despair" and "abandonment" have a much wider resonance in an existential context. And it seems to me that despair or anguish means, to you, something more fundamental than the responsibility of the man who feels he is alone and has to make decisions. It is a state of consciousness of the human predicament which does not arise all the time. That one is choosing whom one is to be, is admitted, but anguish and despair do not appear concurrently.

M. Sartre

Obviously I do not mean that whenever I choose between a millefeuille and a chocolate éclair, I choose in anguish. Anguish is constant in this sense—that my original choice is something constant. Indeed, this anguish is, in my view, the complete absence of justification at the same time as one is responsible in regard to everyone.

Questioner

I was alluding to the point of view of the explanation published in *Action*, in which it seemed to me that your own point of view was somewhat weakened.

M. Sartre

Frankly it is possible that my themes have been rather weakened in

Action. It often happens that people who come and put questions to me are not qualified to do so. I am then presented with two alternatives, that of refusing to answer or that of accepting discussion upon the level of popularisation. I have chosen the latter because, after all, when one expounds theories in a class of philosophy one consents to some weakening of an idea in order to make it understood, and it is not such a bad thing to do. If one has a theory of commitment one must commit oneself to see it through. If in truth existential philosophy is above all a philosophy which says that existence precedes essence, it must be lived to be really sincere; and to live as an existentialist is to consent to pay for this teaching, not to put it into books. If you want this philosophy to he indeed a commitment, you have to render some account of it to people who discuss it upon the political or the moral plane.

You reproach me for using the word "humanism." I do so because that is how the problem presents itself. One must either keep the doctrine strictly to the philosophic plane and rely upon chance for any action upon it, or else, seeing that people demand something else, and since its intention is to be a commitment, one must consent to its popularisation—provided one does not thereby distort it.

Questioner

Those who want to understand you will understand, and those who do not want to will not understand you.

M. Sartre

You seem to conceive the part played by philosophy in this civilisation in a sense that has been outmoded by events. Until recently philosophers were attacked only by other philosophers. The public understood nothing of it and cared less. Now, however, they have made philosophy come right down into the market-place. Marx himself never ceased to popularise his thought. The manifesto is the popularisation of an idea.

Questioner

The original choice of Marx was a revolutionary one.

M. Sartre

He must he a cunning fellow indeed who can say whether Marx chose himself first as a revolutionary and then as a philosopher, or first as a philosopher and as a revolutionary afterwards. He is both a philosopher and a revolutionary—that is a whole. To say that he chose himself first as a revolutionary—what does that mean?

Questioner

The *Communist Manifesto* does not look to me like a popularisation; it is a weapon of war. I cannot believe that it was not an act of commitment.

As soon as Marx concluded that the revolution was necessary, his first action was his *Communist Manifesto*, which was a political action. The *Communist Manifesto* is the bond between the philosophy of Marx and Communism. Whatever may be the morality you hold, one can feel no such close logical connection between that morality and your philosophy as there is between the *Communist Manifesto* and Marx's philosophy.

M. Sartre

We are dealing with a morality of freedom. So long as there is no contradiction between that morality and our philosophy, nothing more is required. Types of commitment differ from one epoch to another. In one epoch, in which to commit oneself was to make revolution, one had to write the *Manifesto*. In such an epoch as ours, in which there are various parties, each advertising itself as the revolution, commitment does not consist in joining one of them, but in seeking to clarify the conception, in order to define the situation and at the same time to try to influence the different revolutionary parties.

M. Naville

The question one must ask oneself, arising from the point of view that you have just indicated, is this: Will not your doctrine present itself, in the period now beginning, as the resurrection of radical-socialism? This may seem fantastic, but it is the way in which one must now frame the question. You place yourself, by the way, at all sorts of points of view; but if one looks for the actual point of convergence, to which all these points of view and aspects of existential thought are tending, I have the impression that it turns out to be a kind of resurrection of liberalism. Your philosophy seeks to revive, in the quite peculiar conditions which are our present historical conditions, what is essential in radical-socialism, in liberal humanism. What gives it its distinctive character, is the fact that the social crisis of the world has gone too far for the old liberalism, it puts liberalism to torture, to anguish. I believe that one could find several rather profound reasons for this evaluation, even if one kept within your own terms. It follows from the present exposition, that existentialism presents itself as a form of humanism and of a philosophy of freedom, which is at bottom a pre-commitment, and that is a purpose undefined. You put in the forefront, as do many others, the dignity of man, the eminent value of personality. These are themes which, all things considered, are not so far from those of the old liberalism. To justify them, you make distinction between two meanings of "the condition of man" and between two meanings of several terms which are in common use. The significance of these terms has, however, a whole history, and their equivocal character is not the result of chance. To rescue them, you would invent new meanings for them. I will pass over all the special questions of philosophic technique which this raises, interesting and important as they are; and, confining myself to the terms that I have just heard, I will fasten upon the fundamental point which shows that, in spite of your distinction between two meanings of humanism, the meaning that you hold is, after all, the old one.

Man presents himself as a choice to be made. Very well. He is, first and foremost, his existence at the present instant, and he stands outside of natural determinism. He is not defined by anything prior to himself, but by his present functioning as an individual. There is no human nature superior to him, but a specific existence is given to him at a given moment. I ask myself whether "existence" taken in this sense is not another form of the concept of human nature which, for historical reasons, is appearing in a novel guise. Is it not very similar—more so than it looks at first sight—to human nature as it was defined in the eighteenth century, the conception which you say you repudiate? For this reappears in and very largely underlies the expression "the condition of man" as it is used in existentialism. Your conception of the human condition is a substitute for human nature, just as you substitute lived experience for common experience or scientific experiment.

If we consider human conditions as conditions defined by X, which is the X of the subject, and not by the natural environment, not by positive determinants, one is considering human nature under another form. It is a nature-condition, if you like, which is not to say that it is definable simply as an abstract type of nature; it is revealed in ways much more difficult to formulate for reasons which, in my view, are historical. In these days, human nature is expressing itself in a social framework that is undergoing a general disintegration of social orders and social classes, in conflicts that cut across them, and in a stirring-together of all races and nations. The notion of a uniform and schematic human nature cannot now be presented with the same character of generality nor take on the same aspect of universality as in the eighteenth century, an epoch when it appeared to be definable upon a basis of continuous progress. In these days we are concerned with an expression of human nature which both thoughtful and simple people call the condition of man. Their presentation of this is vague, chaotic and generally of an aspect that is, so to speak, dramatic; imposed by the circumstances. And, in so far as they do not want to go beyond the general expression of that condition into a deterministic enquiry into what the effective conditions are, they maintain the type and the scheme of an abstract expression, analogous to that of human nature.

This existentialism does depend upon a notion of the nature of man, but this time it is not a nature that has pride in itself, but one that is fearful, uncertain and forlorn. And, indeed, when the existentialist speaks of the condition of man, he is speaking of a condition in which he is not yet really committed to what existentialism calls purposes— and which is, consequently, a pre-condition. We have here a pre-engagement, not a commitment, not even a real condition. It is not by accident, then, that this "condition of man" is defined primarily by its general, humanist character. In the past, when one spoke of human nature, one was thinking of something more limited than if one were speaking of a condition in general. For nature—that is already something else: in a sense it is something more than a condition. Human nature is not a modality in the sense that the condition of man is a modality. For that reason it would be better, in my view, to speak of naturalism than of humanism. In naturalism there is an implication of realities more general than are implied in humanism—at least, in the sense in which you take the term 'humanism'—we are dealing with reality itself. As to human nature, the discussion of it needs to be widened: for the historical point of view must also be considered. The primary reality is that of nature, of which human reality is only one function. But for that, one must admit the truth of history, and the existentialist will not, as a rule, admit the truth of human history any more than that of natural history in general. Nevertheless, it is history which makes individuals: it is because of their actual history, from the moment when they are conceived, that they are neither born nor do they live in a world which provides an abstract condition for them. Because of their history they appear in a world of which they themselves have always been part and parcel, by which they are conditioned and to the conditions of which they contribute, even as the mother conditions her child and the child also conditions her from the beginning of its gestation. It is only from this point of view that we have any right to speak of the condition of man as of a primary reality. One ought rather to say that the primary reality is a natural condition and not a human condition. These are merely current and common opinions that I am repeating, but in no way whatever that I can see does the existential argument refute them. After all, if it is certain that there is no human nature in the abstract, no essence of man apart from or anterior to his existence, it is also certain that there is no human condition in general—not even if you mean by condition a certain set of concrete circumstances or situations, for in your view these are not articulated. In any case, upon this subject Marxism has a different idea, that of nature within man and man within nature, which is not necessarily defined from an individual point of view.

This means that there are laws of the functioning of man, as of every other object of science, which constitute, in the full sense of the word, his nature. That nature is variable, it is true, but bears little resemblance to a phenomenology—that is, to any perception of it that is felt, empirical, or lived, or such as is given by common sense or rather by the assumed common sense of the philosophers. Thus understood, the conception of human nature as the men of the eighteenth century had it, was un-doubtedly much nearer to that of Marx than is its existential substitute, "the condition of man"—which is a pure phenomenology of his situation.

In these days, unfortunately, humanism is a word employed to identify philosophic tendencies, not only in two senses but in three, four, five, or six. We are all humanists to-day, even certain Marxists. Those who reveal themselves as classical rationalists are humanists in a sense that has gone sour on us, derived from the liberal ideas of the last century, a liberalism refracted throughout the contemporary crisis. If Marxists can claim to be humanists, the various religions, Christian, Hindu and many others, also claim above all that they are humanist; so do the existen-tialists in their turn and, in a general way, all the philosophies. Actually, many political movements protest no less that they are humanist. What all this amounts to is a kind of attempt to re-instate a philosophy which, for all its claims, refuses in the last resort to commit itself, not only from the political or social standpoint, but also in the deeper philosophic sense. When Christianity claims to be humanist before all else, it is because it refuses to commit itself, because it cannot—that is, it cannot side with the progressive forces in the conflict, because it is holding on to reactionary positions in face of the revolution. When the pseudo-Marxists or the liberals place the rights of the personality above everything, it is because they recoil before the exigencies of the present world situation. Just so the existentialist, like the liberal, puts in a claim for man in general because he cannot manage to formulate such a position as the events require, and the only progressive position that is known is that of Marxism. Marxism alone states the real problems of the age.

It is not true that a man has freedom of choice, in the sense that by that choice he confers upon his activity a meaning it would not otherwise have. It is not enough to say that men can strive for freedom without knowing that they strive for it—or, if we give the fullest meaning to that recognition, it means that men can engage in the struggle for a cause which over-rules them, which is to say that they can act within a frame greater than themselves, and not merely act out of themselves. For in the end, if a man strives for freedom without knowing it, without being able to say precisely how or to what end he is striving, what does that signify? That his actions are going to bring about a succession of consequences weaving themselves into a whole network of causality of which he cannot grasp all the effects, but which, all the same, round off his action and endow it with a meaning, in function with the activity of others—and not only that of other men, but of the natural environment in which those men act. But, from your point of view, the choice is a pre-choice—I come back again to that prefix, for I think you still interpose a reserve. In this kind of pre-choice one is concerned with the freedom of a prior indifference. But your conception of the condition and the freedom of man is linked to a certain definition of the objective upon which I have a word to say: it is, indeed, upon this idea of the world of objects as utilities that you base everything else. From an image of beings existing in discontinuity, you form a picture of a discontinuous world of objects, in which there is no causality, excepting that strange variety of causal relatedness which is that of utility—passive, incomprehensible and contemptible. Existential man stumbles about in a world of implements, of untidy obstacles, entangled and piled up one upon another in a fantastic desire to make them serve one another, but all branded with the stigma, so frightful in the eyes of idealists, of their so-called pure exteriority. This implemental mode of determinism is, however, a-causal. For where is the beginning or the end of such a world, the definition of which, moreover, is wholly arbitrary and in no way agrees with the data of modern science? For us it neither begins nor ends anywhere, for the separation which the existentialist inflicts upon it—separation from nature, or rather from the condition of man—makes it unreal. There is one world and only one, in our view, and the whole of this world—both men and things, if you must make that distinction—may be seen, in certain variable conditions, under the sign of objectivity. The utility of stars, of anger, of a flower? I will not argue about such things: but I maintain that your freedom, your idealism, is made out of an arbitrary contempt for things. And yet things are very different from the description that you give of them. You admit their existence in their own right, and so far so good. But it is a purely privative existence, one of permanent hostility. The physical and biological universe is never, in your eyes, a condition or a source of conditioning—that word, in its full and practical sense, has no more meaning for you than has the word "cause." That is why the objective universe is, for existential man, nothing but an occasion of vexation, a thing elusive, fundamentally indifferent, a continual mere probability—in short, the very opposite of what it is to the Marxist materialist.

For all these reasons and for some others, you can only conceive the commitment of philosophy as an arbitrary decision which you describe as free. You denature history, even that of Marx, when you say that he has outlined a philosophy because he was committed to it. On the contrary; the commitment, or rather the social and political action, was a determinant of his thinking in a more general sense. It was out of a multiplicity of experiences that he distilled his doctrines. It appears evident to me that the development of philosophic thinking in Marx took place in conscious connection with the development of politics and society. That is more or less the case, moreover, with all previous philosophers. Kant is a systematic philosopher who is known to have refrained from all political activity, but that does not mean that his philosophy did not play a certain political rôle—Kant, the German Robespierre, as Heine called him. And, even to the extent that one might admit, of the epoch of Descartes for example, that the development of philosophy played no direct part in politics—which is however erroneous—it has become impossible to say so since the last century. In these days to seek to re-establish, in any form whatsoever, a position anterior to Marxism—I call that going back to radical-socialism.

In so far as existentialism is engendering a will to revolution it ought, therefore, to undertake first of all a work of self-criticism. I do not think it will do this very cheerfully, but it must be done. It will have to undergo a crisis in the persons of those who advocate it—a dialectical crisis—if it is still to retain, in some sense, certain positions not devoid of value which are held by some of its partisans. That seems to me all the more necessary because I have noted that some of them have been arguing from existentialism to social conclusions that are most disquieting, indeed obviously retrograde. One of them wrote, at the end of an analysis, that phenomenology could perform a special social service to-day, by providing the *petite*-bourgeoisie with a philosophy which would enable them to live and to become the vanguard of the international revolutionary movement. By this interpretation of conscientious intentions, one could give the *petite*-bourgeoisie a philosophy corresponding to its existence, and it could become the advance guard of the world-revolutionary movement! I mention this as an example, and I could give you others of the same kind, showing that a certain number of persons, who are moreover deeply committed, and find themselves much drawn to the existential theme, are beginning to elaborate it into political theories. But after all, and here I come back to what I said at the beginning, these are theories coloured with neo-liberalism, with neo-radical-socialism. That is certainly a danger. What chiefly interests us is not any research into the dialectical coherence between all the different grounds touched upon by existentialism, but to see the orientation of these themes. For little by little, perhaps unknown to their defenders, and undertaken as an enquiry, a theory, as an attitude, they do lead to something. Not, of course, to quietism; to talk of quietism in the present epoch would be a losing game indeed, in fact an impossible one: but to something very like 'attentism.'[3] That may, perhaps, be not inconsistent with certain kinds of individual commitment; but it is inconsistent with any search for a commitment of collective value—especially of a prescriptive value. Why should existentialism not give any directions? In the name of freedom? But if this philosophy tends in the direction indicated by Sartre, it ought to give directives. It ought, in 1945, to tell us whether to join the U.D.S.R.,[4] or the Socialist Party, the Communist Party or another: it ought to say whether it is on the side of the workers or on that of the *petite*-bourgeoisie.

M. Sartre

It is rather difficult to give you a complete answer. You have said so many things. But I will try to reply to a few points that I have noted down. First, I must say that you take up a dogmatic position. You say that we take up a position anterior to Marxism, that we are advancing towards the rear. I consider that what you have to prove is that the position we are seeking to establish is not post-Marxian. As to that I will not argue, but I would like to ask you how you come by your conception of 'the truth.' You think there are some things that are absolutely true, for you present your objections in the name of a certitude. But if all men are objects as you say, whence have you such a certitude? You say it is in the name of human dignity that man refuses to regard man as an object. That is false: it is for a reason of a philosophic and logical order: if you postulate a universe of objects, truth disappears. The objective world is the world of the probable. You ought to recognise that every theory, whether scientific or philosophic, is one of probability. The proof of this is that scientific and historical theses vary, and that they are made in the form of hypotheses. If we admit that the objective world, the world of the probable, is one, we have still no more than a world of probabilities; and in that case since the probability depends upon our having acquired some truths, whence comes the certitude? Our subjectivism allows us some certitudes, and we are thus enabled to rejoin you upon the plane of the probable. We can thus justify the dogmatism which you have demonstrated throughout your discourse, though it is incomprehensible from the position that you take. If you do not define the truth, how can you conceive the theory of Marx otherwise than as a doctrine which appears, disappears, is modified and has no more than theoretical value? How can one make a dialectic of history unless one begins by postulating a certain number of rules? We deduce these from the Cartesian *cogito*: we can only find them by placing ourselves firmly upon the ground of subjectivity. We have never disputed the fact that, continually, man is an object to man. But reciprocally, in order to grasp the object as it is, there must be a subject which attains to itself as subject.

Then, you speak of a condition of man, which you sometimes call a pre-condition, and you speak of pre-determination. What has escaped your notice here, is that we adhere to much that is in the Marxian descriptions. You cannot criticise me as you would criticise the men of the eighteenth century, who were ignorant of the whole question. We have known for a long time all that you have been telling us about determinism. For us the real problem is to define conditions in which there can be universality. Since there is no human nature, how can one preserve, throughout the continual changes of history, universal principles sufficient to interpret, for instance, the phenomenon of Spartacus, which presupposes a minimum understanding of that epoch? We are in agreement upon this point—that there is no human nature; in other words, each epoch develops according to dialectical laws, and men depend upon their epoch and not upon human nature.

M. Naville

When you seek to interpret, you say: "This is so because we are dealing with a particular situation." For our part, we consider what is analogous or different in the social life of that epoch compared with that of our own. If on the other hand, we tried to analyse the analogy itself as a function of some abstract kind, we should never arrive at anything. If you suppose that, after two thousand years, one has no means of analysing the present situation except certain observations upon the condition of man in general, how could one conduct an analysis that was retrospective? One could not do it.

M. Sartre

We have never doubted the need for analysis either of human conditions or of individual intentions. That which we call the situation is, precisely, the whole of the conditions, not only material but psycho-analytic, which, in the epoch under consideration, define it precisely as a whole.

M. Naville

I do not believe that your definition is in conformity with your texts. Anyhow, it clearly appears that your conception of the situation is in no way identifiable, even remotely, with any Marxist conception, in that it denies causality. Your definition is not precise: it often slips cleverly from one position to another, without defining either in a sufficiently rigorous manner. For us, a situation is a totality that is constructed, and that reveals itself, by a whole series of determining factors, and these determinants are causal, including causality of a statistical kind.

M. Sartre

You talk to me about causality of a statistical order. That is meaningless. Will you tell me, precisely and clearly, what you understand by causality? I will believe in the Marxian causality upon the very day when a Marxian explains it to me. Whenever anyone speaks to you of freedom you spend your time in saying, "Excuse me, but there is causality." But of this secret causality, which has no meaning except in Hegel, you can render no account. You have a dream about the Marxian causality.

M. Naville

Do you admit the existence of scientific truth? There may be spheres in which no kind of truth is predicable. But the world of objects—this you will nevertheless admit, I hope—is the world with which the sciences are concerned. Yet for you, this is a world in which there are only probabilities, never amounting to the truth. The world of objects, then, which is that of science, admits of no absolute truth. But it does attain to relative truth. Now, you will admit that the sciences employ the notion of causality?

M. Sartre

Certainly not. The sciences are abstract; they study the variations of factors that are equally abstract, and not real causality. We are concerned with universal factors upon a plane where their relations can always be studied: whereas, in Marxism, one is engaged in the study of a single totality, in which one searches for causality. But it is not at all the same thing as scientific causality.

M. Naville

You gave an example, and developed it at length—that of a young man who came to consult you.

M. Sartre

Was it not a question of freedom?

M. Naville

He ought to have been answered. I would have endeavoured to ascertain what were his capabilities, his age, his financial resources; and to look into his relation to his mother. Perhaps I should have pronounced a merely probable opinion, but I would most certainly have tried to arrive at a definite point of view, though it might have been proved wrong when acted upon. Most certainly I would have urged him to do something.

M. Sartre

If he comes to ask your advice, it is because he has already chosen the answer. Practically, I should have been very well able to give him some advice. But as he was seeking freedom I wanted to let him decide. Besides, I knew what he was going to do, and that is what he did.

Notes

1 Oignez vilain il vous plaindra, poignez vilain il vous oindra.
2 Mouvement Républicain Populaire.
3 The attentistes, as they were called, were those who neither collaborated with the German occupation nor resisted it: but waited (as they said), for the time when the Allies would invade and make resistance more efficacious, or—as their enemies said—waited to join the winning side.
4 Union Des Socialistes Républicains.

3 Phenomenology

The 'existential phenomenology' of *Being and Nothingness* is a synthesis of existentialism and phenomenology. To understand it, we need a grasp of phenomenology before Sartre.

Although the term 'phenomenology' was given currency by the German mathematician and philosopher J. H. Lambert (1728–77), and although phenomenological themes are salient in *Psychology From an Empirical Standpoint* (1874) by the Austrian philosopher and psychologist Franz Brentano (1838–1917), it is Brentano's pupil Edmund Husserl who is accepted as the 'father' of phenomenology. It is controversial whether Hegel's *Phenomenology of Spirit* (1807) contains much phenomenology in the Husserlian sense and whether Kant engaged in phenomenology in his *Critique of Pure Reason* (1781/87), although Husserl thought he did.

Husserl's phenomenology is often thought to exist in three not wholly distinct phases: the distinguishing of phenomenology from both psychology and logic in *Logical Investigations* (1900–1), 'transcendental phenomenonology' in *Ideas I* (1913) and an emphasis on the 'lifeworld' (*Lebenswelt*) in *The Crisis of the European Sciences* (1936).

Husserl's project is partly the Cartesian one of placing all knowledge on indubitable epistemological foundations, partly the Kantian one of explaining how all knowledge is possible. In *Ideas I*, he uses the methodological device of *epoché*, or phenomenological reduction, to suspend or 'put in abeyance' all claims about the reality of the world outside consciousness. This reduction of what is to the appearance of what is facilitates phenomenological description. Husserl hopes to discover the essence of consciousness, the essence of perception, the essence of a physical object and so on. Objects are shown to be transcendentally constituted by consciousness. That there is an objective world available to us is argued to be an achievement of consciousness. It is the positing and constitution of the world that makes knowledge of it possible. If we ask how consciousness itself is possible, then Husserl's answer, increasingly from 1913, is that consciousness is grounded in the *pure ego* (*reine Ich*). The term 'transcendental ego' (*transzendentale Ich*) is first used in the *Erste Philosophie* and *Phanomenologische Psychologie* and appears in the second volume of *Ideas* (which Husserl worked on from 1912–28).

There are three aspects of this Husserlian picture which Sartre crucially rejects: the transcendental ego, the essentialism and the *epoché*. In *The Transcendence of the Ego* (1937) Sartre argues that the existence of the transcendental ego is inconsistent with the unity of consciousness. There is the unity of consciousness, so there is no transcendental ego. The very postulation of the transcendental ego is phenomenologically illegitimate because phenomenology describes only what appears to consciousness and, as subject of consciousness, no transcendental ego appears to consciousness.

Sartre's existentialism, including Roquentin's meditations in *Nausea* on the contingency of things being and being what they are, is an implicit repudiation of Husserl's essentialism. Husserl grounds what is in necessity, Sartre in contingency.

Sartre rejects the phenomenological *epoché* because it entails that conscious states may be coherently studied in abstraction from their real objects in the world. To understand this we need to turn to the phenomenology of Martin Heidegger (1889–1976).

Heidegger's massive and influential *Sein und Zeit* (*Being and Time*) (1927) is an attempt to clarify the *question of being* (*Seinsfrage*). The question of being is not What exists? but What is it for anything to be rather than not be?, What exactly does it consist in for there to be something rather than nothing?. Heidegger thinks the question of being has been forgotten or repressed since Plato and Aristotle. It was thought in a pure form, which should be recovered, by the pre-socratic philosophers, notably Parmenides and Heraclitus. However, Heidegger thinks a prerequisite for the inquiry into being is an inquiry into the being of the inquirer: the being who is capable of raising the question of being. Heidegger's name for one's own being, or the kind of existence exhibited by human being, is *Dasein*.

The being of *Dasein* is *being-in-the-world*. The hyphenation of this expression signals Heidegger's insistence that *being*, *in* and *world* are not ontologically separable. Much of *Being and Time* is taken up with the description of the structures of *being-in-the-world*. *Dasein* is the site, or clearing in the forest (*Lichtung*), where being is disclosed to itself. The *Seinsfrage* is not answered in *Being and Time*, which remained unfinished, but in its closing chapters Heidegger suggests there is a kind of time primordial with regard to being: a transition between future and past that being itself presupposes and is constitutive of *Dasein*.

Sartre's own existential phenomenology is a synthesis of Husserl's and Heidegger's thought. Sartre substitutes the Heideggerian structure *being-in-the-world* for the Husserlian *epoché*. Although Heidegger eschews a psychologistic vocabulary to engage in fundamental ontology, Sartre revives the Husserlian emphasis on consciousness but insists that consciousness is necessarily embedded in the world. It cannot be usefully or coherently abstracted from its objects.

Two extracts are reproduced below, one from *Sketch For a Theory of Emotions* that is accessible, the other from *Being and Nothingness* which is more demanding. In the first, Sartre distinguishes phenomenology from psychology, especially from scientific psychology, which, he feels, cannot in principle explain the distinctively human. In his critique of positivism he freely appropriates the phenomenology of Husserl and the fundamental ontology of Heidegger. Heidegger was uncomfortable with Sartre's use of his thought, and in *Sketch For a Theory of Emotions* we can see why. Heidegger is called a 'psychologist' by Sartre and 'Dasein' is rendered 'human reality'. (The standard French translation of *Sein und Zeit, L'Etre et le temps*, renders 'Dasein' as 'realité humaine'.)

Heidegger is at pains to distance himself from the psychologism and epistemology of the Western intellectual tradition and 'Dasein' denotes a manner of being that is not captured by the empirical connotations of 'human reality'. Nevertheless, Sartre is not concerned with Heideggerian exegesis but with developing a phenomenology through the particular case of emotion.

In the first part of the extract from *Being and Nothingness,* called 'The Phenomenon', Sartre claims phenomenology's reduction of what exists to the appearance of what exists is progress, because it overcomes some *dualisms* (or binary oppositions) constitutive of philosophical problems: interior and exterior, appearance and reality, act and potential, appearance and essence. It reduces these to a prior or more fundamental dualism between the finite and the infinite. An object's being a possible object of experience is its capacity to disclose itself through an infinite number of *profiles* (Husserlian *Abschattungen*) that correspond to the infinity of possible perspectives on it. The reduction of everything to the monism of the phenomenon does not contrast 'phenomenon' with a Kantian 'noumenon' or 'thing-in-itself'.

In the second part of the extract from *Being and Nothingness*, called 'The Phenomenon of Being and the Being of the Phenomenon', Sartre argues that neither of these can be reduced to the other. Husserlian phenomena and the Heideggerian disclosure of being require one another for a phenomenology that is adequate to our being-in-the-world.

In the third and fourth parts, Sartre distinguishes his phenomenology from the idealism of the eighteenth-century Irish philosopher George Berkeley (1685–1753) from whom he nevertheless takes the terminology of *percipere*. It was a slogan of Berkeley's philosophy that in the case of physical objects *esse est percipi, to be is to be perceived*. Sartre introduces Husserl's idea of *intentionality*, the doctrine crucial to phenomenology that all consciousness is consciousness *of* something or other. There is no consciousness that does not take an object, whatever the ontological status of that object should turn out to be. Sartre's descriptions of consciousness here are useful for an understanding of subsequent sections of this anthology, especially Imagination and emotion, Being, Nothingness and The self. In the final section called 'The Ontological Proof' Sartre argues that the consciousness of consciousness not only implies the existence of consciousness but *transphenomenal* being. The existence of consciousness implies the existence of the world.

SKETCH FOR A THEORY OF THE EMOTIONS

Psychology, phenomenology and phenomenological psychology

Psychology is a discipline which claims to be positive; that is, it tries to draw upon the resources of experience alone. We are, of course, no longer in the days of the associationists, and contemporary psychologists do not forbid themselves to *interrogate* and to *interpret*. But they try to confront their subject as the physicist confronts his. We must, however, delimit this concept of experience when we speak of contemporary psychology, for there is, after all, a multitude of diverse experiences and we may, for example, have to decide whether an experience of essences or of values, or a religious experience, really exists or not. The psychologist tries to make use of only two well-defined types of experience: that which is given to us by spatio-temporal experience of organized bodies, and the intuitive knowledge of ourselves which we call reflective experience. When there are debates about method among psychologists they almost always bear upon the problem whether these two kinds of information are complementary. Ought one to be subordinated to the other? Or ought one of them to be resolutely disregarded? But there is agreement upon one essential principle: that their enquiries should begin first of all from the facts. And if we ask ourselves what is a fact, we see that it defines itself in this way: that one must *meet* with it in the course of research, and that it always presents itself as an unexpected enrichment and a novelty in relation to the antecedent facts. We must not then count upon the facts to organize themselves into a synthetic whole which would deliver its meaning by itself. In other words, if what we call anthropology is a discipline which seeks to define the essence of man and the human condition, then psychology—even the psychology of man—is not, and never will be an anthropology. It does not set out to define and limit *a priori* the object of its research. The notion of man that it accepts is quite empirical: all over the world there is a certain number of creatures that offer analogous characteristics. From other sciences, moreover, sociology and physiology, we have learned that certain objective relations exist between these creatures. No more is needed to justify the psychologist in accepting, prudently and as a working hypothesis, the provisional limitation of his researches to this group of creatures. The means of relevant information at our disposal are indeed more easily accessible since they live in society, possess languages and leave records. But the psychologist does not commit himself: he does not know whether the notion of man is arbitrary. It may be too *extensive*; there is nothing to show that the Australian primitive can be placed in the same psychological class as the American workman of 1939. Or it may be *too narrow*; nothing tells us that there is an abyss separating the higher apes from any human creature. In any case, the psychologist strictly forbids himself to consider the men around him as men *like himself*. That notion of likeness, upon which one could perhaps build up an anthropology, seems to him foolish and dangerous. He will gladly admit, with the reservations mentioned above, that he is a man—that is, that he belongs to this provisionally isolated class. But he will think that this human character should be conferred upon him *a posteriori*, and that he cannot, *qua* member of this class, be a privileged object of study, except for experimental convenience. He will learn then *from others* that he is a man: his human nature will not be revealed in any special manner under the pretext that he *is* himself that which he is studying. Introspection here, like "objective" experimentation there, will furnish nothing but facts. If, later on, there ought to be a definitive concept of *man*—which itself is doubtful—this concept is to be envisaged only as the crowning concept of a completed science, which means that it is postponed to infinity. Nor would this be more than a unifying hypothesis invented in order to co-ordinate, hierarchically, the infinite collection of facts brought to light. Which means that the idea of man, if it ever acquires a positive meaning, will be only a conjecture intended to establish connections between the disparate materials and will derive its probability only from its success. Pierce defined the hypothesis as the sum of the experimental results which it enables us to foresee. If, however, some psychologists made use of a certain conception of man *before* this ultimate synthesis was possible, it could be only on their personal account and as a leading idea or, better, as an idea in the Kantian sense, and their primary duty would be never to forget that it was merely a regulative concept.

It follows from all these precautions that psychology, in so far as it claims to be a science, can furnish no more than a sum of heteroclite facts, the majority of which have no link between them. What could be more different, for instance, than the study of the stroboscopic illusion and the study of the inferiority complex? This disorder does not arise by chance, but from the very principles of the science of psychology. To wait upon the *fact* is, by definition, to wait upon the isolated; it is to prefer, positively, the accident to the essential, the contingent to the necessary, disorder to order. It is to discard, in principle, the essential as something in the future—"that is for later on, when we have collected enough facts". The psychologists do not notice, indeed, that it is just as impossible to attain the essence by heaping up the accidents as it is to arrive at unity by the indefinite addition of figures to the right of 0.99. If their only aim is to accumulate observations of detail there is nothing to be said, except that one can see little interest in the collectors' labours. But, if, in their modesty, they are animated by the hope, laudable in itself, that they will eventually realize an anthropological synthesis upon the basis of their monographs, then their aim is completely self-contradictory. They may say that this precisely is the method and the ambition of the natural sciences. To that we must reply that the aim of the sciences of nature is not to know *the world*, but the conditions under which certain general phenomena are possible. It is a good while since the notion of the *world* has succumbed under the criticisms of the methodologists, just because we cannot apply the methods of the positive sciences and at the same time expect them to lead us one day to a discovery of the meaning of the synthetic totality that we call the world. But *man* is a being of the same type as the *world*; it is even possible that, as Heidegger believes, the notions of the world and of "human-reality" *(Dasein)* are inseparable. Precisely for that reason, psychology ought to resign itself to doing without the human-reality, if indeed that human-reality exists.

Applied to a particular example, to the study of the emotions for instance, what is to be gained from the principles and methods of the psychologist? First of all, our knowledge of emotion will be something additional to and *outside* all our other knowledge about psychic being. Emotion will present itself as an irreducible novelty in relation to the phenomena of attention, of memory, etc. You can indeed inspect these phenomena, and the empirical notions that the psychologists lead us to form about them, you can turn and turn them about as you will, but you will not find they have the slightest essential relation to emotion. However, the psychologist admits that man has emotions, he knows that from experience. In this view, emotion is primarily and in principle an *accident*. In treatises on psychology it is the subject of one chapter after the other chapters, much as in chemical treatises calcium might come after hydrogen and sulphur. As for studying the conditions under which an emotion is possible—enquiring, that is, whether the very structure of the human-reality renders the emotions possible and *how* it does so—to the psychologist this would seem needless and absurd. What is the use of enquiring whether emotion is possible, seeing that manifestly it *is*? It is also to experience that the psychologist appeals in order to establish the limits of emotive phenomena and to define them. And, truth to tell, this may well awaken him to the fact that he already has an *idea* of emotion, for after examining the facts, he will draw a line of demarcation between the facts of emotion and those of a quite different order. How could experience supply him with a principle of demarcation if he did not already have one? But the psychologist prefers to hold fast to the belief that the facts fall into groups of themselves under his gaze.

The question now is how to *study* the emotions one has isolated. To this end, let us agree to depict some emotional situations or turn our attention to the particularly emotional subjects offered to us by pathology. We will then try to determine the factors in such complex states: we will isolate the *bodily reactions* (which moreover we can establish with the greatest precision), the *behaviour* and the state of consciousness properly so called. After that, we shall be in a position to formulate our laws and put forward our explanations; that is, we shall try to relate these three types of factors in an irreversible order. If I am partial to the intellectualist theory, for example, I shall set up a constant and irreversible succession between the intimate state of consciousness considered as antecedent and the physiological disturbances considered as consequences. If, on the contrary, I agree with the advocates of the peripheric theory (that "a mother is sad because she weeps"), I shall limit myself; fundamentally, to the reverse order of the factors. What is certain in any case is that I shall not look for the explanation or the laws of emotion in the general structure of the human-reality, but, on the contrary, in the development of the emotion itself, so that, even when duly described and explained, the emotion will never be more than one fact among others, a fact enclosed in itself, which will never enable anyone to understand anything else, nor to look through it into the essential reality of man.

It was in reaction against the insufficiencies of psychology and of psychologism that there grew up, some thirty years ago, a new discipline, that of phenomenology. Its founder, Husserl, was first of all struck by this truth: that there is an incommensurability between essences and facts, and that whoever begins his researches with the facts will never attain to the essences. If I am looking for the psychic facts that underlie the arithmetical attitude of a man who is counting and calculating I shall never succeed in reconstituting the arithmetical essences of unity, of number and of numerical operations. Without, however, renouncing the idea of experience (the principle of phenomenology is to "go to the things themselves", and its method is founded upon the eidetic intuition), it must at least be made more flexible; room must be made for the experience of essences and values; we must even recognize that essences alone enable us to classify and examine facts. If we did not have implicit recourse to the essence of emotion it would be impossible for us to distinguish, among the multitude of psychic facts, this particular group of the facts of emotivity. Since, then, we have anyhow taken implicit recourse to the essence of emotion, phenomenology prescribes that we make our recourse explicit—that we should fix, once for all and by concepts, the content of this essence. It is easy to see that, for phenomenology, the notion of man can no longer be taken as an empirical concept derived from historical generalization; but that on the contrary we are obliged to make use, without saying so, of the *a priori* essence of the *human being* to give a little firm basis to the generalizations of the psychologist. Psychology, moreover, envisaged as the science of certain human facts, cannot be our starting-point, since the psychic facts that we meet with are always prior to it. And these, in their essential structure, are reactions of man against the world: they therefore presuppose man and the world, and cannot take on their true meaning unless those two notions have first been elucidated. If we want to found a psychology we must go beyond the psychic, beyond the situation of man in the world, even to the very source of man, of the world and of the psychic; to the transcendental and constitutive consciousness that we attain through a "phenomenological reduction", or "putting the world in brackets". It is this consciousness that must be interrogated; and what gives value to its answers is that it is *mine.* Husserl knows how to take advantage of that absolute proximity of consciousness to itself; which the psychologists do not choose to profit by. He takes advantage of it wittingly and with absolute confidence, because all consciousness exists precisely to the degree that it is consciousness of existing. But here, as above, he refuses to question consciousness about the *facts*, which would be to find the disorder of psychology again upon the transcendental plane. What he sets out to describe and to fix in concepts are precisely the essences which preside over developments in the transcendental field. Thus there will be, for instance, a phenomenology of emotion which, after "putting the world in brackets", will study emotion as a purely transcendental phenomenon, not addressing itself to particular emotions, but seeking to attain and elucidate the transcendent essence of emotion as an organized type of consciousness.

The absolute proximity of the investigator to the object investigated is also the point of departure for another psychologist, Heidegger. What must differentiate all research into man from other types of strict investigation is precisely this privileged circumstance, that the human-reality is *ourselves*. "The existent that we have to analyse," writes Heidegger, "is ourselves. The being of this existent is *my own*." And it is no negligible matter that this human-reality should be *myself*, because it is precisely for the human reality that to exist is always to *assume* its being; that is, to be responsible for it instead of receiving it from outside, as a pebble does. And since "the human reality" is essentially its own possibility, this existent can itself "choose" what it will be, achieve itself—or lose itself. "This assumption" of itself which characterizes the human reality implies an understanding of the human reality by itself; however obscure an understanding this may be. "In the being of this existent, the latter relates itself to its being." For indeed this under-standing is not a quality that comes to the human reality from without, but is its own mode of existence. Thus the human reality which is myself assumes its own being by understanding it. This understanding is mine. I am, then, first of all, a being who more or less obscurely understands his reality as a man, which means that I make myself a man by understand-ing myself as such. I can therefore question myself and, on the basis of that interrogation, carry out an analysis of the "human reality" which will serve as the basis for an anthropology. Here too, of course, the pro-cedure is not to be one of introspection; firstly, because introspection meets with nothing but facts, and secondly, because my comprehension of the human reality is dim and inauthentic. It has to be made explicit and corrected. In any case, the hermeneutic of existence will be sufficient foundation for an anthropology, and this anthropology will serve as a basis for all psychology. We are thus taking up a position opposite to that of the psychologists, since we *start* from the synthetic totality that man is, and establish the essence of man before beginning our psychology.

At all events, phenomenology is the study of phenomena—not of the facts. And by a phenomenon we are to understand "that which announces itself", that of which the reality precisely is the appearance. And this "announcement of itself" is not that of anything else . . . the being of the existent is not a thing "behind which" there is still something else which "does not yet appear". Indeed, for the human reality, to exist is, according to Heidegger, to assume its own being in an existential mode of understanding. And in Husserl, to exist is, for consciousness, to appear to itself. Since the appearance here is the absolute, it is the appearance which has to be described and enquired into. From this point of view, Heidegger thinks that, in every human attitude—in emotion, for example, since we have been speaking of that—we can rediscover the whole of the human reality, for emotion is the human reality assuming itself and "emotionally-directing" itself towards the world. Husserl, for his part, thinks that a phenomenological description of emotion will reveal the essential structures of consciousness, seeing that an emotion precisely is a consciousness. And reciprocally, a problem will arise that the psychologist does not even suspect: can one conceive of consciousnesses which do not include emotion among their potentialities or must we indeed regard it as an indispensable constituent of consciousness? Thus the phenomenologist will interrogate emotion *about consciousness* or *about man*; he will enquire not only what it is, but what it has to tell us about a being, one of whose characteristics is just this, that it is capable of being moved. And conversely, he will interrogate consciousness, the human reality, about emotion: what must a consciousness be, that emotion should be possible, perhaps that it should even be necessary?

We are now able to understand why the psychologist distrusts phenomenology. The initial precaution of the psychologist is, in effect, to consider the psychic state from an aspect that will divest it of all *signification*. For him a psychic state is always a *fact* and, as such, always accidental. This accidental character is indeed what the psychologist most firmly maintains. If we ask of a scientist: why do bodies attract one another according to Newton's law? he will reply: I know nothing about that; or, because it is so. And if we ask him: what does that attraction signify? he will answer: it does not signify anything; it just is. Similarly, the psychologist, questioned about emotion, is quite proud to affirm: "It exists. Why? I know nothing of that, I simply state the fact. I do not know its signification." To the phenomenologist, on the other hand, every human fact is of its essence significant. If you deprive it of its significance you rob it of its nature as a human fact. The task of the phenomenologist, then, will be to study the significance of emotion. What are we to understand by that?

To signify is to indicate something else; and to indicate it in such a way that in developing the signification one finds precisely the thing signified. For the psychologist emotion signifies nothing, because he studies it as a fact; that is, by separating it from everything else. It will then be non-significant from the start; but if every human fact is in truth significant, this emotion of the psychologists is of its nature dead, non-psychic, inhuman. Whereas, if we want to see emotion as the phenomenologists see it, as a true phenomenon of consciousness, we shall have to consider it as significant first of all; and this means that we shall affirm that it *is* strictly to the degree that it signifies. We shall not begin by losing our way in the study of psychological facts, simply because, taken by themselves and in isolation, they signify *almost* nothing: they are, and that is all. On the contrary, we shall try, by developing the significance of behaviour and of disturbed consciousness, to explain what is signified. And what this is we know from the beginning: an emotion signifies *in its own manner* the whole of the consciousness, or, if we take our stand on the existential plane, of the human reality. It is not an accident, because the human reality is not a sum of facts; it expresses under a definite aspect the synthetic human entirety in its integrity. And by that we must in no wise be understood to mean that it is the effect of the human reality. It is that human reality itself; realizing itself in the form of "emotion". Hence it is impossible to regard emotion as a psycho-physiological disorder. It has its own essence, its peculiar structures, its laws of appearance, its meaning. It cannot possibly come from *outside* the human reality. It is man, on the contrary, who *assumes* his emotion, and emotion is therefore an organized form of human existence.

It is not our intention here to attempt a phenomenological study of emotion. Such a study, if we had one, would deal with affectivity as an existential mode of the human reality. But our ambition is more limited. We would rather try, in one defined and concrete case, that of emotion, to see whether pure psychology could derive a method and some instructions from phenomenology. We will not quarrel with psychology for not bringing man into question or putting the world in brackets. It takes man in the world as he presents himself in a multitude of situations: at the restaurant, in the family, at war. In a general way, what interests psychology is *man in situation*. In itself it is, as we have seen, subordinate to phenomenology, since a truly positive study of man in situation would have first to have elucidated the notions of man, of the world, of being-in-the-world, and of situation. But, after all, phenomenology is hardly born as yet, and all these notions are very far from a definitive elucidation. Ought psychology to wait until phenomenology comes to maturity? We do not think so. But even if it does not wait for the definitive constitution of an anthropology, it should not forget that this anthropology is realisable, and that if one day it is realised, all the psychological disciplines will have to draw upon its resources. For the time being, psychology should endeavour not so much to collect the facts as to interrogate the *phenomena*—that is, the actual psychic events in so far as these are significations, not in so far as they are pure facts. For instance, it should recognize that emotion *does not exist*, considered as a physical phenomenon, for a body cannot be emotional, not being able to attribute a meaning to its own manifestations. Psychology will immediately look for something beyond the vascular or respiratory disturbances, this something beyond being the *meaning* of the joy or sadness. But since this meaning is precisely not a quality superposed from without upon the joy or the sadness, since it exists only to the degree that it appears—namely, to which it is *assumed* by the human-reality—it is the consciousness itself that is to be interrogated, for joy is joy only in so far as it appears as such. And, precisely because psychology is not looking for facts, but for their significations, it will abandon the method of inductive introspection or empirical external observation and seek only to grasp and to fix the essence of the phenomena. Psychology too will then offer itself as an eidetic science. Only, it will not be aiming, through study of the psychic phenomenon, at what is ultimately *signified*, which is indeed the totality of man. It does not dispose of sufficient means to attempt that study. What will interest it, however, and this alone, is the phenomenon *inasmuch as it signifies*. Just so might I seek to grasp the essence of the proletariat through the word "proletariat". In that case I should be doing sociology. But the linguist studies the word "proletariat" *in so far as it means proletariat* and will be worrying himself about the vicissitudes of the word as a transmitter of meaning.

Such a science is perfectly possible. What is lacking for it to become real? To have proved itself. We have seen that if the human-reality appears to the psychologist as a collection of heteroclite data, this is because the psychologist has voluntarily placed himself upon the terrain where the human-reality must look to him like that. But this does not necessarily imply that the human reality is anything else but a collection. What we have proved is only that it *cannot* appear otherwise to the psychologist. We have yet to see whether it will bear, to the depths, a phenomenological investigation—whether emotion, for instance, is in truth a phenomenon that signifies. To come clear about this, there is only one way; that which, moreover, the phenomenologist himself recommends: to "go to the things themselves".

BEING AND NOTHINGNESS

The pursuit of being

I.   The phenomenon

Modern thought has realized considerable progress by reducing the existent to the series of appearances which manifest it. Its aim was to overcome a certain number of dualisms which have embarrassed philosophy and to replace them by the monism of the phenomenon. Has the attempt been successful?

In the first place we certainly thus get rid of that dualism which in the existent opposes interior to exterior. There is no longer an exterior for the existent if one means by that a superficial covering which hides from sight the true nature of the object. And this true nature in turn, if it is to be the secret reality of the thing, which one can have a presentiment of or which one can suppose but can never reach because it is the "interior" of the object under consideration—this nature no longer exists. The appearances which manifest the existent are neither interior nor exterior; they are all equal, they all refer to other appearances, and none of them is privileged. Force, for example, is not a metaphysical conatus of an unknown kind which hides behind its effects (accelerations, deviations, etc.); it is the totality of these effects. Similarly an electric current does not have a secret reverse side; it is nothing but the totality of the physical-chemical actions which manifest it (electrolysis, the incandescence of a carbon filament the displacement of the needle of a galvanometer, etc.). No one of these actions alone is sufficient to reveal it. But no action indicates anything which is *behind itself*; it indicates only itself and the total series.

The obvious conclusion is that the dualism of being and appearance is no longer entitled to any legal status within philosophy. The appearance refers to the total series of appearances and not to a hidden reality which would drain to itself all the *being* of the existent. And the appearance for its part is not an inconsistent manifestation of this being. To the extent that men had believed in noumenal realities, they have presented appearance as a pure negative. It was "that which is not being"; it had no other being than that of illusion and error. But even this being was borrowed, it was itself a pretence, and philosophers met with the greatest difficulty in maintaining cohesion and existence in the appearance so that it should not itself be reabsorbed in the depth of non-phenomenal being. But if we once get away from what Nietzsche called "the illusion of worlds-behind-the-scene," and if we no longer believe in the being-behind-the-appearance, then the appearance becomes full positivity; its essence is an "appearing" which is no longer opposed to being but on the contrary is the measure of it. For the being of an existent is exactly what it appears. Thus we arrive at the idea of the phenomenon such as we can find, for example in the "phenomenology" of Husserl or of Heidegger—the phenomenon or the relative-absolute. Relative the phenomenon remains, for "to appear" supposes in essence somebody to whom to appear. But it does not have the double relativity of Kant's *Erscheinung*. It does not point over its shoulder to a true being which would be, for it, absolute. What it is, it is absolutely, for it reveals itself as it is. The phenomenon can be studied and described as such, for it is *absolutely indicative of itself*.

The duality of potency and act falls by the same stroke. The act is everything. Behind the act there is neither potency nor "hexis"[1] nor virtue. We shall refuse, for example, to understand by "genius"—in the sense in which we say that Proust "had genius" or that he "was" a genius—a particular capacity to produce certain works, which was not exhausted exactly in producing them. The genius of Proust is neither the work considered in isolation nor the subjective ability to produce it; it is the work considered as the totality of the manifestations of the person.

That is why we can equally well reject the dualism of appearance and essence. The appearance does not hide the essence, it reveals it; it *is* the essence. The essence of an existent is no longer a property sunk in the cavity of this existent; it is the manifest law which presides over the succession of its appearances, it is the principle of the series. To the nominalism of Poincaré defining a physical reality (an electric current, for example) as the *sum* of its various manifestations, Duhem rightly opposed his own theory, which makes of the concept the synthetic unity of these manifestations. To be sure phenomenology is anything but a nominalism. But essence, as the principle of the series, is definitely only the concatenation of appearances; that is, itself an appearance. This explains how it is possible to have an intuition of *essences* (the *Wesenchau* of Husserl, for example). The phenomenal being manifests itself; it manifests its essence as well as its existence, and it is nothing but the well connected series of its manifestations.

Does this mean that by reducing the existent to its manifestations we have succeeded in overcoming *all* dualisms? It seems rather that we have converted them all into a new dualism: that of finite and infinite. Yet the existent in fact can not be reduced to a *finite* series of manifestations since each one of them is a relation to a subject constantly changing. Although an *object* may disclose itself only through a single *Abschattung*, the sole fact of there being a subject implies the possibility of multiplying the points of view on that *Abschattung*. This suffices to multiply to infinity the *Abschattung* under consideration. Furthermore if the series of appearances were finite, that would mean that the first appearances do not have the possibility of *reappearing*, which is absurd, or that they can be all given at once, which is still more absurd. Let us understand indeed that our theory of the phenomenon has replaced the *reality* of the thing by the *objectivity* of the phenomenon and that it has based this on an appeal to infinity. The reality of that cup is that it is there and that it *is not me*. We shall interpret this by saying that the series of its appearances is bound by a principle which does not depend on my whim. But the appearance, reduced to itself and without reference to the series of which it is a part, could be only an intuitive and subjective plenitude, the manner in which the subject is affected. If the phenomenon is to reveal itself as *transcendent*, it is necessary that the subject himself transcend the appearance toward the total series of which it is a member. He must seize *Red* through his impression of red. By *Red* is meant the principle of the series—the electric current through the electrolysis, etc. But if the transcendence of the object is based on the necessity of causing the appearance to be always transcended, the result is that on principle an object posits the series of its appearances as infinite. Thus the appearance, which is *finite*, indicates itself in its finitude, but at the same time in order to be grasped as an appearance-of-that-which-appears, it requires that it be surpassed toward infinity.

This new opposition, the "finite and the infinite," or better, "the infinite in the finite," replaces the dualism of being and appearance. What appears in fact is only an *aspect* of the object, and the object is altogether *in* that aspect and altogether outside of it. It is altogether *within*, in that it manifests itself *in* that aspect; it shows itself as the structure of the appearance, which is at the same time the principle of the series. It is altogether outside, for the series itself will never appear nor can it appear. Thus the outside is opposed in a new way to the inside, and the being-which-does-not-appear, to the appearance. Similarly a certain "potency" returns to inhabit the phenomenon and confer on it its very transcendence—a potency to be developed in a series of real or possible appearances. The genius of Proust, even when reduced to the works produced, is no less equivalent to the infinity of possible points of view which one can take on that work and which we will call the "inexhaustibility" of Proust's work. But is not this inexhaustibility which implies a transcendence and a reference to the infinite—is this not an "hexis" at the exact moment when one apprehends it on the object? The essence finally is radically severed from the individual appearance which manifests it, since on principle it is that which must be able to be manifested by an infinite series of individual manifestations.

In thus replacing a variety of oppositions by a single dualism on which they all are based, have we gained or lost? This we shall soon see. For the moment, the first consequence of the "theory of the phenomenon" is that the appearance does not refer to being as Kant's phenomenon refers to the noumenon. Since there is nothing behind the appearance, and since it indicates only itself (and the total series of appearances), it can not be *supported* by any being other than its own. The appearance can not be the thin film of nothingness which separates the being-of-the-subject from absolute-being. If the essence of the appearance is an "appearing" which is no longer opposed to any *being*, there arises a legitimate problem concerning *the being of this appearing*. It is this problem which will be our first concern and which will be the point of departure for our inquiry into being and nothingness.

II. The phenomenon of being and the being of the phenomenon

The appearance is not supported by any existent different from itself; it has its own *being*. The first being which we meet in our ontological inquiry is the being of the appearance. Is it itself an appearance? It seems so at first. The phenomenon is what manifests itself, and being manifests itself to all in some way, since we can speak of it and since we have a certain comprehension of it. Thus there must be for it a *phenomenon of being*, an appearance of being, capable of description as such. Being will be disclosed to us by some kind of immediate access—boredom, nausea, etc., and ontology will be the description of the phenomenon of being as it manifests itself; that is, without intermediary. However for any ontology we should raise a preliminary question: is the phenomenon of being thus achieved identical with the being of phenomena? In other words, is the being which discloses itself to me, which *appears* to me, of the same nature as the being of existents which appear to me? It seems that there is no difficulty. Husserl has shown how an eidetic reduction is always possible; that is, how one can always pass beyond the concrete phenomenon toward its essence. For Heidegger also "human reality" is ontic-ontological; that is, it can always pass beyond the phenomenon toward its being. But the passage from the particular object to the essence is a passage from homogeneous to homogeneous. Is it the same for the passage from the existent to the phenomenon of being: Is passing beyond the existent toward the phenomenon of being actually to pass beyond it toward *its* being, as one passes beyond the particular red toward *its* essence? Let us consider further.

In a particular object one can always distinguish qualities like color, odor, etc. And proceeding from these, one can always determine an essence which they imply, as a sign implies its meaning. The totality "object-essence" makes an organized whole. The essence is not in the object it is the meaning of the object, the principle of the series of appearances which disclose it. But being is neither one of the object's qualities, capable of being apprehended among others, nor a meaning of the object. The object does not refer to being as to a signification; it would be impossible, for example, to define being as a *presence* since *absence* too discloses being, since not to be *there* means still to be. The object does not *possess* being, and its existence is not a participation in being, nor any other kind of relation. It *is*. That is the only way to define its manner of being; the object does not hide being, but neither does it reveal being. The object does not hide it, for it would be futile to try to push aside certain qualities of the existent in order to find the being behind them; being is being of them all equally. The object does not reveal being, for it would be futile to address oneself to the object in order to apprehend its being. The existent is a phenomenon; this means that it designates itself as an organized totality of qualities. It designates itself and not its being. Being is simply the condition of all revelation. It is being-for-revealing (*être-pour-dévoiler*) and not revealed being (*être dévoilé*). What then is the meaning of the surpassing toward the ontological, of which Heidegger speaks? Certainly I can pass beyond this table or this chair toward its being and raise the question of the being-of-the-table or the being-of-the-chair.[2] But at that moment I turn my eyes away from the phenomenon of the table in order to concentrate on the phenomenon of being, which is no longer the condition of all revelation, but which is itself something revealed—an appearance which as such, needs in turn a being on the basis of which it can reveal itself.

If the being of phenomena is not resolved in a phenomenon of being and if nevertheless we can not say anything about being without considering this phenomenon of being, then the exact relation which unites the phenomenon of being to the being of the phenomenon must be established first of all. We can do this more easily if we will consider that the whole of the preceding remarks has been directly inspired by the revealing intuition of the phenomenon of being. By not considering being as the condition of revelation but rather being as an appearance which can be determined in concepts, we have understood first of all that knowledge can not by itself give an account of being; that is, the being of the phenomenon can not be reduced to the phenomenon of being. In a word, the phenomenon of being is "ontological" in the sense that we speak of the *ontological* proof of St. Anselm and Descartes. It is an appeal to being; it requires as phenomenon, a foundation which is trans-phenomenal. The phenomenon of being requires the transphenomenality of being. That does not mean that being is found hidden *behind* phenomena (we have seen that the phenomenon can not hide being), nor that the phenomenon is an appearance which refers to a distinct being (the phenomenon exists only qua appearance; that is, it indicates itself on the foundation of being). What is implied by the preceding considerations is that the being of the phenomenon although coextensive with the phenomenon, can not be subject to the phenomenal condition—which is to exist only in so far as it reveals itself—and that consequently it surpasses the knowledge which we have of it and provides the basis for such knowledge.

III.   *The pre-reflective* cogito *and the being of the* percipere

One will perhaps be tempted to reply that the difficulties mentioned above all pertain to a certain conception of being, to a kind of onto-logical realism entirely incompatible with the very notion of appearance. What determines the being of the appearance is the fact that it appears. And since we have restricted reality to the phenomenon, we can say of the phenomenon that it *is* as it *appears*. Why not push the idea to its limit and say that the being of the appearance is its appearing? This is simply a way of choosing new words to clothe the old "*Esse est percipi*" of Berkeley. And it is in fact just what Husserl and his followers are doing when after having effected the phenomenological reduction, they treat the noema as *unreal* and declare that its *esse* is *percipi*.

It seems that the famous formula of Berkeley can not satisfy us—for two essential reasons, one concerning the nature of the *percipi*, the other that of the *percipere*.

The nature of the percipere

If every metaphysics in fact presupposes a theory of knowledge, every theory of knowledge in turn presupposes a metaphysics. This means among other things that an idealism intent on reducing being to the knowledge which we have of it, ought first to give some kind of guaran-tee for the being of knowledge. If one begins, on the other hand, by taking the knowledge as a given, without being concerned to establish a basis for its being, and if one then affirms that *esse est percipi*, the totality "perceived-perception," lacks the support of a solid being and so falls away in nothingness. Thus the being of knowledge can not be measured by knowledge; it is not subject to the *percipi*.[3] Therefore the foundation-of-being (*l'être-fondement*) for the *percipere* and the *percipi* can not itself be subject to the *percipi*; it must be transphenomenal. Let us return now to our point of departure. We can always agree that the *percipi* refers to a being not subject to the laws of the appearance, but we still maintain that this transphenomenal being is the being of the subject. Thus the *percipi* would refer to the *percipiens*—the known to knowledge and knowledge to the being who knows (in his capacity as *being*, not as being known); that is, knowledge refers to consciousness. This is what Husserl understood; for if the noema is for him an unreal correlate of noesis, and if its ontological law is the *percipi*, the noesis, on the contrary, appears to him as *reality*, of which the principle characteristic is to give itself to the reflection which *knows* it as "having already been there before." For the law of being in the knowing subject is to-be-conscious. Consciousness is not a mode of particular knowledge which may be called an inner meaning or self-knowledge; it is the dimension of transphenomenal being in the subject.

Let us look more closely at this dimension of being. We said that consciousness is the knowing being in his capacity as *being* and not as being known. This means that we must abandon the primacy of knowledge if we wish to establish that knowledge. Of course consciousness can know and know itself. But it is in itself something other than a knowledge turned back upon itself.

All consciousness, as Husserl has shown, is consciousness *of* something. This means that there is no consciousness which is not a *positing* of a transcendent object, or if you prefer, that consciousness has no "content." We must renounce those neutral "givens" which, according to the system of reference chosen, find their place either "in the world" or "in the psyche." A table is not *in* consciousness—not even in the capacity of a representation. A table is *in* space, beside the window, etc. The existence of the table in fact is a center of opacity for consciousness; it would require an infinite process to inventory the total contents of a thing. To introduce this opacity into consciousness would be to refer to infinity the inventory which it can make of itself, to make consciousness a thing, and to deny the cogito. The first procedure of a philosophy ought to be to expel things from consciousness and to reestablish its true connection with the world, to know that consciousness is a positional consciousness of the world. All consciousness is positional in that it transcends itself in order to reach an object, and it exhausts itself in this same positing. All that there is of *intention* in my actual consciousness is directed toward the outside, toward the table; all my judgments or practical activities, all my present inclinations transcend themselves; they aim at the table and are absorbed in it. Not all consciousness is knowledge (there are states of affective consciousness, for example), but all knowing consciousness can be knowledge only of its object.

However, the necessary and sufficient condition for a knowing consciousness to be knowledge *of* its object, is that it be consciousness of itself as being that knowledge. This is a necessary condition, for if my consciousness were not consciousness of being consciousness of the table, it would then be consciousness of that table without consciousness of being so. In other words, it would be a consciousness ignorant of itself, an unconscious—which is absurd. This is a sufficient condition, for my being conscious of being conscious of that table suffices in fact for me to be conscious of it. That is of course not sufficient to permit me to affirm that this table exists *in itself*—but rather that it exists *for me*.

What is this consciousness of consciousness? We suffer to such an extent from the illusion of the primacy of knowledge that we are immediately ready to make of the consciousness of consciousness an *idea ideae* in the manner of Spinoza; that is, a knowledge of knowledge. Alain, wanting to express the obvious "To know is to be conscious of knowing," interprets it in these terms: "To know is to know that one knows." In this way we should have defined *reflection* or positional consciousness of consciousness, or better yet *knowledge of consciousness*. This would be a complete consciousness directed toward something which is not it; that is, toward consciousness as object of reflection. It would then transcend itself and like the positional consciousness *of* the world would be exhausted in aiming at its object. But that object would be itself a consciousness.

It does not seem possible for us to accept this interpretation of the consciousness of consciousness. The reduction of consciousness to knowledge in fact involves our introducing into consciousness the subject-object dualism which is typical of knowledge. But if we accept the law of the knower-known dyad, then a third term will be necessary in order for the knower to become known in turn, and we will be faced with this dilemma: Either we stop at any one term of the series—the known, the knower known, the knower known by the knower, *etc.* In this case the totality of the phenomenon falls into the unknown; that is, we always bump up against a non-self-conscious reflection and a final term. Or else we affirm the necessity of an infinite regress (*idea ideae ideae*, etc.), which is absurd. Thus to the necessity of ontologically establishing consciousness we would add a new necessity: that of establishing it epistemologically. Are we obliged after all to introduce the law of this dyad into consciousness? Consciousness of self is not dual. If we wish to avoid an infinite regress, there must be an immediate, non-cognitive relation of the self to itself.

Furthermore the reflecting consciousness posits the consciousness reflected-on, as its object. In the act of reflecting I pass judgment on the consciousness reflected-on; I am ashamed of it, I am proud of it, I will it, I deny it, *etc.* The immediate consciousness which I have of perceiving does not permit me either to judge or to will or to be ashamed. It does not *know* my perception, does not *posit* it; all that there is of intention in my actual consciousness is directed toward the outside, toward the world. In turn, this spontaneous consciousness of my perception is *constitutive* of my perceptive consciousness. In other words, every positional consciousness of an object is at the same time a non-positional consciousness of itself. If I count the cigarettes which are in that case, I have the impression of disclosing an objective property of this collection of cigarettes: *they are a dozen.* This property appears to my consciousness as a property existing in the world. It is very possible that I have no positional consciousness of counting them. Then I do not know myself as counting. Proof of this is that children who are capable of making an addition spontaneously can not *explain* subsequently how they set about it. Piaget's tests, which show this, constitute an excellent refutation of the formula of Alain—To know is to know that one knows. Yet at the moment when these cigarettes are revealed to me as a dozen, I have a non-thetic consciousness of my adding activity. If anyone questioned me, indeed, if anyone should ask, "What are you doing there?" I should reply at once, "I am counting." This reply aims not only at the instantaneous consciousness which I can achieve by reflection but at those fleeting consciousnesses which have passed without being reflected-on, those which are forever not-reflected-on in my immediate past. Thus reflection has no kind of primacy over the consciousness reflected-on. It is not reflection which reveals the consciousness reflected-on to itself. Quite the contrary, it is the non-reflective consciousness which renders the reflection possible; there is a pre-reflective cogito which is the condition of the Cartesian cogito. At the same time it is the non-thetic consciousness of counting which is the very condition of my act of adding. If it were otherwise, how would the addition be the unifying theme of my consciousnesses? In order that this theme should preside over a whole series of syntheses of unifications and recognitions, it must be present to itself, not as a thing but as an operative intention which can exist only as the revealing-revealed (*révélante-révélée*), to use an expression of Heidegger's. Thus in order to count, it is necessary to be conscious of counting.

Of course, someone may say, but this makes a circle. For is it not necessary that I count *in fact* in order to *be conscious* of counting? That is true. However there is no circle, or if you like, it is the very nature of consciousness to exist "in a circle." The idea can be expressed in these terms: Every conscious existence exists as consciousness of existing. We

understand now why the first consciousness of consciousness is not positional; it is because it is one with the consciousness of which it is consciousness. At one stroke it determines itself as consciousness of
perception and as perception. The necessity of syntax has compelled us
hitherto to speak of the "non-positional consciousness of self." But we
can no longer use this expression in which the "*of self*" still evokes the
idea of knowledge. (Henceforth we shall put the "of" inside parentheses
to show that it merely satisfies a grammatical requirement.)[4]

This self-consciousness we ought to consider not as a new
consciousness, but as *the only mode of existence which is possible for a
consciousness of something*. Just as an extended object is compelled to
exist according to three dimensions, so an intention, a pleasure, a grief
can exist only as immediate self-consciousness. If the intention is not a
thing in consciousness, then the being of the intention can be only
consciousness. It is not necessary to understand by this that on the one
hand, some external cause (an organic trouble, an unconscious impulse,
another *Erlebnis*) could determine that a psychic event—a pleasure, for
example,—produce itself, and that on the other hand, this event so
determined in its material structure should be compelled to produce
itself as self-consciousness. This would be to make the non-thetic
consciousness a *quality* of the positional consciousness (in the sense that
the perception, positional consciousness of that table, would have as
addition the quality of self-consciousness) and would thus fall back into
the illusion of the theoretical primacy of knowledge. This would be
moreover to make the psychic event a thing and to *qualify* it with
"conscious" just as I can qualify this blotter with "red." Pleasure can not
be distinguished—even logically—from consciousness of pleasure.
Consciousness (of) pleasure is constitutive of the pleasure as the very
mode of its own existence, as the material of which it is made, and not as
a form which is imposed by a blow upon a hedonistic material. Pleasure
can not exist "before" consciousness of pleasure—not even in the form
of potentiality or potency. A potential pleasure can exist only as
consciousness (of) being potential. Potencies of consciousness exist only
as consciousness of potencies.

Conversely, as I showed earlier, we must avoid defining pleasure by
the consciousness which I have of it. This would be to fall into an
idealism of consciousness which would bring us by indirect means to the
primacy of knowledge. Pleasure must not disappear behind its own self-
consciousness; it is not a representation, it is a concrete event, full and
absolute. It is no more a quality of self-consciousness than self-
consciousness is a quality of pleasure. There is no more first a consciousness which receives *subsequently* the affect "pleasure" like water

which one stains, than there is first a pleasure (unconscious or psycho-logical) which receives subsequently the quality of "conscious" like a pencil of light rays. There is an indivisible, indissoluble being—definitely not a substance supporting its qualities like particles of being, but a being which is existence through and through. Pleasure is the being of self-consciousness and this self-consciousness is the law of being of pleasure. This is what Heidegger expressed very well when he wrote (though speaking of *Dasein*, not of consciousness): "The 'how' (*essentia*) of this being, so far as it is possible to speak of it generally, must be conceived in terms of its existence (*existentia*)." This means that consciousness is not produced as a particular instance of an abstract possibility but that in rising to the center of being, it creates and supports its essence—that is, the synthetic order of its possibilities.

This means also that the type of being of consciousness is the opposite of that which the ontological proof reveals to us. Since consciousness is not *possible* before being, but since its being is the source and condition of all possibility, its existence implies its essence. Husserl expresses this aptly in speaking of the "necessity of fact." In order for there to be an essence of pleasure, there must be first the *fact* of a consciousness (of) this pleasure. It is futile to try to invoke pretended *laws* of consciousness of which the articulated whole would constitute the essence. A law is a transcendent object of knowledge; there can be consciousness of a law, not a law of consciousness. For the same reasons it is impossible to assign to a consciousness a motivation other than itself. Otherwise it would be necessary to conceive that consciousness to the degree to which it is an effect, is not conscious (of) itself. It would be necessary in some manner that it should be without being conscious (of) being. We should fall into that too common illusion which makes consciousness semi-conscious or a passivity. But consciousness is consciousness through and through. It can be limited only by itself.

This self-determination of consciousness must not be conceived as a genesis, as a becoming, for that would force us to suppose that consciousness is prior to its own existence. Neither is it necessary to conceive of this self-creation as an act, for in that case consciousness would be conscious (of) itself as an act, which it is not. Consciousness is a plenum of existence, and this determination of itself by itself is an essential characteristic. It would even be wise not to misuse the expression "cause of self," which allows us to suppose a progression, a relation of self-cause to self-effect. It would be more exact to say very simply: The existence of consciousness comes from consciousness itself. By that we need not understand that consciousness "derives from nothingness." There can not be "nothingness of consciousness" *before* consciousness. "Before" consciousness one can conceive only of a plenum of being of which no element can refer to an absent consciousness. If there is to be nothingness of consciousness, there must be a consciousness which has been and which is no mote and a witnessing consciousness which poses the nothingness of the first consciousness for a synthesis of recognition. Consciousness is prior to nothingness and "is derived" from being.[5]

One will perhaps have some difficulty in accepting these conclusions. But considered more carefully, they will appear perfectly clear. The paradox is not that there are "self-activated" existences but that there is no other kind. What is truly unthinkable is passive existence; that is, existence which perpetuates itself without having the force either to produce itself or to preserve itself. From this point of view there is nothing more incomprehensible than the principle of inertia. Indeed where would consciousness "come" from if it did "come" from something? From the limbo of the unconscious or of the physiological. But if we ask ourselves how this limbo in its turn can exist and where it derives its existence, we find ourselves faced with the concept of passive existence; that is, we can no more absolutely understand how this non-conscious given (unconscious or physiological) which does not derive its existence from itself, can nevertheless perpetuate this existence and find in addition the ability to produce a consciousness. This demonstrates the great favor which the proof *a contingentia mundi* has enjoyed.

Thus by abandoning the primacy of knowledge, we have discovered the *being* of the *knower* and encountered the absolute, that same absolute which the rationalists of the seventeenth century had defined and logically constituted as an object of knowledge. But precisely because the question concerns an absolute of existence and not of knowledge, it is not subject to that famous objection according to which a known absolute is no longer an absolute because it becomes relative to the knowledge which one has of it. In fact the absolute here is not the result of a logical construction on the ground of knowledge but the subject of the most concrete of experiences. And it is not at all *relative* to this experience because it *is* this experience. Likewise it is a non-substantial absolute. The ontological error of Cartesian rationalism is not to have seen that if the absolute is defined by the primacy of existence over essence, it can not be conceived as a substance. Consciousness has nothing substantial, it is pure "appearance" in the sense that it exists only to the degree to which it appears. But it is precisely because consciousness is pure appearance, because it is total emptiness (since the entire world is outside it)—it is because of this identity of appearance and existence within it that it can be considered as the absolute.

IV. The being of the percipi

It seems that we have arrived at the goal of our inquiry. We have reduced things to the united totality of their appearances, and we have established that these appearances lay claim to a being which is no longer itself appearance. The *"percipi"* referred us to a *percipiens*, the being of which has been revealed to us as consciousness. Thus we have attained the ontological foundation of knowledge, the first being to whom all other appearances appear, the absolute in relation to which every phenomenon is relative. This is no longer the subject in Kant's meaning of the term, but it is subjectivity itself, the immanence of self in self. Henceforth we have escaped idealism. For the latter, being is measured by knowledge, which subjects it to the law of duality. There is only *known* being; it is a question of thought itself. Thought appears only through its own products; that is, we always apprehend it only as the signification of thoughts produced, and the philosopher in quest of thought must question the established sciences in order to derive it from them as the condition of their possibility. We, on the other hand, have apprehended a being which is not subject to knowledge and which founds knowledge, a thought which is definitely not given as a representation or a signification of expressed thoughts, but which is directly apprehended such as it is—and this mode of apprehension is not a phenomenon of knowledge but is the structure of being. We find ourselves at present on the ground of the phenomenology of Husserl although Husserl himself has not always been faithful to his first intuition. Are we satisfied? We have encountered a transphenomenal being, but is it actually the being to which the phenomenon of being refers? Is it indeed the being of the phenomenon? In other words is consciousness sufficient to provide the foundation for the appearance qua appearance? We have extracted its being from the phenomenon in order to give it to consciousness, and we anticipated that consciousness would subsequently restore it to the phenomenon. Is this possible? We shall find our answer in the examination of the ontological exigencies of the *percipi*.

Let us note first that there is a being of the thing perceived—*as perceived*. Even if I wished to reduce this table to a synthesis of subjective impressions, I must at least remark that it reveals itself *qua table* through this synthesis, that it is the transcendent limit of the synthesis—the reason for it and its end. The table is before knowledge and can not be identified with the knowledge which we have of it; otherwise it would be consciousness—*i.e.*, pure immanence—and it would disappear *as* table. For the same cause even if a pure distinction of reason is to separate the table from the synthesis of subjective impressions through which I apprehend it, at least it can not *be* this synthesis; that would be to reduce it to a synthetic activity of connection. In so far then as the known can not be reabsorbed into knowledge, we must discover for it a *being*. This being, we are told, is the *percipi*. Let us recognize first of all that the being of the *percipi* can not be reduced to that of the *percipiens—i.e.*, to consciousness—any more than the table is reduced to the bond of representations. At most we can say that it is *relative* to this being. But this *relativity* does not render unnecessary an examination of the being of the *percipi*.

Now the mode of the *percipi* is the passive. If then the being of the phenomenon resides in its *percipi*, this being is passivity. Relativity and passivity—such are the characteristic structures of the *esse* in so far as this is reduced to the *percipi*. What is passivity? I am passive when I undergo a modification of which I am not the origin; that is, neither the source nor the creator. Thus my being supports a mode of being of which it is not the source. Yet in order for me to support, it is still necessary that I exist, and due to this fact my existence is always situated on the other side of passivity. "To support passively," for example, is a conduct which I assume and which engages my liberty as much as to "reject resolutely." If I am to be for always "the-one-who-has-been-offended," I must per-severe in my being; that is, I myself assume my existence. But all the same I respond on my own account in some way and I assume my offense; I cease to be passive in relation to it. Hence we have this choice of alternatives: either, indeed, I am not passive in my being, in which case I become the foundation of my affections even if at first I have not been the origin of them—or I am affected with passivity in my very existence, my being is a received being, and hence all falls into nothingness. Thus passivity is a doubly relative phenomenon, relative to the activity of the one who acts and to the existence of the one who suffers. This implies that passivity can not affect the actual being of the passive existent; it is a relation of one being to another being and not of one being to a nothingness. It is impossible that *the percipere affects the perceptum* of being, for in order for the *perceptum* to be affected it would of necessity have to be already given in some way and exist before having received being. One can conceive of a *creation* on condition that the created being recover itself, tear itself away from the creator in order to close in on itself immediately and assume its being; it is in this sense that a book exists as distinct from its author. But if the act of creation is to be continued indefinitely, if the created being is to be supported even in its inmost parts, if it does not have its own independence, if it is *in itself* only nothingness—then the creature is in no way distinguished from its creator; it is absorbed in him; we are dealing with a false transcendence, and the creator can not have even an illusion of getting out of his subjectivity.[6]

Furthermore the passivity of the recipient demands an equal passivity on the part of the agent. This is expressed in the principle of action and reaction; it is because my hand can be crushed, grasped, cut, that my hand can crush, cut, grasp. What element of passivity can we assign to perception, to knowledge? They are all activity, all spontaneity. It is precisely because it is pure spontaneity, because nothing can get a grip on it that consciousness can not act upon anything. Thus the *esse est percipi* would require that consciousness, pure spontaneity which can not *act* upon anything, give being to a transcendent nothingness, at the same time keeping it in its state of nothingness. So much nonsense! Husserl has attempted to overcome these objections by introducing passivity into the *noesis*; this is the *hyle* or pure flux of experience and the matter of the passive syntheses. But he has only added an additional difficulty to those which we have mentioned. He has introduced in fact those neutral givens, the impossibility of which we have shown earlier. To be sure, these are not "contents" of consciousness, but they remain only so much the more unintelligible. The *hyle* in fact could not be consciousness, for it would disappear in translucency and could not offer that resisting basis of impressions which must be surpassed toward the object. But if it does not belong to consciousness, where does it derive its being and its opacity? How can it preserve at once the opaque resistance of things and the subjectivity of thought? Its *esse* can not come to it from a *percipi* since it is not even perceived, for consciousness transcends it toward the objects. But if the *hyle* derives its being from itself alone we meet once again the insoluble problem of the connection of consciousness with exist-tents independent of it. Even if we grant to Husserl that there is hyletic stratum for the noesis, we can not conceive how consciousness can transcend this subjective toward objectivity. In giving to the *hyle* both the characteristics of a thing and the characteristics of consciousness, Husserl believed that he facilitated the passage from the one to the other, but he succeeded only in creating a hybrid being which consciousness rejects and which can not be a part of the world.

Furthermore, as we have seen, the *percipi* implies that the law of being of the *perceptum* is relativity. Can we conceive that the being of the thing known is relative to the knowledge? What can the relativity of being mean for an existent if not that the existent has its own being in something other than in itself; that is, *in an existent which it is not*. Certainly it would not be inconceivable that a being should be external to itself if one means that this being is *its own* externality. But such is not the case here. The perceived being is before consciousness; consciousness can not reach it, and it can not enter into consciousness; and as the perceived being is cut off from consciousness, it exists cut off from its own existence. It would be no use to make of it an unreal in the manner of Husserl; even as unreal it must exist.

Thus the two determinations of *relativity* and of *passivity*, which can concern modes of being, can on no account apply to being. The *esse* of the phenomenon can not be its *percipi*. The transphenomenal being of consciousness can not provide a basis for the transphenomenal being of the phenomenon. Here we see the error of the phenomenalists: having justifiably reduced the object to the connected series of its appearances, they believed they had reduced its being to the succession of its modes of being. That is why they have explained it by concepts which can be applied only to the modes of being, for they are pointing out the relations between a plurality of already existing beings.

V. The ontological proof

Being has not been given its due. We believed we had dispensed with granting transphenomenality to the being of the phenomenon because we had discovered the transphenomenality of the being of consciousness. We are going to see, on the contrary, that this very transphenomenality requires that of the being of the phenomenon. There is an "ontological proof" to be derived not from the reflective *cogito* but from the *pre-reflective* being of the *percipiens*. This we shall now try to demonstrate.

All consciousness is consciousness *of* something. This definition of consciousness can be taken in two very distinct senses: either we understand by this that consciousness is constitutive of the being of its object, or it means that consciousness in its inmost nature is a relation to a transcendent being. But the first interpretation of the formula destroys itself: to be conscious *of* something is to be confronted with a concrete and full presence which *is not* consciousness. Of course one can be conscious of an absence. But this absence appears necessarily as a pre-condition of presence. As we have seen, consciousness is a real subjectivity and the impression is a subjective plenitude. But this subjectivity can not go out of itself to posit a transcendent object in such a way as to endow it with a plenitude of impressions.[7] If then we wish at any price to make the being of the phenomenon depend on consciousness, the object must be distinguished from consciousness not by its *presence* but by its *absence*, not by its plenitude, but by its nothingness. If being belongs to consciousness, the object is not consciousness, not to the extent that it is another being, but that it is non-being. This is the appeal to the infinite of which we spoke in the first section of this work. For Husserl, for example, the animation of the hyletic nucleus by the only intentions which can find their fulfilment (*Erfüllung*) in this *hyle* is not enough to bring us outside of subjectivity. The truly objectifying intentions are empty intentions, those which aim beyond the present subjective appearance at the infinite totality of the series of appearances.

We must further understand that the intentions aim at appearances which are never to be given at one time. It is an impossibility on principle for the terms of an infinite series to exist all at the same time before consciousness, along with the real absence of all these terms except for the one which is the foundation of objectivity. If present these impressions—even in infinite number-would dissolve in the subjective; it is their absence which gives them objective being. Thus the being of the object is pure non-being. It is defined as a *lack*. It is that which escapes, that which by definition will never be given, that which offers itself only in fleeting and successive profiles.

But how can non-being be the foundation of being? How can the absent, *expected* subjective become thereby the objective? A great joy which I hope for, a grief which I dread, acquire from that fact a certain transcendence. This I admit. But that transcendence in immanence does not bring us out of the subjective. It is true that things give themselves in profile; that is, simply by appearances. And it is true that each appearance refers to other appearances. But each of them is already in itself alone a *transcendent being*, not a subjective material of impressions—a *plenitude of being*, not a lack—a presence, not an absence. It is futile by a sleight of hand to attempt to found the *reality* of the object on the subjective plenitude of impressions and its *objectivity* on non-being; the objective will never come out of the subjective nor the transcendent from immanence, nor being from non-being. But, we are told, Husserl defines consciousness precisely as a transcendence. In truth he does. This is what he posits. This is his essential discovery. But from the moment that he makes of the *noema* an *unreal*, a correlate of the *noesis*, a noema whose *esse* is *percipi*, he is totally unfaithful to his principle.

Consciousness is consciousness *of* something. This means that transcendence is the constitutive structure of consciousness; that is, that consciousness is born *supported by* a being which is not itself. This is what we call the ontological proof. No doubt someone will reply that the existence of the demand of consciousness does not prove that this demand ought to be satisfied. But this objection can not hold up against an analysis of what Husserl calls intentionality, though, to be sure, he misunderstood its essential character. To say that consciousness is consciousness of something means that for consciousness there is no being outside of that precise obligation to be a revealing intuition of something—*i.e.*, of a transcendent being. Not only does pure subjectivity, if initially given, fail to transcend itself to posit the objective; a "pure" subjectivity disappears. What can properly be called subjectivity is consciousness (of) consciousness. But this consciousness (of being) consciousness must be qualified in some way, and it can be qualified only as revealing intuition or it is nothing. Now a revealing intuition implies something revealed. Absolute subjectivity can be established only in the face of something revealed; immanence can be defined only within the apprehension of a transcendent. It might appear that there is an echo here of Kant's refutation of problematical idealism. But we ought rather to think of Descartes. We are here on the ground of being, not of knowledge. It is not a question of showing that the phenomena of inner sense imply the existence of objective spatial phenomena, but that consciousness implies in its being a non-conscious and transphenomenal being. In particular there is no point in replying that in fact subjectivity implies objectivity and that it constitutes itself in constituting the objective; we have seen that subjectivity is powerless to constitute the objective. To say that consciousness is consciousness of something is to say that it must produce itself as a revealed-revelation a being which is not it and which gives itself as already existing when consciousness reveals it.

Thus we have left pure appearance and have arrived at full being. Consciousness is a being whose existence posits its essence, and inversely it is consciousness of a being, whose essence implies its existence; that is, in which appearance lays claim to *being*. Being is everywhere. Certainly we could apply to consciousness the definition which Heidegger reserves for *Dasein* and say that it is a being such that in its being, its being is in question. But it would be necessary to complete the definition and formulate it more like this: *consciousness is a being such that in its being, its being is in question in so far as this being implies a being other than itself*.

We must understand that this being is no other than the transphenomenal being of phenomena and not a noumenal being which is hidden behind them. It is the being of this table of this package of tobacco of the lamp, more generally the being of the world which is implied by consciousness. It requires simply that being of that which *appears* does not exist *only* in so far as it appears. The transphenomenal being of what exists for consciousness is itself in itself (*lui-même en soi*).

Notes

1 From Greek εξις. Sartre seems to have ignored the rough breathing and writes "exis." Tr.

2   Perhaps a more intelligible paraphrase would be, "the question of what it means to be a table or a chair." Tr.
3   It goes without saying that any attempt to replace the *percipere* by another *attitude* from human reality would be equally fruitless. If we granted that being is revealed to man in "acting," it would still be necessary to guarantee the being of acting apart from the action.
4   Since English syntax does not require the "of," I shall henceforth freely translate *conscience (de) soi* as "self-consciousness." Tr.
5   That certainly does not mean that consciousness is the foundation of its being. On the contrary, as we shall see later, there is a full contingency of the being of consciousness. We wish only to show (1) That *nothing* is the cause of consciousness. (2) That consciousness is the cause of its own way of being.
6   It is for this reason that the Cartesian doctrine of substance finds its logical culmination in the work of Spinoza.
7   I.e., in such a way that the impressions are objectified into qualities of the thing. Tr.

4   Imagination and emotion

Understanding the application of Sartre's phenomenology to imagination and emotion requires further clarification of the concept of intentionality and the distinction between reflexive and pre-reflexive consciousness introduced in the last chapter.

By 'intentionality' is meant the alleged property of consciousness always taking some object or other. All consciousness is consciousness of something, whether real or imaginary. All perception is perception of, all thinking is thinking of, all loving is loving something, all hating, hating something. For any act of consciousness, that act could not exist unless it were directed towards some object. The object need not be a physical object, it could be a fictional character, an abstract object like a number, or an imaginary being.

Brentano had used the concept of intentionality to demarcate the mental from the non-mental (including the physical) by claiming that all and only mental phenomena exhibit intentionality. Husserl thought intentionality is the essence of consciousness. Intentionality was first formulated systematically by the thirteenth-century scholastic philosopher St. Thomas Aquinas (1224–74), but anticipations may be found in Plato and Aristotle. Sartre, following Husserl, allows some exceptions to the doctrine all mental states are intentional. Sensations of pain, and certain moods, for example are not 'about' anything. (This leaves both Sartre and Husserl with the problem of what non-intentional phenomena being mental consists in.)

Sartre makes a crucial break with the doctrines of Brentano and Husserl when he insists that the intended objects of consciousness *exist*. Brentano had thought that they 'inexist' as presented to consciousness, that is, neither exist nor do not exist. Husserl suspended belief and disbelief in the existence of objects in the external world by his *epoché* in order to describe consciousness purely. Sartre regards these positions as confused. Even if an object is fictional or abstract or imaginary, it exists. It is rather than is not. In failing to see this, Husserl misunderstood intentionality's essential character.

Husserl also fails to see the impossibility of the *epoché* or phenomeno-logical reduction. No object can be reduced to the consciousness of it, not even to an infinity of acts of consciousness of it, because consciousness cannot be that of which it is conscious. The object, in some non-spatial sense of 'outside', is always irreducibly 'outside' consciousness.

If the objects of consciousness are not 'in' consciousness as Brentano and Husserl supposed then where are they? As we have seen, Sartre thinks our fundamental mode of being is truly captured by the Heidegerian notion of *being-in-the-world*. If our being is *being-in-the-world* then it is impossible that we might persist in abstraction from the world of objects and subjects that surrounds us. The objects of our consciousness are in the world so, essentially, consciousness is consciousness of something outside itself.

Nevertheless, consciousness is a consciousness of consciousness, a consciousness of itself 'in the face of being'. The implicit consciousness of itself called 'pre-reflexive consciousness' and the overt self-consciousness called 'reflexive consciousness' are possible only because consciousness is directed towards objects outside itself. Although I am a consciousness of being, nothing separates me from being.

Sartre is a realist about the objects of consciousness. Idealism, the doctrine that only consciousness and its mental contents exist, is incoherent. Husserl thought that consciousness constitutes its objects; it makes them be what they are. It was his quasi-Kantian view that, although Berkeleyan idealism is false because objects do not depend on consciousness for their existence, nevertheless what objects are to us is largely due to our transcendental constitution.

Sartre treads a careful path between naive realism and Husserl's neo-Kantianism. He is concerned to resolve the apparent paradox that even though an object enters my visual perception as complete, I nevertheless see it only one side (or profile) at a time. When I see a physical object I see it only from a certain angle. For example if I am looking at a cube I can see a maximum of three sides simultaneously. Nevertheless, there is a real sense in which I perceive the whole physical object. Sartre should have put the point this way: I see the whole physical object but I do not see the whole of the physical object.

Sartre, like Husserl, argues that being aware of the whole physical object depends on the possible awareness of its parts, (empirically and realistically its sides or, phenomenologically, its available *profiles* or *Abschattungen*). However, Sartre insists that the object really exists outside consciousness. It is our awareness of the object as a whole that is constituted by the actual and possible mental acts we direct towards it. The object itself is not constituted by consciousness. It is really there.

We can now see the sense in which the object of the perception constantly overflows or exceeds the consciousness of it. There is always more to an object than the consciousness of it. It is incoherent to suppose an object could be the consciousness of it. Also, an object systematically exceeds what it directly presents to consciousness. In the visual case, a front implies a back and some sides. The whole exceeds the momentarily presented parts.

Sartre's phenomenology of perception is a realist transformation of Husserl's theory of the constitution of objects. Sartre retains from Husserl what we could call a kind of 'perspectivism'. An object is always perceived from a point of view and always presents an aspect to that point of view. It follows that 'the object appears only in a series of profiles, or projections' (*The Psychology of Imagination*, p. 9). The profile is however part of the object. The profile is any part of the object that appears to a point of view at a time.

Husserl thought that an object is constituted by the infinity of possible points of view on it. Sartre thinks the object really exists, independently of any point of view. Nevertheless, it is only ever seen as presenting an aspect that both implies and excludes an infinite number of other points of view. What I see exists even when unseen. Other points of view are excluded in the sense that at any one time I may adopt just one and not any other of them. Other points of view are included in the sense that at other times I could adopt any one of them.

It is the object that makes possible the points of view on it. The points of view do not make the object possible, even though they make possible the perception of it. So, when Sartre argues in *The Psychology of Imagination* that an object itself is a synthesis of all the appearances of it, an appearance is nothing mental. The appearances of an object are the parts of it that can appear.

Husserl was wrong to claim that consciousness constitutes objects. Rather, objects constitute consciousness. In *The Transcendence of the Ego* (1937) Sartre argues that consciousness constitutes itself *in the face of* objects. The presentation of objects is a necessary condition for the unity of consciousness. If there were no world, there could be no consciousness.

Sartre's realism therefore entails a kind of externalism. What consciousness is depends upon the objects of consciousness that lie outside it. Objects transcend consciousness, there is more to them than both the consciousness of them and what is directly presented in the consciousness of them. Transcendence is the constitutive structure of consciousness. An object is transcendent if and only if it is not exhausted by the consciousness of it. Sartre thinks consciousness is supported by a being which is not itself. A necessary condition for the existence and nature of consciousness is the existence of objects for consciousness that exist independently of consciousness.

It follows straightforwardly from this externalism that consciousness is not a *substance*. If something is a substance then it depends on nothing outside itself, but consciousness depends on its external objects, so consciousness is not a substance. Sartre's existential phenomenology is inconsistent with the Cartesian doctrine that consciousness is a mental substance capable of existing independently of physical objects. If consciousness is not any kind of substance then consciousness is not a mental substance. If Sartre is right, Cartesian mind–body dualism is false.

Nevertheless, Sartre's realism is not immune to objection. Even if it is part of common sense, and may be sustained by philosophical argument, that physical objects exist independently of the perception of them, this view looks far less plausible when applied to mental images, fictional characters, imaginary beings and perhaps abstract objects such as numbers. On the face of it these items are 'internal' rather than 'external'. Arguably their existence depends upon consciousness rather than vice versa.

Sartre's reply is to draw attention to what he calls the *illusion of immanence* in *The Psychology of Imagination*. From the fact that there are mental images and abstract objects it does not follow that there are non-physical objects that exist within consciousness.

In fact, according to Sartre, the mental image is not an object towards which acts of consciousness are directed. The image is itself a mental act, embedded by and embedding further mental acts. An image is not an object of awareness, it is a kind of awareness, a way of being aware. It posits its own object as non-existent, as absent or as existing elsewhere. It follows that the image itself includes an act of belief, an act of positing (or not positing) an object. The image is a relation, not an object. It is a relation between subject and object.

Succumbing to the illusion of immanence involves thinking of consciousness as a place, and thinking of images as 'in' consciousness. Sartre thinks of Hume as the paradigm case of someone who commits this fallacy. However, he thinks it widespread in philosophy, psychology and common sense.

Because he denies that consciousness is a place, a strange non-physical place, in *The Psychology of Imagination* Sartre regards expressions of the form 'a mental image of Peter' as philosophically misleading and 'the imaginative consciousness of Peter' as philosophically perspicuous even if Peter does not exist. Imagining an imaginary object is logically parasitic on imagining a real object, rather as holding a false belief depends upon being capable of holding a true belief.

In the extract from *The Psychology of Imagination* called 'Conscious-ness and Imagination' reprinted below, we see Sartre's existential pheno-menology applied to the mental image. He also introduces the concept of *negation* which is important for understanding Chapter 6 of this book.

In the extract from *Sketch For a Theory of the Emotions* Sartre applies the doctrine of intentionality to emotion and draws distinctions between being conscious and being conscious of being conscious. He argues that an emotion is a *transformation of the world*. Although it is always part of our existential predicament to choose, to act, the world frustrates us in our preferences. At that moment we choose an emotion in an effort to transform the world as if by magic. Disturbingly, it follows that we are *responsible* for our emotions. We see here not only the repudiation of scientific psychology, but that Sartrean fusion of existentialism and phenomenology called 'existential phenomenology'.

THE PSYCHOLOGY OF THE IMAGINATION

Consciousness and imagination

We are now in a position to raise the metaphysical question which has been gradually shaping itself through these studies of phenomenological psychology. We may formulate it as follows: what are the characteristics that can be attributed to consciousness from the fact that it is a consciousness capable of *imagining*. This question can be taken in the sense of a critical analysis under the form: of what nature must a con-sciousness be in general if the construction of an image should always be possible? And no doubt it is in this form that our minds, accustomed to raising philosophical questions in the Kantian perspective, will best understand it. But, as a matter of fact, the problem in its deepest meaning can only be grasped from a phenomenological point of view.

After the phenomenological reduction we find ourselves in the presence of the transcendental consciousness which unveils itself to our reflective descriptions. We can thus *fix* by concepts the result of our eidetic intuition of the essence "consciousness". Now, phenomen-ological descriptions can discover, for instance, that the very structure of the transcendental consciousness implies that this consciousness is constitutive *of a world*. But it is evident that they will not teach us that consciousness must be constitutive of *such* a world, that is to say, exactly the one where we are, with its earth, its animals, its men and the story of these men. We are here in the presence of a primary and irreducible fact which presents itself as a contingent and irrational specification of the essence of the *world* as we know it. And many phenomenologists will call "metaphysics" the investigation whose aim it is to uncover this contingent existent in its entirety. This is not exactly what we would call metaphysics, but that is of little importance here. What will concern us is this: is the function of imagination a contingent and metaphysical specification of the essence "consciousness" or should it rather be described as a constitutive structure of that essence? In other words: can we conceive of a consciousness which would never imagine and which would be completely absorbed in its intuitions of the real—in that case the possibility of imagining, which appears as one quality among others of *our* consciousnesses, would be a contingent enrichment or rather, as soon as we posit a consciousness, must it be posited as always being able to imagine? We should be able to settle this question by the simple reflective inspection of the essence "consciousness", and it is thus in fact that we would attempt to settle it, were we not addressing ourselves to a public as yet but little accustomed to phenomenological methods. But since the idea of eidetic intuition is still repugnant to many French readers, we shall resort to a subterfuge, that is, to a method somewhat more complex. We shall begin with the question: what must a consciousness be in order for it to possess the power to imagine, which we shall try to develop by the usual procedures of critical analysis, that is, by a regressive method. Next we shall compare the results we obtain with those the Cartesian intuition gives us of the consciousness realized by the cogito, and we shall see whether the necessary conditions for realizing an imaginative consciousness are *the same* or *different* from the conditions of possibility of a consciousness in general.

Indeed, the problem stated thus may appear to be completely new and even trifling to French psychologists. And, in fact, as long as we are the victims of the illusion of immanence, there is no general problem of imagination. Images are in fact supplied, in these theories, by a type of existence strictly like that of things. They are reborn sensations which may differ in degree, in cohesion, in meaning from primary sensations, but which belong, as do sensations, to the *intra-mundane* existence. The image is as real as any other existence. The only question concerning the image is the problem of its relationship to other existences but, whatever this relationship may be, the existence of the image remains intact. This is like saying that whether the portrait of King Charles VI is or is not a true likeness, whether the king is dead or alive or even whether he ever existed, the portrait is nevertheless something that exists in the world. There is therefore no existential problem of the image.

But if the image is looked upon as we have viewed it in this work, the existential problem of the image can no longer be sidetracked. In fact, to the existence of an object for consciousness there corresponds noetically a hypothesis or position of existence. Now, the hypothesis of the imaginative consciousness is radically different from the hypothesis of a consciousness of the real. This means that the type of existence of the object of the image *as long as it is imagined*, differs in nature from the type of existence of the object grasped as real. And surely, if I now form an image of Peter, my imaginative consciousness includes a certain positing of the existence of Peter, in so far as he is now at this very moment in Berlin or London. But while he *appears to me as an image*, this Peter who is in London *appears to me absent*. This absence in actuality, this essential nothingness of the imagined object, is enough to distinguish it from the object of perception. What then must the nature of a consciousness be in order that it be able successively to posit *real* objects and *imagined* objects?

We must at once make an important observation, which the reader may have made himself if he has studied the problem of the relationships between perception and imagery, as outlined in Chapter 2. For an object or any element of an object there is a great difference between *being grasped as nothing* and *being-given-as-absent*. In a perception of whatever sort many empty intentions are directed, from the elements of the object now given, towards other aspects and other elements of the object which no longer reveal themselves to our intuition. For instance, the arabesques of the rug I am viewing are both in part given to my intuition. The legs of the armchair which stands before the window conceal certain curves, certain designs. But I nevertheless seize these hidden arabesques as *existing now*, as hidden but not at all as absent. And I grasp them not for themselves in trying to present them by means of an analogue but in the very way in which I grasp what has been given me of their continuation. I *perceive* the beginnings and the endings of the hidden arabesques (which appear to me before and behind the leg of the chair) as *continuing* under the legs of the chair. It is therefore *in the way in which I grasp the data* that I posit that which is not given as being real. Real by the same right as the data, as that which gives it its meaning and its very nature. Likewise the successive tones of a melody are grasped by appropriate retentions as that which makes of the tone now heard exactly what it is. In this sense, to perceive this or that real datum is to perceive it on the foundation of total reality *as a whole*. This reality never becomes the object of any special act of my attention, but it is co-present as an essential condition of the existence of the reality actually perceived. Here we see that the imaginative act is the reverse of the act of reality. If I want to imagine the hidden arabesques, I direct my attention upon them and isolate them, just as I isolate on the foundation of an undifferentiated universe the thing I actually perceive. I cease to grasp them as empty but constituting the sense of the perceived reality; instead *I present them to myself*, in themselves. But at the moment that I cease to conceive them as continuous present in order to grasp them in themselves, I grasp them as *absent*. Of course they really exist over there, under the chair, and it is over there that I think of them, but in thinking of them where they are not given to me, I grasp them as *nothing for me*. Thus the imaginative act is at once *constitutive*, *isolating* and *annihilating*.

It is this which turns the problem of memory and that of anticipation into two problems which are radically different from the problem of imagination. No doubt recollection is in many respects very close to the image, and at times we were able to draw our examples from memory to clarify the nature of the image. There is nevertheless an essential difference between the theme of recollection and that of the image. If I recall an incident of my past life I do not imagine it, I *recall* it. That is, I do not posit it as *given-in-its absence*, but as *given-now-as-in-the-past*. The handshake of Peter of last evening in leaving me did not turn into an unreality as it became a thing of the past: it simply *went into retirement*; it is always real but *past*. It exists *past*, which is one mode of real existence among others. And when I want to apprehend it anew I pursue it *where it is*, I direct my consciousness towards that past object which is *yesterday*, and, at the heart of that object, I recover the event I am looking for, the handshake of Peter. In a word, just as when I want actually to *see* the hidden arabesques under the chair I have to look for them where they are, that is, move the chair; so when I recall this or that memory I do not *call it forth* but I betake myself to where it is, I direct my consciousness to the past where it awaits me as a real event in retirement. But if I imagine Peter as he might be at this moment in Berlin—or simply Peter as he exists at this moment (and not as he was yesterday on leaving me), I grasp an object which is not at all given to me or which is given to me simply as being beyond reach. There I grasp *nothing*, that is, I posit *nothingness*. In this sense the imaginative consciousness of Peter in Berlin (what is he doing at this moment? I imagine he is walking in the Kurfürstendamm, etc.), is very much closer to that of the centaur (whose complete non-existence I proclaim), than the recollection of Peter as he was the day he left. What is common between Peter as an image and the centaur as an image is that they are two aspects of Nothingness. And this it is that also distinguishes the living future from the imagined future. There are in fact two sorts of futures: the one is but the temporal ground on which my present perception develops, the other is posited for itself but as *that which* is *not yet*. When I play tennis I see my opponent hit the ball with his racket and I run to the net. Here there is real anticipation since I foresee the course of the ball. But this anticipation does not posit for itself the passage of the ball to this or that point. In reality the future is here only the *real* development of a form induced by the gesture of my opponent, and the real gesture of this opponent communicates its reality to the whole form. In other words, the real form with its zones of real-past and real-future is effected entirely as a result of his gesture. *As for my prevision also being reality*, I continue to carry out the form by foreseeing it, because my prevision is a real gesture within the form. Thus, step by step, there is always a real future which occurs simply as the real past, the sense of an actual form in development, or, in other words, as the meaning of the universe. And, in this sense, it makes no difference whether we think of the unperceived real aspects of objects as a present which is real but empty, or as a real future. The arabesques hidden by the chair are the real complement of the gesture by which I remove the chair, as the present and latent existence hidden by the chair. All real existence occurs with present, past and future structures, therefore past and future as essential structures of the real are equally real, that is, they are correlatives of a realizing theme. But if, on the contrary, while lying on my bed I anticipate what might happen when my friend Peter returns from Berlin, I detach the future from the present whose meaning it constitutes. I posit it for itself and I present it to myself. But I give it to myself precisely while it is not, yet, that is to say, as absent, or if one prefers, as nothing. Thus, I can live the same future in reality as a ground of the present (as, for instance, when I look for Peter at the station and all my acts have for their real meaning the arrival of Peter at 7:35 p.m.), or, on the other hand, I can isolate it and posit it for itself but by cutting it off from all reality and by annihilating it, by *presenting it as nothingness*.

We can now see what the essential requisite is in order that a consciousness may be able to imagine; it must possess the possibility of positing an hypothesis of unreality. But we must clarify this requisite. It does not mean that consciousness must cease being consciousness *of* something. It is of the very nature of consciousness to be intentional and a consciousness that ceased to be consciousness *of* something would for that very reason cease to exist. But consciousness should be able to form and posit objects possessing a certain trait of nothingness in relation to the whole or reality. In fact, we recall that the imaginary object can be posited as non-existent or as absent or as existing elsewhere or not posited as existing. We note that the common property of these four theses is that they include the entire category of negation, though at different degrees. Thus the negative act is constitutive of the image. We have already mentioned, in fact, that the theme is not added to the image but that it is its most intimate structure. But in relation to what is the negation carried out? To answer this question we need but consider for a moment what happens when I grasp the portrait of Charles VIII *as an image* of Charles VIII. Immediately I stop considering the picture as forming a part of a real world, it is no longer possible that the perceived object *on* the picture can be altered by the changes of the milieu surrounding it. The picture itself, as a *real thing*, can be more or less brightened, its colours can peel off, it can burn. This is because it possesses—due to lack of a "being-in-the-world" which is restricted to consciousness—a "being-in-the-midst-of-the-world". Its objective nature depends upon reality grasped as a spatio-temporal whole. But if, on the other hand, I grasp Charles VIII as an image on the picture, the object apprehended can no longer be subjected to changes in brightness for instance. It is not true that I can more or less brighten the *cheek* of Charles VIII.

In fact the brightening of that cheek has been established in the unreal by the painter once and for all. It is the unreal sun—or the unreal candle placed by the painter at this or that distance from the face being painted —which determines the degree of the brightness of the cheek. All that a real projector can do is to brighten the part of the real picture that corresponds to the cheek of Charles VIII. Likewise, if the picture burns, it is not Charles VIII as an image who is burning but only the material object which serves as analogue for the manifestation of the imagined object. Thus the unreal object appears immediately to be beyond the reach of reality. We therefore see that in order to produce the object "Charles VIII" as an image, consciousness must be able to deny the reality of the picture, and that it could deny that reality only by retreating from reality grasped as a whole. To posit an image is to construct an object on the fringe of the whole of reality, which means therefore to hold the real at a distance, to free oneself from it, in a word, to deny it. Or, in other words, to deny that an object belongs to the real is to deny the real in positing the object; the two negations are complementary, the former being the condition for the latter. We know, besides, that the totality of the real, so long as it is grasped by consciousness as a synthetic *situation* for that consciousness, is the world. There is then a two-fold requisite if consciousness is to imagine: it must be able to posit the world in its synthetic totality, and it must be able to posit the imagined object as being out of reach of this synthetic totality, that is, posit the world as a nothingness in relation to the image. From this it follows clearly that all creation of the imaginary would be completely impossible to a consciousness whose nature was precisely to be "in-the-midst-of-the-world". If we assume a consciousness placed in the very bosom of the world as one existence among others, we must conceive it hypothetically as completely subjected to the action of a variety of realities—without its being able to avoid the detail of these realities by an intuition capable of grasping their totality. This consciousness could therefore contain only real modifications aroused by real actions, and all imagination would be prohibited to it, exactly in the degree to which it was engulfed in the real. This conception of an imagination enmired in the world is not unknown to us, since it is precisely that of psychological determinism. We can affirm fearlessly that if consciousness is a succession of determined psychical facts it is entirely impossible for it ever to produce anything but the real. For consciousness to be able to imagine, it must be able to escape from the world by its very nature; it must be able by its own efforts to withdraw from the world. In a word it must be free. Thus the thesis of unreality has yielded us the possibility of negation as its condition. Now, the latter is possible only by the "negation" of the world as a whole, and this negation has revealed itself to us as the reverse of the very freedom of consciousness. But at this point several comments force themselves to the fore: first of all, we must bear in mind that the act of positing the world as a synthetic totality and the act of "taking perspective" from the world are one and the same. If we may use a comparison, it is precisely by placing oneself at a convenient distance from the picture that the impressionist painter disengages the whole "forest" or the "white water lilies" from the multitude of small strokes he has placed on the canvas. But, reciprocally, the possibility of constructing a whole is given as the primary structure of the act of taking perspective. Therefore merely to be able to posit reality as a synthetic whole is enough to enable one to posit oneself as free from it; and this going-beyond is freedom itself since it could not happen if consciousness were not free. Thus to posit the world *as* a world, or to "negate" it, is one and the same thing. In this sense Heidegger can say that nothingness is the constitutive structure of existence. To be able to imagine, it is enough that consciousness be able to surpass the real in constituting it as a world, since the negating of the real is always implied by its constitution in the world. But this surpassing cannot be brought about by just any means, and the freedom of consciousness must not be confused with the arbitrary. For an image is not purely and simply the *world-negated*, it is always *the world negated from a certain point of view*, namely, the one that permits the positing of the absence or the non-existence of the object presented "as an image". The arbitrary positing of the real as a world will not of itself cause the appearance of the centaur as an unreal object. For the centaur to emerge as unreal, the world must be grasped as a world-where-the-centaur-is-not, and this can happen only if consciousness is led by different motivations to grasp the world as being exactly the sort in which the centaur has no place. Likewise, if my friend Peter is to be given me as absent I must be led to grasp the world as that sort of a whole in which Peter cannot *actually exist* and *be present to me*. (He can actually be present for others—in Berlin, for instance.) What motivates the appearance of the unreal is not necessarily nor most often the *representative* intuition of the world from some point of view. Consciousness in fact has many other ways of *surpassing the real in order to make a world of it*: the surpassing can and should happen at first by affectivity or by action. The appearance of a dead friend as unreal, for instance, is built on the foundation of affective expectation of the real as an *empty world* from this point of view.

We shall give the name of "situations" to the different immediate ways of apprehending the real as a world. We can therefore say that the essential prerequisite that enables consciousness to imagine is that it be "situated in the world", or more briefly, that it "be-in-the-world". It is the situation-in-the-world, grasped as a concrete and individual reality of consciousness, which is the motivation for the construction of any unreal object whatever and the nature of that unreal object is circumscribed by this motivation. Thus the *situation* of consciousness does not need to appear as a pure and abstract condition of possibility for all imagination but as the concrete and exact motivation for the appearance of a certain particular imagination.

From this point of view we finally grasp the relation between the unreal and the real. At first; even if an image is not produced at this moment, every apprehension of the real as a world tends of its own accord to end up with the production of unreal objects because it is always, in one sense, a free negation of the world and that always *from a particular point of view*. Thus, if consciousness is free, the intelligible correlative of its freedom should be the *world* which carries in itself its possibility of negation, at each moment and from each point of view, by means of an image, even while the image must as yet be constructed by a particular intention of consciousness. But, reciprocally, an image, being a negation of the world from a particular point of view, can never appear except *on the foundation of the world* and in connection with the foundation. Naturally the appearance of the image demands that the particular perceptions should be diluted in the syncretic wholeness *world* and that this wholeness should withdraw. But it is exactly the withdrawal of the wholeness which turns it into a foundation, the foundation from which the unreal form must detach itself. Thus, although as a result of producing the unreal, consciousness can appear momentarily delivered from "being-in-the-world", it is just this "being-in-the-world" which is the necessary condition for the imagination.

Thus the critical analysis of the conditions that made all imagination possible has led us to the following discoveries: in order to imagine, consciousness must be free from all specific reality and this freedom must be able to define itself by a "being-in-the-world" which is at once the constitution and the negation of the world; the concrete situation of consciousness in the world must at each moment serve as the singular motivation for the constitution of the unreal. Thus the unreal—which is always a two-fold nothingness: nothingness of itself in relation to the world, nothingness of the world in relation to itself—must always be constituted on the foundation of the world which it denies, it being well understood, moreover, that the world does not present itself only to a representative intuition, and that this synthetic foundation demands to be lived as a situation. If these are the conditions that make imagination possible, do they correspond to a specification, to an enrichment contingent upon the essence "consciousness" or are they nothing else but the very essence of that consciousness considered from a particular point of view? It seems that the answer lies in the question. Indeed, what is this free consciousness whose nature is to be the consciousness *of* something, but which, for this very reason, constructs itself before the real and which surpasses it at each moment because it can exist only by "being-in-the-world", that is, by living its relation to the real as *situation*, what is it, indeed, if not simply consciousness such as it reveals itself to itself in the cogito?

Is not doubt the very primary condition of the cogito, that is, at once the constitution of the real as a world and its negation from this same point of view, and does not a reflective grasp of the doubt as doubt coincide with the indisputable intuition of freedom?

We may therefore conclude that imagination is not a contingent and superadded power of consciousness, it is the whole of consciousness as it realizes its freedom; every concrete and real situation of consciousness in the world is pregnant with imagination in as much as it always presents itself as a withdrawing from the real. It does not follow that all perception of the real must reverse itself in imagination, but as consciousness is always "in a situation" because it is always free, it always and at each moment has the concrete *possibility* of producing the unreal. These are the various motivations which decide at each moment whether consciousness will only be realized or whether it will imagine. The unreal is produced outside the world by a consciousness which *stays in the world* and it is because he is transcendentally free that man can imagine.

But, in its turn, the imagination, which has become a psychological and empirical function, is the necessary condition for the freedom of empirical man in the midst of the world. For, if the negating function belonging to consciousness—which Heidegger calls surpassing—is what makes the act of imagination possible, it must be added that this function can manifest itself *only* in an imaginative act. There can be no intuition of nothingness just because nothingness is nothing and because all consciousness, intuitive or not, is consciousness of something. Nothingness can present itself only as an infra-structure of something. The experience of nothingness is not, strictly speaking, an indirect one, it is an experience which is in principle given "with" and "in". Bergson's analyses are pertinent in this connection: any attempt to conceive death or the nothingness of existence directly is by nature bound to fail.

The gliding of the world into the heart of nothingness and the emergence of human reality in this very nothingness can happen only through the positing of *something* which is nothingness in relation to the world, and in relation to which the world is nothing. By this we evidently define the structure of the imagination. It is the appearance of the imaginary before consciousness which permits the grasping of the process of turning the world into nothingness as its essential condition and as its primary structure. If it were possible to conceive for a moment a consciousness which does not imagine, it would have to be conceived as completely engulfed in the existent and without the possibility of grasping anything but the existent. But it is exactly that which cannot be and could never be: all existence is surpassed by itself as soon as it is posited. But it must retreat *towards something*. The imaginary is in every case the "something" concrete toward which the existent is surpassed. When the imaginary is not posited as a fact, the surpassing and the nullifying of the existent are swallowed up in the existent; the surpassing and the freedom *are there* but are not revealed; the person is crushed in the world, run through by the real, he is closest to the thing. However, as soon as he apprehends in one way or another (most of the time without representation) the whole as a *situation*, he retreats from it towards that in relation to which he is *a lack*, an *empty space*, etc. In a word, the concrete motivation of the imaginative consciousness itself presupposes the imaginative structure of consciousness; the realizing consciousness always includes a retreat towards a particular imaginative consciousness which is like the reverse of the situation and in relation to which the situation is defined. For instance, if I desire to see my friend Peter who is not here now the situation defines itself as a "being-in-the-world" such as Peter is not now given, and Peter is this because the whole of the real is surpassed in order to make a world. But it is not at all the real Peter who, on the contrary, if he were given as present or as placed on the edge of reality by empty but presentifying intentions (for instance, if I heard his steps outside the door), would be a part of the situation: this Peter in relation to whom the situation becomes defined is exactly the *absent* Peter.

The imaginary thus represents at each moment the implicit meaning of the real. The imaginative act itself consists in positing the imaginary for itself, that is, in making that meaning explicit—as when Peter as an image rises suddenly before me—but this specific positing of the imaginary will be accompanied by a collapsing of the world which is then no more than the negated foundation of the unreal. And if the negation is the unconditioned principle of all imagination, it itself can never be realized except in and by an act of imagination. That which is denied must be imagined. In fact, the object of a negation cannot be *real* because that would be affirming what is being denied—but neither can it be a complete nothing, since it is *something* that is being denied. So the object of a negation must be posited as imaginary. And this is true for the logical forms of negation (doubt, restriction, etc.) as it is for its active and affective forms (defence, consciousness of impotence, of deprivation, etc.).

Now we are at the point of understanding the meaning and the value of the imaginary. The imaginary appears "on the foundation of the world", but reciprocally all apprehension of the real as world implies a hidden surpassing towards the imaginary. All imaginative consciousness uses the world as the negated foundation of the imaginary and reciprocally all consciousness of the world calls and motivates an imaginative consciousness as grasped from the particular *meaning* of the situation. The apprehension of nothingness could not occur by an immediate unveiling, it develops in and by the free succession of acts of consciousness, the nothingness is the material of the surpassing of the world towards the imaginary. It is as such that it is *lived*, without ever being posited for itself. There could be no developing consciousness without an imaginative consciousness, and vice versa. So imagination, far from appearing as an accidental characteristic of consciousness, turns out to be an essential and transcendental condition of consciousness. It is as absurd to conceive of a consciousness which did not imagine as it would be to conceive of a consciousness which could not realize the cogito.

SKETCH FOR A THEORY OF THE EMOTIONS

[. . .] emotion is not the accidental modification of a subject who is surrounded by an unchanged world. It is easy to see that no emotional apprehension of an object as frightening, irritating, saddening, etc. can arise except against the background of a complete alteration of the world. For an object to appear *formidable*, indeed, it must be realized as an immediate and magical presence *confronting* the consciousness. For example, this face that I see ten yards away behind the window must be lived as an immediate, present threat to myself. But this is possible only in an act of consciousness which destroys all the structures of the world that might dispel the magic and reduce the event to reasonable proportions. It would require, for instance, that the window *as* "object that must first be broken" and the ten yards *as* "distance that must first be covered" should be annihilated. This does not mean in the least that the consciousness in its terror brings the face *nearer*, in the sense of reducing the distance between it and my body. To reduce a distance is still to be thinking in terms of distance. Similarly, although the terrified subject might think, about the window, "it could easily be broken", or "it could be opened from outside", these are only rational explanations that he might offer for his fear. In reality, the window and the distance are seized *simultaneously* in the act of consciousness which catches sight of the face at the window: but in this very act of catching sight of it, window and distance are emptied of their "usable" and necessary character. They are grasped in another way. The distance is no longer grasped as distance— for it is not thought of as "that which would first have to be traversed", it is grasped as the *background* united with the horrible. The window is no longer grasped as "that which would first have to be opened", it is grasped simply as the *frame* of the frightful visage. And in a general way, areas form themselves around me out of which the horrible makes itself felt. For the horrible is *not possible* in the deterministic world of the usable. The horrible can appear only in a world which is such that all the things existing in it are magical by nature, and the only defences against them are magical. This is what we experience often enough in the universe of dreams, where doors, locks and walls are no protection against the threats of robbers or wild animals for they are all grasped in one and the same act of horror. And since the act which is to disarm them is the same as that which is creating them, we see the assassins passing through doors and walls; we press the trigger of our revolver in vain, no shot goes off. In a word, to experience any object as horrible, is to see it against the background of a world which reveals itself as *already* horrible.

Thus consciousness can "be-in-the-world" in two different ways. The world may appear before it as an organized complex of utilizable things, such that, if one wants to produce a predetermined effect, one must act upon the determinate elements of that complex. As one does so, each "utensil" refers one to other utensils and to the totality of utensils; there is no absolute action, no radical change that one can introduce immediately into this world. We have to modify one particular utensil, and this by means of another which refers in its turn to yet another, and so on to infinity. But the world may also confront us at one non-utilizable whole; that is, as only modifiable without intermediation and by great masses. In that case, the categories of the world act immediately upon the consciousness, they are present to it *at no distance* (for example, the face that frightens us through the window acts upon us *without* any means; there is no need for the window to open, for a man to leap into the *room* or to walk across the *floor*). And, conversely, the consciousness tries to combat these dangers or to modify these objects at no distance and without means, by some absolute, massive modification of the world. This aspect of the world is an entirely coherent one; this is the *magical* world. Emotion may be called a sudden fall of consciousness into magic; or, if you will, emotion arises when the world of the utilizable vanishes abruptly and the world of magic appears in its place. We must not, therefore, see in emotion a passing disorder of the organism and the mind which enters and upsets them *from outside*. On the contrary, it is the return of consciousness to the magical attitude, one of the great attitudes which are essential to it, with the appearance of the correlative world—the magical world. Emotion is not an accident, it is a mode of our conscious existence, one of the ways in which consciousness understands (in Heidegger's sense of *Verstehen)* its Being-in-the-World.

A reflective consciousness can always direct its attention upon emotion. In that case, emotion is seen as a structure of consciousness. It is not a pure, ineffable quality like brick-red or the pure feeling of pain— as it would have to be according to James's theory. It has a meaning, it *signifies something in my psychic life*. The purifying reflection of phenomenological reduction enables us to perceive emotion at work constituting the magical form of the world. "I find him hateful *because* I am angry." But that reflection is rare, and depends upon special motivations. In the ordinary way, the reflection that we direct towards the emotive consciousness is accessory after the fact. It may indeed recognize the consciousness *qua* consciousness, but only as it is motivated by the object: "I am angry because *he* is hateful." It is from that kind of reflection that passion is constituted.

5   Being

The question What is being? is not the question What exists? or What is there?. It cannot be answered by producing a list of things that exist. The question is: What exactly have we said about anything when we have said that it is rather than is not?.

In *Being and Time* (*Sein und Zeit*, 1927) Heidegger calls What is being? 'the question of being' (*Seinsfrage*) and the attempt to answer it 'fundamental ontology'. Traditional ontology is the attempt to establish what exists and what does not exist. Fundamental ontology seeks to establish what it is for what is to be. Heidegger thinks that because Western philosophy, since at least Plato and Aristotle, has forgotten and surpressed the question of being in favour of epistemology and traditional ontology, What is it to be? has slipped all too readily into What exists?. The meaning of the *Seinsfrage* has to be recovered and rethought with pre-socratic purity because our technocratic and means-to-end modes of thinking make us largely oblivious to the puzzlement of just being.

We know that Sartre read and re-read Heidegger, partly in the original and partly in the translation *l'Etre et le Temps*. In *Being and Nothingness* Sartre does not answer the *Seinsfrage* but produces phenomenological descriptions of being. The subtitle of *Being and Nothingness* is *An Essay in Phenomenological Ontology*, a concatenation of words which would have made no sense to Husserl because he insists it is necessary to suspend or bracket ontology to engage in phenomenology. For Husserl it is necessary to ignore what is in order to reveal what appears to be – the phenomenon. Sartre eschews Husserl's methodological solipsism and uses Heidegger's fundamental existential category *being-in-the-world* to characterise our human existence and thus puts phenomenology back into the world. For this reason the philosophy of *Being and Nothingness* is existential phenomenology.

Sartre thinks there are fundamentally two manners of being: *being-for-itself* (*l'être-pour-soi*) and *being-in-itself* (*l'être-en-soi*). Other modes of being, such as *being-for-others*, are parasitic on these. Roughly, *being-for-itself* is subjective being and *being-in-itself* is objective being. *Being-for-itself* is the kind of being that pertains to one's own existence. *Being-in-itself* is the manner in which the world external to one's own reality exists.

More precisely, *being-for-itself* entails the existence of consciousness, and consciousness of itself. It is that present centre of conscious awareness that each of us finds him or herself to be. It is being in the sense of being someone, the kind of being of which it makes sense to say 'I am it'. Because *being-for-itself* entails consciousness, it entails that directedness towards the world called 'intentionality' which consciousness entails. *Being-for-itself* is partly constituted by presence to *being-in-itself*. It is what it is over and against the world.

Being-for-itself possesses three existential structures: *facticity, temporality* and *transcendence*. Facticity is the unchosen condition or situation of the *for-itself* in which freedom is exercised. Temporality is the totality past, present, future, and transcendence is the controversial fact about *being-for-itself*: that *it is what it is not and is not what it is*. Sartre means that I am, in a sense, constantly projected towards the future in my free self-definition.

Being for itself is free and entails a kind of lack or *nothingness*. *Being-for-itself* does not so much *have* choice as *is* choice. An essential part of my ownmost ontology is my constant capacity to choose, no matter how unpleasant and constrained the choices available. I am a kind of nothingness because there is nothing that I am independently of my self constitution through those choices. My consciousness is a kind of interior phenomenological space of non-being, surrounded by the plentitude of the world.

Being-in-itself is opaque, objective, inert and entails a massive fullness or plentitude of being. *Being-in-itself* is uncreated, meaning that although it is, it never began to be and there is no cause and no reason for it to be. *Being-in-itself* is not subject to temporality because past, present and future pertain uniquely to *being-for-itself*. (However, the human past is *in-itself*, not *for-itself*, because it is fixed and unalterable.) *Being-in-itself* is undifferentiated, solid and opaque to itself and filled with itself. Sartre sums up these ascriptions in the quasi-tautological thought: *it is what it is*. In *being-in-itself* there is no difference between its being and its being what it is. Existence and essence coincide.

Sartre thinks all being is contingent. Whatever is might not have been. Whatever is might not have been what it is. As Roquentin realises in *Nausea*, there might not have been any conscious beings including oneself. There might not have been anything. That there is something rather than nothing is a fact that could have been otherwise. That there is what there is rather than something else is a fact that could have been otherwise. Humanity seeks to evade its contingency in the inauthentic denial of freedom called 'bad faith' described in Chapter 11 below. Sartre thinks that the fundamental human aspiration is to be a synthesis of *being-for-itself* and *being-in-itself,* the perpetually frustrated aspiration, in fact, to be God.

In order to appreciate Sartre's distinctions between manners of being, in the passages from *Being and Nothingness* which follow, it is necessary to pay close and direct attention to one's own existence and the surrounding world. It is not possible to understand them by thinking in any abstract, objective, or quasi-scientific way. They are entailed by phenomenological descriptions, not theories.

BEING AND NOTHINGNESS

Being-in-itself

We can now form a few definite conclusions about the phenomenon of being, which we have considered in order to make the preceding observations. Consciousness is the revealed-revelation of existents, and existents appear before consciousness on the foundation of their being. Nevertheless the primary characteristic of the being of an existent is never to reveal itself completely to consciousness. An existent can not be stripped of its being; being is the ever present foundation of the existent; it is every-where in it and nowhere. There is no being which is not the being of a certain mode of being, none which can not be apprehended through the mode of being which manifests being and veils it at the same time. Consciousness can always pass beyond the existent, not toward its being, but toward the *meaning of this being.* That is why we call it ontic-ontological, since a fundamental characteristic of its transcendence is to transcend the ontic toward the ontological. The meaning of the being of the existent in so far as it reveals itself to consciousness is the phenomenon of being. This meaning has itself a being, based on which it manifests itself.

It is from this point of view that we can understand the famous scholastic argument according to which there is a vicious circle in every proposition which concerns being, since any judgment about being already implies being. But in actuality there is no vicious circle, for it is not necessary again to pass beyond the being of this meaning toward its meaning; the meaning of being is valid for the being of every phenomenon, including its own being. The phenomenon of being is not being, as we have already noted. But it indicates being and requires it— although, in truth, the ontological proof which we mentioned above is not valid *especially* or *uniquely* for it; there is one ontological proof valid for the whole domain of consciousness. But this proof is sufficient to justify all the information which we can derive from the phenomenon of being. The phenomenon of being, like every primary phenomenon, is immediately disclosed to consciousness. We have at each instant what Heidegger calls a pre-ontological comprehension of it; that is, one which is not accompanied by a fixing in concepts and elucidation. For us at present, then, there is no question of considering this phenomenon for the sake of trying to fix the meaning of being. We must observe always:

(1) That this elucidation of the meaning of being is valid only for the being of the phenomenon. Since the being of consciousness is radically different, its meaning will necessitate a particular elucidation, in terms of the revealed-revelation of another type of being, being-for-itself (*l'être-pour-soi*), which we shall define later and which is opposed to the being-in-itself (*l'être-en-soi*) of the phenomenon.

(2) That the elucidation of the meaning of being-in-itself which we are going to attempt here can be only provisional. The aspects which will be revealed *imply* other significations which ultimately we must apprehend and determine. In particular the preceding reflections have permitted us to distinguish two absolutely separated regions of being: the being of the *pre-reflective cogito* and the being of the phenomenon. But although the concept of being has this peculiarity of being divided into two regions without communication, we must nevertheless explain how these two regions can be placed under the same heading. That will necessitate the investigation of these two types of being, and it is evident that we can not truly grasp the meaning of either one until we can establish their true connection with the notion of being in general and the relations which unite them. We have indeed established by the examination of non-positional self-consciousness that the being of the phenomenon can on no account act upon consciousness. In this way we have ruled out a realistic conception of the relations of the phenomenon with consciousness.

We have shown also by the examination of the spontaneity of the non-reflective cogito that consciousness can not get out of its subjectivity if the latter has been initially given, and that consciousness can not act upon transcendent being nor without contradiction admit of the passive elements necessary in order to constitute a transcendent being arising from them. Thus we have ruled out the *idealist* solution of the problem. It appears that we have barred all doors and that we are now condemned to regard transcendent being and consciousness as two closed totalities without possible communication. It will be necessary to show that the problem allows a solution other than realism or idealism.

A certain number of characteristics can be fixed on immediately because for the most part they follow naturally from what we have just said.

A clear view of the phenomenon of being has often been obscured by a very common prejudice which we shall call "creationism." Since people supposed that God had given being to the world, being always appeared tainted with a certain passivity. But a creation *ex nihilo* can not explain the coming to pass of being; for if being is conceived in a subjectivity, even a divine subjectivity, it remains a mode of intra-subjective being. Such subjectivity can not have even the *representation* of an objectivity, and consequently it can not even be affected with the *will* to create the objective. Furthermore being, if it is suddenly placed outside the subjective by the fulguration of which Leibniz speaks, can only affirm itself as distinct from and opposed to its creator; otherwise it dissolves in him. The theory of perpetual creation, by removing from being what the Germans call *Selbständigkeit*, makes it disappear in the divine subjectivity. If being exists as over against God, it is its own support; it does not preserve the least trace of divine creation. In a word, even if it had been created, being-in-itself would be *inexplicable* in terms of creation; for it assumes its being beyond the creation.

This is equivalent to saying that being is uncreated; But we need not conclude that being creates itself, which would suppose that it is prior to itself. Being can not be *causa sui* in the manner of consciousness. Being is *itself*. This means that it is neither passivity nor activity. Both of these notions are *human* and designate human conduct or the instruments of human conduct. There is activity when a conscious being uses means with an end in view. And we call those objects passive on which our activity is exercised, in as much as they do not spontaneously aim at the end which we make them serve. In a word, man is active and the means which he employs are called passive. These concepts, put absolutely, lose all meaning. In particular, being is not active; in order for there to be an end and means, there must be being. For an even stronger reason it can not be passive, for in order to be passive, it must be. The self-consistency of being is beyond the active as it is beyond the passive.

Being is equally beyond negation as beyond affirmation. Affirmation is always affirmation of something; that is, the act of affirming is distinguished from the thing affirmed. But if we suppose an affirmation in which the affirmed comes to fulfill the affirming and is confused with it, this affirmation can not be affirmed—owing to too much of plenitude and the immediate inherence of the noema in the noesis. It is there that we find being-if we are to define it more clearly-in connection with consciousness. It is the noema in the noesis; that is, the inherence in itself without the least distance. From this point of view, we should not call it "immanence," for immanence in spite of all *connection* with self is still that very slight withdrawal which can be realized—away from the self. But being is not a connection with itself. It is *itself*. It is an immanence which can not realize itself, an affirmation which can not affirm itself, an activity which can not act, because it is glued to itself. Everything happens as if, in order to free the affirmation *of* self from the heart of being, there is necessary a decompression of being. Let us not, however, think that being is merely *one* undifferentiated self-affirmation; the undifferentiation of the in-itself is beyond an infinity of self-affirmations, inasmuch as there is an infinity of modes of self-affirming. We may summarize these first conclusions by saying that being is in itself.

But if being is in itself, this means that it does not refer to itself as self-consciousness does. It is this self. It is itself so completely that the per-petual reflection which constitutes the self is dissolved in an identity. That is why being is at bottom beyond the *self*, and our first formula can be only an approximation due to the requirements of language. In fact being is opaque to itself precisely because it is filled with itself. This can be better expressed by saying that *being is what it is*. This statement is in appearance strictly analytical. Actually it is far from being reduced to that principle of identity which is the unconditioned principle of all analytical judgments. First the formula designates a particular region of being, that of *being in-itself*. We shall see that the being of *for-itself* is defined, on the contrary, as being what it is not and not being what it is. The question here then is of a regional principle and is as such syn-thetical. Furthermore it is necessary to oppose this formula—being in-itself *is* what it is—to that which designates the being of consciousness. The latter in fact, as we shall see, *has to be* what it is.

This instructs us as to the special meaning which must be given to the "is" in the phrase, being *is* what it is. From the moment that beings exist who have to be what they are, the fact of being what they are is no longer a purely axiomatic characteristic; it is a contingent principle of being in-itself. In this sense, the principle of identity, the principle of analytical judgments, is also a regional synthetical principle of being. It designates the opacity of being-in-itself. This opacity has nothing to do with our *position* in relation to the in-itself; it is not that we are obliged to *apprehend it and to observe it* because we are "without." Being-in-itself has no *within* which is opposed to a *without* and which is analogous to a judgment, a law, a consciousness of itself. The in-itself has nothing secret; it is *solid* (*massif*). In a sense we can designate it as a synthesis. But it is the most indissoluble of all: the synthesis of itself with itself.

The result is evidently that being is isolated in its being and that it does not enter into any connection with what is not itself. Transition, becoming, anything which permits us to say that being is not yet what it will be and that it is already what it is not—all that is forbidden on principle. For being is the being of becoming and due to this fact it is beyond becoming. It is what it is. This means that by itself it can not even be what it is not; we have seen indeed that it can encompass no negation. It is full positivity. It knows no otherness; it never posits itself as *other-than-another-being*. It can support no connection with the other. It is itself indefinitely and it exhausts itself in being. From this point of view we shall see later that it is not subject to temporality. It is, and when it gives way, one can not even say that it no longer is. Or, at least, a consciousness can be conscious of it as no longer being, precisely because consciousness is temporal. But being itself does not exist as a lack there where it was; the full positivity of being is re-formed on its giving way. It was and at present other beings are: that is all.

Finally—this will be our third characteristic—being-in-itself *is*. This means that being can neither be derived from the possible nor reduced to the necessary. Necessity concerns the connection between ideal propositions but not that of existents. An existing phenomenon can never be derived from another existent qua existent. This is what we shall call the *contingency* of being-in-itself. But neither can being-in-itself be derived from a *possibility*. The possible is a structure of the *for-itself*; that is, it belongs to the other region of being. Being-in-itself is never either possible or impossible. It *is*. This is what consciousness expresses in anthropomorphic terms by saying that being is superfluous (*de trop*)—that is, that consciousness absolutely can not derive being from anything, either from another being, or from a possibility, or from a necessary law. Uncreated, without reason for being, without any connection with another being, being-in-itself is *de trop* for eternity.

Being is. Being is in-itself. Being is what it is. These are the three characteristics which the preliminary examination of the phenomenon of being allows us to assign to the being of phenomena. For the moment it is impossible to push our investigation further. This is not yet the examination of the *in-itself*—which is never anything but what it is—which will allow us to establish and to explain its relations with the for-itself. Thus we have left "appearances" and have been led progressively to posit two types of being, the in-itself and the for-itself, concerning which we have as yet only superficial and incomplete information. A multitude of questions remain unanswered: What is the ultimate meaning of these two types of being? For what reasons do they both belong to *being* in general? What is the meaning of that being which includes within itself these two radically separated regions of being? If idealism and realism both fail to explain the relations which *in fact* unite these regions which *in theory* are without communication, what other solution can we find for this problem? And how can the being of the phenomenon be transphenomenal?

Immediate structures of the for-itself

I.   *Presence to self*

[...] Now the *cogito* never gives out anything other than what we ask of it. Descartes questioned it concerning its functional aspect—*"I doubt, I think."* And because he wished to pass without a conducting thread from this functional aspect to existential dialectic, he fell into the error of substance. Husserl, warned by this error, remained timidly on the plane of functional description. Due to this fact he never passed beyond the pure description of the appearance as such; he has shut himself up inside the *cogito* and deserves—in spite of his denial—to be called a phenomenalist rather than a phenomenologist. His phenomenalism at every moment borders on Kantian idealism. Heidegger, wishing to avoid that descriptive phenomenalism which leads to the Megarian, antidialectic isolation of essences, begins with the existential analytic without going through the *cogito*. But since the *Dasein* has from the start been deprived of the dimension of consciousness, it can never regain this dimension. Heidegger endows human reality with a self-understanding which he defines as an "ekstatic pro-ject" of its own possibilities. It is certainly not my intention to deny the existence of this project. But how could there be an understanding which would not in itself be the consciousness (of) being understanding? This ekstatic character of human reality will lapse into a thing-like, blind in-itself unless it arises from the consciousness of ekstasis. In truth the *cogito* must be our point of departure, but we can say of it, parodying a famous saying, that it leads us only on condition that we get out of it. Our preceding study, which concerned the conditions for the possibility of certain types of conduct, had as its goal only to place us in a position to question the *cogito* about its being and to furnish us with the dialectic instrument which would enable us to find in the *cogito* itself the means of escaping from instantaneity toward the totality of being which constitutes human reality. Let us return now to description of non-thetic self-consciousness; let us examine its results and ask what it means for consciousness that it must necessarily be what it is not and not be what it is.

"The being of consciousness," we said in the Introduction, "is a being such that in its being, its being is in question." This means that the being of consciousness does not coincide with itself in a full equivalence. Such equivalence, which is that of the in-itself, is expressed by this simple formula: being is what it is. In the in-itself there is not a particle of being which is not wholly within itself without distance. When being is thus conceived there is not the slightest suspicion of duality in it; this is what we mean when we say that the density of being of the in-itself is infinite. It is a fullness. The principle of identity can be said to be synthetic not only because it limits its scope to a region of definite being, but in particular because it masses within it the infinity of density. "A is A" means that A exists in an infinite compression with an infinite density. Identity is the limiting concept of unification: it is not true that the in-itself has any need of a synthetic unification of its being; at its own extreme limit, unity disappears and passes into identity. Identity is the ideal of "one," and "one" comes into the world by human reality. The in-itself is full of itself, and no more total plenitude can be imagined, no more perfect equivalence of content to container. There is not the slightest emptiness in being, not the tiniest crack through which nothingness might slip in.

The distinguishing characteristic of consciousness, on the other hand, is that it is a decompression of being. Indeed it is impossible to define it as coincidence with itself. Of this table I can say only that it is purely and simply *this* table. But I can not limit myself to saying that my belief is belief; my belief is the consciousness (of) belief. It is often said that the act of reflection alters the fact of consciousness on which it is directed. Husserl himself admits that the fact "of being seen" involves a total modification for each *Erlebnis*. But I believe that I have demonstrated that the first condition of all reflection is a pre-reflective *cogito*. This *cogito*, to be sure, does not posit an object; it remains within consciousness. But it is nonetheless homologous with the reflective *cogito* since it appears as the first necessity for non-reflective consciousness to be seen by itself. Originally then the *cogito* includes this nullifying characteristic of existing for a witness, although the witness for which consciousness exists is itself. Thus by the sole fact that my belief is apprehended as belief, it is *no longer only belief*; that is, it is already no longer belief, it is troubled belief. Thus the ontological judgment "belief is consciousness (of) belief" can under no circumstances be taken as a statement of identity; the subject and the attribute are radically different though still within the indissoluble unity of one and the same being.

Very well, someone will say, but at least we must say that consciousness (of) belief is consciousness (of) belief. We rediscover identity and the in-itself on this level. It was only a matter of choosing the appropriate plane on which we should apprehend our object. But that is not true: to affirm that the consciousness (of) belief is consciousness (of) belief is to dissociate consciousness from belief, to suppress the parenthesis, and to make belief an object for consciousness; it is to launch abruptly on to the plane of reflectivity. A consciousness (of) belief which would be only consciousness (of) belief would in fact have to assume consciousness (of) itself as consciousness (of) belief. Belief would become a pure transcending and noematic qualification of consciousness; consciousness would be free to determine itself as it pleased in the face of that belief. It would resemble that impassive regard which, according to Victor Cousin, consciousness casts on psychic phenomena in order to elucidate them one by one. But the analysis of methodical doubt which Husserl attempted has clearly shown the fact that only reflective consciousness can be dissociated from what is posited by the consciousness reflected-on. It is on the reflective level only that we can attempt an ἐποχή,[1] a putting between parentheses, only there that we can refuse what Husserl calls the *mitmachen*.[2] The consciousness (of) belief, while irreparably altering belief, does not distinguish itself from belief; it *exists in order to* perform the act of faith. Thus we are obliged to admit that the consciousness (of) belief is belief. At its origin we have apprehended this double game of reference: consciousness (of) belief is belief and belief is consciousness (of) belief. On no account can we say that consciousness is consciousness or that belief is belief. Each of the terms refers to the other and passes into the other, and yet each term is different from the other. We have seen that neither belief nor pleasure nor joy can exist *before* being conscious; consciousness is the measure of their being; yet it is no less true that belief, owing to the very fact that it can exist only as *troubled*, exists from the start as escaping itself, as shattering the unity of all the concepts in which one can wish to inclose it.

Thus consciousness (of) belief and belief are one and the same being, the characteristic of which is absolute immanence. But as soon as we wish to grasp this being, it slips between our fingers, and we find ourselves faced with a pattern of duality, with a game of reflections. For consciousness is a reflection *(reflet)*, but *qua* reflection it is exactly the one reflecting *(réfléchissant)*, and if we attempt to grasp it as reflecting, it vanishes and we fall back on the reflection. This structure of the reflection—reflecting *(reflet-reflétant)* has disconcerted philosophers, who have wanted to explain it by an appeal to infinity—either by positing it as an *idea-ideae* as Spinoza did, who calls it an *idea-ideae-ideae*, etc., or by defining it in the manner of Hegel as a return upon itself, as the veritable infinite. But the introduction of infinity into consciousness, aside from the fact that it fixes the phenomenon and obscures it, is only an explicative theory expressly designed to reduce the being of consciousness to that of the in-itself. Yet if we accept the objective existence of the reflection—reflecting as it is given, we are obliged to conceive a mode of being different from that of the in-itself, not a unity which contains a duality, not a synthesis which surpasses and lifts the abstract moments of the thesis and of the antithesis, but a duality which *is* unity, a reflection *(reflet)* which *is* its own reflecting *(reflection)*. In fact if we seek to lay hold on the total phenomenon (*i.e.*, the unity of this duality or consciousness (of) belief), we are referred immediately to one of the terms, and this term in turn refers us to the unitary organization of immanence. But if on the contrary we wish to take our point of departure from duality as such and to posit consciousness and belief as a dyad, then we encounter the *idea-ideae* of Spinoza and we miss the pre-reflective phenomenon which we wished to study. This is because pre-reflective consciousness is self-consciousness. It is this same notion of *self* which must be studied, for it defines the very being of consciousness.

Let us note first that the term in-itself, which we have borrowed from tradition to designate the transcending being, is inaccurate. At the limit of coincidence with itself, in fact, the self vanishes to give place to identical being. The *self* can not be a property of being-in-itself. By nature it is a reflexive, as syntax sufficiently indicates—in particular the logical rigor of Latin syntax with the strict distinctions imposed by grammar between the uses of *ejus* and *sui*. The self refers, but it refers precisely to the *subject*. It indicates a relation between the subject and himself, and this relation is precisely a duality, but a particular duality since it requires particular verbal symbols. But on the other hand, the *self* does not designate being either as subject or as predicate. If indeed I consider the "*se*" in "*il s'ennuie,*"[3] for example, I establish that it opens up to allow the subject himself to appear behind it. It is not the subject, since the subject without relation to himself would be condensed into the identity of the in-itself; neither is it a consistent articulation of the real, since it allows the subject to appear behind it. In fact the *self* cannot be apprehended as a real existent; the subject can not *be* self, for coincidence with self, as we have seen, causes the self to disappear. But neither can it *not be* itself since the self is an indication of the subject himself. The *self* therefore represents an ideal distance within the immanence of the subject in relation to himself, a way of *not being his own coincidence*, of escaping identity while positing it as unity—in short, of being in a perpetually unstable equilibrium between identity as absolute cohesion without a trace of diversity and unity as a synthesis of a multiplicity. This is what we shall call presence to itself. The law of being of the *for-itself*, as the ontological foundation of consciousness, is to be itself in the form of presence to itself.

This presence to itself has often been taken for a plenitude of existence, and a strong prejudice prevalent among philosophers causes them to attribute to consciousness the highest rank in being. But this postulate can not be maintained after a more thorough description of the notion of presence. Actually *presence to* always implies duality, at least a virtual separation. The presence of being to itself implies a detachment on the part of being in relation to itself. The coincidence of identity is the veritable plenitude of being exactly because in this coincidence there is left no place for any negativity. Of course the principle of identity can involve the principle of noncontradiction as Hegel has observed. The being which is what it is must be able to be the being which is not what it is not. But in the first place this negation, like all others, comes to the surface of being through human reality, as we have shown, and not through a dialectic appropriate just to being. In addition this principle can denote only the relations of being with the *external*, exactly because it presides over the relations of being with what it is not. We are dealing then with a principle constitutive of *external relations* such that they can appear to a human reality present to being-in-itself and engaged in the world. This principle does not concern the internal relations of being; these relations, inasmuch as they would posit an otherness, do not exist. The principle of identity is the negation of every species of relation at the heart of being-in-itself.

Presence to self, on the contrary, supposes that an impalpable fissure has slipped into being. If being is present to itself, it is because it is not wholly itself. Presence is an immediate deterioration of coincidence, for it supposes separation. But if we ask ourselves at this point *what it is* which separates the subject from himself, we are forced to admit that it is *nothing*. Ordinarily what separates is a distance in space, a lapse of time, a psychological difference, or simply the individuality of two co-presents—in short, a *qualified* reality. But in the case which concerns us, *nothing* can separate the consciousness (of) belief from belief, since belief is *nothing other* than the consciousness (of) belief. To introduce into the unity of a pre-reflective *cogito* a qualified element external to this *cogito* would be to shatter its unity, to destroy its translucency; there would then be in consciousness something of which it would not be conscious and which would not exist in itself as consciousness. The separation which separates belief from itself can not be grasped or even conceived in isolation. If we seek to reveal it, it vanishes. We find belief once more as pure immanence. But if, on the other hand, we wish to apprehend belief as such, then the fissure is there, appearing when we do not wish to see it, disappearing as soon as we seek to contemplate it. This fissure then is the pure negative. Distance, lapse of time, psychological difference can be apprehended in themselves and include as such elements of positivity; they have a simple negative *function*. But the fissure within consciousness is a nothing except for the fact that it denies and that it can have being only as we do not see it.

This negative which is the nothingness of being and the nihilating power both together, is nothingness. Nowhere else can we grasp it in such purity. Everywhere else in one way or another we must confer on it being-in-itself as *nothingness*. But the nothingness which arises in the heart of consciousness *is not*. It *is made-to-be*. Belief, for example, is not the contiguity of one being with another being; it is *its own* presence to itself, its own decompression of being. Otherwise the unity of the for-itself would dissolve into the duality of two in-itselfs.[4] Thus the for-itself must be its own nothingness. The being of consciousness qua consciousness is to exist *at a distance from itself* as a presence to itself, and this empty distance which being carries in its being is Nothingness. Thus in order for a *self* to exist, it is necessary that the unity of this being include its own nothingness as the nihilation of identity. For the nothingness which slips into belief is *its* nothingness, the nothingness of belief as belief in itself, as belief blind and full, as "simple faith." The for-itself is the being which determines itself to exist inasmuch as it can not coincide with itself.

Hence we understand how it was that by questioning the pre-reflective *cogito* without any conducting thread, we could not find nothingness anywhere. One does not *find*, one does not *disclose* nothingness in the manner in which one can find, disclose a being. Nothingness is always an *elsewhere*. It is the obligation for the for-itself never to exist except in the form of an elsewhere in relation to itself, to exist as a being which perpetually effects in itself a break in being. This break does not refer us elsewhere to another being; it is only a perpetual reference of self to self, of the reflection to the reflecting, of the reflecting to the reflection. This reference, however, does not provoke an infinite movement in the heart of the for-itself but is given within the unity of a single act. The infinite movement belongs only to the reflective regard which wants to apprehend the phenomenon as a totality and which is referred from the reflection to the reflecting, from the reflecting to the reflection without being able to stop. Thus nothingness is this hole of being, this fall of the in-itself toward the self, the fall by which the for-itself is constituted. But this nothingness can only "be made-to-be" if its borrowed existence is correlative with a nihilating act on the part of being. This perpetual act by which the in-itself degenerates into presence to itself we shall call an ontological act. Nothingness is the putting into question of being by being—that is, precisely consciousness or for-self. It is an absolute event which comes to being by means of being and which without having being, is perpetually sustained by being. Since being-in-itself is isolated in its being by its total positivity no being can produce being and nothing can happen to being through being—except for nothingness. Nothingness is the peculiar possibility of being and its unique possibility. Yet this original possibility appears only in the absolute act which realizes it. Since nothingness is nothingness of being, it can come to being only through being itself. Of course it comes to being through a particular being, which is human reality. But this being is constituted as human reality inasmuch as this being is nothing but the original project of its own nothingness. Human reality is being in so far as within its being and for its being it is the unique foundation of nothingness at the heart of being.

II.   *The facticity of the for-itself*

Yet the for-itself *is*. It is, we may say, even if it is a being which is not what it is and which is what it is not. It is since whatever reefs there may be to cause it to founder, still the project of sincerity is at least conceivable. The for-itself is, in the manner of an event, in the sense in which I can say that Philip II *has been*, that my friend Pierre is or exists. The for-itself *is*, in so far as it appears in a condition, which it has not chosen, as Pierre is a French bourgeois in 1942, as Schmitt was a Berlin worker in 1870; it *is* in so far as it is thrown into a world and abandoned in a "situation;" it *is* as pure contingency inasmuch as for it as for things in the world, as for this wall, this tree, this cup, the original question can be posited: "Why is this being exactly such and not otherwise?" It *is* in so far as there is in it something of which it is not the foundation—its *presence to the world*.

Being apprehends itself as not being its own foundation, and this apprehension is at the basis of every *cogito*. In this connection it is to be noted that it reveals itself immediately to the *reflective cogito* of Descartes. When Descartes wants to profit from this revelation, he apprehends himself as an imperfect being "since he doubts." But in this imperfect being, he establishes the presence of the idea of perfection. He apprehends then a cleavage between the type of being which he can conceive and the being which he is. It is this cleavage or lack of being which is at the origin of the second proof of the existence of God. In fact if we get rid of the scholastic terminology, what remains of this proof?

The very clear indication that the being which possesses in itself the idea of perfection can not be its own foundation, for if it were, it would have produced itself in conformance with that idea. In other words, a being which would be its own foundation could not suffer the slightest discrepancy between what it is and what it conceives, for it would produce itself in conformance with its comprehension of being and could conceive only of what it is.

But this apprehension of being as a lack of being in the face of being is first a comprehension on the part of the *cogito* of its own contingency. I think, therefore I am. What am I? A being which is not its own foundation, which qua being, could be other than it is to the extent that it does not account for its being. This is that first intuition of our own contingency which Heidegger gives as the first motivation for the passage from the un-authentic to the authentic.[5] There is restlessness, an appeal to the conscience *(Ruf des Gewissens)*, a feeling of guilt. In truth Heidegger's description shows all too clearly his anxiety to establish an ontological foundation for an Ethics with which he claims not to be concerned, as also to reconcile his humanism with the religious sense of the transcendent. The intuition of our contingency is not identical with a feeling of guilt. Nevertheless it is true that in our own apprehension of ourselves, we appear to ourselves as having the character of an unjustifiable fact.

Earlier, however, we apprehended ourselves as consciousness—that is, as a "being which exists by itself."[6] How within the unity of one and the same upsurge into being, can we be that being which exists by itself as not being the foundation of its being? Or in other words, since the for-itself-in so far as it *is*—is not its own being (*i.e.*, is not the foundation of it), how can it as for-itself, be the foundation of its own nothingness? The answer is in the question.

While being is indeed the foundation of nothingness as the nihilation of its own being, that is not the same as saying that it is the foundation of its being. To found its own being it would have to exist at a distance from itself, and that would imply a certain nihilation of the being founded as of the being which founds—a duality which would be unity; here we should fall back into the case of the for-itself. In short, every effort to conceive of the idea of a being which would be the foundation of its being results inevitably in forming that of a being which contingent as being-in-itself, would be the foundation of its own nothingness. The act of causation by which God is *causa sui* is a nihilating act like every recovery of the self by the self, to the same degree that the original relation of necessity is a return to *self*, a reflexivity. This original necessity in turn appears on the foundation of a contingent being, precisely that being which *is in order to* be the cause of itself. Leibniz' effort to define necessity in terms of possibility—a definition taken up again by Kant—is undertaken from the point of view of knowledge and not from the point of view of being. The passage from possibility to being such as Leibniz conceives it (the necessary is a being whose possibility implies its existence) marks the passage from our ignorance to knowledge. In fact since possibility precedes existence, it can be possibility only with respect to our thought. It is an external possibility in relation to the being whose possibility it is, since being unrolls from it like a consequence from a principle. But we pointed out earlier that the notion of possibility could be considered in two aspects. We can make of it a subjective indication. The statement, "It is possible that Pierre is dead," indicates that I am in ignorance concerning Pierre's fate, and in this case it is a witness who decides the possible in the presence of the world. Being has its possibility outside of itself in the pure regard which gauges its chances of being; possibility can indeed be given *to us* before being; but it is *to us* that it is given and it is in no way the possibility *of* this being. The billiard ball which rolls on the table does not possess the possibility of being turned from its path by a fold in the cloth; neither does the possibility of deviation belong to the cloth; it can be established only by a witness synthetically as an external relation. But possibility can also appear to us as an ontological structure of the real. Then it belongs to certain beings as *their* possibility; it is the possibility which they are, which they have to be. In this case being sustains its own possibilities in being; it is their foundation, and the necessity of being can not then be derived from its possibility. In a word, God, if he exists, is contingent.

Thus the being of consciousness; since this being is in itself *in order to* nihilate itself in for-itself, remains contingent; that is, it is not the role of consciousness either to give being to itself or to receive it from others. In addition to the fact that the ontological proof like the cosmological proof fails to establish a necessary being, the explanation and the foundation of my being—in so far as I am *a particular being*—can not be sought in necessary being. The premises, "Everything which is contingent must find a foundation in a necessary being. Now I am contingent," mark a desire to find a foundation and do not furnish the explicative link with a real foundation. Such premises could not in any way account for *this* contingency but only for the abstract idea of contingency in general. Furthermore the question here is one of value, not fact.[7] But while being in-itself is contingent, it recovers itself by degenerating into a for-itself. It *is*, in order to lose itself in a for-itself. In a word being *is* and can only be. But the peculiar possibility of being—that which is revealed in the nihilating act—is of being the foundation of itself as consciousness through the sacrificial act which nihilates being. The for-itself is the in-itself losing itself as in-itself in order to found itself as consciousness. Thus consciousness holds within itself its own being-as-consciousness, and since it is its own nihilation, it can refer only to itself; but *that which is annihilated*[8] in consciousness—though we can not call it the foundation of consciousness—is the contingent in-itself. The in-itself can not provide the foundation for anything; if it founds itself, it does so by giving itself the modification of the for-itself. It is the foundation of itself in so far as it is *already no longer* in-itself, and we encounter here again the origin of every foundation. If being in-itself can be neither its own foundation nor that of other beings, the whole idea of foundation comes into the world through the for-itself. It is not only that the for-itself as a nihilated in-itself is itself given a foundation, but with it foundation appears for the first time.

It follows that this in-itself, engulfed and nihilated in the absolute event which is the appearance of the foundation or upsurge of the for-itself, remains at the heart of the for-itself as its original contingency. Consciousness is its own foundation but it remains contingent *in order that there may be* a consciousness rather than an infinity of pure and simple in-itself. The absolute event or for-itself is contingent in its very being. If I decipher the givens of the pre-reflective *cogito*, I establish, to be sure, that the for-itself refers to itself. Whatever the for-itself may be, it is this in the mode of consciousness of being. Thirst refers to the consciousness of thirst, which it *is*, as to its foundation—and conversely. But the totality "reflected–reflecting," if it could be given, would be contingency and in-itself. But this totality can not be attained, since I can not say either that the consciousness of thirst is consciousness of thirst, or that thirst is thirst. It is there as a nihilated totality, as the evanescent unity of the phenomenon. If I apprehend the phenomenon as plurality, this plurality indicates itself as a total unity, and hence its meaning is its contingency. That is, I can ask myself, "Why am I thirsty? Why am I conscious of this glass? Of this Me?" But as soon as I consider this totality in in-itself, it nihilates itself under my regard. It *is not*; it *is* in order not to be, and I return to the for-itself apprehended in its suggestion of duality as the foundation of itself. I am angry because I produce myself as consciousness of anger. Suppress this self-causation which constitutes the being of the for-itself, and you will no longer find anything, not even "anger-in-itself;" for anger exists by nature as for-itself. Thus the for-itself is sustained by a perpetual contingency for which it assumes the responsibility and which it assimilates without ever being able to suppress it. This perpetually evanescent contingency of the in-itself which, without ever allowing itself to be apprehended, haunts the for-itself and reattaches it to being-in-itself—this contingency is what we shall call the *facticity* of the for-itself. It is this facticity which permits us to say that the for-itself *is*, that it *exists*, although we can never *realize* the facticity and although we always apprehend it through the for-itself.

We indicated earlier that we can be nothing without playing at being.[9] "If I am a café waiter," we said, "this can be only in the mode of *not being* one." And that is true. If I could *be* a café waiter, I should suddenly constitute myself as a contingent block of identity. And that I am not. This contingent being in-itself always escapes me. But in order that I may freely give a meaning to the obligations which my state involves, then in one sense at the heart of the for-itself, as a perpetually evanescent totality, being-in-itself must be given as the evanescent contingency of my *situation*. This is the result of the fact that while I must *play at being* a café waiter in order to be one, still it would be in vain for me to play at being a diplomat or a sailor, for I would not be one. This inapprehensible *fact* of my condition, this impalpable difference which distinguishes this drama of realization from drama pure and simple is what causes the for-itself, while choosing the meaning of its situation and while constituting itself as the foundation of itself in situation, *not to choose* its position. This part of my condition is what causes me to apprehend myself simultaneously as totally responsible for my being— inasmuch as I am its foundation—and as totally unjustifiable. Without facticity consciousness could choose attachments to the world in the same way as the souls in Plato's *Republic* choose their condition. I could determine myself to "be born a worker" or to "be born a bourgeois." But on the other hand facticity can not constitute me as *being* a bourgeois or *being* a worker. It is not even strictly speaking a *resistance* of fact since it is only by recovering it in the substructure of the *pre-reflective cogito* that I confer on it its meaning and its resistance. Facticity is only one indication which I give myself of the being to which I must reunite myself in order to be what I am.

It is impossible to grasp facticity in its brute nudity, since all that we will find of it is already recovered and freely constructed. The simple fact "of being there," at that table, in that chair is already the pure object of a limiting-concept and as such can not be grasped. Yet it is contained in my "consciousness of being-there," as its full contingency, as the nihilated in-itself on the basis of which the for-itself produces itself as consciousness of being there. The for-itself looking deep into itself as the consciousness of being there will never discover anything in itself but *motivations*; that is, it will be perpetually referred to itself and to its constant freedom. (I am there in order to . . . *etc.*) But the contingency which paralyzes these motivations to the same degree as they totally found themselves is the facticity of the for-itself. The relation of the for-itself, which is its own foundation qua for-itself, to facticity can be correctly termed a factual necessity. It is indeed this factual necessity which Descartes and Husserl seized upon as constituting the evidence of the *cogito*. The for-itself is necessary in so far as it provides its own foundation. And this is why it is the object reflected by an apodictic intuition. I can not doubt that I am. But in so far as this for-itself as such could also not be, it has all the contingency of fact. Just as my nihilating freedom is apprehended in anguish, so the for-itself is conscious of its facticity. It has the feeling of its complete gratuity; it apprehends itself as being there *for nothing*, as being *de trop*.

We must not confuse facticity with that Cartesian substance whose attribute is thought. To be sure, thinking substance exists only as it thinks; and since it is a created thing, it participates in the contingency of the *ens creatum*. But it *is*. It preserves the character of being-in-itself in its integrity, although the for-itself is its attribute. This is what is called Descartes' substantialist illusion. For us, on the other hand, the appearance of the for-itself or absolute event refers indeed to the effort of an in-itself to found itself; it corresponds to an attempt on the part of being to remove contingency from its being. But this attempt results in the nihilation of the in-itself, because the in-itself can not found *itself* without introducing the *self* or a reflective, nihilating reference into the absolute identity of its being and consequently degenerating into *for-itself*. The for-itself corresponds then to an expanding de-structuring of the in-itself, and the in-itself is nihilated and absorbed in its attempt to found itself. Facticity is not then a substance of which the for-itself would be the attribute and which would produce thought without exhausting itself in that very production. It simply resides in the for-itself as a memory of being, as its unjustifiable *presence in the world*. Being-in-itself can found its nothingness but not its being. In its decompression it nihilates itself in a for-itself which becomes qua for-itself its own foundation; but the contingency which the for-itself has derived from the in-itself remains out of reach. It is what *remains* of the in-itself in the for-itself as facticity and what causes the for-itself to have only a factual necessity; that is, it is the foundation of its *consciousness-of-being* or *existence*, but on no account can it found its *presence*. Thus consciousness can in no case prevent itself from being and yet it is totally responsible for its being.

In-itself and for-itself: metaphysical implications

We are finally in a position to form conclusions. [. . .] we discovered consciousness as an appeal to being, and we showed that the *cogito* refers immediately to a being-in-itself which is the *object* of consciousness. But after our description of the In-itself and the For-itself, it appeared to us difficult to establish a bond between them, and we feared that we might fall into an insurmountable dualism. This dualism threatened us again in another way. In fact to the extent that it can be said of the For-itself that it is, we found ourselves confronting two radically distinct modes of being: that of the For-itself which has to be what it is—*i.e.*, which is what it is not and which is not what it is—and that of the In-itself which is what it is. We asked then if the discovery of these two types of being had resulted in establishing an hiatus which would divide Being (as a general category belonging to all existents) into two incommunicable regions, in each one of which the notion of Being must be taken in an original and unique sense.

Our research has enabled us to answer the first of these questions: the For-itself and the In-itself are reunited by a synthetic connection which is nothing other than the For-itself itself. The For-itself, in fact, is nothing but the pure nihilation of the In-itself; it is like a hole of being at the heart of Being. One may be reminded here of that convenient fiction by which certain popularizers are accustomed to illustrate the principle of the conservation of energy. If, they say, a single one of the atoms which constitute the universe were annihilated, there would result a catastrophe which would extend to the entire universe, and this would be, in particular, the end of the Earth and of the solar system. This metaphor can be of use to us here. The For-itself is like a tiny nihilation which has its origin at the heart of Being; and this nihilation is sufficient to cause a total upheaval to *happen* to the In-itself. This upheaval is the world. The for-itself has no reality save that of being the nihilation of being. Its sole qualification comes to it from the fact that it is the nihilation of an individual and particular In-itself and not of a being in general. The For-itself is not nothingness in general but a particular privation; it constitutes itself as the privation of *this being*. Therefore we have no business asking about the way in which the for-itself can be united with the in-itself since the for-itself is in no way an autonomous substance. As a nihilation it *is made-to-be* by the in-itself; as an internal negation it must by means of the in-itself make known to itself what it is not and consequently what it has to be. If the *cogito* necessarily leads outside the self, if consciousness is a slippery slope on which one cannot take one's stand without immediately finding oneself tipped outside onto being-in-itself, this is because consciousness does not have by itself any sufficiency of being as an absolute subjectivity; from the start it refers to the thing.

For consciousness there is no being except for this precise obligation to be a revealing intuition of something. What does this mean except that consciousness is the Platonic *Other*? We may recall the fine description which the Stranger in the *Sophist* gives of this "other,"[10] which can be apprehended only "as in a dream," which has no being except its being-other (*i.e.*, which enjoys only a borrowed being), which if considered by itself disappears and which takes on a marginal existence only if one fixes his look on being, this other which is exhausted in being other than itself and other than being. It even seems that Plato perceived the dynamic character which the otherness of the other presented in relation to itself, for in certain passages he sees in this the origin of motion. But he could have gone still further; he would have seen then that the other, or relative non-being, could have a semblance of existence only by virtue of consciousness. To be other than being is to be self-consiousness in the unity of the temporalizing ekstases. Indeed what can the otherness be if not that game of musical chairs played by the reflected and the reflecting which we described as at the heart of the for-itself? For the only way in which the other can exist as other is to be consciousness (of) being other. Otherness is, in fact, an internal negation, and only a consciousness can be constituted as an internal negation. Every other conception of otherness will amount to positing it as an in-itself-that is, establishing between it and being an external relation which would necessitate the presence of a witness so as to establish that the other is other than the in-itself. However the other can not be other without emanating from being; in this respect it is relative to the in-itself. But neither can it be other without *making itself other*; otherwise its otherness would become a given and therefore a being capable of being considered in-itself. In so far as it is relative to the in-itself, the other is affected with facticity; in so far as it makes itself, it is an absolute. This is what we pointed out when we said that the for-itself is not the foundation of its being-as-nothingness-of-being but that it perpetually founds its nothingness-of-being. Thus the for-itself is an absolute *Unselbständig*, what we have called a non-substantial absolute. Its reality is purely *interrogative*. If it can posit questions this is because it is itself always *in question*; its being is never *given* but *interrogated* since it is always separated from itself by the nothingness of otherness. The for-itself is always in suspense because its being is a perpetual reprieve. If it could ever join with its being, then the otherness would by the same stroke disappear and along with it possibles, knowledge, the world. Thus the *ontological* problem of knowledge is resolved by the affirmation of the ontological primacy of the in-it-self over the for-itself.

But this immediately gives rise to a *metaphysical* interrogation. The upsurge of the for-itself starting from the in-itself is in no way comparable to the *dialectical* genesis of the Platonic Other starting from being. "Being" and "other" are, for Plato, *genera*. But we, on the contrary, have seen that being is an individual venture. Similarly the appearance of the for-itself is the absolute event which comes to being. There is therefore room here for a *metaphysical problem which could be formulated* thus: Why does the for-itself arise in terms of being? We, indeed, apply the term "metaphysical" to the study of individual processes which have given birth to *this* world as a concrete and particular totality. In this sense metaphysics is to ontology as history is to sociology. We have seen that it would be absurd to ask why being is other, that the question can have meaning only within the limits of a for-itself and that it even supposes the ontological priority of nothingness over being. It can be posited only if combined with another question which is externally analogous and yet very different: Why is it that *there is* being? But we know now that we must carefully distinguish between these two questions. The first is devoid of meaning: all the "Whys" in fact are subsequent to being and presuppose it. Being is without reason, without cause, and without necessity; the very definition of being releases to us its original contingency. To the second question we have already replied, for it is not posited on the metaphysical level but on that of ontology: "There is" being because the for-itself is such that there is being. The character of a *phenomenon* comes to being through the for-itself.

But while questions on the origin of being or on the origin of the world are either devoid of meaning or receive a reply within the actual province of ontology, the case is not the same for the origin of the for-itself. The for-itself is such that it has the right to turn back on itself toward its own origin. The being by which the "Why" comes into being has the right to posit its own "Why" since it is itself an interrogation, a "Why." To this question ontology can not reply, for the problem here is to explain an event, not to describe the structures of a being. At most it can point out that the nothingness which *is made-to-be* by the in-itself is not a simple emptiness devoid of meaning. The meaning of the nothingness of the nihilation is to-be-made-to-be in order to found being. Ontology furnishes us two pieces of information which serve as the basis for metaphysics: first, that every process of a foundation of the self is a rupture in the identity-of-being of the in-itself, a withdrawal by being in relation to itself and the appearance of presence to self or consciousness. It is only by making itself for-itself that being can aspire to be the cause of itself.

Consciousness as the nihilation of being appears therefore as one stage in a progression toward the immanence of causality—*i.e.*, toward being a self-cause. The progression, however, stops there as the result of the insufficiency of being in the for-itself. The temporalization of consciousness is not an ascending progress toward the dignity of the *causa sui*; it is a surface run-off whose origin is, on the contrary, the impossibility of being a self-cause. Also the *ens causa sui* remains as the *lacked*, the indication of an impossible *vertical* surpassing which by its very non-existence conditions the flat movement of consciousness; in the same way the vertical attraction which the moon exercises on the ocean has for its result the horizontal displacement which is the tide. The second piece of information which metaphysics can draw from ontology is that the for-itself is *effectively* a perpetual project of founding itself qua being and a perpetual failure of this project. Presence to itself with the various directions of its nihilation (the ekstatic nihilation of the three temporal dimensions, the twin nihilation of the dyad reflected-reflecting) represents the primary upsurge of this project; reflection represents the splitting of the project which turns back on itself in order to found itself at least as a project, and the aggravation of the nihilating hiatus by the failure of this project itself. "Doing" and "having," the cardinal categories of human reality, are immediately or mediately reduced to the project of being. Finally the plurality of both *can* be interpreted as human reality's final attempt to found itself, resulting in the radical separation of being and the consciousness of being.

Thus ontology teaches us two things: (1) *If* the in-itself were to found itself, it could attempt to do so only by making itself consciousness; that is, the concept of *causa sui* includes within it that of presence to self—*i.e.*, the nihilating decompression of being; (2) Consciousness is *in fact* a project of founding itself; that is, of attaining to the dignity of the in-itself-for-itself or in-itself-as-self-cause. But we can not derive anything further from this. Nothing allows us to affirm on the ontological level that the nihilation of the in-itself in for-itself has for its meaning—from the start and at the very heart of the in-itself—the project of being its own self-cause. Quite the contrary. Ontology here comes up against a profound contradiction since it is through the for-itself that the possibility of a foundation comes to the world. In order to be a project of founding itself, the in-itself would of necessity have to be originally a presence to itself—*i.e.*, it would have to be already consciousness. Ontology will therefore limit itself to declaring that *everything takes place as if* the in-itself in a project to found itself gave itself the modification of the for-itself. It is up to metaphysics to form the *hypotheses* which will allow us to conceive of this process as the absolute event which comes to crown the individual venture which is the existence of being. It is evident that these hypotheses will remain hypotheses since we can not expect either further validation or invalidation. What will make their *validity* is only the possibility which they will offer us of unifying the *givens* of ontology. This unification naturally must not be constituted in the perspective of an historical becoming since temporality comes into being through the for-itself. There would be therefore no sense in asking what being was *before* the appearance of the for-itself. But metaphysics must nevertheless attempt to determine the nature and the meaning of this prehistoric process, the source of all history, which is the articulation of the individual venture (or existence of the in-itself) with the absolute event (or up-surge of the for-itself). In particular the task belongs to the metaphysician of deciding whether the movement is or is not a first "attempt" on the part of the in-itself to found itself and to determine what are the relations of motion as a "malady of being" with the for-itself as a more profound malady pushed to nihilation.

It remains for us to consider the second problem which we formulated in our Introduction: If the in-itself and the for-itself are two modalities of *being*, is there not an hiatus at the very core of the idea of being? And is its comprehension not severed into two incommunicable parts by the very fact that its extension is constituted by two radically heterogenous classes? What is there in common between the being which is what it is, and the being which is what it is not and which is not what it is? What can help us here, however, is the conclusion of our preceding inquiry. We have just shown in fact that the in-itself and the for-itself are not juxtaposed. Quite the contrary, the for-itself without the in-itself is a kind of abstraction; it could not exist any more than a color could exist without form or a sound without pitch and without timbre. A consciousness which would be consciousness of nothing would be an absolute nothing. But if consciousness is bound to the in-itself by an internal relation, doesn't this mean that it is articulated with the in-itself so as to constitute a totality, and is it not this totality which would be given the name *being* or reality? Doubtless the for-itself is a nihilation, but as a nihilation it *is*; and it is in *a priori* unity with the in-itself. Thus the Greeks were accustomed to distinguish cosmic reality, which they called Τò πᾶυ, from the totality constituted by this and by the infinite void which surrounded it—a totality which they called Τò ὅλου. To be sure, we have been able to call the for-itself a nothing and to declare that there is "outside of the in-itself" *nothing* except a reflection of this nothing which is itself polarized and defined by the in-itself—inasmuch as the for-itself is precisely the nothingness of *this in-itself*. But here as in Greek philosophy a question is raised: which shall we call *real*? To which shall we attribute *being*? To the cosmos or to what we called Tò ὅλου? To the pure in-itself or to the in-itself surrounded by that shell of nothingness which we have designated by the name of the for-itself?

But if we are to consider total being as constituted by the synthetic organization of the in-itself and of the for-itself, are we not going to encounter again the difficulty which we wished to avoid? And as for that hiatus which we revealed in the concept of being, are we not going to meet it at present in the existent itself? What definition indeed are we to give to an existent which as in-itself would be what it is and as for-itself would be what it is not?

If we wish to resolve these difficulties, we must take into account what is required of an existent if it is to be considered as a totality: it is necessary that the diversity of its structures be held within a unitary synthesis in such a way that each of them considered apart is only an abstraction. And certainly consciousness considered apart is only an abstraction; but the in-itself has no need of the for-itself in order to be; the "passion" of the for-itself only causes *there to be* in-itself. The *phenomenon* of in-itself is an abstraction without consciousness but its *being* is not an abstraction.

If we wish to conceive of a synthetic organization such that the for-itself is inseparable from the in-itself and conversely such that the in-itself is indissolubly bound to the for-itself, we must conceive of this synthesis in such a way that the in-itself would receive its existence from the nihilation which caused there to be consciousness of it. What does this mean if not that the indissoluble totality of in-itself and for-itself is conceivable only in the form of a being which is its own "self-use"? It is this being and no other which could be valid absolutely as that ὅλου of which we spoke earlier. And if we can raise the question of the being of the for-itself articulated in the in-itself, it is because we define ourselves *a priori* by means of a pre-ontological comprehension of the *ens causa sui*. Of course this *ens causa sui* is *impossible*, and the concept of it, as we have seen, includes a contradiction. Nevertheless the fact remains that since we raise the question of the being of the ὅλου by adopting the point of view of the *ens causa sui*, it is from this point of view that we must set about examining the credentials of this ὅλου. Has it not appeared due to the mere fact of the upsurge of the for-itself, and is not the for-itself originally a project of being its own self-use? Thus we begin to grasp the nature of total reality. Total being, the concept of which would not be cleft by an hiatus and which would nevertheless not exclude the nihilating-nihilated being of the for-itself, that being whose existence would be a unitary synthesis of the in-itself and of consciousness—this ideal being would be the in-itself founded by the for-itself and identical with the for-itself which founds it—i.e., the *ens causa sui*. But precisely because we adopt the point of view of this ideal being in order to judge the *real* being which we call ὅλου, we must establish that the real is an abortive effort to attain to the dignity of the self-cause. Everything happens as if the world, man, and man-in-the-world succeeded in realizing only a missing God. Everything happens therefore as if the in-itself and the for-itself were presented in a state of disintegration in relation to an ideal synthesis. Not that the integration has ever *taken place* but on the contrary precisely because it is always indicated and always impossible.

It is this perpetual failure which explains both the indissolubility of the in-itself and of the for-itself and at the same time their relative independence. Similarly when the unity of the cerebral functions is shattered, phenomena are produced which simultaneously present a relative autonomy and which at the same time can be manifested only on the ground of the disintegration of a totality. It is this failure which explains the hiatus which we encounter both in the concept of being and in the existent. If it is impossible to pass from the notion of being-in-itself to that of being-for-itself and to reunite them in a common genus, this is because the *passage in fact* from the one to the other and their reuniting can not be effected. We know that for Spinoza and for Hegel, for example, if a synthesis is arrested before its completion and the terms fixed in a relative dependence and at the same time in a relative independence, then the synthesis is constituted suddenly as an error. For example, it is in the notion of a sphere that for Spinoza the rotation of a semicircle around its diameter finds its justification and its meaning. But if we imagine that the notion of a sphere is on principle out of reach, then the phenomenon of the rotation of the semicircle becomes *false*. It has been decapitated; the idea of rotation and the idea of a circle are held together without being able to be united in a synthesis which surpasses them and justifies them; the one remains irreducible to the other. This is precisely what happens here. We shall say therefore that the ὅλου we are considering is like a decapitated notion in perpetual disintegration. And it is in the form of a disintegrated ensemble that it presents itself to us in its ambiguity—that is, so that one can *ad libitum* insist on the dependence of the beings under consideration or on their independence. There is here a passage which is not completed, a short circuit.

On this level we find again that notion of a detotalized totality which we have already met in connection with the for-itself itself and in connection with the consciousnesses of others. But this is a third type of detotalization. In the simply detotalized totality of reflection the reflective *had to be* reflected-on, and the reflected-on had to be the reflected. The double negation remained evanescent. In the case of the for-others the (reflection-reflecting) reflected was distinguished from the (reflection-reflecting) reflecting in that each one *had to not-be* the other. Thus the for-itself and the-other-for-itself constitute a being in which each one confers the being-other on the other by making himself other. As for the totality of the for-itself and the in-itself, this has for its characteristic the fact that the for-itself makes itself *other* in relation to the in-itself but that the in-itself is in no way other than the for-itself in its being; the in-itself purely and simply is. If the relation of the in-itself to the for-itself were the reciprocal of the relation of the for-itself to the in-itself, we should fall into the case of being-for-others. But this is definitely not the case, and it is this absence of reciprocity which characterizes the ὅλου of which we spoke earlier. To this extent it is not absurd to raise the question of the totality. In fact when we studied the for-others, we established that it was necessary that there be a being which was an "other-me" and which had to be the reflective scissiparity of the for-others. But at the same time this being which is an other-me appeared to us as being able to exist only if it included an inapprehensible non-being of exteriority. We asked then if the paradoxical character of the totality was in itself an irreducible and if we could posit the mind as the being which is and which is not. But we decided that the question of the synthetic unity of consciousnesses had no meaning, for it presupposed that it was possible for us to assume a point of view on the totality; actually we exist on the foundation of this totality and as engaged in it.

But if we can not "adopt a point of view on the totality," this is because the Other on principle denies that he is I as I deny that I am he. It is the reciprocity of the relation which prevents me from ever grasping it in its integrity. In the case of the internal negation for-itself-in-itself, on the contrary, the relation is not reciprocal, and I am both one of the terms of the relation and the relation itself. I apprehend being, I *am* the apprehension of being, I am *only* an apprehension of being. And the being which I apprehend is not posited *against* me so as to apprehend me in turn; it is what is apprehended. Its *being* simply does not coincide in any way with its being-apprehended. In one sense therefore I can pose the question of the totality. To be sure, I exist here as *engaged* in this totality, but I can be an *exhaustive consciousness* of it since I am at once consciousness of the being and self-consciousness. This question of the totality, however, does not belong to the province of ontology. For ontology the only regions of being which can be elucidated are those of the in-itself, of the for-itself, and the ideal region of the "self-cause." For ontology it makes no difference whether we consider the for-itself articulated in the in-itself as a well marked *duality* or as a disintegrated being.

It is up to metaphysics to decide which will be more profitable for knowledge (in particular for phenomenological psychology, for anthropology, *etc.*): will it deal with a being which we shall call the *phenomenon* and which will be provided with two dimensions of being, the dimension in-itself and the dimension for-itself (from this point of view there would be *only one* phenomenon: the world), just as in the physics of Einstein it has been found advantageous to speak of an *event* conceived as having spatial dimensions and a temporal dimension and as determining its space in a space-time; or, on the other hand will it remain preferable despite all to preserve the ancient duality "consciousness-being." The only observation which ontology can hazard here is that in case it appears useful to employ the new notion of a phenomenon as a disintegrated totality, it will be necessary to speak of it *both* in terms of immanence and in terms of transcendence. The danger, in fact, would be of falling into either a doctrine of pure immanence (Husserlian idealism) or into one of pure transcendence which would look on the *phenomenon* as a new kind of *object*. But immanence will be always limited by the phenomenon's dimension in-itself, and transcendence will be limited by its dimension for-itself.

After having decided the question of the origin of the for-itself and of the nature of the phenomenon of the world, the metaphysician will be able to attack various problems of primary importance, in particular that of action. Action, in fact, is to be considered simultaneously on the plane of the for-itself and on that of the in-itself, for it involves a project which has an immanent origin and which determines a modification in the being of the transcendent. It would be of no use to declare that the action modifies only the phenomenal appearance of the thing. If the phenomenal appearance of a cup can be modified up to the annihilation of the cup qua cup, and if the being of the cup is nothing but its *quality*, then the action envisaged must be capable of modifying the very being of the cup. The problem of action therefore supposes the elucidation of the transcendent efficacy of consciousness, and it puts us on the path of its veritable relation of being with being. It reveals to us also, owing to the repercussions of an act in the world, a relation of being with being which, although apprehended in exteriority by the physicist, is neither pure exteriority nor immanence but which refers us to the notion of the Gestalt *form*. It is therefore in these terms that one might attempt a metaphysics of nature.

Notes

1 Correction for ἐπόχη, an obvious misprint. Tr.

2 "To take part in," "to participate." Tr.
3 Literally the "self" in "he bores himself" (*il s'ennuie*), a familiar construction in the many French reflexive verbs. *Cf.* English "he washes himself." Tr.
4 *Deux en-soi*. Ungrammatical as the expression "in-itselfs" admittedly is, it seems to me the most accurate translation. "In-themselves" would have a different meaning, for it would suggest a unity of two examples of being-in-itself, and Sartre's point here is their duality and isolation from each other. Tr.
5 I have corrected what must surely be a misprint. "From the authentic to the authentic," as the text actually reads, would make no sense. Tr.
6 *Cf. Introduction*, section III.
7 This reasoning indeed is explicitly based on the *exigencies* of reason.
8 Sartre says "annihilated" here, but I feel that he must have meant "nihilated" since he has told us earlier that being cannot be annihilated. Tr.
9 Part One, chapter II, section ii. "Patterns of Bad Faith."
10 "The other" in this passage must of course not be confused with "The Other" discussed in connection with the problem of human relationships. Tr.

6   Nothingness

The title of Sartre's *Being and Nothingness* is taken from the opening paragraphs of Hegel's dialectic. In the 1812–16 *Science of Logic* (*Wissenschaft der Logik*) Hegel argues that *Being* (*Sein*) and *Nothing* (*Nichts*) are the fundamental concepts because without them there are no concepts. Being and nothing are dialectically antithetical because semantically, psychologically and ontologically opposed yet mutually dependent. They are indeterminate because being is pure being and nothing pure nothing. Being and nothing are *aufgehoben* (synthesised, relieved, abolished, retained, taken up) in becoming (*Werden*). Becoming is the *transition* between being and nothingness.

Sartre subjects this clean Hegelian dialectical reasoning to Heideggerian criticism in *Being and Nothingness*. The phenomenological concept of nothingness is not the dialectical concept of nothingness. Nevertheless, in reading the ways in which nothingness is introduced into the world by being-in-itself it is useful to see Sartre distancing himself from the Hegelian picture.

Sartre takes from Heidegger's *Being and Time* the idea of the *question*. In raising the question of being, Heidegger had said that there is no inquiry without an inquirer, no search without a seeker and, in at least a minimal hermeneutic sense, the questioner already knows the answer to the question in order to seek for it. Sartre argues in the passages below from *Being and Nothingness* that it is *questioning* that fundamentally discloses nothingness. Nothingness is presupposed by questioning in three ways: The answer to the question may be negative, the questioner is (paradigmatically) in a state of ignorance or non-knowledge, truth is limited by non-truth, or the false. It is Sartre's view that negative existential propositions depend upon non-being or nothingness rather than the reverse. The phenomenological is prior to the linguistic.

Although it is sometimes said about Sartre that he reifies nothingness, writes as though nothing were a thing, or something called 'nothing' exists, it is not his overt or professed view. Indeed, he is conscious of it as a possible misunderstanding and tries to rule it out by saying 'Nothingness is not'. He tries to improve on Heidegger's famous, or infamous, dictum in *What is Metaphysics?* (*Was ist Metaphysik?*, 1929) that 'nothingness nihilates' (*Das Nichts selbst nichtet*) by saying 'Nothing does not nihilate itself; Nothingness "is nihilated"'. Heidegger too is trying to avoid the charge of holding that nothing in some sense exists but Sartre thinks Heidegger makes a mistake in his formulation. By saying 'nothing nihilates' Heidegger imparts an agency to nothing; the power to nihilate, but this agency could hardly be efficacious unless it or that which exercises it existed. Sartre's 'Nothingness is nihilated' does not carry the logical or grammatical connotation of accomplishment. It is a putative affirmation of nothing's non-being logically consistent with that of the Eleatic pre-socratic philosopher Parmenides (*c.* 480 BC). Sartre fails to observe that his passive rendering of Heidegger's active voice may have equally incoherently construed nothing as a subject of anihilation, and hence, something that exists.

Nonetheless, it is true according to Sartre that there are absences. There are refusals and denials, acts of imagining that things could be otherwise. For example, in the celebrated passage from *Being and Nothingness* reproduced below Sartre is expecting his friend Pierre to be in a café but Pierre is not there. Sartre encounters nothingness. Sartre wonders whether this is a judgement or thought that Pierre is absent or whether there is an experience of Pierre's absence, an intuition of nothingness. Sartre knows there is a *prima facie* absurdity in speaking of the experience of nothing. Nothing is not anything, so an experience of nothing would not be an experience of anything. Nevertheless, Sartre decides that it is by sight that the absence of Pierre was detected. There was at least the phenomenon of *seeing that* Pierre is absent, even if not a seeing of Pierre's absence.

It is *as if* nothingness existed. Non-being is a component of the real. Nothingness is real even though nothingness is not. We may speak of absent friends, holes in the ground, negative and false propositions, purely imaginary states of affairs, fictional characters *as though* they existed because nothingness possesses an appearance of being, a being it borrows from being. The appearance of nothingness depends upon the appearance of being. For example, a hole in a wall exists in a borrowed sense because it is nothing over and above the arrangement of the remaining parts of the wall. An earthquake destroys a city and ontologically this is a re-distribution of beings that to human beings is disastrous. Sartre says after a storm there is no *less* than before, there is something *else*. It is the presence of human reality in the world, being-for-itself, that makes the redistributions of beings called 'storms' and 'earthquakes' into cases of *destruction*.

Nothingness depends upon consciousness. Consciousness depends upon *being-for-itself* so nothingness is ultimately introduced into the world by *being-for-itself*. In the café, we are aware of the absence of Pierre because we expect to see him there; as a figure against a background. Sartre distinguishes clearly between non-existence that depends on consciousness and non-existence that does not. After all, many people are absent from the café. The Duke of Wellington and Paul Valéry are absent. But they are only thought to be absent, in the abstract, or not even thought. Pierre's absence is experienced. In these ways, according to Sartre, consciousness is *prior* to nothingness.

Consciousness is defined by negation. This is partly the modal point that its being and its being what it is depend upon its not being what it is not. It is partly the psychological claim that its imaginative power to negate is one of its essential properties. Unless we could think or imagine what is absent we could not intuit that which is present.

There is a more profound connection between consciousness and nothingness. I am my consciousness and my consciousness is a kind of nothingness; a nothingness at the heart of being. The being of consciousness contrasts with the kind of being of Sartre calls 'en-soi' or 'in-itself'. Being-in-itself is massive, opaque, full, dense and inert. It confronts me and it surrounds me. If I try to locate myself as consciousness, in contrast, I am strangely absent. Phenomenologically, I seem to be a subjective region of non-being within the plenitude of being. Consciousness is a kind of emptiness or non being. Consciousness is certainly not one object amongst others that I could encounter in the course of my experience. Sartre thinks nothingness distances me from being-in-itself and I am nothing but consciousness of being.

Sartre often speaks as though consciousness *is* a kind of nothingness or emptiness. Sometimes he says consciousness is a *prerequisite* for nothingness. Sometimes he says nothingness *confronts* consciousness. For example, when in *Being and Nothingness* he says consciousness is total emptiness because the whole world is outside it, he implies that consciousness is a kind of non-being, an absence of being-in-itself. All these views may be exhibited as mutually consistent. Sartre is establishing a hierarchy of dependencies between kinds of absence. Consciousness is a kind of absence that depends on being: *being-in-itself*. Consciousness essentially involves the power of negation: the possibility of denial through imagination. This in turn makes possible the experience of absence as a kind of quasi-being.

It is through its power of negation that consciousness distinguishes itself from its own objects. This distinction makes possible consciousness' intentionality which, as we saw in the last two chapters, is essential to what consciousness is.

BEING AND NOTHINGNESS

The origin of negation

I.   The question

Our inquiry has led us to the heart of being. But we have been brought to an impasse since we have not been able to establish the connection between the two regions of being which we have discovered. No doubt this is because we have chosen an unfortunate approach. Descartes found himself faced with an analogous problem when he had to deal with the relation between soul and body. He planned then to look for the solution on that level where the union of thinking substance and extended substance was actually effected—that is, in the imagination. His advice is valuable. To be sure, our concern is not that of Descartes and we do not conceive of imagination as he did. But what we can retain is the reminder that it is not profitable first to separate the two terms of a relation in order to try to join them together again later. The relation is a synthesis. Consequently the *results* of analysis can not be covered over again by the *moments* of this synthesis.

M. Laporte says that an abstraction is made when something not capable of existing in isolation is thought of as in an isolated state. The concrete by contrast is a totality which can exist by itself alone. Husserl is of the same opinion; for him *red* is an abstraction because color can not exist without form. On the other hand, a spatial-temporal *thing*, with all its determinations, is an example of the concrete. From this point of view, consciousness is an abstraction since it conceals within itself an ontological source in the region of the in-itself, and conversely the phenomenon is likewise an abstraction since it must "appear" to consciousness. The concrete can be only the synthetic totality of which consciousness, like the phenomenon, constitutes only moments. The concrete is man within the world in that specific union of man with the world which Heidegger, for example, calls "being-in-the-world." We deliberately begin with the abstract if we question "experience" as Kant does, inquiring into the conditions of its possibility—or if we effect a phenomenological reduction like Husserl, who would reduce the world to the state of the noema-correlate of consciousness. But we will no more succeed in restoring the concrete by the summation or organization of the elements which we have abstracted from it than Spinoza can reach substance by the infinite summation of its modes.

The relation of the regions of being is an original emergence and is a part of the very structure of these beings. But we discovered this in our first observations. It is enough now to open our eyes and question ingenuously this totality which is man-in-the-world. It is by the description of this totality that we shall be able to reply to these two questions: (1) What is the synthetic relation which we call being-in-the-world? (2) What must man and the world be in order for a relation between them to be possible? In truth, the two questions are interdependent, and we can not hope to reply to them separately. But each type of human conduct, being the conduct of man in the world, can release for us simultaneously man, the world, and the relation which unites them, only on condition that we envisage these forms of conduct as realities objectively apprehensible and not as subjective affects which disclose themselves only in the face of reflection.

We shall not limit ourselves to the study of a single pattern of conduct. We shall try on the contrary to describe several and proceeding from one kind of conduct to another, attempt to penetrate into the profound meaning of the relation "man-world." But first of all we should choose a single pattern which can serve us as a guiding thread in our inquiry.

Now this very inquiry furnishes us with the desired conduct; this man that *I am*—if I apprehend him such as he is at this moment in the world, I establish that he stands before being in an attitude of interrogation. At the very moment when I ask, "Is there any conduct which can reveal to me the relation of man with the world?" I pose a question. This question I can consider objectively, for it matters little whether the questioner is myself or the reader who reads my work and who is questioning along with me. But on the other hand, the question is not simply the objective totality of the words printed on this page; it is indifferent to the symbols which express it. In a word, it is a human attitude filled with meaning. What does this attitude reveal to us?

In every question we stand before a being which we are questioning. Every question presupposes a being who questions and a being which is questioned. This is not the original relation of man to being-in-itself, but rather it stands within the limitations of this relation and takes it for granted. On the other hand, this being which we question, we question about something. That *about which* I question the being participates in the transcendence of being. I question being about its ways of being or about its being. From this point of view the question is a kind of expectation; I expect a reply from the being questioned. That is, on the basis of a pre-interrogative familiarity with being, I expect from this being a revelation of its being or of its way of being. The reply will be a "yes" or a "no". It is the existence of these two equally objective and contradictory possibilities which on principle distinguishes the question from affirmation or negation. There are questions which on the surface do not permit a negative reply—like, for example, the one which we put earlier, "What does this attitude reveal to us?" But actually we see that it is always possible with questions of this type to reply, "Nothing" or "Nobody" or "Never." Thus at the moment when I ask, "Is there any conduct which can reveal to me the relation of man with the world?" I admit *on principle* the possibility of a negative reply such as, "No, such a conduct does not exist." This means that we admit to being faced with the transcendent fact of the non-existence of such conduct.

One will perhaps be tempted not to believe in the objective existence of a non-being; one will say that in this case the fact simply refers me to my subjectivity; I would learn from the transcendent being that the conduct sought is a pure fiction. But in the first place, to call this conduct a pure fiction is to disguise the negation without removing it. "To be pure fiction" is equivalent here to "to be only a fiction." Consequently to destroy the reality of the negation is to cause the reality of the reply to disappear. This reply, in fact, is the very being which gives it to me; that is, reveals the negation to me. There exists then for the questioner the permanent objective possibility of a negative reply. In relation to this possibility the questioner by the very fact that he is questioning, posits himself as in a state of indetermination; he *does not know* whether the reply will be affirmative or negative. Thus the question is a bridge set up between two non-beings: the non-being of knowing in man, the possibility of non-being of being in transcendent being. Finally the question implies the existence of a truth. By the very question the questioner affirms that he expects an objective reply, such that we can say of it, "It is thus and not otherwise." In a word the truth, as differentiated from being, introduces a third non-being as determining the question—the non-being of limitation. This triple non-being conditions every question and in particular the metaphysical question, which is *our* question.

We set out upon our pursuit of being, and it seemed to us that the series of our questions had led us to the heart of being. But behold, at the moment when we thought we were arriving at the goal, a glance cast on the question itself has revealed to us suddenly that we are encompassed with nothingness. The permanent possibility of non-being, outside us and within, conditions our questions about being. Furthermore it is non-being which is going to limit the reply. What being *will be* must of necessity arise on the basis of what *it is not*. Whatever being is, it will allow this formulation: "Being is *that* and outside of that, *nothing*."

Thus a new component of the real has just appeared to us—non-being. Our problem is thereby complicated, for we may no longer limit our inquiry to the relations of the human being to being in-itself, but must include also the relations of being with non-being and the relations of human non-being with transcendent-being. But let us consider further.

II. *Negations*

Someone will object that being-in-itself can not furnish negative replies. Did not we ourselves say that it was beyond affirmation as beyond negation? Furthermore ordinary experience reduced to itself does not seem to disclose any non-being to us. I think that there are fifteen hundred francs in my wallet, and I find only thirteen hundred; that does not mean, someone will tell us, that experience had discovered for me the non-being of fifteen hundred francs but simply that I have counted thirteen hundred-franc notes. Negation proper (we are told) is unthinkable; it could appear only on the level of an act of judgment by which I should establish a comparison between the result anticipated and the result obtained. Thus negation would be simply a quality of judgment and the expectation of the questioner would be an expectation of the judgment-response. As for Nothingness, this would derive its origin from negative judgments; it would be a concept establishing the transcendent unity of all these judgments, a propositional function of the type, "X is not."

We see where this theory is leading; its proponents would make us conclude that being-in-itself is full positivity and does not contain in itself any negation. This negative judgment, on the other hand, by virtue of being a subjective act, is strictly identified with the affirmative judgment. They can not see that Kant, for example, has distinguished in its internal texture the negative act of judgment from the affirmative act. In each case a synthesis of concepts is operative; that synthesis, which is a concrete and full event of psychic life, is operative here merely in the manner of the copula "is" and there in the manner of the copula "is not." In the same way the manual operation of sorting out (separation) and the manual operation of assembling (union) are two objective conducts which possess the same reality of fact. Thus negation would be "at the end" of the act of judgment without, however, being "in" being. It is like an unreal encompassed by two full realities neither of which claims it; being-in-itself, if questioned about negation, refers to judgment, since being is only what it is—and judgment, a *wholly* psychic positivity, refers to being since judgment formulates a negation which concerns being and which consequently is transcendent. Negation, the result of concrete psychic operations, is supported in existence by these very operations and is incapable of existing by itself; it has the existence of a noema-correlate; its *esse* resides exactly in its *percipi*. Nothingness, the conceptual unity of negative judgments, can not have the slightest trace of reality, save that which the Stoics confer on their "lecton."[1] Can we accept this concept?

The question can be put in these terms: Is negation as the structure of the judicative proposition at the origin of nothingness? Or on the contrary is nothingness as the structure of the real, the origin and foundation of negation? Thus the problem of being had referred us first to that of the question as a human attitude, and the problem of the question now refers us to that of the being of negation.

It is evident that non-being always appears within the limits of a human expectation. It is because I expect to find fifteen hundred francs that I find *only* thirteen hundred. It is because a physicist *expects* a certain verification of his hypothesis that nature can tell him no. It would be in vain to deny that negation appears on the original basis of a relation of man to the world. The world does not disclose its non-beings to one who has not first posited them as possibilities. But is this to say that these non-beings are to be reduced to pure subjectivity? Does this mean to say that we ought to give them the importance and the type of existence of the Stoic "lecton," of Husserl's noema? We think not.

First it is not true that negation is only a quality of judgment. The question is formulated by an interrogative judgment, but it is not itself a judgment; it is a pre-judicative attitude. I can question by a look, by a gesture. In posing a question I stand facing being in a certain way and this relation to being is a relation of being; the judgment is only one optional expression of it. At the same time it is not necessarily a person whom the questioner questions about being; this conception of the question by making of it an intersubjective phenomenon, detaches it from the being to which it adheres and leaves it in the air as pure modality of dialogue. On the contrary; we must consider the question in dialogue to be only a particular species of the genus "question;" the being in question is not necessarily a thinking being. If my car breaks down, it is the *carburetor*, the *spark plugs*, etc., that I question. If my watch stops, I can question the watchmaker about the cause of the stopping, but it is the various mechanisms of the watch that the watchmaker will in turn question. What I expect from the carburetor, what the watchmaker expects from the works of the watch, is not a judgment; it is a disclosure of being on the basis of which we can make a judgment. And if I *expect* a disclosure of being, I am prepared at the same time for the eventuality of a disclosure of a non-being. If I question the carburetor, it is because I consider it possible that "there is nothing there" in the carburetor. Thus my question by its nature envelops a certain pre-judicative comprehension of non-being; it is in itself a relation of being with non-being, on the basis of the original transcendence; that is, in a relation of being with being.

Moreover if the proper nature of the question is obscured by the fact that questions are frequently put by one man to other men, it should be pointed out here that there are numerous non-judicative conducts which present this immediate comprehension of non-being on the basis of being—in its original purity. If, for example, we consider *destruction*, we must recognize that it is an *activity* which doubtless could utilize judgment as an instrument but which can not be defined as uniquely or even primarily judicative. "Destruction" presents the same structure as "the question." In a sense, certainly, man is the only being by whom a destruction can be accomplished. A geological plication, a storm do not destroy—or at least they do not destroy *directly*; they merely modify the distribution of masses of beings. There is no *less* after the storm than before. There is *something else*. Even this expression is improper, for to posit otherness there must be a witness who can retain the past in some manner and compare it to the present in the form of *no longer*. In the absence of this witness, there is being before as after the storm—that is all. If a cyclone can bring about the death of certain living beings, this death will be destruction only if it is experienced as such. In order for destruction to exist, there must be first a relation of man to being—*i.e.*, a transcendence; and within the limits of this relation, it is necessary that man apprehend one being as destructible. This supposes a limiting cutting into being by a being, which, as we saw in connection with truth, is already a process of nihilation. The being under consideration is *that* and outside of that *nothing*. The gunner who has been assigned an objective carefully points his gun in a certain direction *excluding* all others. But even this would still be nothing unless the being of the gunner's objective is revealed as *fragile*. And what is fragility if not a certain probability of non-being for a given being under determined circumstances. A being is fragile if it carries in its being a definite possibility of non-being. But once again it is through man that fragility comes into being, for the individualizing limitation which we mentioned earlier is the condition of fragility; one being is fragile and not *all* being, for the latter is beyond all possible destruction. Thus the relation of individualizing limitation which man enters into with *one* being on the original basis of his relation to being causes fragility to enter into this being as the appearance of a permanent possibility of non-being. But this is not all. In order for destructibility to exist, man must determine himself in the face of this possibility of non-being, either positively or negatively; he must either take the necessary measures to realize it (destruction proper) or, by a negation of non-being, to maintain it always on the level of a simple possibility (by preventive measures). Thus it is man who renders cities destructible, precisely because he posits them as fragile and as precious and because he adopts a system of protective measures with regard to them. It is because of this ensemble of measures that an earthquake or a volcanic eruption can destroy these cities or these human constructions. The original meaning and aim of war are contained in the smallest building of man. It is necessary then to recognize that destruction is an essentially human thing and that *it is man* who destroys his cities through the agency of earthquakes or directly, who destroys his ships through the agency of cyclones or directly. But at the same time it is necessary to acknowledge that destruction supposes a pre-judicative comprehension of nothingness as such and a conduct *in the face of nothingness*. In addition destruction although coming into being through man, is an *objective fact* and not a thought. Fragility has been impressed upon the very being of this vase, and its destruction would be an irreversible absolute event which I could only verify. There is a transphenomenality of non-being as of being. The examination of "destruction" leads us then to the same results as the examination of "the question."

But if we wish to decide with certainty, we need only to consider an example of a negative judgment and to ask ourselves whether it causes non-being to appear at the heart of being or merely limits itself to determining a prior revelation. I have an appointment with Pierre at four o'clock. I arrive at the café a quarter of an hour late. Pierre is always punctual. Will he have waited for me? I look at the room, the patrons, and I say, "He is not here." Is there an intuition of Pierre's absence, or does negation indeed enter in only with judgment? At first sight it seems absurd to speak here of intuition since to be exact there could not be an intuition of *nothing* and since the absence of Pierre is this nothing. Popular consciousness, however, bears witness to this intuition. Do we not say, for example, "I suddenly saw that he was not there." Is this just a matter of misplacing the negation? Let us look a little closer.

It is certain that the café by itself with its patrons, its tables, its booths, its mirrors, its light, its smoky atmosphere, and the sounds of voices, rattling saucers, and footsteps which fill it—the café is a fullness of being. And all the intuitions of detail which I can have are filled by these odors, these sounds, these colors, all phenomena which have a transphenomenal being. Similarly Pierre's actual presence in a place which I do not know is also a plenitude of being. We seem to have found fullness everywhere. But we must observe that in perception there is always the construction of a figure on a ground. No one object, no group of objects is especially designed to be organized as specifically either ground or figure; all depends on the direction of my attention. When I enter this café to search for Pierre, there is formed a synthetic organization of all the objects in the café on the ground of which Pierre is given as about to appear. This organization of the café as the ground is an original nihilation. Each element of the setting, a person, a table, a chair, attempts to isolate itself, to lift itself upon the ground constituted by the totality of the other objects, only to fall back once more into the undifferentiation of this ground; it melts into the ground. For the ground is that which is seen only in addition, that which is the object of a purely marginal attention. Thus the original nihilation of all the figures which appear and are swallowed up in the total neutrality of a *ground* is the necessary condition for the appearance of the principle figure, which is here the person of Pierre. This nihilation is given to my intuition; I am witness to the successive disappearance of all the objects which I look at—in particular of the faces, which detain me for an instant (Could this be Pierre?) and which as quickly decompose precisely because they "are not" the face of Pierre. Nevertheless if I should finally discover Pierre, my intuition would be filled by a solid element, I should be suddenly arrested by his face and the whole café would organize itself around him as a discrete presence.

But now Pierre is not here. This does not mean that I discover his absence in some precise spot in the establishment. In fact Pierre is absent from the *whole* café; his absence fixes the café in its evanescence; the café remains *ground*; it persists in offering itself as an undifferentiated totality to my only marginal attention; it slips into the background; it pursues its nihilation. Only it makes itself ground for a determined figure; it carries the figure everywhere in front of it, presents the figure everywhere to me. This figure which slips constantly between my look and the solid, real objects of the café is precisely a perpetual disappearance; it is Pierre raising himself as nothingness on the ground of the nihilation of the café. So that what is offered to intuition is a flickering of nothingness; it is the nothingness of the ground, the nihilation of which summons and demands the appearance of the figure, and it is the figure—the nothingness which slips as a *nothing* to the surface of the ground. It serves as foundation for the judgment—"Pierre is not here." It is in fact the intuitive apprehension of a double nihilation. To be sure, Pierre's absence supposes an original relation between me and this café; there is an infinity of people who are without any relation with this café for want of a real expectation which establishes their absence. But, to be exact, I myself expected to see Pierre, and my expectation has caused the absence of Pierre *to happen* as a real event concerning this cafe. It is an objective fact at present that I have *discovered* this absence, and it presents itself as a synthetic relation between Pierre and the setting in which I am looking for him. Pierre absent haunts this café and is the condition of its self-nihilating organization as ground. By contrast, judgments which I can make subsequently to amuse myself, such as, "Wellington is not in this café, Paul Valéry is no longer here, *etc.*"—these have a purely abstract meaning; they are pure applications of the principle of negation without real or efficacious foundation, and they never succeed in establishing a *real* relation between the cafe and Wellington or Valéry. Here the relation "is not" is merely *thought*. This example is sufficient to show that non-being does not come to things by a negative judgment; it is the negative judgment, on the contrary, which is conditioned and supported by non-being.

How could it be otherwise? How could we even conceive of the negative form of judgment if all is plenitude of being and positivity? We believed for a moment that the negation could arise from the comparison instituted between the result anticipated and the result obtained. But let us look at that comparison. Here is an original judgment, a concrete, positive psychic act which establishes a fact: "There are 1300 francs in my wallet." Then there is another which is something else, no longer it but an establishing of fact and an affirmation: "I expected to find 1500 francs." There we have real and objective facts, psychic, and positive events, affirmative judgments. Where are we to place negation? Are we to believe that it is a pure and simple application of a category? And do we wish to hold that the mind in itself possesses the *not* as a form of sorting out and separation? But in this case we remove even the slightest suspicion of negativity from the negation. If we admit that the category of the "not" which exists *in fact* in the mind and is a positive and concrete process to brace and systematize our knowledge, if we admit first that it is suddenly released by the presence in us of certain affirmative judgments and then that it comes suddenly to mark with its seal certain thoughts which result from these judgments—by these considerations we will have carefully stripped negation of all negative function. For negation is a refusal of existence. By means of it a being (or a way of being) is posited, then thrown back to nothingness. If negation is a category, if it is only a sort of plug set indifferently on certain judgments, then how will we explain the fact that it can nihilate a being, cause it suddenly to arise, and then appoint it to 'be thrown back to non-being? If prior judgments establish fact, like those 'which we have taken for examples, negation must be like a free discovery, it must tear us away from this wall of positivity which encircles us. Negation is an abrupt break in continuity which can not in any case *result* from prior affirmations; it is an original and irreducible event. Here we are in the realm of consciousness. Consciousness moreover can not produce a negation except in the form of consciousness of negation. No category can "inhabit" consciousness and reside there in the manner of a thing. The *not*, as an abrupt intuitive discovery, appears as consciousness (of being), consciousness of the *not*. In a word, if being is everywhere, it is not only Nothingness which, as Bergson maintains, is inconceivable; for negation will never be derived from being. The necessary condition for our saying *not* is that non-being be a perpetual presence in us and outside of us, that nothingness haunt being.

Note

1 An abstraction or something with purely nominal existence—like space or time. Tr.

7   The self

What is this subjective being that I am? The distinction between reflexive consciousness (*la conscience réflexive*) and pre-reflexive consciousness (*la conscience préréflexive*) is essential to understanding Sartre's phenomenology of the self. It finds its original and clearest expression not in *Being and Nothingness* but in Sartre's short 1937 work *The Transcendence of the Ego*.

There Sartre argues against Husserl, that there is no transcendental ego, no irreducibly subjective and psychic self, no hidden inner source of one's own mental states. Husserl's transcendental ego is transcendental in two senses. On quasi-Kantian grounds, Husserl argues in *Cartesian Meditations* and elsewhere that there exists an ego that is a necessary condition for experience. The ego also transcends our ordinary pre-phenomenological consciousness. It is not to be found within the world of the *natural attitude*. It is revealed as the source of the transcendental field, or subjective consciousness, by the application of the *epoché* or transcendental reduction. It is the subjective 'pole' of my mental states and does not exist without them. It explains my numerical identity over time. It is what I ultimately am.

In *The Transcendence of the Ego* Sartre brings this argument against Husserl: Phenomenology is the description of what appears to consciousness, without any preconception about the objective reality of what thus appears. But no transcendental ego is given to consciousness, not before the phenomenological *epoché* and not after it. Rather, Husserl assumes or postulates the transcendental ego as an explanation of how consciousness is possible. It is not the role of phenomenology to postulate but to describe. Ironically, the transcendental ego falls before the *epoché*.

It does not follow from this argument alone that there is no transcendental ego, only that there are no consistent phenomenological grounds for postulating one. Nevertheless, Sartre insists on subjectivity: that which is conscious is not what consciousness is consciousness of. The subject of consciousness, is not an object of that consciousness.

Sartre thinks that the existence of the transcendental is inconsistent with the unity of consciousness. There is a unity of consciousness, so there is no transcendental ego. He perhaps overestimates the role of the transcendental ego in unifying consciousness in Husserl's philosophy. Husserl thinks that acts of consciousness are parts of the same consciousness through the horizontal and vertical intentionalities of time consciousness. However, Husserl does think that some mental act's being mine is its source being a particular transcendental ego. Sartre suggests instead that it is the intentional object of acts of consciousness that accounts for their unity. Consciousness unifies itself in the face of its objects and that is as much unity as consciousness has. Neither thinker has resolved the ultimate problem of what it is for acts of consciousness to be *mine*.

Sartre also argues that the existence of the transcendental ego is inconsistent with the freedom of consciousness. Consciousness is free, so there is no transcendental ego. Consciousness is a free spontaneity or play of nothingness. If conscious states were directed by a transcendental ego this spontaneity would be impossible.

The Transcendence of the Ego shows that Husserl misread Kant's theory of the self in *The Critique of Pure Reason* and that Sartre understood Kant correctly. Kant, like Sartre, rejected the transcendental ego although most commentators, like Husserl, mistakenly ascribe it to Kant. In the Paralogisms chapter of the *Critique of Pure Reason* Kant insists that there is no substantial, subjective, quasi-Cartesian self. Kant's distinction between the noumenal self and the phenomenal self is only the distinction between how I am and how I appear to myself. The noumenal self is not an extra entity.

The psychic subject according to Sartre, far from being the subjective source of consciousness, is itself a product of consciousness. It is in fact the result of consciousness being turned on consciousness in reflexive consciousness. The I is not a psychic subject but a psychic object: the intentional object of reflexive consciousness. In reflection I appear to myself as an ego. Independently of reflection I am *the me*. In the world, as the me, I am a psycho-physical totality, a flesh and blood thinking, feeling, moving, human being.

Pre-reflexive consciousness is the ordinary awareness of objects in the external world that we exercise typically from morning to night. Reflexive consciousness is consciousness of consciousness: a new act of consciousness directed by consciousness onto itself. Reflexive consciousness is only intermittently exercised on pre-reflexive consciousness so the picture so far seems reasonably clear: There is pre-reflexive consciousness whenever we are conscious. From time to time we are self-conscious in that a new act of consciousness is directed onto consciousness by itself.

Sartre complicates this picture by saying that *every* consciousness is a consciousness of existing. Pre-reflexive consciousness is conscious of itself and reflexive consciousness is conscious of itself. In addition to this, reflexive consciousness is an intermittent consciousness of pre-reflexive consciousness.

Why does Sartre present us with this complicated and barely coherent picture? He says, for example, consciousness is consciousness of itself rather than consciousness is conscious of itself, meaning that it is *identical with* the awareness it has of itself. What is the subject and the object of this awareness?

Sartre's motivation is Cartesian and anti-Freudian. As we shall see in the discussions of bad faith and psychoanalysis (Chapters 11 and 13 below), Sartre thinks there is no unconscious. Indeed the idea of an unconscious mental state is contradictory and so impossible. He agrees with Descartes that if I am a mental state then I am aware of that mental state. All consciousness is therefore self-intimating or transparent. If that is so however, reflexive consciousness would seem to be redundant. Pre-reflexive, consciousness is already 'a consciousness of itself' so there is no need for reflection to inspect its states.

There are important differences between the self-intimations of pre-reflexive consciousness and the acts of reflexive consciousness. Not only is reflexive consciousness presented with an ego and pre-reflexive conscious-ness not presented with an ego (except, sometimes, the ego of another). Reflexive consciousness consists in a set of mental acts extra to or in addition to those of pre-reflexive consciousness. Reflexive-consciousness always only takes conscious states and the ego as its objects. Pre-reflexive consciousness takes external objects as its objects, as well as intimating its own mental states.

The findings of acts of reflective consciousness are incorrigible. The findings of acts of pre-reflexive consciousness are corrigible in so far as they are directed towards external objects. Sartre endorses the Cartesian epistemological thesis that if I believe I am in a mental state, internally or psychologically described, then that belief cannot be false. That awareness cannot be non-veridical. In the case of awareness of objects in the external world, however, there is always room for error. I may misidentify an object, ascribe to it a property it lacks or think there is an object where there is none. Reflexive consciousness delivers knowledge that is absolutely certain. If I believe I am in a conscious state it is impossible for me to be mistaken.

It is doubtful that this doctrine is true. Obviously, if it is true that I believe I am in a mental state then it follows validly that I am in at least one mental state *viz.* that state of belief. Not much more than this can be said with certainty however. This is not just because Sartre might be wrong about the non-existence of an unconscious mind. It is also because I may be caused to believe I am in a mental state by something other than my being in it. If Sartre is wrong and there is an unconscious mind then I may be in a mental state and not know I am in it, and I may believe I am in a mental state and that belief may be false.

Sartre, however, thinks the corrigible/incorrigible distinction marks another important difference between reflexive and pre-reflexive consciousness. Pre-reflexive conscious of external objects is corrigible. Reflexive conscious of consciousness is incorrigible.

This picture of self-consciousness depends on there being consciousness of objects outside the mind. Consciousness unifies itself only through its objects and only as unified can it be its own object. Intentionality depends upon on external objects, a unified consciousness depends on intentionality and self-consciousness depends upon a unified consciousness. Self-consciousness is therefore not only consistent with consciousness being embedded in the world, it presupposes it. We see here another way in which our being is being-in-the-world.

THE TRANSCENDENCE OF THE EGO

The I and the me

The cogito *as reflective consciousness*

The Kantian *I Think* is a condition of possibility. The *Cogito* of Descartes and of Husserl is an apprehension of fact. We have heard of the "factual necessity" of the *Cogito*, and this phrase seems to me most apt. Also, it is undeniable that the *Cogito* is personal. In the *I Think* there is an *I* who thinks. We attain here the *I* in its purity, and it is indeed from the *Cogito* that an "Egology" must take its point of departure. The fact that can serve for a start is, then, this one: each time we apprehend our thought, whether by an immediate intuition or by an intuition based on memory, we apprehend an I which is the *I* of the apprehended thought, and which is given, in addition, as transcending this thought and all other possible thoughts. If, for example, I want to remember a certain landscape perceived yesterday from the train, it is possible for me to bring back the memory of that landscape as such. But I can also recollect that *I* was seeing that landscape. This is what Husserl calls, in *Vorlesungen Zur Phänomenologie Des Inneren Zeitbewusstseins*, the possibility of *reflecting in memory*. In other words, I can always perform any recollection whatsoever in the personal mode, and at once the *I* appears. Such is the *factual* guarantee of the Kantian claim *concerning validity*. Thus it seems that there is not one of my consciousnesses which I do not apprehend as provided with an *I*.

But it must be remembered that all the writers who have described the *Cogito* have dealt with it as a reflective operation, that is to say, as an operation of the second degree. Such a *Cogito* is performed by a consciousness *directed upon consciousness*, a consciousness which takes consciousness as an object. Let us agree: the certitude of the *Cogito* is absolute, for, as Husserl said, there is an indissoluble unity of the reflecting consciousness and the reflected consciousness (to the point that the reflecting consciousness could not exist without the reflected consciousness). But the fact remains that we are in the presence of a synthesis of two consciousnesses, one of which is consciousness *of* the other. Thus the essential principle of phenomenology, "all consciousness is consciousness *of* something," is preserved. Now, my reflecting consciousness does not take itself for an object when I effect the *Cogito*. What it affirms concerns the reflected consciousness. Insofar as my reflecting consciousness is consciousness of itself, it is *non-positional* consciousness. It becomes positional only by directing itself upon the reflected consciousness which itself was not a positional consciousness of itself before being reflected. Thus the consciousness which says *I Think* is precisely not the consciousness which thinks. Or rather it is not *its own* thought which it posits by this thetic act. We are then justified in asking ourselves if the *I* which thinks is common to the two superimposed consciousnesses, or if it is not rather the *I* of the reflected consciousness. All reflecting consciousness is, indeed, in itself unreflected, and a new act of the third degree is necessary in order to posit it. Moreover, there is no infinite regress here, since a consciousness has no need at all of a reflecting consciousness in order to be conscious of itself. It simply does not posit itself as an object.

But is it not precisely the reflective act which gives birth to the *me* in the reflected consciousness? Thus would be explained how every thought apprehended by intuition possesses an *I*, without falling into the difficulties noted in the preceding section. Husserl would be the first to acknowledge that an unreflected thought undergoes a radical modification in becoming reflected. But need one confine this modification to a loss of "naïveté"? Would not the appearance of the *I* be what is essential in this change?

One must evidently revert to a concrete experience, which may seem impossible, since by definition such an experience is reflective, that is to say, supplied with an *I*. But every unreflected consciousness, being non-thetic consciousness of itself, leaves a non-thetic memory that one can consult. To do so it suffices to try to reconstitute the complete moment in which this unreflected consciousness appeared (which by definition is always possible). For example, I was absorbed just now in my reading. I am going to try to remember the circumstances of my reading, my attitude, the lines that I was reading. I am thus going to revive not only these external details but a certain depth of unreflected consciousness, since the objects could only have been perceived *by* that consciousness and since they remain relative to it. That consciousness must not be posited as object of a reflection. On the contrary, I must direct my attention to the revived objects, but *without losing sight of the unreflected consciousness*, by joining in a sort of conspiracy with it and by drawing up an inventory of its content in a non-positional manner. There is no doubt about the result: while I was reading, there was consciousness *of* the book, *of* the heroes of the novel, but the *I* was not inhabiting this consciousness. It was only consciousness of the object and non-positional consciousness of itself. I can now make these a-thetically apprehended results the object of a thesis and declare: there was no *I* in the unreflected consciousness. It should not be thought that this operation *is* artificial or conceived for the needs of the case. Thanks to this operation, evidently, Titchener could say in his *Textbook of Psychology* that the *me* was very often absent from his consciousness. He went no further, however, and did not attempt to classify the states of consciousness lacking a *me*.

It is undoubtedly tempting to object that this operation, this non-reflective apprehension of one consciousness by another consciousness, can evidently take place only by memory, and that therefore it does not profit from the absolute certitude inherent in a reflective act. We would then find ourselves, *on the one hand*, with an absolutely certain act which permits the presence of the *I* in the reflected consciousness to be affirmed, and, *on the other hand*, with a questionable memory which would purport to show the absence of the *I* from the unreflected consciousness. It would seem that we have no right to oppose the latter to the former. But I must point out that the memory of the unreflected consciousness is not opposed to the data of the reflective consciousness. No one would deny for a moment that the *I* appears in a reflected consciousness. It is simply a question of opposing a reflective memory of my reading ("I was reading"), which is itself of a questionable nature, to a non-reflective memory. The validity of a present reflection, in fact, does not reach beyond the consciousness presently apprehended. And reflective memory, to which we are obliged to have recourse in order to reinstate elapsed consciousnesses, besides its questionable character owing to its nature as memory, remains suspect since, in the opinion of

Husserl himself, reflection *modifies* the spontaneous consciousness. Since, in consequence, all the non-reflective memories of unreflected consciousness show me a consciousness *without a me*, and since, on the other hand, theoretical considerations concerning consciousness which are based on intuition of essence have constrained us to recognize that the *I* cannot be a part of the internal structure of *Erlebnisse*, we must therefore conclude: there is no *I* on the unreflected level. When I run after a streetcar, when I look at the time, when I am absorbed in contemplating a portrait, there is no *I*. There is consciousness *of the streetcar-having-to-be-overtaken*, etc., and non-positional consciousness of consciousness. In fact, I am then plunged into the world of objects; it is they which constitute the unity of my consciousnesses; it is they which present themselves with values, with attractive and repellent qualities— but *me*, I have disappeared; I have annihilated myself. There is no place for *me* on this level. And this is not a matter of chance, due to a momentary lapse of attention, but happens because of the very structure of consciousness.

This is what a description of the *Cogito* will make even more obvious to us. Can one say, indeed, that the reflective act apprehends the *I* and the thinking consciousness to the same degree and in the same way? Husserl insists on the fact that the certitude of the reflective act comes from apprehending consciousness without facets, without profiles, completely (without *Abschattungen*). This is evidently so. On the contrary, the spatio-temporal object always manifests itself through an infinity of aspects and is, at bottom, only the ideal unity of this infinity. As for meanings, or eternal truths, they affirm their transcendence in that the moment they appear they are given as independent of time, whereas the consciousness which apprehends them is, on the contrary, individuated through and through in duration. Now we ask: when a reflective consciousness apprehends the *I Think*, does it apprehend a full and concrete consciousness gathered into a real moment of concrete duration? The reply is clear: the *I* is not given as a concrete moment, a perishable structure of my actual consciousness. On the contrary, it affirms its permanence beyond this consciousness and all consciousnesses, and— although it scarcely resembles a mathematical truth—its type of existence comes much nearer to that of eternal truths than to that of consciousness.

Indeed, it is obvious that Descartes passed from the *Cogito* to the idea of thinking substance because he believed that *I* and *think* are on the same level. We have just seen that Husserl, although less obviously, is ultimately subject to the same reproach. I quite recognize that Husserl grants to the *I* a special transcendence which is not the transcendence of the object, and which one could call a transcendence "from above." But by what right? And how account for this privileged treatment of the *I* if not by metaphysical and Critical preoccupations which have nothing to do with phenomenology? Let us be more radical and assert without fear that *all transcendence* must fall under the ἐποχή; thus, perhaps, we shall avoid writing such awkward chapters as Section Sixty-one of *Ideen Zu Einer Reinen Phänomenologischen Philosophie*. If the *I* in the *I think* affirms itself as transcendent, this is because the *I* is not of the same nature as transcendental consciousness.

Let us also note that the *I Think* does not appear to reflection as the reflected consciousness: it is given *through* reflected consciousness. To be sure, it is apprehended by intuition and is an object grasped with evidence. But we know what a service Husserl has rendered to philosophy by distinguishing diverse kinds of evidence. Well, it is only too certain that the *I* of the *I Think* is an object grasped with neither apodictic nor adequate evidence. The evidence is not apodictic, since by saying *I* we affirm far more than we know. It is not adequate, for the *I* is presented as an opaque reality whose content would have to be unfolded. To be sure, the *I* manifests itself as the source of consciousness. But that alone should make us pause. Indeed, for this very reason the *I* appears veiled, indistinct through consciousness, like a pebble at the bottom of the water. For this very reason the *I* is deceptive from the start, since we know that nothing but consciousness can be the source of consciousness.

In addition, if the *I* is a part of consciousness, there would then be *two I*'s: the *I* of the reflective consciousness and the *I* of the reflected consciousness. Fink, the disciple of Husserl, is even acquainted with a third *I*, disengaged by the ἐποχή, the *I* of transcendental consciousness. Hence the problem of the three *I*'s, whose difficulties Fink agreeably mentions. For us, this problem is quite simply insoluble. For it is inadmissible that any communication could be established between the reflective *I* and the reflected *I* if they are real elements of consciousness; above all, it is inadmissible that they may finally achieve identity in one unique *I*.

By way of conclusion to this analysis, it seems to me that one can make the following statements:

First, the *I* is an *existent*. It has a concrete type of existence, undoubtedly different from the existence of mathematical truths, of meanings, or of spatio-temporal beings, but no less real. The *I* gives itself as transcendent.

Second, the *I* proffers itself to an intuition of a special kind which apprehends it, always inadequately, behind the reflected consciousness.

Third, the *I* never appears except on the occasion of a reflective act. In this case, the complex structure of consciousness is as follows: there is an unreflected act of reflection, without an *I*, which is directed on a reflected consciousness. The latter becomes the object of the reflecting consciousness without ceasing to affirm its own object (a chair, a mathematical truth, etc.). At the same time, a new object appears which is the occasion for an affirmation by reflective consciousness, and which is consequently not on the same level as the unreflected consciousness (because the latter consciousness is an absolute which has no need of reflective consciousness in order to exist), nor on the same level as the object of the reflected consciousness (chair, etc.). This transcendent object of the reflective act is the *I*.

Fourth, the transcendent *I* must fall before the stroke of phenomenological reduction. The *Cogito* affirms too much. The certain content of the pseudo-"Cogito" is not "*I have* consciousness of this chair," but "There *is* consciousness of this chair." This content is sufficient to constitute an infinite and absolute field of investigation for phenomenology.

BEING AND NOTHINGNESS

The immediate structure of the for-itself

Any study of human reality must begin with the *cogito*. But the Cartesian "I think" is conceived in the instantaneous perspective of temporality. Can we find in the heart of the *cogito* a way of transcending this instantaneity? If human reality were limited to the being of the "I think," it would have only the truth of an instant. And it is indeed true that with Descartes the *cogito* is an instantaneous totality, since by itself it makes no claim on the future and since an act of continuous "creation" is necessary to make it pass from one instant to another. But can we even conceive of the truth of an instant? Does the *cogito* not in its own way engage both past and future? Heidegger is so persuaded that the "I think" of Husserl is a trap for larks, fascinating and ensnaring, that he has completely avoided any appeal to consciousness in his description of Dasein. His goal is to show it immediately as *care*; that is, as escaping itself in the project of self toward the possibilities which it *is*. It is this projection of the self outside the self which he calls "understanding" (*Verstand*) and which permits him to establish human reality as being a "revealing-revealed." But this attempt to show *first* the escape from self of the Dasein is going to encounter in turn insurmountable difficulties; we cannot *first* suppress the dimension "consciousness," not even if it is in order to re-establish it subsequently. Understanding has meaning only if it is consciousness of understanding. My possibility can exist as *my* possibility only if it is my consciousness which escapes itself toward my possibility. Otherwise the whole system of being and its possibilities will fall into the unconscious—that is into the in-itself. Behold, we are thrown back again towards the *cogito*. We must make this our point of departure. Can we extend it without losing the benefits of reflective evidence? What has the description of the for-itself revealed to us?

First we have encountered a nihilation in which the being of the for-itself is affected in its being. This revelation of nothingness did not seem to us to pass beyond the limits of the *cogito*. But let us consider more closely.

The for-itself can not sustain nihilation without determining itself as a *lack of being.* This means that the nihilation does not coincide with a simple introduction of emptiness into consciousness. An external being has not expelled the in-itself from consciousness; rather the for-itself is perpetually determining itself *not to be* the in-itself. This means that it can establish itself only in terms of the in-itself and against the in-itself. Thus since the nihilation is the nihilation of being, it represents the original connection between the being of the for-itself and the being of the in-itself. The concrete, real in-itself is wholly present to the heart of consciousness as that which consciousness determines itself not to be. The *cogito* must necessarily lead us to discover this total, out-of-reach presence of the in-itself. Of course the fact of this presence will be the very transcendence of the for-itself. But it is precisely the nihilation which is the origin of transcendence conceived as the original bond between the for-itself and the in-itself. Thus we catch a glimpse of a way of getting out of the *cogito*. We shall see later indeed that the profound meaning of the *cogito* is essentially to refer outside itself. But it is not yet time to describe this characteristic of the for-itself. What our ontological description has immediately revealed is that this being is the foundation of itself as a lack of being; that is, that it determines its being by means of a being which it is not.

Nevertheless there are many ways of not being and some of them do not touch the inner nature of the being which is not what it is not. If, for example, I say of an inkwell that it is not a bird, the inkwell and the bird remain untouched by the negation. This is an external relation which can be established only by a human reality acting as witness. By contrast, there is a type of negation which establishes an internal relation between what one denies and that concerning which the denial is made.[1]

Of all internal negations, the one which penetrates most deeply into being, the one which constitutes *in its being* the being concerning which it makes the denial along with the being which it denies—this negation is *lack*. This lack does not belong to the nature of the in-itself, which is all positivity. It appears in the world only with the upsurge of human reality. It is only in the human world that there can be lacks. A lack presupposes a trinity: that which is missing or "the lacking," that which misses what is lacking or "the existing," and a totality which has been broken by the lacking and which would be restored by the synthesis of "the lacking" and "the existing"—this is "the lacked."[2] The being which is released to the intuition of human reality is always that to which *some thing is lacking*—i.e., the existing. For example, if I say that the moon is not full and that one quarter is lacking, I base this judgment on full intuition of the crescent moon. Thus what is released to intuition is an in-itself which by itself is neither complete nor incomplete but which simply is what it *is*, without relation with other beings. In order for this in-itself to be grasped as the crescent moon, it is necessary that a human reality surpass the given toward the project of the realized totality—here the disk of the full moon—and return toward the given to constitute it as the crescent moon; that is, in order to realize it in its being in terms of the totality which becomes its foundation. In this same surpassing the lacking will be posited as that whose synthetic addition to the existing will reconstitute the synthetic totality of the lacked. In this sense the lacking is of the same nature as the existing; it would suffice to reverse the situation in order for it to become the existing to which the lacking is missing, while the existing would become the lacking. This lacking as the complement of the existing is determined in its being by the synthetic totality of the lacked. Thus *in the human world*, the incomplete being which is released to intuition as lacking is constituted in its being by the lacked—that is, by what it is not. It is the full moon which confers on the crescent moon its being as crescent; what-is-not determines what-is. It is in the being of the existing, as the correlate of a human transcendence, to lead outside itself to the being which it is not—as to its meaning.

Human reality by which lack appears in the world must be itself a lack. For lack can come into being only through lack; the in-itself can not be the occasion of lack in the in-itself. In other words, in order for being to be lacking or lacked, it is necessary that a being make itself its own lack; only a being which lacks can surpass being toward the lacked.

The existence of desire as a human fact is sufficient to prove that human reality is a lack. In fact how can we explain desire if we insist on viewing it as a psychic state; that is, as a being whose nature is to be what it is? A being which is what it is, to the degree that it is considered as being what it is, summons nothing to itself in order to complete itself. An incomplete circle does not call for completion unless it is surpassed by human transcendence. In-itself it is complete and perfectly positive as an open curve. A psychic state which existed with the sufficiency of this curve could not possess in addition the slightest "appeal to" something else; it would be itself without any relation to what is not it. In order to constitute it as hunger or thirst, an external transcendence surpassing it toward the totality "satisfied hunger" would be necessary, just as the crescent moon is surpassed toward the full moon.

We will not get out of the difficulty by making desire a *conatus* conceived in the manner of a physical force. For the *conatus* once again, even if we grant it the efficiency of a cause, can not possess in itself the character of a reaching out toward another state. The *conatus* as the *producer* of states can not be identified with desire as the *appeal* from a state. Neither will recourse to psycho-physiological parallelism enable us better to clear away the difficulties. Thirst as an organic phenomenon, as a "physiological" need of water, does not exist. An organism deprived of water presents certain positive phenomena: for example, a certain coagulating thickening of the blood, which provokes in turn certain other phenomena. The ensemble is a positive state of the organism which refers only to itself, exactly as the thickening of a solution from which the water has evaporated can not be considered by itself as the solution's desire of water. If we suppose an exact correspondence between the mental and the physiological, this correspondence can be established only on the basis of ontological identity, as Spinoza has seen. Consequently the being of psychic thirst will be the being in itself of a state, and we are referred once again to a transcendent witness. But then the thirst will be desire for this transcendence but not for itself; it will be desire in the eyes of another. If desire is to be able to be desire to itself it must necessarily be itself transcendence; that is, it must by nature be an escape from itself toward the desired object. In other words, it must be a lack—but not an object-lack, a lack undergone, created by the surpassing which it is not; it must be its own lack of —. Desire is a lack of being. It is haunted in its inmost being by the being of which it is desire. Thus it bears witness to the existence of lack in the being of human reality. But if human reality is lack, then it is through human reality that the trinity of the existing, the lacking and the lacked comes into being. What exactly are the three terms of this trinity?

That which plays here the role of the existing is what is released to the *cogito* as the immediate of the desire; for example, it is this for-itself which we have apprehended as not being what it is and being what it is not. But how are we to define the lacked?

To answer this question, we must return to the idea of lack and determine more exactly the bend which unites the existing to the lacking. This bond can not be one of simple contiguity. If what is lacking is in its very absence still profoundly present at the heart of the existing, it is because the existing and the lacking are at the same moment apprehended and surpassed in the unity of a single totality. And that which constitutes itself as lack can do so only by surpassing itself toward one great broken form. Thus lack is appearance on the ground of a totality. Moreover it matters little whether this totality has been originally given and is now broken (*e.g.* "The arms of the Venus di Milo are now *lacking*") or whether it has never yet been realized. (*e.g.* "He lacks courage.") What is important is only that the lacking and the existing are given or are apprehended as about to be annihilated in the unity of the totality which is lacked. Everything which is lacking is lacking *to* — *for* —. What is given in the unity of a primitive upsurge is the *for*, conceived as not yet being or as not being any longer, an absence toward which the curtailed existing surpasses itself or is surpassed and thereby constitutes itself as curtailed. What is the *for* of human reality?

The for-itself, as the foundation of itself, is the upsurge of the negation. The for-itself founds itself in so far as it denies *in relation to itself* a certain being or a mode of being. What it denies or nihilates, as we know, is being-in-itself. But no matter *what* being-in-itself: human reality is before all else its own nothingness. What it denies or nihilates *in relation to* itself as for-itself can be only *itself*. The meaning of human reality as nihilated is constituted by this nihilation and this presence in it of what it nihilates; hence the self-as-being-in-itself is what human reality lacks and what makes its meaning. Since human reality in its primitive relation to itself is not what it is, its relation to itself is not primitive and can derive its meaning only from an original relation which is the *null relation* or identity. It is the self which would be what it is which allows the for-itself to be apprehended as not being what it is; the relation denied in the definition of the for-itself—which as such should be first posited—is a relation (given as perpetually absent) between the for-itself and itself in the mode of identity. The meaning of the subtle confusion by which thirst escapes and is not thirst (in so far as it is consciousness of thirst), is a thirst which would be thirst and which haunts it. What the for-itself lacks is the self—or itself as in-itself.

Nevertheless we must not confuse this missing in itself (the lacked) with that of facticity. The in-itself of facticity in its failure to found itself is reabsorbed in pure presence in the world on the part of the for-itself The missing in-itself, on the other hand is pure absence. Moreover the failure of the act to found the in-itself has caused the for-itself to rise up from the in-itself as the foundation of its own nothingness. But the meaning of the missing act of founding remains as transcendent. The for-itself in its being is failure because it is the foundation only of itself as nothingness. In truth this failure is its very being, but it has meaning only if the for-itself apprehends itself as failure *in the presence of* the being which it has failed to be; that is, of the being which would be the foundation of its being and no longer merely the foundation of its nothingness—or, to put it another way, which would be its foundation as coincidence with itself. By nature the *cogito* refers to the lacking and to the lacked, for the *cogito* is haunted by being, as Descartes well realized.

Such is the origin of transcendence. Human reality is its own surpassing toward what it lacks; it surpasses itself toward the particular being which it would be if it were what it is. Human reality is not something which exists first in order afterwards to lack this or that; it exists first as lack and in immediate, synthetic connection with what it lacks. Thus the pure event by which human reality rises as a presence in the world is apprehended by itself as *its* own *lack*. In its coming into existence human reality grasps itself as an incomplete being. It apprehends itself as being in so far as it is not, in the presence of the particular totality which it lacks and which it is in the form of not being it and which is what it is. Human reality is a perpetual surpassing toward a coincidence with itself which is never given. If the *cogito reaches* toward being, it is because by its very thrust it surpasses itself toward being by qualifying itself in its being as the being to which coincidence with self is lacking in order for it to be what it is. The *cogito* is indissolubly linked to being-in-itself, not as a thought to its object—which would make the in-itself relative—but as a lack to that which defines its lack. In this sense the second Cartesian proof is rigorous. Imperfect being surpasses itself toward perfect being; the being which is the foundation only of its nothingness surpasses itself toward the being which is the foundation of its being. But the being toward which human reality surpasses itself is not a transcendent God; it is at the heart of human reality; it is only human reality itself as totality.

This totality is not the pure and simple contingent in-itself of the transcendent. If what consciousness apprehends as the being toward which it surpasses itself were the pure in-itself, it would coincide with the annihilation of consciousness. But consciousness does not surpass itself toward it annihilation; it does not want to lose itself in the in-itself of identity at the limit of its surpassing. It is for the for-itself as such that the for-itself lays claim to being-in-itself.

Thus this perpetually absent being which haunts the for-itself is itself fixed in the in-itself. It is the impossible synthesis of the for-itself and the in-itself: it would be its own foundation not as nothingness but as being and would preserve within it the necessary translucency of consciousness along with the coincidence with itself of being-in-itself. It would preserve in it that turning back upon the self which conditions every necessity and every foundation. But this return to the self would be without distance; it would not be presence to itself, but identity with itself. In short, this being would be exactly the *self* which we have shown can exist only as a perpetually evanescent relation, but it would be this self as substantial being. Thus human reality arises as such in the presence of its own totality or self as a lack of that totality. And this totality can not be given by nature, since it combines in itself the incompatible characteristics of the in-itself and the for-itself.

Let no one reproach us with capriciously inventing a being of this kind; when by a further movement of thought the being and absolute absence of this totality are hypostasized as transcendence beyond the world, it takes on the name of God. Is not God a being who is what he is—in that he is all positivity and the foundation of the world—and at the same time a being who is not what he is and who is what he is not—in that he is self-consciousness and the necessary foundation of himself? The being of human reality is suffering because it rises in being as perpetually haunted by a totality which it is without being able to be it, precisely because it could not attain the in-itself without losing itself as for-itself. Human reality therefore is by nature an unhappy consciousness with no possibility of surpassing its unhappy state.

Notes

1   Hegelian opposition belongs to this type of negation. But this opposition must itself be based on an original internal negation; that is, on lack. For example, if the non-essential becomes in its turn the essential, this is because it is experienced as a lack in the heart of the essential.

2   *Le manquant*, "the lacking," *l'existant*, "the existing"; *le manqué*, "the lacked." *Le manque* is "the lack." At times when *manqué* is used as an adjective, I have translated it as "missing," e.g., *l'en-soi manqué*, "the missing in-itself." Tr.

8 Temporality

The phenomenology of time entails the description of kinds of time that are scientifically inexplicable: paradigmatically, subjective or human time. Although the Newtonian understanding of the objective ordering *before, simultaneous with*, and *after* has been shown to be incomplete by Einstein's Special and General theories of relativity, physics is still powerless to say anything about *past, present* and *future* or subjective time.

Understanding Sartre's phenomenology of time in Part Two, Chapter Two, of *Being and Nothingness*, extracts of which are reprinted below, requires a grasp of Husserl's *Lectures on the Phenomenology of Internal Time Consciousness (Vorlesungen zur Phänomenologie des innern Zeitbewusstseins*, delivered from 1905) and 'temporality' (*Temporalität*) in Heidegger's *Being and Time*.

Husserl's lectures, which facilitate a transition from the early phenomenology of *Logical Investigations* (1900–1) to the 'transcendental' phenomenology of *Ideas* (1913), are a putative explanation of how objective time may be apprehended. The temporal ordering of events in the external world is not the temporal ordering of one's own experiences: I think *this thought*, am distracted by *that sensation*, etc., but outside of my mind *this physical event* occurs then *that physical event*. Arguably anyone is only ever directly acquainted with the temporal ordering of their own experiences, yet believes in an objective ordering of event chains. The problem is: How is the apprehension of such an objective time order possible ?

In a partial anticipation of his 1913 use of *epoché*, Husserl adopts a methodological suspension of belief in objective time to explain its possibility as an object for consciousness. World time, real time, the time of nature, scientific and psychological time are all suspended but phenomenological time, or time as it is directly given to consciousness, is treated as an absolute, indubitable, datum. The objective temporality of an event is then explained as an achievement of consciousness. A melody, in

Husserl's example, is apprehended as an objective event through *retention* and *protention*. The past course of the melody is partly retained and the future course of the melody is partly anticipated in the present apprehension of the melody. The melody is constituted as an objective temporal object for consciousness by this retentive and anticipatory 'reading into' the present. Knowledge of the objective time dealt with commonsensically, measured by clocks and studied by science, presupposes phenomenological time.

As we have seen, Heidegger's aim in *Being and Time* is the clarification of the meaning of the *question of being* (*Seinsfrage*). What is it to be? is difficult to answer once we appreciate that *being is not being something*. Being is not being red, or being perceived, or being spatio–temporal. The possession of these properties is neither necessary nor sufficient for being rather than not being.

Heidegger assumes that a necessary preliminary to the inquiry into being is an inquiry into the kind of being that can pose the *Seinsfrage*, our own being or *Dasein*. Much of *Being and Time* is then taken up with description of the existential structures of Dasein's being-in-the-world. However, towards the end of the book Heidegger comes close to answering the *Seinsfrage* by claiming a temporality that is primordial with regard to being, a kind of time presupposed by being. This is a kind of becoming that is not so much between the future and the past as the becoming past of the future. One's own being or *Dasein* entails this process.

Sartre is profoundly influenced by both Husserl's and Heidegger's phenomenology of time. His views are partly their synthesis, or a reconciliation of tensions between them.

Sartre seeks to avoid a paradox which vitiates the philosophy of time: The past does not exist because it is over. The future does not exist because it has not happened yet. The present does not exist because there is no time interval between the past and the future. Nevertheless, the appearance of all three temporal ekstases as real is existentially compelling.

Sartre's solution, in the chapter of *Being and Nothingness* reproduced below, is to argue that past present and future all exist, but as an *original synthesis*. He means that past, present and future can not exist in abstraction from one another but only as a temporal whole. Any atomistic account of time that fails to recognise this will fail.

Although past, present and future all *are*, they exist in three radically different fashions. The past belongs to that fixed, inert and passive mode of being that Sartre calls *being-in-itself*. The present is part of the spontaneous, free, subjective, conscious, manner of being called *being-for-itself*. The being of the future is neither being-in-itself nor being-for-itself. The future exists as pure *possibility*. Nevertheless, being-for-itself has an ontologically privileged role in the constitution of temporality. The past is someone's past. The present is someone's present and the future is someone's future. If there were no subjective conscious beings, there would be no past, present or future.

To see this, we need to draw a sharp distinction between past, present and future on the one hand and before, simultaneous with and after, on the other. If there is past, present and future then there is before, simultaneous with and after but from the fact that there is before, simultaneous with and after it does not follow that there is past, present and future. 'Past' means 'before now' and 'future' means 'after now' but 'now' means roughly 'when I am', or 'simultaneous with this thought/utterance of "now"'. A historical figure, say Louis XIV, uses 'past', 'present' and 'future' indexed to his time. We use them indexed to ours. 'Before', 'simultaneous with', and 'after' may be used to denote an ordering that arguably obtains independently of tense.

Sartre says that I am my past and I am my future, and the for-itself can be defined in terms of presence to being. My being is therefore intimately bound up with my being temporal. I am my past because I am, so far, the totality of my exercised choices in situations. I am my future because that is what my present possibilities consist in. The being of the for-itself is present in both senses of 'present'. I am present in the sense that now is when I am but I am present in the sense of in the presence of being. In the first sense, I am present in a sense that contrasts with past and future. In the second sense, I am present in a sense that contrasts with absent.

Sartre's insistence that the ekstases of time are inseparable incorporates Husserl's distinction between 'retention' and 'protention' but Sartre rejects Husserl's view that subjective time may be even methodologically separated from objective time.

In this he endorses the Heideggerian doctrine that our being is fundamentally being-in-the world.

BEING AND NOTHINGNESS

Temporality

I. The Past

What then is the meaning of "was"? We see first of all that it is transitive. If I say, "Paul is fatigued," one might perhaps argue that the copula has an ontological value, one might perhaps want to see there only an indication of inherence. But when we say, "Paul *was* fatigued," the essential meaning of the "was" leaps to our eyes: the present Paul is actually responsible for having had this fatigue in the past. If he were not sustaining this fatigue with his being, he would not even have forgotten that state; there would be rather a "no-longer-being" strictly identical with a "not-being." The fatigue would be *lost*. The present being therefore is the foundation of its own past; and it is the present's character as a foundation which the "was" manifests. But we are not to understand that the present founds the past in the mode of indifference and without being profoundly modified by it. "Was" means that the present being has to be in its being the foundation of its past while *being* itself this past What does this mean? How can the present *be* the past?

The crux of the question lies evidently in the term "was," which, serving as intermediary between the present and the past, is itself neither wholly present nor wholly past. In fact it can be neither the one nor the other since in either case it would be contained inside the tense which would denote its being. The term "was" indicates the ontological leap from the present into the past and represents an original synthesis of these two temporal modes. What must we understand by this synthesis?

I see first that the term "was" is a mode of being. In this sense I *am* my past. I do not have it; I am it. A remark made by someone concerning an act which I performed yesterday or a mood which I had does not leave me indifferent; I am hurt or flattered, I protest or I let it pass; I am touched to the quick. I do not dissociate myself from my past. Of course, in time I can attempt this dissociation; I can declare that "I am no longer what I was," argue that there has been a change, progress. But this is a matter of a secondary reaction which is given as such. To deny my solidarity of being with my past at this or that particular point is to affirm it for the whole of my life. At my limit, at that infinitesimal instant of my death, I shall be no more than my past. It alone will define me. This is what Sophocles wants to express in the *Trachiniae* when he has Deianeira say, "It is a proverb current for a long time among men that one cannot pass judgment on the life of mortals and say if it has been happy or unhappy, until their death." This is also the meaning of that sentence of Malraux' which we quoted earlier. "Death changes life into Destiny." Finally this is what strikes the Believer when he realizes with terror that at the moment of death the chips are down, there remains not a card to play. Death reunites us with ourselves. Eternity has changed us into ourselves. At the moment of death we *are*; that is, we are defenceless before the judgments of others. They can decide *in truth* what we are; ultimately we have no longer any chance of escape from what an all knowing intelligence could do. A last hour repentance is a desperate effort to crack all this being which has slowly congealed and solidified *around us*, a final leap to dissociate ourselves from what we *are*. In vain. Death fixes this leap along with the rest; it does no more than to enter into combination with what has preceded it, as one factor among others, as one particular determination which is understood only in terms of the totality. By death the for-itself is changed forever into an in-itself in that it has slipped entirely into the past. Thus the past is the ever growing totality of the in-itself which we are.

Nevertheless so long as we are not dead, we are not this in-itself in the mode of identity. We *have to be it*. Ordinarily a grudge against a man ceases with his death; this is because he has been reunited with his past; he *is it* without, however, being responsible for it. So long as he lives, he is the object of my grudge; that is, I reproach him for his past not only in so far as he *is it* but in so far as he reassumes it at each instant and sustains it in being, in so far as he is *responsible* for it. It is not true that the grudge fixes the man in what he was; otherwise it would survive death. It is addressed to the living man who in his being is freely what he was. I am my past and if I were not, my past would not exist any longer either *for me* or *for anybody*. It would no longer have any relation with the present. That certainly does not mean that it would not be but only that its being would be undiscoverable. I am the one by whom my past arrives in this world. But it must be understood that I do not give being to it. In other words it does not exist as "my" representation. It is not because I "represent" my past that it exists. But it is because I *am* my past that it enters into the world, and it is in terms of its being-in-the-world that I can by applying a particular psychological process represent it to myself.

The past is what I have to be, and yet its nature is different from that of my possibles. The possible, which also I have to be, remains as my concrete possible, that whose opposite is equally possible—although to a less degree. The past, on the contrary, is that which is without possibility of any sort; it is that which has consumed its possibilities. *I have to be* that which no longer depends on my being-able-to-be, that which is already in itself all which it can be. The past which I am, I have to be with no possibility of not being it. I assume the total responsibility for it as if I could change it, and yet I can not be anything other than it. We shall see later that we continually preserve the possibility of changing the *meaning* of the past in so far as this is an ex-present *which has had* a future. But from the content of the past as such I can remove nothing, and I can add nothing to it. In other words the past which *I was* is what it is; it is an in-itself like the things in the world. The relation of being which I have to sustain with the past is a relation of the type of the in-itself—that is, an identification with itself.

On the other hand I am not my past. I *am* not it because I *was* it. The malice of others always surprises me and makes me indignant. How can they hate in the person who I am now that person who I was? The wisdom of antiquity has always insisted on this fact: I can make no pronouncement on myself which has not already become false at the moment when I pronounce it.

II.   The Present

In contrast to the Past which is in-itself, the Present is for-itself. What is its being? There is a peculiar paradox in the Present: On the one hand we willingly define it as *being*; what is present *is*—in contrast to the future which is not yet and to the past which is no longer. But on the other hand, a rigorous analysis which would attempt to rid the present of all which is not it—*i.e.*, of the past and of the immediate future—would find that nothing remained but an infinitesimal instant. As Husserl remarks in his *Essays on the Inner Consciousness of Time*, the ideal limit of a division pushed to infinity is a nothingness. Thus each time that we approach the study of human reality from a new point of view we rediscover that indissoluble dyad, Being and Nothingness.

What is the fundamental meaning of the Present? It is clear that what exists in the present is distinguished from all other existence by the characteristic of *presence*. At rollcall the soldier or the pupil replies "Present!" in the sense of *adsum*. *Present* is opposed to *absent* as well as to *past*. Thus the meaning of *present* is presence to ——. It is appropriate then to ask ourselves to *what* the present is presence and *who* or *what* is present. That will doubtless enable us to elucidate subsequently the very being of the present.

My present is to be present. Present to what? To this table, to this room, to Paris, to the world, in short to being-in-itself. But can we say conversely that being-in-itself is present to *me* and to the being-in-itself which it is not? If that were so, the present would be a reciprocal relation of presences. But it is easy to see that it is nothing of the sort. Presence to —— is an internal relation between the being which is present and the beings to which it is present. In any case it can not be a matter of a simple external relation of contiguity. Presence to —— indicates existence outside oneself near to ——. Anything which can be present to —— must be such in its being that there is in it a relation of being with other beings. I can be present to this chair only if I am united to it in an ontological relation of synthesis, only if I am there in the being of the chair as *not being* the chair. A being which is present to —— can not be at rest "in-itself;" the in-itself cannot be present any more than it can be Past. It simply *is*. There can be no question of any kind of simultaneity between one in-itself and another in-itself except from the point of view of a being which would be co-present with two in-itselfs and which would have in it the power of presence. The Present therefore can be only the presence of the For-itself to being in-itself. And this presence can not be the effect of an accident, of a concomitance: on the contrary it is presupposed by all concomitance, and it must be an ontological structure of the For-itself. This table must be present to that chair in a world which human reality haunts as a presence. In other words one cannot conceive of a type of existent which would be *first* For-itself in order *subsequently* to be present to being. But the For-itself makes itself presence to being by making itself be For-itself and it ceases to be presence by ceasing to be for-itself. The For-itself is defined as presence to being.

To what being does the For-itself make itself presence? The answer is clear: the For-itself is presence to all of being-in-itself. Or rather the presence of the For-itself is what makes being-in-itself exist as a totality. For by this very mode of presence to being qua being, every possibility is removed whereby the For-itself might be *more present* to one privileged than to all other beings. Even though the facticity of its existence causes it to be *there* rather than elsewhere, being *there* is not the same as being *present*. *Being there* determines only the perspective by which presence to the totality of the in-itself is realized. By means of the *there* the For-itself causes beings to be *for* one and the same presence. Beings are revealed as co-present in a world where the For-itself unites them with its own blood by that total ekstatic sacrifice of the self which is called presence. "Before" the sacrifice of the For-itself it would have been impossible to say that beings existed either together or separated. But the For-itself is the being by which the present enters into the world; the beings of the world are co-present; in fact, just in so far as one and the same for-itself is at the same time present to all of them. Thus for the in-itselfs what we ordinarily call Present is sharply distinguished from their being although it is *nothing more* than their being. For their Present means only their co-presence in so far as a For-itself is present to them.

We know now *what is present* and *to what* the present is present. But what is *presence*?

We have seen that this can not be the pure co-existence of two existents, conceived as a simple relation of exteriority, for that would require a third term to establish the co-existence. This third term exists in the case of the co-existence of things in the midst of the world; it is the For-itself which establishes this co-existence by making itself co-present to all. But in the case of the Presence of the For-itself to being-in-itself, there can not be a third term. No witness—not even God—could *establish* that presence; even the For-itself can know it only if the presence *already is*. Nevertheless presence can not be in the mode of the in-itself. This means that originally the For-itself is presence to being in so far as the For-itself is to itself its own witness of co-existence. How are we to understand this? We know that the For-itself is the being which exists in the form of a witness of its being. Now the For-itself is present to being if it is intentionally directed outside itself upon that being. And it must adhere to being as closely as is possible without identification. This adherence, as we shall see in the next chapter, is realistic, due to the fact that the For-itself realizes its birth in an original bond with being; it is a witness to itself of itself as *not being* that being. Due to this fact it is outside that being, upon being and within being as not being that being.

In addition we can deduce the following conclusions as to the meaning of Presence: Presence to a being implies that one is bound to that being by an internal bond; otherwise no connection between Present and being would be possible. But this internal bond is a negative bond and denies, as related to the present being, that one is the being to which one is present. If this were not so, the internal bond would dissolve into pure and simple identification. Thus the For-itself's Presence to being implies that the For-itself is a witness of itself in the presence of being as not being that being; presence to being is the presence of the For-itself in so far as the For-itself is not. For the negation rests not on a difference in mode of being which would distinguish the For-itself from being but on a difference of being. This can be expressed briefly by saying that the Present *is not*.

What is meant by this non-being of the Present and of the For-itself? To grasp this we must return to the For-itself, to its mode of existing, and outline briefly a description of its ontological relation to being. Concerning the For-itself as such we should never say, "It *is*" in the sense that we say, for example, "It *is* nine o'clock;" that is, in the sense of the total equivalence of being with itself which posits and suppresses the self and which gives the external aspect of passivity. For the For-itself has the existence of an appearance coupled with a witness of a reflection which refers to a reflecting without there being any object of which the reflection would be the reflection. The For-itself does not have being because its being is always at a distance: its being is there in the reflecting, if you consider appearance, which is appearance or reflection only *for* the reflecting; it is there in the reflection if you consider the reflecting, which is no longer in itself anything more than a pure function of reflecting *this* reflection. Furthermore in itself the For-itself is not being, for it makes itself be explicitly for-itself as not being being. It is consciousness of —— as the internal negation of ——. The structure at the basis of intentionality and of selfness is the negation, which is the *internal* relation of the For-itself to the thing. The For-itself constitutes itself outside in terms of the thing as the negation of that thing; thus its first relation with being-in-itself is negation. It "is" in the mode of the For-itself; that is, as a separated existent inasmuch as it reveals itself as not being being. It doubly escapes being, by an internal disintegration and by express negation. The present is precisely this negation of being, this escape from being inasmuch as being is *there* as that from which one escapes. The For-itself is present to being in the form of flight; the Present is a perpetual flight in the face of being. Thus we have precisely defined the fundamental meaning of the Present: the Present *is not*. The present instant emanates from a realistic and reifying conception of the For-itself; it is this conception which leads us to denote the For-itself according to the mode of that which is and that to which it is present—for example, of that hand on the face of the clock. In this sense it would be absurd to say that it is nine o'clock for the For-itself, but the For-itself can be present to a hand pointed at nine o'clock. What we falsely call the Present is the being to which the present is presence. It is impossible to grasp the Present in the form of an instant, for the instant would be the moment when the present *is*. But the present is not; it makes itself present in the form of flight.

But the present is not only the For-itself's non-being making itself present. As For-itself it has its being outside of it, before and behind. Behind, it *was* its past; and before, it *will be* its future. It is a flight outside of co-present being and from the being which it was toward the being which it will be. At present it is not what it is (past) and it is what it is not (future). Here then we are referred to the Future.

III. The Future

We must not understand by the future a "now" which is not yet. If we did so, we should fall back into the in-itself, and even worse we should have to envisage time as a given and static container. The future is *what I have to be* in so far as I can not be it. Let us recall that the For-itself makes itself present before being as not being this being and as having been its own being in the past. This presence is flight. We are not dealing here with a belated presence at rest near being but with an escape outside of being towards ——. And this flight is two-fold, for in fleeing the being which it is not, Presence flees the being which it was. Toward *what* is it fleeing? We must not forget that in so far as it makes itself present to being in order to flee it the For-itself is a lack. The possible is *that which* the For-itself lacks in order to be itself or, if you prefer, the appearance of what I am—at a distance. Thus we grasp the meaning of the flight which is Presence; it is a flight toward *its being*; that is, toward the self which it will be by coincidence with what it lacks. The Future is the lack which wrenches it as lack away from the in-itself of Presence. If Presence did not lack anything, it would fall back into being and would lose *presence to being* and acquire in exchange the isolation of complete identity. It is lack as such which permits it to be presence. Because Presence is outside of itself toward something lacking which is beyond the world, it can be outside itself as presence to an in-itself which it is not.

The Future is the determining being which the For-itself has to be beyond being. There is a Future because the For-itself *has to be* its being instead of simply being it. This being which the For-itself has to be can not be in the mode of the cc-present in-itselfs; for in that case it would be without being made-to-be; we could not then imagine it as a completely defined state to which presence alone would be lacking, as Kant says that existence adds nothing more to the object of the concept. But this being would no longer be able to exist, for in that case the For-itself would be only a given. This being is because the For-itself makes itself be by perpetually apprehending itself for itself as unachieved in relation to it. It is this which at a distance haunts the dyad reflection-reflecting and which causes the reflection to be apprehended by the reflecting (and conversely) as a Not-yet. But it is necessary that this lacking be given in the unity of a single upsurge with the For-itself which lacks; otherwise there would be nothing in relation to which the For-itself might apprehend itself as not-yet. The Future is revealed to the For-itself as that which the For-itself is not yet, inasmuch as the For-itself constitutes itself non-thetically for itself as a not-yet in the perspective of this revelation, and inasmuch as it makes itself be as a project of itself outside the Present toward that which it is not yet. To be sure, the Future can not be without this revelation. This revelation itself requires being revealed to itself; that is, it requires the revelation of the For-itself to itself, for otherwise the ensemble revelation-revealed would fall into the unconscious—*i.e.*, into the In-itself. Thus only a being which is its own revealed to itself—that is, whose being is in question for itself—can have a Future. But conversely such a being can be for itself only in the perspective of a Not-yet, for it apprehends itself as a nothingness—that is, as a being whose complement of being is at a distance from itself. At a distance means beyond being. Thus everything which the For-itself is beyond being is the Future.

What is the meaning of this "beyond?" In order to understand it we must note that the Future has one essential characteristic of the For-itself: it is presence (future) to being. And it is Presence of this particular For-itself, of the For-itself for which it is the future. When I say, "*I* shall be happy," it is this present For-itself which will be happy; it is the actual *Erlebnis* with all which it was and which it drags behind it. It will be happy as presence to being; that is, as future Presence of the For-itself to a co-future being. So that what has been given me as the meaning of the present For-itself is ordinarily the co-future being in so far as it will be revealed to the future For-itself as that to which this For-itself will be present. For the For-itself is the thetic consciousness of the world in the form of presence and non-thetic self-consciousness. Thus what is ordinarily revealed to consciousness is the *future world* without consciousness' being aware that it is the world in so far as it will appear to a consciousness, the world in so far as it is posited as future by the presence of a For-itself to come. This world has meaning as future only in so far as I am present to it as *another* who I *will be*, in another position, physical, emotional, social, etc. Yet it is this which is at the end of my present For-itself and beyond being-in-itself, and this is the reason why we have a tendency first to present the future as a state of the world and to make it appear subsequently on the ground of the world. If I write, I am conscious of the words as written and as about to be written. The words alone seem to be the future which awaits me. But the very fact that they appear as *to be written* implies that writing, as a non-thetic self-consciousness, is the possibility which I am. Thus the Future as the future presence of a For-itself to a being drags being-in-itself along with it into the future. This being to which the For-itself will be present is the meaning of the in-itself co-present with the present For-itself, as the future is the meaning of the For-itself. The Future is presence to a co-future being because the For-itself can exist only outside itself at the side of being and because the future is a future For-itself. But thus through the Future a particular future arrives in the World; that is, the For-itself *is* its meaning as Presence to being which is beyond being. Through the For-itself, a Beyond of being is revealed next to which the For-itself has to be what it is. As the saying goes, "I must become what I was;" but I must become what I was-in a world that has become and in a world that has become *from the standpoint of* what it is. This means that I give to the world its own possibilities in terms of the state which I apprehend on it. Determinism appears on the ground of the futurizing project of myself. Thus the future will be distinguished from the imaginary, where similarly I am what I am not, where similarly I find my meaning in a being which I have to be but where this For-itself which I have to be emerges on the ground of the nihilation of the world, *apart from* the world of being.

But the Future is not solely the presence of the For-itself to a being situated beyond being. It is something which waits for the For-itself which I am. This something is myself. When I say that *I* will be happy, we understand that it is the present "I," dragging its Past after it, who will be happy. Thus the Future is "I" in as much as I await myself as presence to a being beyond being. I project myself toward the Future in order to merge there with that which I lack; that is, with that which if synthetically added to my Present would make me be what I am. Thus what the For-itself has to be as presence to being beyond being is its own possibility. The Future is the ideal point where the sudden infinite compression of facticity (Past), of the For-itself (Present), and of its possible (a particular Future) will at last cause the *Self* to arise as the existence in-itself of the For-itself. The project of the For-itself toward the future which it *is* is a project toward the In-itself. In this sense the For-itself has to be its future because it can be the foundation of what it is only before itself and beyond being. It is the very nature of the For-itself that it must be "an always future hollow." For this reason it will never have *become*, in the Present, what it had to be, in the Future. The entire future of the present For-itself falls into the Past as the future along with this For-itself itself. It will be the past future of a particular For-itself or a former future. This future is not *realized*. What is realized is a For-itself which is *designated* by the Future and which is constituted in connection with this future. For example, my final position on the tennis court has determined on the ground of the future all my intermediary positions, and finally it has been reunited with an ultimate position identical with what it was in the future as the meaning of my movements. But, precisely, this "reuniting" is purely ideal; it is not really operative. The future does not allow itself to be rejoined; it slides into the Past as a bygone future, and the Present For-itself in all its facticity is revealed as the foundation of its own nothingness and once again as the lack of a new future. Hence comes that ontological disillusion which awaits the For-itself at each emergence into the future. "Under the Empire how beautiful was the Republic!" Even if my present is strictly identical in its content with the future toward which I projected myself beyond being, it is not *this* present toward which I was projecting myself; for I was projecting myself toward the future qua future—that is, as the point of the reuniting of my being, as the place of the upsurge of the *Self.*

Now we are better able to raise the question of the being of the Future since this Future which I have to be is simply my *possibility* of presence to being beyond being. In this sense the Future is strictly opposed to the Past. The Past is, to be sure, the being which I am outside of myself, but it is the being which I am without the possibility of not being it. This is what we have defined as being its past *behind* itself. The being of the Future which I have to be, on the contrary, is such that I *can only* be it; for my freedom gnaws at its being from below. This means that Future constitutes the meaning of my present For-itself, as the project of its possibility, but that it in no way predetermines my For-itself which is to-come, since the For-itself is always abandoned to the nihilating obligation of being the foundation of its nothingness. The Future can only effect a pre-outline of the limits within which the For-itself will make itself be as a flight making itself present to being in the direction of another future. The future is what I would be if I were not free and what I can *have to be* only because I am free. It appears on the horizon to announce to me what I am from the standpoint of what I shall be. ("What are you doing? I am in the process of tacking up this tapestry, of hanging this picture on the wall"). Yet at the same time by its nature as a future present-for-itself, it is disarmed; for the For-itself which will be, will be in the mode of determining itself to be, and the Future, then become a past future as a pre-outline of this for-itself, will be able only as the past to influence it to be what it makes itself be. In a word, I am my Future in the constant perspective of the possibility of not being it. Hence that anguish which we have described above which springs from the fact that I am not sufficiently that Future which I have to be and which gives its meaning to my present: it is because I am a being whose meaning is always problematic. In vain would the For-itself long to be enchained to its Possibility, as to the being which it is outside itself but which it is *surely* outside itself. The For-itself can never be its Future except problematically, for it is separated from it by a Nothingness which it is. In short the For-itself is free, and its Freedom is to itself its own limit. To be free is to be condernned to be free. Thus the Future qua Future does not have to be. It is not *in itself,* and neither is it in the mode of being of the For-itself since it is the *meaning* of the For-itself. The Future is not, it *is possibilized.*

The Future is the continual possibilization of possibles—as the meaning of the present For-itself in so far as this meaning is problematic and as such radically escapes the present For-itself.

The Future thus defined does not correspond to a homogeneous and chronologically ordered succession of moments to come. To be sure, there is a hierarchy of my possibles. But this hierarchy does not correspond to the order of universal Temporality such as will be established on the bases of original Temporality. I *am* an infinity of possibilities, for the meaning of the For-itself is complex and cannot be contained in one formula. But a particular possibility may be more determinant for the meaning of the present For-itself than another which is nearer in universal time. For example, the possibility of going at two o'clock to see a friend whom I ve not seen for two years—this is truly a possible which I am. But the nearer possibilities—the possibilities of going there in a taxi, by bus, by subway, on foot—all these at present remain undertermined. I *am not* any one of these possibilities. Also there are gaps in the series of my possibilities. In the order of knowledge the gaps will be filled by the constitution of an homogeneous time without lacuna; in the order of action they will be filled by the will—that is, by rational, thematizing choice in terms of my possibles, and of possibilities which are not and will never be *my possibilities* and which I will realize in the mode of total indifference *in order to be reunited* with a possible which I am.

9 Freedom

Sartre is usually misunderstood as having an exaggerated view of human freedom, no doubt because of the claims in the *Existentialism and Humanism* lecture that there is no determinism; we are free, we are freedom, we are condemned to be free. The only sense in which we are not free, it seems, is that we are not free not to be free. After the war Sartre caused outrage by saying that the French people had never been so free as during the Nazi occupation. In his play *Men Without Shadows* (*Morts sans sepulture*, 1946) French resistance fighters confront their own freedom in being tortured by Nazi collaborators. How can this be?

In *Being and Nothingness* Sartre draws a crucial distinction between freedom and *power*. Although my freedom is absolute my power may be severely constrained. There is no situation in which I do not have a choice, no matter how unpleasant. Indeed in Sartre's examples, the reality of choice is frequently agonising; a resistance fighter under torture may choose to betray comrades or remain silent for a moment longer. Freedom, for Sartre, is not comfortable. It is a capacity to choose that never leaves us so long as we exist. Scientific determinism is a theoretical abstraction when put by the side of the lived reality of human dilemmas. Even if scientific determinism were true, it would be of no practical help to us in making our commitments.

Sartrean freedom can not be understood without understanding the *situation*. (Sartre calls his volumes of literary, political and philosophical essays that appeared from 1947 *Situations*.) A human being is not separable from the human condition. A person divorced from the totality of their situations is an intellectual abstraction that can only be partly achieved. I am what I am only in relation to my situations. The totality of situations is the world and the kind of being that I have is *being-in-the-world*. What I make myself is inseparably bound up with my projects, with my surroundings as I take them to be. Situations obtain in hierarchies: Sartre's being about to smoke depends upon the existence of smoking as a practice in mid-twentieth-century France. Keeping an appointment depends upon friendships or meetings. These in turn depend upon the existence of human beings, their projects and situations. All of these depend fundamentally upon being-in-the-world, the situation of all situations.

Sartre's concept of a situation is anti-Cartesian. Descartes thinks a person could in principle exist in abstraction from their physical and social environment and it makes sense to specify someone's mental states without reference to the ways in which those states are embedded in the world, without reference to what they are typically or paradigmatically about. Sartre's use of 'situation' and 'being-in-the-world' is sharply opposed to this picture. As a mental and physical agent what I do only makes sense if I am existentially related to an external and public world populated by other people who are similar agents.

In our unreflective taken-for-granted living we do not think of the situation as *constituted* by our freedom. It is my acquiescence in authority, rather than any objective constraint, that determines my behaviour. Once I recognise my freedom to disobey, to rebel, I am deconditioned. The fixed cognitive contribution of my acquiescence is stripped from the world and the possibility of my changing it is opened up.

In Sartre's existentialism, human being and human situation form a mutually dependent totality. The relations between a human being and his or her situation are dialectical or reciprocal. The situation presents the agent with a range of possibilities. The agent acts to realise some of these possibilities and this action alters the situation and thereby presents a new range of possibilities. Agency constitutes both the agent and the situation. The situation only exists as a situation for some agent. The agent only exists as an agent in some situation so to be in a situation is to choose oneself in a situation. It follows that the relation between agent and situation is very close. The reciprocal relation is not only causal. It is not even only constitutive. Agent and situation may only be adequately understood as two aspects of one reality. Sartre does not put it this way, but it is as though the agent is the inside of the situation and the situation is the outside of the agent.

In order to reconcile this dialectical relation between agent and environment with Sartre's absolute libertarianism we need to invoke his distinction between freedom and power. Although our freedom is absolute, our power is limited. Although there is no situation in which we do not have a choice, there is no situation which does not limit our power. Sartre spells this out clearly in the 1947 essay *Cartesian Freedom* (*La Liberté Cartésienne* in *Situations I*) when he insists that the situation of a person and their powers can neither increase or limit their freedom. Although what I can do is limited by where as well as when I am, that I can do something rather than nothing is in no way affected. I retain the dispositional property of being a choosing agent even though which choices I may exercise varies from situation to situation. Clearly some choices may be unpleasant to me but, logically, an unpleasant choice is nevertheless a choice. The expression 'I had no choice' is misleading.

The theme that freedom is unimpaired by constraints on power pervades Sartre's literature. Sometimes his characters are horribly constrained: the tortured resistance fighters in *Men Without Shadows*, Mathieu and his comrades trapped in the clock tower in the 1949 volume of *The Roads to Freedom; Iron in the Soul*. As their power is reduced their awareness of freedom increases.

In Sartre's existentialism, the recognition of freedom is a lonely first person singular phenomenon for which recourse to others provides no respite. For example, also in *Iron in the Soul*, Sartre has Odette shift swiftly from the first person plural thought 'What ought we to want?' to the first person singular thought 'What ought I to want ?' (p. 185) against the background 'situation' of the May 1940 invasion of France. Odette is expressing the ethical tenet of *Being and Nothingness* that 'It is I who sustain values in being'. Sartre did not write 'It is we who sustain values in being'. For all his repudiation of Descartes in 'Cartesian Freedom' the primacy and inescapability of the first person singular exercise of, and confrontation with, freedom remains thoroughly Cartesian.

Sometimes, the existence of freedom is depicted as dependent upon its acknowledgement or recognition by the agent. For example, in *The Flies* Sartre has Zeus say of Orestes 'Orestes knows that he is free' and Aegistheus replies 'He knows he is free? Then to lay hands on him, to put him in irons, is not enough'.[1] Although, as we shall see, Sartre thinks there is a pervasive human tendency to deny one's own freedom, it is the fact of a person's freedom not their knowledge of it that makes freedom unconstrained. Freedom is entailed by knowledge of freedom but not vice versa. An agent aware of their freedom can act authentically.

Sartre endorses Heidegger's view that we are 'thrown' into the world. We are but we did not choose to be. Seemingly inconsistently with this, he says in *Being and Nothingness* that in a sense I choose to be born. Clearly, any kind of Platonic pre-existence is out of the question here. Sartre thinks it is false that we pre-date (and post-date) our empirical existence. Drawing a distinction between existence and essence, Sartre means that what my birth is, or is to me, largely depends on how I freely think of it. Its significance is the significance I bestow upon it. Freedom does not pre-date existence. Freedom is existence, and in it existence precedes the essence we freely choose.

In *Being and Nothingness* a person is their freedom. Sartre identifies *the upsurge of freedom, choice,* and *the person himself,* as one and the same being. One existent is subsumed under three descriptions. I do not *have* my freedom. I *am* it. The will has no role in the exercise of Sartrean freedom. The moment the will operates, the decision is already taken. Sartre's libertarianism entails that human actions are unpredictable. The only respect in which I am not free is that I am not free not to be free. I am not able not to choose.

We could refrain from action, or omit to act. Would this not be a way of escaping one's own freedom? Sartre's position is that refraining from action pre-supposes the choice not to act. This is what *refraining* is. There exists an infinity of actions I am not performing. I am only refraining from doing some of them. In *Iron in the Soul* Sartre has Ivich and Boris agree about the French soldiers caught up the May 1940 invasion of France 'they chose to have this war' (p. 69). They did nothing to prevent it.

Sartre believes those who live in the developed countries are causally responsible for the death, by starvation and malnutrition, of those who live in the Third World. To fail to save life is as causally efficacious and as morally culpable, as to actively take life. This kind of reasoning leads Sartre to justify political violence by, or on behalf of, oppressed groups, for example in the Preface he wrote for Frantz Fanon's *The Wretched of the Earth* (*Les Damnés de la Terre,* 1961) and to support the Baader Meinhof gang in the early 1970s. Sartre denies that the distinction between our acts and our omissions marks a distinction between what we are and are not responsible for.

How is Sartre's libertarianism to be reconciled with his post-war Marxism? A human individual retains the capacity to choose whatever their situation, whatever the constraints on their power. Our power is constrained because we are alienated. He endorses the view of the early Marx that members of capitalist society are psychologically estranged from their work, the products of their work, nature, and each other. This alienation is an obstacle to the construction of what Sartre would call a free society: a society we would freely choose rather than historically inherit. Our dispositional capacity to choose continues to ontologically differentiate us from naturally occurring objects and artefacts even though we are denied the power to create a free society in Sartre's sense.

Freedom is exercised in history. It is not an option for me to freely act in the situation of a late-nineteenth-century German coal miner if I am a mid-twentieth-century French intellectual. My historical location opens for me a range of actions I may perform but there is an infinity of actions which are closed. There is a dialectical dependency between freedom and truth. There is no truth without freedom and no freedom without truth. A human being is free but at the same time in bondage; a chooser whose power is politically and historically constrained. It is only at the moment of death that a human being is complete. Before death a brave person could become a coward or a coward could become brave. Only death brings an end to freedom.

BEING AND NOTHINGNESS

Being and doing: freedom

[. . .] at the outset we can see what is lacking in those tedious discussions between determinists and the proponents of free will. The latter are concerned to find cases of decision for which there exists no prior cause, or deliberations concerning two opposed acts which are equally possible and possess causes (and motives) of exactly the same weight. To which the determinists may easily reply that there is no action without a *cause* and that the most insignificant gesture (raising the right hand rather than the left hand, etc.) refers to causes and motives which confer its meaning upon it. Indeed the case could not be otherwise since every action must be *intentional*; each action must, in fact, have an end and the end in turn is referred to a cause. Such indeed is the unity of the three temporal ekstases; the end or temporalization of my future implies a cause (or motive); that is, it points toward my past, and the present is the upsurge of the act. To speak of an act without a cause is to speak of an act which would Jack the intentional structure of every act; and the proponents of free will by searching for it on the level of the act which is in the process of being performed can only end up by rendering the act absurd. But the determinists in turn are weighting the scale by stopping their investigation with the mere designation of the cause and motive. The essential question in fact lies beyond the complex organization "cause-intention-act-end"; indeed we ought to ask how a cause (or motive) can be constituted as such.

Now we have just seen that if there is no act without a cause, this is not in the sense that we can say that there is no phenomenon without a cause. In order to be a *cause,* the *cause* must be *experienced* as such. Of course this does not mean that it is to be thematically conceived and made explicit as in the case of deliberation. But at the very least it means that the for-itself must confer on it its value as cause or motive. And, as we have seen, this constitution of the cause as such can not refer to another real and positive existence; that is, to a prior cause. For otherwise the very nature of the act as engaged intentionally in non-being would disappear. The motive is understood only by the end; that is, by the non-existent. It is therefore in itself a négatité. If I accept a niggardly salary it is doubtless because of fear; and fear is a motive. But it is *fear of dying from starvation*; that is, this fear has meaning only outside itself in an end ideally posited, which is the preservation of a life which I apprehend as "in danger." And this fear is understood in turn only in relation to the *value which I* implicitly give to this life; that is, it is referred to that hierarchal system of ideal objects which are values. Thus the motive makes itself understood as what it is by means of the ensemble of beings which "are not," by ideal existences, and by the future. Just as the future turns back upon the present and the past in order to elucidate them, so it is the ensemble of my projects which turns back in order to confer upon the *motive* its structure as a motive. It is only because I escape the in-itself by nihilating myself toward my possibilities that this in-itself can take on value as cause or motive. Causes and motives have meaning only inside a projected ensemble which is precisely an ensemble of non-existents. And this ensemble is ultimately myself as transcendence; it is Me in so far as I have to be myself outside of myself.

If we recall the principle which we established earlier—namely that it is the apprehension of a revolution as possible which gives to the work-man's suffering its value as a motive—we must thereby conclude that it is by fleeing a situation toward our possibility of changing it that we organize this situation into complexes of causes and motives. The nihilation by which we achieve a withdrawal in relation to the situation is the same as the ekstasis by which we project ourselves toward a modification of this situation. The result is that it is in fact impossible to find an act without a motive but that this does not mean that we must conclude that the motive causes the act; the motive is an integral part of the act. For as the resolute project toward a change is not distinct from the act, the motive, the act, and the end are all constituted in a single upsurge. Each of these three structures claims the two others as its meaning. But the organized totality of the three is no longer explained by any particular structure, and its upsurge as the pure temporalizing nihilation of the in-itself is one with freedom. It is the act which decides its ends and its motives, and the act is the expression of freedom.

We cannot, however, stop with these superficial considerations; if the fundamental condition of the act is freedom, we must attempt to describe this freedom more precisely. But at the start we encounter a great difficulty. Ordinarily, to describe something is a process of making explicit by aiming at the structures of a particular essence. Now freedom has no essence. It is not subject to any logical necessity; we must say of it what Heidegger said of the *Dasein* in general: "In it existence precedes and commands essence." Freedom makes itself an act, and we ordinarily attain it across the act which it organizes with the causes, motives, and ends which the act implies. But precisely because this act has an essence, it appears to us as *constituted*; if we wish to reach the constitutive power, we must abandon any hope of finding it an essence. That would in fact demand a new constitutive power and so on to infinity. How then are we to describe an existence which perpetually makes itself and which refuses to be confined in a definition? The very use of the term "freedom" is dangerous if it is to imply that the word refers to a concept as words ordinarily do. Indefinable and unnamable, is freedom also indescribable?

Earlier when we wanted to describe nothingness and the being of the phenomenon, we encountered comparable difficulties. Yet they did not deter us. This is because there can be descriptions which do not aim at the essence but at the existent itself in its particularity. To be sure, I could not describe a freedom which would be common to both the Other and myself; I could not therefore contemplate an essence of freedom. On the contrary, it is freedom which is the foundation of all essences since man reveals intra-mundane essences by surpassing the world toward his own possibilities. But actually the question is of *my* freedom. Similarly when I described consciousness, I could not discuss a nature common to certain individuals but only *my* particular consciousness, which like my freedom is beyond essence, or—as we have shown with considerable repetition—for which *to be* is to have been. I discussed this consciousness so as to touch it in its very existence as a particular experience—the *cogito*. Husserl and Descartes, as Gaston Berger has shown, demand that the *cogito* release to them a *truth as essence*: with Descartes we achieve the connection of two simple natures; with Husserl we grasp the eidetic structure of consciousness.[2] But if in consciousness its existence must precede its essence, then both Descartes and Husserl have committed an error. What we can demand from the *cogito* is only that it discover for us a factual necessity. It is also to the *cogito* that we appeal in order to determine freedom as the freedom which is *ours*, as a pure factual necessity; that is, as a contingent existent but one which I *am not able* not to experience. I am indeed an existent who *learns* his freedom through his acts, but I am also an existent whose individual and unique existence temporalizes itself as freedom. As such I am necessarily a consciousness (of) freedom since nothing exists in consciousness except as the non-thetic consciousness of existing. Thus my freedom is perpetually in question in my being; it is not a quality added on or a *property* of my nature. It is very exactly the stuff of my being; and as in my being, my being is in question, I must necessarily possess a certain comprehension of freedom. It is this comprehension which we intend at present to make explicit.

In our attempt to reach to the heart of freedom we may be helped by the few observations which we have made on the subject in the course of this work and which we must summarize here. In the first chapter we established the fact that if negation comes into the world through human-reality, the latter must be a being who can realize a nihilating rupture with the world and with himself; and we established that the permanent possibility of this rupture is the same as freedom. But on the other hand, we stated that this permanent possibility of nihilating what I am in the form of "having-been" implies for man a particular type of existence. We were able then to determine by means of analyses like that of bad faith that human reality is its own nothingness. For the for-itself, to be is to nihilate the in-itself which it is. Under these conditions freedom can be nothing other than this nihilation. It is through this that the for-itself escapes its being as its essence; it is through this that the for-itself is always something other than what can be *said* of it. For in the final analysis the For-itself is the one which escapes this very denomination, the one which is already beyond the name which is given to it, beyond the property which is recognized in it. To say that the for-itself has to be what it is, to say that it is what it is not while not being what it is, to say that in it existence precedes and conditions essence or inversely according to Hegel, that for it "Wesen ist was gewesen ist"—all this is to say one and the same thing: to be aware that man is free. Indeed by the sole fact that I am conscious of the causes which inspire my action, these causes are already transcendent objects for my consciousness; they are outside. In vain shall I seek to catch hold of them; I escape them by my very existence. I am condemned to exist forever beyond my essence, beyond the causes and motives of my act. I am condemned to be free. This means that no limits to my freedom can be found except freedom itself or, if you prefer, that we are not free to cease being free. To the extent that the for-itself wishes to hide its own nothingness from itself and to incorporate the in-itself as its true node of being, it is trying also to hide its freedom from itself.

The ultimate meaning of determinism is to establish within us an unbroken continuity of existence in itself. The motive conceived as a psychic act—*i.e.*, as a full and given reality—is, in the deterministic view, artienated without any break with the decision and the act, both of which are equally conceived as psychic givens. The in-itself has got hold of all these "data"; the motive provokes the act as the physical cause its effect; everything is real, everything is full. Thus the refusal of freedom can be conceived only as an attempt to apprehend oneself as being-in-itself; it amounts to the same thing. Human reality may be defined as a being such that in its being its freedom is at stake because human reality perpetually tries to refuse to recognize its freedom. Psychologically in each one of us this amounts to trying to take the causes and motives as *things*. We try to confer permanence upon them. We attempt to hide from ourselves that their nature and their weight depend each moment on the meaning which I give to them; we take them for constants. This amounts to considering the meaning which I gave to them just now or yesterday—which is irremediable because it is *past*—and extrapolating from it a character fixed still in the present. I attempt to persuade myself that the cause *is* as it was. Thus it would pass whole and untouched from my past consciousness to my present consciousness. It would inhabit my consciousness. This amounts to trying to give an essence to the for-itself. In the same way people will posit ends as transcendences, which is not an error. But instead of seeing that the transcendences there posited are maintained in their being by my own transcendence, people will assume that I encounter them upon my surging up in the world; they come from God, from nature, from "my" nature, from society. These ends ready made and pre-human will therefore define the meaning of my act even before I conceive it, just as causes as pure psychic givens will produce it without my even being aware of them.

Cause, act, and end constitute a *continuum*, a *plenum*. These abortive attempts to stifle freedom under the weight of being (they collapse with the sudden upsurge of anguish before freedom) show sufficiently that freedom in its foundation coincides with the nothingness which is at the heart of man. Human-reality is free because it *is not enough*. It is free because it is perpetually wrenched away from itself and because it has been separated by a nothingness from what it is and from what it will be. It is free, finally, because its present being is itself a nothingness in the form of the "reflection-reflecting." Man is free because he is not himself but presence to himself. The being which is what it is can not be free. Freedom is precisely the nothingness which is *made-to-be* at the heart of man and which forces human-reality *to make itself* instead of *to be*. As we have seen, for human reality, to be is to *choose oneself*; nothing comes to it either from the outside or from within which it can *receive or accept*. Without any help whatsoever, it is entirely abandoned to the intolerable necessity of making itself be—down to the slightest detail. Thus freedom is not a being; it is *the being* of man—*i.e.*, his nothingness of being. If we start by conceiving of man as a plenum, it is absurd to try to find in him afterwards moments or psychic regions in which he would be free. As well look for emptiness in a container which one has filled beforehand up to the brim! Man can not be sometimes slave and sometimes free; he is wholly and forever free or he is not free at all.

These observations can lead us, if we know how to use them, to new discoveries. They will enable us first to bring to light the relations between freedom and what we call the "will." There is a fairly common tendency to seek to identify free acts with voluntary acts and to restrict the deterministic explanation to the world of the passions. In short the point of view of Descartes. The Cartesian will is free, but there are "passions of the soul." Again Descartes will attempt a physiological interpretation of these passions. Later there will be an attempt to instate a purely psychological determinism. Intellectualistic analyses such as Proust, for example, attempts with respect to jealousy or snobbery can serve as illustrations for this concept of the passional "mechanism." In this case it would be necessary to conceive of man as simultaneously free and determined, and the essential problem would be that of the relations between this unconditioned freedom and the determined processes of the psychic life: how will it master the passions, how will it utilize them for its own benefit? A wisdom which comes from ancient times—the wisdom of the Stoics—will teach us to come to terms with these passions so as to master them; in short it will counsel us how to conduct ourselves with regard to affectivity as man does with respect to nature in general when he obeys it in order better to control it. Human reality therefore appears as a free power besieged by an ensemble of determined processes. One will distinguish wholly free acts, determined processes over which the free will has power, and processes which on principle escape the human-will.

It is clear that we shall not be able to accept such a conception. But let us try better to understand the reasons for our refusal. There is one objection which is obvious and which we shall not waste time in developing; this is that such a trenchant duality is inconceivable at the heart of the psychic unity. How in fact could we conceive of a being which could be *one* and which nevertheless on the one hand would be constituted as a series of facts determined by one another—hence existents in exteriority—and which on the other hand would be constituted as a spontaneity determining itself to be and revealing only itself? *A priori* this spontaneity would be capable of no action on a determinism already *constituted*. On what could it act? On the object itself (the present psychic fact)? But how could it modify an in-itself which by definition is and can be only what it is? On the actual law of the process? This is self-contradictory. On the antecedents of the process? But it amounts to the same thing whether we act on the present psychic fact in order to modify it in itself or act upon it in order to modify its consequences. And in each case we encounter the same impossibility which we pointed out earlier. Moreover, what instrument would this spontaneity have at its disposal? If the hand can clasp, it is because it can be clasped. Spontaneity, since by definition it is *beyond reach* can not in turn *reach*; it can produce only itself. And if it could dispose of a special instrument, it would then be necessary to conceive of this as of an intermediary nature between free will and determined passions—which is not admissible. For different reasons the passions could get no hold upon the will. Indeed it is impossible for a determined process to act upon a spontaneity, exactly as it is impossible for objects to act upon consciousness. Thus any synthesis of two types of existents is impossible; they are not homogeneous; they will remain each one in its incommunicable solitude. The only bond which a nihilating spontaneity could maintain with mechanical processes would be the fact that it *produces itself by an internal negation directed toward these existents*. But then the spontaneity will exist precisely only in so far as it denies concerning itself that it is these passions. Henceforth the ensemble of the determined πάθος will of necessity be apprehended by spontaneity as a pure transcendent; that is, as what is necessarily *outside*, as what *is not* it.[3] This internal negation would therefore have for its effect only the dissolution of the πάθος in the world, and the πάθος would exist as some sort of object in the midst of the world for a free spontaneity which would be simultaneously will and consciousness. This discussion shows that two solutions and only two are possible: either man is wholly determined (which is inadmissible, especially because a determined consciousness—*i.e.*, a consciousness externally motivated—becomes itself pure exteriority and ceases to be consciousness) or else man is wholly free.

But these observations are still not our primary concern. They have only a negative bearing. The study of the will should, on the contrary, enable us to advance further in our understanding of freedom. And this is why the fact which strikes us first is that if the will is to be autonomous, then it is impossible for us to consider it as a *given* psychic fact; that is, in-itself. It can not belong to the category defined by the psychologist as "states of consciousness." Here as everywhere else we assert that the state of consciousness is a pure idol of a positive psychology. If the will is to be freedom, then it is of necessity negativity and the power of nihilation. But then we no longer can see why autonomy should be preserved for the will. In fact it is hard to conceive of those holes of nihilation which would be the volitions and which would surge up in the otherwise dense and full web of the passions and of the πάθος in general. If the will is nihilation, then the ensemble of the psychic must likewise be nihilation. Moreover—and we shall soon return to this point—where do we get the idea that the "fact" of passion or that pure, simple desire is not nihilating? Is not passion first a project and an enterprise? Does it not exactly posit a state of affairs as intolerable? And is it not thereby forced to effect a withdrawal in relation to this state of affairs and to nihilate it by isolating it and by considering it in the light of an end—*i.e.*, of a non-being? And does not passion have its own ends which are recognized precisely at the same moment at which it posits them as non-existent? And if nihilation is precisely the being of freedom, how can we refuse autonomy to the passions in order to grant it to the will?

But this is not all: the will, far from being the unique or at least the privileged manifestation of freedom, actually—like every event of the for-itself—must presuppose the foundation of an original freedom in order to be able to constitute itself as will. The will in fact is posited as a reflective decision in relation to certain ends. But it does not create these ends. It is rather a mode of being in relation to them: it decrees that the pursuit of these ends will be reflective and deliberative. Passion can posit the same ends. For example, if I am threatened, I can run away at top speed because of my fear of dying. This passional fact nevertheless posits implicitly as a supreme end the value of life. Another person in the same situation will, on the contrary, understand that he must remain at his post even if resistance at first appears more dangerous than flight; he "will stand firm." But his goal, although better understood and explicitly posited, remains the same as in the case of the emotional reaction. It is simply that the methods of attaining it are more clearly conceived; certain of them are rejected as dubious or inefficacious, others are more solidly organized. The difference here depends on the choice of means and on the degree of reflection and of making explicit, not on the end. Yet the one who flees is said to be "passionate," and we reserve the term "voluntary" for the man who resists. Therefore the question is of a difference of subjective attitude in relation to a transcendent end. But if we wish to avoid the error which we denounced earlier and not consider these transcendent ends as pre-human and as an *a priori* limit to our transcendence, then we are indeed compelled to recognize that they are the temporalizing projection of our freedom. Human reality can not receive its ends, as we have seen, either from outside or from a so-called inner "nature." It chooses them and by this very choice confers upon them a transcendent existence as the external limit of its projects. From this point of view—and if it is understood that the existence of the *Dasein* precedes and commands its essence—human reality in and through its very upsurge decides to define its own being by its ends. It is therefore the positing of my ultimate ends which characterizes my being and which is identical with the sudden thrust of the freedom which is mine. And this thrust is an *existence;* it has nothing to do with an essence or with a property of a being which would be engendered conjointly with an idea.

Thus since freedom is identical with my existence, it is the foundation of ends which I shall attempt to attain either by the will or by passionate efforts. Therefore it can not be limited to voluntary acts. Volitions, on the contrary, like passions are certain subjective attitudes by which we attempt to attain the ends posited by original freedom. By original freedom, of course, we should not understand a freedom which would be *prior* to the voluntary or passionate act but rather a foundation which is strictly contemporary with the will or the passion and which these *manifest*, each in its own way. Neither should we oppose freedom to the will or to passion as the "profound self" of Bergson is opposed to the superficial self; the for-itself is wholly selfness and can not have a "profound self," unless by this we mean certain transcendent structures of the psyche. Freedom is nothing but the *existence* of our will or of our passions in so far as this existence is the nihilation of facticity; that is, the existence of a being which is its being in the mode of having to be it. We shall return to this point. In any case let us remember that the will is determined within the compass of motives and ends already posited by the for-itself in a transcendent projection of itself toward its possibles. If this were not so, how could we understand deliberation, which is an evaluation of means in relation to already existing ends?

If these ends are already posited, then what remains to be decided at each moment is the way in which I shall conduct myself with respect to them; in other words, the attitude which I shall assume. Shall I act by volition or by passion? Who can decide except me? In fact, if we admit that circumstances decide for me (for example, I can act by volition when faced with a minor danger but if the peril increases, I shall fall into passion), we thereby suppress all freedom. It would indeed be absurd to declare that the will is autonomous when it appears but that external circumstances strictly determine the moment of its appearance. But, on the other hand, how can it be maintained that a will which does not yet exist can suddenly decide to shatter the chain of the passions and suddenly stand forth on the fragments of these chains? Such a conception would lead us to consider the will as a *power* which sometimes would manifest itself to consciousness and at other times would remain hidden, but which would in any case possess the permanence and the existence "in-itself" of a property. This is precisely what is inadmissible. It is, however, certain that common opinion conceives of the moral life as a struggle between a will-thing and passion-substances. There is here a sort of psychological Manichaeism which is absolutely insupportable.

Actually it is not enough to will; it is necessary to will to will. Take, for example, a given situation: I can react to it emotionally. We have shown elsewhere that emotion is not a physiological tempest;[4] it is a reply adapted to the situation; it is a type of conduct, the meaning and form of which are the object of an intention of consciousness which aims at attaining a particular end by particular means. In fear, fainting and cataplexie[5] aim at suppressing the danger by suppressing the consciousness of the danger. There is an *intention* of losing consciousness in order to do away with the formidable world in which consciousness is engaged and which comes into being through consciousness. Therefore we have to do with magical behavior provoking the symbolic satisfactions of our desires and revealing by the same stroke a magical stratum of the world. In contrast to this conduct voluntary and rational conduct will consider the situation scientifically, will reject the magical, and will apply itself to realizing determined series and instrumental complexes which will enable us to resolve the problems. It will organize a system of means by taking its stand on instrumental determinism. Suddenly it will reveal a technical world; that is, a world in which each instrumental-complex refers to another larger complex and so on. But what will make me decide to choose the magical aspect or the technical aspect of the world? It can not be the world itself, for this in order to be manifested waits to be discovered. Therefore it is necessary that the for-itself in its project must choose being the one by whom the world is revealed as magical or rational; that is, the for-itself must as a free project of itself give to itself magical or rational existence. It is responsible for either one, for the for-itself can be only if it has chosen itself. Therefore the for-itself appears as the free foundation of its emotions as of its volitions. My fear *is* free and manifests my freedom; I have put all my freedom into my fear, and I have chosen myself as fearful in this or that circumstance. Under other circumstances I shall exist as deliberate and courageous, and I shall have put all my freedom into my courage. In relation to freedom there is no privileged psychic phenomenon. All my "modes of being" manifest freedom equally since they are all ways of being my own nothingness.

Notes

1   Jean-Paul Sartre *Altona and Other Plays: Altona, Men Without Shadows, The Flies* (Penguin, in association with Hamish Hamilton, Harmondsworth, 1962) p. 292.
2   Gaston Berger, *Le Cogito chez Husserl et chez Descartes*, 1940.
3   *I.e.*, is not spontaneity. Tr.
4   *Esquisse d'une théorie phénoménologique des émotions*, Hermann, 1939. In English, *The Emotions: Outline of a Theory*. Tr. by Bernard Frechtman. Philosophical Library, 1948.
5   A word invented by Preyer to refer to a sudden inhibiting numbness produced by any shock. Tr.

10 Responsibility

Sartre maintains that ethical values are invented, not discovered. He thinks there is no God so no divine authority on the distinction between right and wrong, and it is an act of bad faith to endorse a pre-established value system such as Christianity, humanism, or Communism. Rather, each person is radically free to create their own values through action. Ethics is something that exists only within the world of things human. Indeed, in the *Existentialism and Humanism* Lecture (Chapter 2 above) he says there is no universe except the human universe and we can not escape human subjectivity. We can not look outside our lives to answer the question of how to live. We can only do that by freely choosing how to live.

Superficially, Sartre might appear to be a naive relativist about morality. Relativism in morality is the thesis that it makes no sense to speak of some actions as right and some wrong, only of some individual or some society holding them to be right or wrong. Relativism embodies a mistake. From the obvious and uncontroversial historical truth that value systems vary from person to person and from society to society it is invalidly concluded that these systems can not themselves be right or wrong. It is important to refute relativism because, although it is sometimes misidentified as a liberal and tolerant doctrine, it in fact precludes our condemning individuals or regimes that practice genocide, torture, arbitrary imprisonment and other atrocities. On the relativist view these practices are, so to speak, 'right for them but wrong for us'; a putative claim that makes no sense.

Sartre's moral philosophy opens a conceptual space between absolute God-given morality on the one hand and naive relativism on the other. He insists that values belong only to the human world, and that we are uncomfortably free to invent them, yet he provides us with strict criteria for deciding between right and wrong.

The essential concept in the establishment of this middle path is responsibility. To say that someone is responsible for what they do is to say that they do it, they could have refrained from doing it, and they are answerable to others for doing it. (This last component of 'responsibility' is apparent in the word's etymology. It means 'answerability'.) It is a consequence of Sartre's theses that existence precedes essence in the case of humanity, and people have an ineliminable freedom, that we are responsible for what we are. We are nothing else but what we make of ourselves. It follows that everyone is wholly and solely responsible for everything they do.

Responsibility for Sartre includes another, crucial, dimension. In choosing for myself I am implicitly choosing for others. By joining a trade union, by joining the communist party, by getting married, by becoming a Christian, by fighting in the French resistance, by anything I do, I am implicitly prescribing the same course of action to the rest of humanity. To put it another way, all my actions are recommendations. By acting I set an example for all similarly placed others to follow. I am obliged at every instant to perform actions which are examples.

This implicit recommendation to others is called in moral philosophy 'universalisability', and finds its most sophisticated expression in Kant's ethical works, the *Groundwork of the Metaphysics of Morals* (*Grundlegung zur Metaphysik der Sitten*, 1785) and the *Critique of Practical Reason* (*Kritik der Praktischen Vernunft*, 1788). Kant, like Sartre, tries to found an objective morality that does not rely on theological premises. In Sartre's texts, universalisability admits of two interpretations, one causal the other logical.

On the causal interpretation we take literally Sartre's notion of setting an example. By joining a trade union I may cause others to join a trade union, and so my responsibility is in a direct sense a responsibility for what I make others do, not just for what I do myself.

On the logical interpretation, in order to be *consistent* we have to accept that persons similarly placed to ourselves should do as we do. A person is only one person amongst others and it would be inconsistent to maintain that one person but not others should follow a course of action where all those people are similarly placed. There would be something incoherent about someone who freely chose to join a trade union, or who became a convert to Christianity, but disapproved of people making just those choices. Of course Sartre accepts that that may happen. One form of religious or political commitment might be suitable for one person but not another but, *prima facie,* if it is right for one person to do something then it is right for any similar and similarly placed person to do the same. Being just one person rather than another can not make a moral difference.

The causal and the logical interpretations are mutually consistent. For any action, say joining the French resistance, it may both be causally efficacious in encouraging others to join, and exhibit the rule that if I join then I do not judge similarly placed others to be under no obligation to join, on pain of inconsistency.

Consistency is a condition for ethics according to Sartre. Acting immorally, that is, in a way that can not be universalised, results in incoherence. Following Kant, Sartre says the act of lying implies the universal value which it denies. Not only is there no lying without truth-telling but lying can not be universalised. The implicit recommendation to everyone to lie could never be adopted. If there was no truth-telling the distinction between lies and truth would break down and there could be no lying either. Because consistency is a constraint on morality what can not be universalised is immoral. In fashioning myself I fashion humanity as a whole.

Universalisability provides us with a test to distinguish between the rightness and the wrongness of our actions. If an action cannot be consistently universalised then it is immoral. If the action can be consistently universalised it is not immoral. In trying to resolve a moral dilemma, we have to ask what the consequences would be of everyone adopting our action as a rule.

Realising the full burden of our responsibility to humanity provokes in us the deepest sense of dread and anxiety. This discomfort is why we plunge ourselves into bad faith. Facing our freedom requires facing our responsibility. We can hardly bear to face our responsibility so we deny our freedom.

We are free and responsible despite our refusal to accept these objective facts about us. They endure through our pretence so we are in anguish.

In this way, Sartre emerges as a moral objectivist despite his rejection of theological premises for ethics. His moral philosophy is in many ways a humanistic transformation of Christian ethics. To take one conspicuous example, instead of being responsible before God a person is responsible before humanity. Instead of God watching our every action everything happens to each person as though the whole human race was watching what they are doing. Sartre's humanity, like Christian humanity, is a fallen humanity, but Sartre's Fall is a secular Fall. We are not fallen from any perfect natural state; we fall short of our own possibilities of acting freely and responsibly. To admit this freedom is to become committed (*engagé*).

The section called 'Freedom and Responsibility' is taken from *Being and Nothingness*. The section called 'The Good and Subjectivity' is from *Notebooks for an Ethics*.

BEING AND NOTHINGNESS

Being and doing: freedom

Freedom and responsibility

Although the considerations which are about to follow are of interest primarily to the ethicist, it may nevertheless be worthwhile after these descriptions and arguments to return to the freedom of the for-itself and to try to understand what the fact of this freedom represents for human destiny.

The essential consequence of our earlier remarks is that man being condemned to be free carries the weight of the whole world on his shoulders; he is responsible for the world and for himself as a way of being. We are taking the word "responsibility" in its ordinary sense as "consciousness (of) being the incontestable author of an event or of an object." In this sense the responsibility of the for-itself is overwhelming since he[1] is the one by whom it happens that *there is* a world; since he is also the one who makes himself be, then whatever may be the situation in which he finds himself, the for-itself must wholly assume this situation with its peculiar coeffecient of adversity, even though it be insupportable. He must assume the situation with the proud consciousness of being the author of it, for the very worst disadvantages or the worst threats which can endanger my person have meaning only in and through my project; and it is on the ground of the engagement which I am that they appear. It is therefore senseless to think of complaining since nothing foreign has decided what we feel, what we live, or what we are.

Furthermore this absolute responsibility is not resignation; it is simply the logical requirement of the consequences of our freedom. What happens to me happens through me, and I can neither affect myself with it nor revolt against it nor resign myself to it. Moreover everything which happens to me is *mine*. By this we must understand first of all that I am always equal to what happens to me *qua* man, for what happens to a man through other men and through himself can be only human. The most terrible situations of war, the worst tortures do not create a non-human state of things; there is no non-human situation. It is only through fear, flight, and recourse to magical types of conduct that I shall decide on the non-human, but this decision is human, and I shall carry the entire responsibility for it. But in addition the situation is mine because it is the image of my free choice of myself, and everything which it presents to me is *mine* in that this represents me and symbolizes me. Is it not I who decide the coefficient of adversity in things and even their unpredictability by deciding myself?

Thus there are no *accidents* in a life; a community event which suddenly bursts forth and involves me in it does not come from the outside. If I am mobilized in a war, this war is *my* war; it is in my image and I deserve it. I deserve it first because I could always get out of it by suicide or by desertion; these ultimate possibles are those which must always be present for us when there is a question of envisaging a situation. For lack of getting out of it, I have *chosen* it. This can be due to inertia, to cowardice in the face of public opinion, or because I prefer certain other values to the value of the refusal to join in the war (the good opinion of my relatives, the honor of my family, *etc.*). Anyway you look at it, it is a matter of a choice. This choice will be repeated later on again and again without a break until the end of the war. Therefore we must agree with the statement by J. Romains, "In war there are no innocent victims."[2] If therefore I have preferred war to death or to dishonor, everything takes place as if I bore the entire responsibility for this war. Of course others have declared it, and one might be tempted perhaps to consider me as a simple accomplice. But this notion of complicity has only a juridical sense, and it does not hold here. For it depended on me that for me and by me this war should not exist, and I have decided that it does exist. There was no compulsion here, for the compulsion could have got no hold on a freedom. I did not have any excuse; for as we have said repeatedly in this book, the peculiar character of human-reality is that it is without excuse. Therefore it remains for me only to lay claim to this war.

But in addition the war is *mine* because by the sole fact that it arises in a situation which I cause to be and that I can discover it there only by engaging myself for or against it, I can no longer distinguish at present the choice which I make of myself from the choice which I make of the war. To live this war is to choose myself through it and to choose it through my choice of myself. There can be no question of considering it as "four years of vacation" or as a "reprieve," as a "recess," the essential part of my responsibilities being elsewhere in my married, family, or professional life. In this war which I have chosen I choose myself from day to day, and I make it mine by making myself. If it is going to be four empty years, then it is I who bear the responsibility for this.

Finally, as we pointed out earlier, each person is an absolute choice of self from the standpoint of a world of knowledges and of techniques which this choice both assumes and illumines; each person is an absolute upsurge at an absolute date and is perfectly unthinkable at another date. It is therefore a waste of time to ask what I should have been if this war had not broken out, for I have chosen myself as one of the possible meanings of the epoch which imperceptibly led to war. I am not distinct from this same epoch; I could not be transported to another epoch without contradiction. Thus *I am* this war which restricts and limits and makes comprehensible the period which preceded it. In this sense we may define more precisely the responsibility of the for-itself if to the earlier quoted statement, "There are no innocent victims," we add the words, "We have the war we deserve." Thus, totally free, undistinguishable from the period for which I have chosen to be the meaning, as profoundly responsible for the war as if I had myself declared it, unable to live without integrating it in *my* situation, engaging myself in it wholly and stamping it with my seal, I must be without remorse or regrets as I am without excuse; for from the instant of my upsurge into being, I carry the weight of the world by myself alone without anything or any person being able to lighten it.

Yet this responsibility is of a very particular type. Someone will say, "I did not ask to be born." This is a naive way of throwing greater emphasis on our facticity. I am responsible for everything, in fact, except for my very responsibility, for I am not the foundation of my being. Therefore everything takes place as if I were compelled to be responsible. I am *abandoned* in the world, not in the sense that I might remain abandoned and passive in a hostile universe like a board floating on the water, but rather in the sense that I find myself suddenly alone and without help, engaged in a world for which I bear the whole responsibility without being able, whatever I do, to tear myself away from this responsibility for an instant. For I am responsible for my very desire of fleeing responsibilities. To make myself passive in the world, to refuse to act upon things and upon Others is still to choose myself, and suicide is one mode among others of being-in-the-world. Yet I find an absolute responsibility for the fact that my facticity (here the fact of my birth) is directly inapprehensible and even inconceivable, for this fact of my birth never appears as a brute fact but always across a projective reconstruction of my for-itself. I am ashamed of being born or I am astonished at it or I rejoice over it, or in attempting to get rid of my life I affirm that I live and I assume this life as bad. Thus in a certain sense I *choose* being born. This choice itself is integrally affected with facticity since I am not able not to choose, but this facticity in turn will appear only in so far as I surpass it toward my ends. Thus facticity is everywhere but inapprehensible; I never encounter anything except my responsibility. That is why I can not ask, "*Why* was I born?" or curse the day of my birth or declare that I did not ask to be born, for these various attitudes toward my birth—*i.e.*, toward the *fact* that I realize a presence in the world—are absolutely nothing else but ways of assuming this birth in full responsibility and of making it *mine*. Here again I encounter only myself and my projects so that finally my abandonment—*i.e.*, my facticity—consists simply in the fact that I am condemned to be wholly responsible for myself. I am the being which *is* in such a way that in its being its being is in question. And this "is" of my being *is* as present and inapprehensible.

Under these conditions since every event in the world can be revealed to me only as an *opportunity* (an opportunity made use of, lacked, neglected, *etc.*), or better yet since everything which happens to us can be considered as a chance (*i.e.*, can appear to us only as a way of realizing this being which is in question in our being) and since others as transcendences-transcended are themselves only *opportunities* and *chances*, the responsibility of the for-itself extends to the entire world as a peopled-world. It is precisely thus that the for-itself apprehends itself in anguish; that is, as a being which is neither the foundation of its own being nor of the Other's being nor of the in-itselfs which form the world, but a being which is compelled to decide the meaning of being-within it and everywhere outside of it. The one who realizes in anguish his condition as *being* thrown into a responsibility which extends to his very abandonment has no longer either remorse or regret or excuse; he is no longer anything but a freedom which perfectly reveals itself and whose being resides in this very revelation. But as we pointed out at the beginning of this work, most of the time we flee anguish in bad faith.

NOTEBOOKS FOR AN ETHICS

The Good and Subjectivity

16 December 45[3]

The Good has to be done. This signifies that it is the end of an act, without a doubt. But also that it does not exist apart from the act that does it. A Platonic Good that would exist in and by itself makes no sense. One would like to say that it is beyond Being, in fact it would be *a* Being and, as such, in the first place it would leave us completely indifferent, we would slide by it without knowing what to make of it; for another thing it would be contradictory as an aberrant synthesis of being and ought-to-be. And in parallel to the Christian Good, which has over the former the superiority of emanating from a subjectivity, if it does perhaps escape contradiction, it would still not be able to move us, for God does not do the Good: he *is* it. Otherwise would we have to refuse to attribute perfection to the divine essence?

What we can take from the examination of this idea that "the Good has to be done" is that the agent of Good *is not* the Good. Nor is he Evil, which will lead us back in an indirect way to posing the problem of the being of the Good. He is poor over against the Good, he is its disgraced creator, for his act does not turn back on him to qualify him. No doubt, if he does it often, it will be said that he is good or just. But "good" does not mean: one who possesses the Good, but: one who does it. Just does not mean: who possesses justice, but: who renders it. So the original relation of man to the Good is the same type as transcendence, that is, the Good presents itself as what has to be posited as an objective reality through the effort of a subjectivity. The Good is necessarily that toward which we transcend ourselves, it is the noema of that particular noesis that is an act. The relation between acting subjectivity and the Good is as tight as the intentional relation that links consciousness to its object, or the one that binds man to the world in being-in-the-world.

The Good cannot be conceived apart from an acting subjectivity, and yet it is beyond this subjectivity. Subjective in that it must always emanate from a subjectivity and never impose itself on this subjectivity from the outside, it is objective in that it is, in its universal essence, strictly independent of this subjectivity. And, reciprocally, any act whatsoever originally presupposes a choice of the Good. Every act, in effect, presupposes a separation and a withdrawal of the agent in relation to the real and an evaluating appraisal of what is in the name of what should be. So man has to be considered as the being through which the Good comes into the world. Not inasmuch as consciousness can be contemplative but inasmuch as the human reality is a project.

This explains why many people are tempted to confuse the Good with what takes the most effort. An ethics of effort would be absurd. In what way would effort be a sign of the Good? It would cost me more in effort to strangle my son than to live with him on good terms. Is this why I should strangle him? And if between equally certain paths that both lead to virtue I choose the more difficult, have I not confused means and ends? For what is important is to act, not to act with difficulty. And if I consider effort as a kind of ascetic exercise, I am yielding first to a naturalistic ethics of exercise, of the gymnastics of the soul. I have the *thinglike* [*choisiste*] idea of profiting from an acquisition, like the gymnast who does fifteen repetitions today so as to be able to do twenty the day after tomorrow. But in ethics there is neither trampoline nor acquisition. Everything is always new. Hero today, coward tomorrow if he is not careful. It is just that, if effort has this price in the eyes of so many (aside from an old Christian aroma of mortification), it is because in forcing myself I experience my act to a greater degree in its relation to the Good. The less I make an effort, the more the Good toward which I strive seems to me given, to exist in the manner of a thing. The more I make an effort, the more this Good that oscillates and fades and bumps along from obstacle to obstacle is something I feel myself to be making. It is in effort that the relation of subjectivity to the Good gets uncovered for me. By escaping destruction, I sense that the Good runs the risk of being destroyed along with me; each time one of my attempts miscarries, I sense that the Good is not done, that it is called into question. Effort reveals the essential fragility of the Good and the primordial importance of subjectivity.

Thus it matters little whether the Good *is*. What is necessary is that it *be through us*. Not that there is here some turning back of subjectivity on itself or that it wants to participate in the Good it posits. Reflective reversals take place after the fact and manifest nothing other than a kind of flight, a preference for oneself. Rather, simply, subjectivity finds its meaning outside of itself in this Good that never *is* and that it perpetually realizes. It chooses itself in choosing the Good and it cannot be that in choosing itself it does not choose the Good that defines it. For it is always through the transcendent that I define myself.

Thus, when someone accuses us of favoring whims, they are following the prejudice that would have it that man is initially fully armed, fully ready, and that thus he chooses his Good afterwards, which would leave him a freedom of indifference faced with contrary possibilities. But if man qualifies himself by his choice, caprice no longer has a meaning for, insofar as it is produced by an already constituted personality that is "in the world," it gets inserted within an already existing choice of oneself and the Good. It is an instantaneous attention to the instant. But for there to be attention to the instant, there must be a duration that temporalizes itself, that is, an original choice of the Good and of myself in the face of the Good.

This is what allows us to comprehend that so many people devoted to the Good of a cause do not willingly accept that this Good should be realized apart from them and by ways that they have not thought of. I will go so far as to sacrifice myself entirely so that the person I love finds happiness, but I do not wish that it come to him by chance and, so to speak, apart from me.

In truth, there is incertitude about subjectivity. What is certain is that the Good must be done by some human reality. But is it a question of my individual reality, of that of my party, or of that of concrete humanity? In truth, the Good being universal, if I could melt into the human totality as into an indissoluable synthesis, the ideal would be that the Good was the result of the *doing* of this totality. But, on the one hand, this concrete humanity is in reality a detotalized totality, that is, it will never exist as a synthesis—it is stopped along the way. With the result that the very ideal of a humanity doing the Good is impossible. But, what is more, the quality of universality of the Good necessarily implies the positing of the Other. If the Other and I were to melt into a single human reality, humanity conscious of being a unique and individual historical adventure could no longer posit the Good except as the object of *its* own will. Or to rediscover the universal structure of the Good, it will have to postulate other human realities, on the Moon or on the planet Mars and therefore, once again, Another person.

Note that the universal structure of the Good is necessary as that which gives it its transcendence and its objectivity. To posit the Good in doing it is to posit Others as having to do it. We cannot escape this. Thus, to conclude, it is concrete subjectivity (the isolated subject or the group, the party) that has to do the Good in the face of others, for others, and in demanding from the diversity of others that they do it too. The notion of Good demands the plurality of consciousnesses and even the plurality of commitments.

If indeed, without going so far as to presuppose the synthetic totalization of consciousnesses and the end of History, we simply imagine a unanimous accord occurring about the nature of the Good to be done and furthermore an identity of actions, the Good preserves its universality, but it loses its reality of "having-to-be-done," for it has at present, for each concrete subjectivity, an *outside*. It is always for me what I have to do, but it is also what everyone else *does*. Which is to say that it appears as natural and as supernatural at the same time. This is, in one sense, the ambiguous reality of what are called *customs*. So the Good is necessarily the quest of concrete subjectivities existing in the world amidst other hostile or merely diversely oriented subjectivities. Not only is it my ideal, it is also my ideal that it become the ideal of others. Its universality is not de facto, it is de jure like its other characteristics.

Monday 17 December

It follows
1st, that no man wants the Good for the sake of the Good;
2nd, no man wants to do the Good so as to profit from it egoistically (*amour-propre*).

In both cases it is wrong to assume that man is initially fully made and that afterward he enters into a centripetal or centrifugal relation with the Good. Instead, since it is from this relation (which is the original choice) that both man and the Good are born, we can set aside both hypotheses. The interested man of the ethics of interest, for example, chooses, due to motivating factors that have to do with existential psychoanalysis, both to be interested and that the Good be his interest. He defines himself by this interest in the very moment that he defines the world and ethics by this interest. For me, he will never be an *interested man*, but rather a man who chooses to be interested. And we shall truly know what this interest is when we have made explicit the metaphysical reasons one might have for reducing the human condition to interest. At the level of his choice, the interested man is disinterested; that is, he does not explain himself in terms of an interest.

Analyze (existential psychoanalysis):

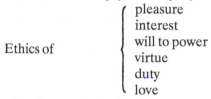

Ethics of
{
pleasure
interest
will to power
virtue
duty
love
}

Study a few types of value:

values of life
{
nobility
grace
}

values of action
{
generosity
devotion
frankness—purity—innocence
}

From this it also necessarily follows that the person is inseparable from the Good he has chosen. The person is the agent of this Good. Take this Good away from him, he is nothing at all, just as if you were to take the world away from consciousness, it would no longer be consciousness of anything, therefore no longer consciousness at all. But the person does not cling to his Good to preserve himself. Instead it is in projecting himself toward his Good that he makes and preserves himself. Thus the person is the bridge between being and the ought-to-be. But as such, he is necessarily unjustifiable. This is why he chooses to hypostasize the essential characteristics of his Good in order to give this Good an ontological priority over himself. Then, existing as the servant of this *a priori* Good, man exists by right. He is in some way raised up by the Good to serve it. We see this clearly in religion—for God has raised up man to reflect his glory.

Paulhan speaks of the illusion of totality that makes us believe in the presence of the armadillo when we see *the* armadillo.[4] But this illusion of totality is not just a fact of knowing something. We find it in every domain. Everything we experience, we experience as though it were our whole life and this is why across our experiences we grasp a meaning of the human condition. This sad street, with its large barracklike buildings, which I am walking along, extends out of sight for me, it is my life, it is life. And my solitude at Bordeaux was *solitude*, *the* forlornness of man.

Difficulty: there are two orders. The man in hell and the saved man. Once we allow that freedom is built up on the ground of the passions, this difficulty no longer exists: there is natural man with his determinism, and freedom appears when he escapes the infernal circle. But if you are not a Stoic, if you think that man is free even in hell, how then can you explain that there is a hell?

To put it another way, why does man almost always *first* choose hell, inauthenticity? Why is salvation the fruit of a new beginning neutralizing the first one? Let us consider this. What we are here calling inauthenticity is in fact the initial project or original choice man makes of himself in choosing his Good. His project is inauthentic when man's project is to rejoin an In-itself-for-itself and to identify it with himself; in short, to be God and his own foundation, and when at the same time he posits the Good as preestablished. This project is first in the sense that it is the very structure of my existence. I exist as a choice. But as this choice is precisely the positing of a transcendent, it takes place on the unreflective plane. I cannot appear at first on the reflective plane since reflection presupposes the appearance of the reflected upon, that is, of an *Erlebnis* that is given always as having been there before and on the unreflective plane. Thus I am free and responsible for my project with the reservation that it is precisely as having been there first.

In fact, it is not a question of a restriction on freedom since, in reality, it is just the form in which it is freedom that is the object of this reservation. Being unreflective, this freedom does not posit itself as freedom. It posits its object (the act, the end of the act) and it is haunted by its value. At this level it realizes itself therefore as a choice of being. And it is in its very existence that it is such. Nor is it a question of a determinism or of an obligation, but rather that freedom realizes itself in the first place on the unreflective plane. And there is no sense in asking if it might first realize itself on the reflective plane since this by definition implies the unreflective. It would be equally useless to speak of a constraint on the mind of a mathematician because he, being able to conceive of a circle or a square, cannot conceive of a square circle. It is not a question of a limit which freedom trips over, but rather, in freely making itself, it does so unreflectively, and as it is a nihilating escape from being toward the In-itself-for-itself and a perpetual nihilation, it cannot do anything unless it posits the In-itself-for-itself as the Good existing as *selbständig*.

Whence the real problem: "can one escape from hell?" cannot be posed on any other level than the reflective level. But since reflection emanates from an already constituted freedom, there is already a question of salvation, depending on whether reflection will take up for its own account the initial project of freedom or not take it up, whether it will be a purifying reflection refusing to "go along with" this project. It is obvious that we are here in the presence of a free choice among alternatives of the type that classical psychology has habituated us to consider. *"Mitmachen oder nicht mitmachen"* [to take or not to take part]. Except the two terms here do not exist before the decision. And as they take their source from the nonthetic consciousness that freedom has of itself, it is clear that accessory reflection is just the prolongation of the bad faith found nonthetically within the primitive project, whereas pure reflection is a break with this projection and the constitution of a freedom that takes itself as its end. This is why, although it would be much more advantageous to live on the plane of freedom that takes itself for its end, most people have a difficulty. . . .

Notes

1   I am shifting to the personal pronoun here since Sartre is describing the for-itself in concrete personal terms rather than as a metaphysical entity. Strictly speaking, of course, this is his position throughout, and the French *"il"* is indifferently "he" or "it." Tr.

2   J. Romains: *Les hommes de bonne volonté*; "Prélude à Verdun."

3   Sartre left for his second trip to the United States on 12 December 1945 (*The Writings of Jean-Paul Sartre*, p. 13). He traveled across the Atlantic by Liberty ship, a voyage that took eighteen days; hence this document, the second part of which is dated 17 December, must have been written during that voyage.

4   Jean Paulhan, *Entretien sur des faits Divers* (Paris: Gallimard, 1945), pp. 24–25.

11 Bad faith

The reality of our freedom is so unbearable that we refuse to face it. Instead of realising our identities as free conscious subjects we pretend to ourselves that we are mechanistic, determined objects. Refusing to freely make ourselves what we are, we masquerade as fixed essences by the adoption of hypocritical social roles and inert value systems. This denial of freedom is called by Sartre 'bad faith' (*mauvaise foi*). Almost a secularisation of the Christian Fall, bad faith is pervasive.

It is depicted in merciless detail in Sartre's fiction and in the chapter on bad faith from *Being and Nothingness*, partly reprinted below, which contains the *locus classicus*: a café waiter whose exaggerated movements and affected manner make it clear that he is *playing at* being a café waiter. Several kinds of bad faith are displayed by the waiter. He behaves mechanically as though he were a thing rather than a person. He is acting a role, playing a part. His relationship to himself is as false as that of an actor to his part in a play. His behaviour is a display before others, a set of routines which make him comfortable in his own eyes and in the eyes of others.

In another of Sartre's examples, the soldier at attention is in bad faith when he turns himself into a mechanical soldier-thing with a fixed unseeing gaze. A woman on a date with a certain man for the first time is presented with the moment of choice. The man takes her hand. For her to leave her hand in his is to choose a sexual direction for the relationship. To withdraw it is to reject this possibility. Instead of choosing, instead of exercising her real choice, she refuses to face it, leaving her hand to rest, neither accepting nor rejecting: a thing.

Sartre's philosophical literature is strewn with characters in bad faith: Goetz in *The Devil and the Good Lord*, Hugo in *Dirty Hands*, the bourgeoisie of Bouville in *Nausea* and Kean in the play of that name. In the biographies *Baudelaire* and *Saint Genet: Comedian and Martyr* the self-justifying bourgeois hypocrisy of the nineteenth-century poet is contrasted with the recognition of freedom by the thieving and streetfighting proletarian homosexual playwright from Brest. Genet's disreputable and criminal behaviour is eulogised by Sartre as a model of good faith – the real exercise of freedom. Baudelaire's law abiding conformity is condemned as the denial of freedom – bad faith. Sartre's distinction between the moral and the immoral cuts across socially acceptable legal and ethical mores. The moral is the free and authentic; the immoral is the conformist, the obsequious, the inauthentic.

Sartre says bad faith is a lie to oneself. This raises the philosophical paradox of self-deception because I know I am free but I hide my freedom from myself. In some sense, I both know and do not know I am free. How is this possible?

Sartre rejects one solution straight away: the psychoanalytical idea that there exists both a conscious and an unconscious mind. The Freudian allows that we know something unconsciously but remain ignorant of it and deny it consciously, and so dissolves the paradox of self-deception. Sartre can not possibly follow this route because it is a central tenet of his theory of consciousness that no unconscious exists. Sartre's phenomenology implies that every mental state is necessarily a conscious state.

Sartre's solution is as follows. The respect in which I know I am free is different from the respect in which I do not know I am free. I know that I am free in that I have the capacity to make choices. However, I mask this capacity from myself by the adoption of everyday roles, by conforming to the fixed image others have of me, by pretending to be a mechanism or a thing. I am fully possessed of the propositional knowledge of my own capacity to act freely but behave rigidly to prevent the realisation of that capacity. I pretend I am not free.

In bad faith I am in relation to myself as the actor is to Hamlet. We are all actors. An actor knows he is an actor but in so far as he performs he is not his real self. In bad faith I know I am free but adopt a role which masks my freedom. Bad faith is a representation for others and for myself. Paradoxically, human reality is what it is not (its authentic self-defining project) and is not what it is (its hypocritical social role).

Sartre distinguishes between two kinds of people in bad faith. One kind he calls 'cowards' ('*les lâches*'). They hide from their freedom in a facade of solemnity or with deterministic excuses. Those who deny not only their own freedom but that of others Sartre calls 'swine' ('*les salauds*'). In *Nausea*, for example, Roquentin concludes his tour of the portraits of the bourgeois officials in the city museum with the comment 'you bastards' ('*salauds*'). They felt they had the natural or God-given right to exist, to occupy their social location of wealth and privilege and suppress the freedom of others. The denial of freedom is immoral because it is inauthentic and hypocritical. Freedom brings with it a heavy and terrible responsibility described in the last chapter. Bad faith is also therefore an evasion of responsibility.

BEING AND NOTHINGNESS

Bad faith

I.   Bad faith and falsehood

The human being is not only the being by whom *négatités* are disclosed in the world; he is also the one who can take negative attitudes with respect to himself. In our Introduction we defined consciousness as "a being such that in its being, its being is in question in so far as this being implies a being other than itself." But now that we have examined the meaning of "the question," we can at present also write the formula thus: "Consciousness is a being, the nature of which is to be conscious of the nothingness of its being." In a prohibition or a veto, for example, the human being denies a future transcendence. But this negation is not explicative. My consciousness is not restricted to *envisioning* a *négatité*. It constitutes itself in its own flesh as the nihilation of a possibility which another human reality projects as *its* possibility. For that reason it must arise in the world as a *Not*; it is as a Not that the slave first apprehends the master, or that the prisoner who is trying to escape sees the guard who is watching him. There are even men (*e.g.*, caretakers, overseers, gaolers) whose social reality is uniquely that of the Not, who will live and die, having forever been only a Not upon the earth. Others so as to make the Not a part of their very subjectivity, establish their human personality as a perpetual negation. This is the meaning and function of what Scheler calls "the man of resentment"—in reality, the Not. But there exist more subtle behaviors, the description of which will lead us further into the inwardness of consciousness. Irony is one of these. In irony a man annihilates what he posits within one and the same act; he leads us to believe in order not to be believed; he affirms to deny and denies to affirm; he creates a positive object but it has no being other than its nothingness. Thus attitudes of negation toward the self permit us to raise a new question: What are we to say is the being of man who has the possibility of denying himself? But it is out of the question to discuss the attitude of "self-negation" in its universality. The kinds of behavior which can be ranked under this heading are too diverse; we risk retaining only the abstract form of them. It is best to choose and to examine one determined attitude which is essential to human reality and which is such that consciousness instead of directing its negation outward turns it toward itself. This attitude, it seems to me, is *bad faith* (*mauvaise foi*).

Frequently this is identified with falsehood. We say indifferently of a person that he shows signs of bad faith or that he lies to himself. We shall willingly grant that bad faith is a lie to oneself, on condition that we distinguish the lie to oneself from lying in general. Lying is a negative attitude, we will agree to that. But this negation does not bear on consciousness itself; it aims only at the transcendent. The essence of the lie implies in fact that the liar actually is in complete possession of the truth which he is hiding. A man does not lie about what he is ignorant of; he does not lie when he spreads an error of which he himself is the dupe; he does not lie when he is mistaken. The ideal description of the liar would be a cynical consciousness, affirming truth within himself, denying it in his words, and denying that negation as such. Now this doubly negative attitude rests on the transcendent; the fact expressed is transcendent since it does not exist, and the original negation rests on a *truth*; that is, on a particular type of transcendence. As for the inner negation which I effect correlatively with the affirmation for myself of the truth, this rests on words; that is, on an event in the world. Furthermore the inner disposition of the liar is positive; it could be the object of an affirmative judgment. The liar intends to deceive and he does not seek to hide this intention from himself nor to disguise the translucency of consciousness; on the contrary, he has recourse to it when there is a question of deciding secondary behavior. It explicitly exercises a regulatory control over all attitudes. As for his flaunted intention of telling the truth ("I'd never want to deceive you! This is true! I swear it!")—all this, of course, is the object of an inner negation, but also it is not recognized by the liar as *his* intention. It is played, imitated, it is the intention of the character which he plays in the eyes of his questioner, but this character, precisely because he *does not exist*, is a transcendent. Thus the lie does not put into the play the inner structure of present consciousness; all the negations which constitute it bear on objects which by this fact are removed from consciousness. The lie then does not require special ontological foundation, and the explanations which the existence of negation in general requires are valid without change in the case of deceit. Of course we have described the ideal lie; doubtless it happens often enough that the liar is more or less the victim of his lie, that he half persuades himself of it. But these common, popular forms of the lie are also degenerate aspects of it; they represent intermediaries between falsehood and bad faith. The lie is a behavior of transcendence.

The lie is also a normal phenomenon of what Heidegger calls the *"Mit-sein."*[1] It presupposes my existence, the existence of the *Other*, my existence *for* the Other, and the existence of the Other *for* me. Thus there is no difficulty in holding that the liar must make the project of the lie in entire clarity and that he must possess a complete comprehension of the lie and of the truth which he is altering. It is sufficient that an over-all opacity hide his intentions from the *Other*; it is sufficient that the Other can take the lie for truth. By the lie consciousness affirms that it exists by nature as *hidden from the Other*; it utilizes for its own profit the ontological duality of myself and myself in the eyes of the Other.

The situation can not be the same for bad faith if this, as we have said, is indeed a lie to oneself. To be sure, the one who practices bad faith is hiding a displeasing truth or presenting as truth a pleasing untruth. Bad faith then has in appearance the structure of falsehood. Only what changes everything is the fact that in bad faith it is from myself that I am hiding the truth. Thus the duality of the deceiver and the deceived does not exist here. Bad faith on the contrary implies in essence the unity of a *single* consciousness. This does not mean that it can not be conditioned by the *Mit-sein* like all other phenomena of human reality, but the *Mit-sein* can call forth bad faith only by presenting itself as *a situation* which bad faith permits surpassing; bad faith does not come from outside to human reality. One does not undergo his bad faith; one is not infected with it; it is not a *state*. But consciousness affects itself with bad faith. There must be an original intention and a project of bad faith; this project implies a comprehension of bad faith as such and a pre-reflective apprehension (of) consciousness as affecting itself with bad faith. It follows first that the one to whom the lie is told and the one who lies are one and the same person, which means that I must know in my capacity as deceiver the truth which is hidden from me in my capacity as the one deceived. Better yet I must know the truth very exactly *in order* to conceal it more carefully—and this not at two different moments, which at a pinch would allow us to reestablish a semblance of duality—but in the unitary structure of a single project. How then can the lie subsist if the duality which conditions it is suppressed?

To this difficulty is added another which is derived from the total translucency of consciousness. That which affects itself with bad faith must be conscious (of) its bad faith since the being of consciousness is consciousness of being. It appears then that I must be in good faith, at least to the extent that I am conscious of my bad faith. But then this whole psychic system is annihilated. We must agree in fact that if I deliberately and cynically attempt to lie to myself, I fail completely in this undertaking; the lie falls back and collapses beneath my look; it is ruined *from behind* by the very consciousness of lying to myself which pitilessly constitutes itself well within my project as its very condition. We have here an *evanescent* phenomenon which exists only in and through its own differentiation. To be sure, these phenomena are frequent and we shall see that there is in fact an "evanescence" of bad faith, which, it is evident, vacillates continually between good faith and cynicism: Even though the existence of bad faith is very precarious, and though it belongs to the kind of psychic structures which we might call "metastable,"[2] it presents nonetheless an autonomous and durable form. It can even be the normal aspect of life for a very great number of people. A person can *live* in bad faith, which does not mean that he does not have abrupt awakenings to cynicism or to good faith, but which implies a constant and particular style of life. Our embarrassment then appears extreme since we can neither reject nor comprehend bad faith.

To escape from these difficulties people gladly have recourse to the unconscious. In the psychoanalytical interpretation, for example, they use the hypothesis of a censor, conceived as a line of demarcation with customs, passport division, currency control, *etc.*, to reestablish the duality of the deceiver and the deceived. Here instinct or, if you prefer, original drives and complexes of drives constituted by our individual history, make up *reality*. It is neither *true* nor *false* since it does not *exist for itself*. It simply *is,* exactly like this table, which is neither true nor false *in itself* but simply *real*. As for the conscious symbols of the instinct, this interpretation takes them not for appearances but for real psychic facts. Fear, forgetting, dreams exist really in the capacity of concrete facts of consciousness in the same way as the words and the attitudes of the liar are concrete, really existing patterns of behavior. The subject has the same relation to these phenomena as the deceived to the behavior of the deceiver. He establishes them in their reality and must interpret them. There is a *truth* in the activities of the deceiver; if the deceived could reattach them to the situation where the deceiver establishes himself and to his project of the lie, they would become integral parts of truth, by virtue of being lying conduct. Similarly there is a truth in the symbolic acts; it is what the psychoanalyst discovers when he reattaches them to the historical situation of the patient, to the unconscious complexes which they express, to the blocking of the censor. Thus the subject deceives himself about the *meaning* of his conduct, he apprehends it in its concrete existence but not in its *truth*, simply because he cannot derive it from an original situation and from a psychic constitution which remain alien to him.

By the distinction between the "id" and the "ego," Freud has cut the psychic whole into two. I *am* the ego but I *am not* the id. I hold no privileged position in relation to my unconscious psyche. I *am* my own psychic phenomena in so far as I establish them in their conscious reality. For example I am the impulse to steal this or that book from this bookstall. I am an integral part of the impulse; I bring it to light and I determine myself hand-in-hand with it to commit the theft. But I *am* not those psychic facts, in so far as I receive them passively and am obliged to resort to hypotheses about their origin and their true meaning, just as the scholar makes conjectures about the nature and essence of an external phenomenon. This theft, for example, which I interpret as an immediate impulse determined by the rarity, the interest, or the price of the volume which I am going to steal—it is in truth a process derived from self-punishment, which is attached more or less directly to an Oedipus complex. The impulse toward the theft contains a truth which can be reached only by more or less probable hypotheses. The criterion of this truth will be the number of conscious psychic facts which it explains; from a more pragmatic point of view it will be also the success of the psychiatric cure which it allows. Finally the discovery of this truth will necessitate the cooperation of the psychoanalyst, who appears as the *mediator* between my unconscious drives and my conscious life. The Other appears as being able to effect the synthesis between the unconscious thesis and the conscious antithesis. I can know myself only through the mediation of the other, which means that I stand in relation to *my* "id," in the position of the *Other*. If I have a little knowledge of psychoanalysis, I can, under circumstances particularly favorable, try to psychoanalyze myself. But this attempt can succeed only if I distrust every kind of intuition, only if I apply to my case *from the outside*, abstract schemes and rules already learned. As for the results, whether they are obtained by my efforts alone or with the cooperation of a technician, they will never have the certainty which intuition confers; they will possess simply the always increasing probability of scientific hypotheses. The hypothesis of the Oedipus complex, like the atomic theory, is nothing but an "experimental idea;" as Pierce said, it is not to be distinguished from the totality of experiences which it allows to be realized and the results which it enables us to foresee. Thus psychoanalysis substitutes for the notion of bad faith, the idea of a lie without a liar; it allows me to understand how it is possible for me to be lied to without lying to myself since it places me in the same relation to myself that the Other is in respect to me; it replaces the duality of the deceiver and the deceived, the essential condition of the lie, by that of the "id" and the "ego." It introduces into my subjectivity the deepest intersubjective structure of the *Mit-sein*. Can this explanation satisfy us?

Considered more closely the psychoanalytic theory is not as simple as it first appears. It is not accurate to hold that the "id" is presented as a thing in relation to the hypothesis of the psychoanalyst, for a thing is indifferent to the conjectures which we make concerning it, while the "id" on the contrary is sensitive to them when we approach the truth. Freud in fact reports resistance when at the end of the first period the doctor is approaching the truth. This resistance is objective behavior apprehended from without: the patient shows defiance, refuses to speak, gives fantastic accounts of his dreams, sometimes even removes himself completely from the psychoanalytic treatment. It is a fair question to ask what part of himself can thus resist. It can not be the "Ego," envisaged as a psychic totality of the facts of consciousness; this could not suspect that the psychiatrist is approaching the end since the ego's relation to the *meaning* of its own reactions is exactly like that of the psychiatrist himself. At the very most it is possible for the ego to appreciate objectively the degree of probability in the hypotheses set forth, as a witness of the psychoanalysis might be able to do, according to the number of subjective facts which they explain. Furthermore, this probability would appear to the ego to border on certainty, which he could not take offence at since most of the time it is he who by a *conscious* decision is in pursuit of the psychoanalytic therapy. Are we to say that the patient is disturbed by the daily revelations which the psychoanalyst makes to him and that he seeks to remove himself, at the same time pretending in his own eyes to wish to continue the treatment? In this case it is no longer possible to resort to the unconscious to explain bad faith; it is there in full consciousness, with all its contradictions. But this is not the way that the psychoanalyst means to explain this resistance; for him it is secret and deep, it comes from afar; it has its roots in the very thing which the psychoanalyst is trying to make clear.

Furthermore it is equally impossible to explain the resistance as emanating from the complex which the psychoanalyst wishes to bring to light. The complex as such is rather the collaborator of the psychoanalyst since it aims at expressing itself in clear consciousness, since it plays tricks on the censor and seeks to elude it. The only level on which we can locate the refusal of the subject is that of the censor. It alone can comprehend the questions or the revelations of the psychoanalyst as approaching more or less near to the real drives which it strives to repress—it alone because it alone *knows* what it is repressing.

If we reject the language and the materialistic mythology of psychoanalysis, we perceive that the censor in order to apply its activity with discernment must know what it is repressing. In fact if we abandon all the metaphors representing the repression as the impact of blind forces, we are compelled to admit that the censor must choose and in order to choose must be aware of so doing. How could it happen otherwise that the censor allows lawful sexual impulses to pass through, that it permits needs (hunger, thirst, sleep) to be expressed in clear consciousness? And how are we to explain that it can relax its surveillance, that it can even be deceived by the disguises of the instinct? But it is not sufficient that it discern the condemned drives; it must also apprehend them *as to be repressed*, which implies in it at the very least an awareness of its activity. In a word, how could the censor discern the impulses needing to be repressed without being conscious of discerning them? How can we conceive of a knowledge which is ignorant of itself? To know is to know that one knows, said Alain. Let us say rather: All knowing is consciousness of knowing. Thus the resistance of the patient implies on the level of the censor an awareness of the thing repressed as such, a comprehension of the end toward which the questions of the psychoanalyst are leading, and an act of synthetic connection by which it compares the *truth* of the repressed complex to the psychoanalytic hypothesis which aims at it. These various operations in their turn imply that the censor is conscious (of) itself. But what type of self-consciousness can the censor have? It must be the consciousness (of) being conscious of the drive to be repressed, but precisely *in order not be conscious of it*. What does this mean if not that the censor is in bad faith?

Psychoanalysis has not gained anything for us since in order to overcome bad faith, it has established between the unconscious and consciousness an autonomous consciousness in bad faith. The effort to establish a veritable duality and even a trinity (*Es, Ich, Ueberich* expressing themselves through the censor) has resulted in a mere verbal terminology. The very essence of the reflexive idea of hiding something from oneself implies the unity of one and the same psychic mechanism and consequently a double activity in the heart of unity, tending on the one hand to maintain and locate the thing to be concealed and on the other hand to repress and disguise it. Each of the two aspects of this activity is complementary to the other; that is, it implies the other in its being. By separating consciousness from the unconscious by means of the censor, psychoanalysis has not succeeded in dissociating the two phases of the act, since the libido is a blind conatus toward conscious expression and since the conscious phenomenon is a passive, faked result. Psychoanalysis has merely localized this double activity of repulsion and attraction on the level of the censor.

Furthermore the problem still remains of accounting for the unity of the total phenomenon (repression of the drive which disguises itself and "passes" in symbolic form), to establish comprehensible connections among its different phases. How can the repressed drive "disguise itself" if it does not include (1) the consciousness of being repressed, (2) the consciousness of having been pushed back because it is what it is, (3) a project of disguise? No mechanistic theory of condensation or of transference can explain these modifications by which the drive itself is affected, for the description of the process of disguise implies a veiled appeal to finality. And similarly how are we to account for the pleasure or the anguish which accompanies the symbolic and conscious satisfaction of the drive if consciousness does not include—beyond the censor— an obscure comprehension of the end to be attained as simultaneously desired and forbidden. By rejecting the conscious unity of the psyche, Freud is obliged to imply everywhere a magic unity linking distant phenomena across obstacles, just as sympathetic magic unites the spellbound person and the wax image fashioned in his likeness. The unconscious drive (*Trieb*) through magic is endowed with the character "repressed" or "condemned," which completely pervades it, colors it, and magically provokes its symbolism. Similarly the conscious phenomenon is entirely colored by its symbolic meaning although it can not apprehend this meaning by itself in clear consciousness.

Aside from its inferiority in principle, the explanation by magic does not avoid the coexistence—on the level of the unconscious, on that of the censor, and on that of consciousness—of two contradictory, complementary structures which reciprocally imply and destroy each other. Proponents of the theory have hypostasized and "reified" bad faith; they have not escaped it. This is what has inspired a Viennese psychiatrist, Steckel, to depart from the psychoanalytical tradition and to write in *La femme frigide*:[3] "Every time that I have been able to carry my investigations far enough, I have established that the crux of the psychosis was conscious." In addition the cases which he reports in his work bear witness to a pathological bad faith which the Freudian doctrine can not account for. There is the question, for example, of women whom marital infidelity has made frigid; that is, they succeed in hiding from themselves not complexes deeply sunk in half physiological darkness, but acts of conduct which are objectively discoverable, which they can not fail to record at the moment when they perform them. Frequently in fact the husband reveals to Steckel that his wife has given objective signs of pleasure, but the woman when questioned will fiercely deny them. Here we find a pattern of *distraction*. Admissions which Steckel was able to draw out inform us that these pathologically frigid women apply themselves to becoming distracted in advance from the pleasure which they dread; many for example at the time of the sexual act, turn their thoughts away toward their daily occupations, make up their household accounts. Will anyone speak of an unconscious here? Yet if the frigid woman thus distracts her consciousness from the pleasure which she experiences, it is by no means cynically and in full agreement with herself; *it is in order to prove to herself that she is frigid*. We have in fact to deal with a phenomenon of bad faith since the efforts taken in order not to be present to the experienced pleasure imply the recognition that the pleasure is experienced; they imply it *in order to deny it*. But we are no longer on the ground of psychoanalysis. Thus on the one hand the explanation by means of the unconscious, due to the fact that it breaks the psychic unity, can not account for the facts which at first sight it appeared to explain. And on the other hand, there exists an infinity of types of behavior in bad faith which explicitly reject this kind of explanation because their essence implies that they can appear only in the translucency of consciousness. We find that the problem which we had attempted to resolve is still untouched.

II. Patterns of bad faith

If we wish to get out of this difficulty, we should examine more closely the patterns of bad faith and attempt a description of them. This description will permit us perhaps to fix more exactly the conditions for the possibility of bad faith; that is, to reply to the question we raised at the outset: "What must be the being of man if he is to be capable of bad faith?"

Take the example of a woman who has consented to go out with a particular man for the first time. She knows very well the intentions which the man who is speaking to her cherishes regarding her. She knows also that it will be necessary sooner or later for her to make a decision. But she does not want to realize the urgency; she concerns herself only with what is respectful and discreet in the attitude of her companion. She does not apprehend this conduct as an attempt to achieve what we call "the first approach;" that is, she does not want to see possibilities of temporal development which his conduct presents. She restricts this behavior to what is in the present; she does not wish to read in the phrases which he addresses to her anything other than their explicit meaning. If he says to her, "I find you so attractive!" she disarms this phrase of its sexual background; she attaches to the conversation and to the behavior of the speaker, the immediate meanings, which she imagines as objective qualities. The man who is speaking to her appears to her sincere and respectful as the table is round or square, as the wall coloring is blue or gray. The qualities thus attached to the person she is listening to are in this way fixed in a permanence like that of things, which is no other than the projection of the strict present of the qualities into the temporal flux.

This is because she does not quite know what she wants. She is profoundly aware of the desire which she inspires, but the desire cruel and naked would humiliate and horrify her. Yet she would find no charm in a respect which would be only respect. In order to satisfy her, there must be a feeling which is addressed wholly to her *personality*—i.e., to her full freedom—and which would be a recognition of her freedom. But at the same time this feeling must be wholly desire; that is, it must address itself to her body as object. This time then she refuses to apprehend the desire for what it is; she does not even give it a name; she recognizes it only to the extent that it transcends itself toward admiration, esteem, respect and that it is wholly absorbed in the more refined forms which it produces, to the extent of no longer figuring anymore as a sort of warmth and density. But then suppose he takes her hand. This act of her companion risks changing the situation by calling for an immediate decision. To leave the band there is to consent in herself to flirt, to engage herself. To withdraw it is to break the troubled and unstable harmony which gives the hour its charm. The aim is to postpone the moment of decision as long as possible. We know what happens next; the young woman leaves her hand there, but she *does not notice* that she is leaving it. She does not notice because it happens by chance that she is at this moment all intellect. She draws her companion up to the most lofty regions of sentimental speculation; she speaks of Life, of her life, she shows herself in her essential aspect—a personality, a consciousness. And during this time the divorce of the body from the soul is accomplished; the hand rests inert between the warm hands of her companion—neither consenting nor resisting—a thing.

We shall say that this woman is in bad faith. But we see immediately that she uses various procedures in order to maintain herself in this bad faith. She has disarmed the actions of her companion by reducing them to being only what they are; that is, to existing in the mode of the in-itself. But she permits herself to enjoy his desire, to the extent that she will apprehend it as not being what it is, will recognize its transcendence. Finally while sensing profoundly the presence of her own body—to the degree of being disturbed perhaps—she realizes herself as *not being* her own body, and she contemplates it as though from above as a passive object to which events can *happen* but which can neither provoke them nor avoid them because all its possibilities are outside of it. What unity do we find in these various aspects of bad faith? It is a certain art of forming contradictory concepts which unite in themselves both an idea and the negation of that idea. The basic concept which is thus engendered, utilizes the double property of the human being, who is at once a *facticity* and a *transcendence*. These two aspects of human reality are and ought to be capable of a valid coordination. But bad faith does not wish either to coordinate them nor to surmount them in a synthesis. Bad faith seeks to affirm their identity while preserving their differences. It must affirm facticity as *being* transcendence and transcendence as *being* facticity, in such a way that at the instant when a person apprehends the one, he can find himself abruptly faced with the other.

We can find the prototype of formulae of bad faith in certain famous expressions—which have been rightly conceived to produce their whole effect in a spirit of bad faith. Take for example the title of a work by Jacques Chardonne, *Love Is Much More than Love.*[4] We see here how unity is established between present love in its facticity—"the contact of two skins," sensuality, egoism, Proust's mechanism of jealousy, Adler's battle of the *sexes, etc.*—and love as transcendence—Mauriac's "river of fire," the longing for the infinite, Plato's *eros*, Lawrence's deep cosmic intuition, etc. Here we leave facticity to find ourselves suddenly beyond the present and the factual condition of man, beyond the psychological, in the heart of metaphysics. On the other hand, the title of a play by Sarment, *I Am Too Great for Myself,*[5] which also presents characters in bad faith, throws us first into full transcendence in order suddenly to imprison us within the narrow limits of our factual essence. We will discover this structure again in the famous sentence: "He has become what he was" or in its no less famous opposite: "Eternity at last changes each man into himself."[6] It is well understood that these various formulae have only the appearance of bad faith; they have been conceived in this paradoxical form explicitly to shock the mind and discountenance it by an enigma. But it is precisely this appearance which is of concern to us. What counts here is that the formulae do not constitute new, solidly structured ideas; on the contrary, they are formed so as to remain in perpetual disintegration and so that we may slide at any time from naturalistic present to transcendence and *vice versa.*

We can see the use which bad faith can make of these judgments which all aim at establishing that I am not what I am. If I were only what I *am*, I could, for example, seriously consider an adverse criticism which someone makes of me, question myself scrupulously, and perhaps be compelled to recognize the truth in it. But thanks to transcendence, I am not subject to all that I am. I do not even have to discuss the justice of the reproach. As Suzanne says to Figaro, "To prove that I am right would be to recognize that I can be wrong." I am on a plane where no reproach can touch me since what I really am is my transcendence. I flee from myself, I escape myself, I leave my tattered garment in the hands of the fault-finder. But the ambiguity necessary for bad faith comes from the fact that I affirm here that I *am* my transcendence in the mode of being of a thing. It is only thus, in fact, that I can feel that I escape all reproaches. It is in the sense that our young woman purifies the desire of anything humiliating by being willing to consider it only as pure transcendence, which she avoids even naming. But inversely "I Am Too Great for Myself," while showing our transcendence changed into facticity, is the source of an infinity of excuses for our failures or our weaknesses. Similarly the young coquette maintains transcendence to the extent that the respect, the esteem manifested by the actions of her admirer are already on the plane of the transcendent. But she arrests this transcendence, she glues it down with all the facticity of the present; respect is nothing other than respect, it is an arrested surpassing which no longer surpasses itself toward anything.

But although this *metastable* concept of "transcendence-facticity" is one of the most basic instruments of bad faith, it is not the only one of its kind. We can equally well use another kind of duplicity derived from human reality which we will express roughly by saying that its being-for-itself implies complementarily a being-for-others. Upon any one of my conducts it is always possible to converge two looks, mine and that of tile Other. The conduct will not present exactly the same structure in each case. But as we shall see later, as each look perceives it, there is between these two aspects of my being, no difference between appearance and being—as if I were to my self the truth of myself and as if the Other possessed only a deformed image of me. The equal dignity of being, possessed by my being-for-others and by my being-for-myself permits a perpetually disintegrating synthesis and a perpetual game of escape from the for-itself to the for-others and from the for-others to the for-itself. We have seen also the use which our young lady made of our being-in-the-midst-of-the-world—*i.e.*, of our inert presence as a passive object among other objects—in order to relieve herself suddenly from the functions of her being-in-the-world—that is, from the being which causes there to be a world by projecting itself beyond the world toward its own possibilities. Let us note finally the confusing syntheses which play on the nihilating ambiguity of these temporal ekstases, affirming at once that I am what I have been (the man who deliberately *arrests himself* at one period in his life and refuses to take into consideration the later changes) and that I am not what I have been (the man who in the face of reproaches or rancor dissociates himself from his past by insisting on his freedom and on his perpetual re-creation). In all these concepts, which have only a transitive role in the reasoning and which are eliminated from the conclusion (like hypochondriacs in the calculations of physicians), we find again the same structure. We have to deal with human reality as a being which is what it is not and which is not what it is.

But what exactly is necessary in order for these concepts of disintegration to be able to receive even a pretence of existence, in order for them to be able to appear for an instant to consciousness, even in a process of evanescence? A quick examination of the idea of sincerity, the antithesis of bad faith, will be very instructive in this connection. Actually sincerity presents itself as a demand and consequently is not a *state*. Now what is the ideal to be attained in this case? It is necessary that a man be *for himself* only what he *is*. But is this not precisely the definition of the in-itself—or if you prefer—the principle of identity? To posit as an ideal the being of things, is this not to assert by the same stroke that this being does not belong to human reality and that the principle of identity, far from being a universal axiom universally applied, is only a synthetic principle enjoying a merely regional universality? Thus in order that the concepts of bad faith can put us under illusion at least for an instant, in order that the candor of "pure hearts" (*cf.* Gide, Kessel) can have validity for human reality as an ideal, the principle of identity must not represent a constitutive principle of human reality and human reality must not be necessarily what it is but must be able to be what it is not. What does this mean?

If man is what he is, bad faith is for ever impossible and candor ceases to be his ideal and becomes instead his being. But is man what he is? And more generally, how can he *be* what he is when he exists as consciousness of being? If candor or sincerity is a universal value, it is evident that the maxim "one must be what one is" does not serve solely as a regulating principle for judgments and concepts by which I express what I am. It posits not merely an ideal of knowing but an ideal of *being*; it proposes for us an absolute equivalence of being with itself as a prototype of being. In this sense it is necessary that we *make ourselves* what we are. But what *are we* then if we have the constant obligation to make ourselves what we are, if our mode of being is having the obligation to be what we are?

Let us consider this waiter in the café. His movement is quick and forward, a little too precise, a little too rapid. He comes toward the patrons with a step a little too quick. He bends forward a little too eagerly; his voice, his eyes express an interest a little too solicitous for the order of the customer. Finally there he returns, trying to imitate in his walk the inflexible stiffness of some kind of automaton while carrying his tray with the recklessness of a tight-rope-walker by putting it in a perpetually unstable, perpetually broken equilibrium which he perpetually reestablishes by a light movement of the arm and hand. All his behavior seems to us a game. He applies himself to chaining his movements as if they were mechanisms, the one regulating the other; his gestures and even his voice seem to be mechanisms; he gives himself the quickness and pitiless rapidity of things. He is playing, he is amusing himself. But what is he playing? We need not watch long before we can explain it: he is playing *at being* a waiter in a café. There is nothing there to surprise us. The game is a kind of marking out and investigation. The child plays with his body in order to explore it, to take inventory of it; the waiter in the café plays with his condition in order to *realize* it. This obligation is not different from that which is imposed on all tradesmen. Their condition is wholly one of ceremony. The public demands of them that they realize it as a ceremony; there is the dance of the grocer, of the tailor, of the auctioneer, by which they endeavour to persuade their clientele that they are nothing but a grocer, an auctioneer, a tailor. A grocer who dreams is offensive to the buyer, because such a grocer is not wholly a grocer. Society demands that he limit himself to his function as a grocer, just as the soldier at attention makes himself into a soldier-thing with a direct regard which does not see at all, which is no longer meant to see, since it is the rule and not the interest of the moment which determines the point he must fix his eyes on (the sight "fixed at ten paces"). There are indeed many precautions to imprison a man in what he is, as if we lived in perpetual fear that he might escape from it, that he might break away and suddenly elude his condition.

In a parallel situation, from within, the waiter in the café can not be immediately a café waiter in the sense that this inkwell *is* an inkwell, or the glass *is* a glass. It is by no means that he can not form reflective judgments or concepts concerning his condition. He knows well what it "means:" the obligation of getting up at five o'clock, of sweeping the floor of the shop before the restaurant opens, of starting the coffee pot going, *etc*. He knows the rights which it allows: the right to the tips, the right to belong to a union, *etc*. But all these concepts, all these judgments refer to the transcendent. It is a matter of abstract possibilities, of rights and duties conferred on a "person possessing rights." And it is precisely this person *who I have to be* (if I am the waiter in question) and who I am not. It is not that I do not wish to be this person or that I want this person to be different. But rather there is no common measure between his being and mine. It is a "representation" for others and for myself, which means that I can be he only in *representation*. But if I represent myself as him, I am not he; I am separated from him as the object from the subject, separated *by nothing*, but this nothing isolates me from him. I can not be he, I can only play *at being* him; that is, imagine to myself that I am he. And thereby I affect him with nothingness. In vain do I fulfill the functions of a café waiter. I can be he only in the neutralized mode, as the actor is Hamlet, by mechanically making the *typical gestures* of my state and by aiming at myself as an imaginary café waiter through those gestures taken as an "analogue."[7] What I attempt to realize is a being-in-itself of the café waiter, as if it were not just in my power to confer their value and their urgency upon my duties and the rights of my position, as if it were not my free choice to get up each morning at five o'clock or to remain in bed, even though it meant getting fired. As if from the very fact that I sustain this role in existence I did not transcend it on every side, as if I did not constitute myself as one *beyond* my condition. Yet there is no doubt that I *am* in a sense a café waiter—otherwise could I not just as well call myself a diplomat or a reporter? But if I am one, this can not be in the mode of being in-itself. I am a waiter in the mode of *being what I am not*.

Furthermore we are dealing with more than mere social positions; I am never any one of my attitudes, any one of my actions. The good speaker is the one who *plays* at speaking, because he can not *be speaking*. The attentive pupil who wishes to *be* attentive, his eyes riveted on the teacher, his ears open wide, so exhausts himself in playing the attentive tole that he ends up by no longer hearing anything. Perpetually absent to my body, to my acts, I am despite myself that "divine absence" of which Valéry speaks. I can not say either that I *am* here or that I *am* not here, in the sense that we say "that box of matches *is* on the table;" this would be to confuse my "being-in-the-world" with a "being-in the midst of the world." Nor that I *am* standing, nor that I *am* seated; this would be to confuse my body with the idiosyncratic totality of which it is only one of the structures. On all sides I escape being and yet—I am.

Notes

1   A "being-with" others in the world. Tr.
2   Sartre's own word, meaning subject to sudden changes or transitions. Tr.
3   N.R.F.
4   *L'amour, c'est beaucoup plus que l'amour.*
5   *Je suis trop grand pour moi.*
6   *Il est devenu ce qu'il était. Tel qu'en lui-même enfin l'éternité le change.*
7   Cf. *L'Imaginaire.* Conclusion.

12 Others

The distinction between *being-for-itself* and *being-in-itself*, although mutually exclusive, is not collectively exhaustive. There exists a third manner of being called 'being-for-others' (*l'être-pour-autrui*). *Being-for-others* is exhibited by exactly the same beings whose being is *being-for-itself*: human beings. In *being-for-others* I am in a state that entails the existence of someone else. Under the heading of 'Being-for-others' Sartre attempts a refutation of solipsism, offers a phenomenology of the body, and a rather pessimistic ontology of human relations. I say something about each of these in turn.

Solipsism is the doctrine that only my mind exists. Putative refutations of solipsism usually either maintain, inductively, that other people have minds because they look and behave like me and I have a mind, or, it is argued that the formulation of solipsism as a theory presupposes its falsity. For example, Hegel argues in *The Phenomenology of Spirit* that one consciousness being a self-consciousness depends upon an encounter with another consciousness. Solipsism presupposes self-consciousness, so solipsism presupposes at least one other consciousness and so is false. Wittgenstein in *Philosophical Investigations* (1953) argues that solipsism presupposes a logically private language for its formulation. A logically private language is impossible because any language presupposes a public language. A public language presupposes other language users, therefore solipsism may be formulated just on condition it is false.

Sartre takes neither of these routes. His refutation is based upon human emotion, paradigmatically, *shame*. Sartre invites us to imagine that listening through a door and looking through a keyhole I suddenly hear footsteps behind me. I am under the gaze of the other. I feel shame. Shame however is shame *before another*. In this situation it is not a psychological option for me to sincerely doubt that other people exist or have minds.

Sartre's phenomenology of the body is a description of the asymmetries which obtain between one's own body, the body that I am, and the bodies of others: the bodies I may observe or encounter in a third person way. My own body is not for me *a thing*. It is a thing from the perspective of another, and another's body is a thing from my perspective, but my own body is not presented to me as an object in the world; as something I could encounter or straightforwardly observe.

Sartre is not denying that each of us experiences his own body. I have a limited visual perspective onto the front of my body from the shoulders downwards. However, I can not see my own head and back. I also have a kinaesthetic awareness of the relative positions of the parts of my body, but not of their locations in the world.

As subject the body cannot be object and as object the body cannot be subject. For example, the eyes that are seeing can not see themselves. Although I can see using my eyes I can not see my seeing. There could be a human being, or an operation on a human being, such that one of the two eyes could watch the other while the other watched objects in the world. Nevertheless, in such a case, I am adopting the standpoint of the other in relation to one of my eyes. The eye that sees still does not see the eye that sees.

Similarly, my hand may touch objects in the world, and I may touch one of my hands with the other. However, my hand can not touch itself, or, at least, the part that is touching is not touching itself. Sartre says 'we are dealing with two essentially different orders of reality. To touch and to be touched' (*Being and Nothingness*, p. 304). Always, being the subject of an experience precludes being simultaneously the object of that same experience.

We see here a new level on which *being-for-itself* and *being in itself* are incommensurable. My body as I experience it is *pour-soi*. My body as experienced by another is *en-soi*. There are not two numerically distinct bodies, but there are two radically distinct modes of being exhibited by one and the same body: subjective and objective, free and mechanical, lived and observed.

This is a dualism of perspectives, not a dualism of entities. The phenomenology of the human body derived from *being one* is radically distinct from that derived from *observing one*, encountering one as a thing in the external world.

What is the relation between conscious and this body that I am? Sartre's view is that *being-for-itself* is primordial with regard to both consciousness and the body. Unless there were the subjective type of being called 'Being-for-itself' there could not obtain the distinction between consciousness and the body.

By 'being-for-others' Sartre means my mode of being, my overall state of experience, when I take myself to be as others perceive me, or when I make myself be as others perceive me, or both. My taking myself to be an object or 'thing' in the world is a paradigm case of being-for-others. It is adopting towards myself the kind of perspective that others have on me. Being-for-others is therefore a kind of bad faith. It is not a false belief about myself because there is a way in which I appear to others and this is thinkable by me. However, it is not how I am and it is not how I experience myself to be. To this extent it is inauthentic and unreal. It does not correspond to my own lived experience.

Consciously or not, the phenomenology of human relations that Sartre offers essentially operates with the parameters of Hegel's *Master and Slave Dialectic* in the 1807 *The Phenomenology of Spirit*. There self-conscious beings are depicted as mutually constituting through a struggle for recognition: a power struggle where one party may bestow or withhold psychological identity from another, a complex dialectic where the freedom of one is sought in the control of the other.

Sartre says that his descriptions of human relations have to be understood within the perspective of conflict. The possibility, if not the actuality, of conflict is a necessary condition for there being any human relations whatsoever. Conflict is ultimately conflict over freedom. In trying to define my own essence through the exercise of free choice I try to repress the freedom of the other. Simultaneously, the other is doing the same. It follows that the perverse form of bad faith called 'being a swine' ('salaud') is at the root of human relations.

It is Sartre's view that there is no human encounter where one party does not psychologically dominate the other: one is master and one is slave. If two strangers pass in the street 'the look' ('*le regard*') of one will make the other uncomfortably subservient.

This is not simply a psychological generalisation. Sartre has philosophical premises for why it should be so. He subscribes to the Hegelian doctrine that my being what I am is partly due to the recognition or acceptance by others of what I am. This is a kind of bad-faith according to Sartre because I really or authentically am what my freedom makes me. Nevertheless, my being a waiter, a woman, a soldier, a leader, or my adopting any role, depends upon the acquiescence of others. The other holds the secret of what I am. It follows that the other may choose to bestow or withhold his recognition of what I am. My psychological security, my social identity as a person, is subject to the freedom of the other. The other 'has a hold' over me.

For this reason I try to deny the freedom of the other and the other tries to deny mine. In denying each other's freedom we are exercising our own. This is the antagonistic power-struggle that pervades all human relations according to Sartre. It has no optimistic resolution.

Why, we might object, should not conflict be overcome in love? Why should not two human beings, who perhaps care more for each other than they do for themselves, feel secure in each other's freedom and not threaten one another's psychological security? Sartre's reply is that love is a conflict.

Love is a conflict because the love of the lover can always be withdrawn. There is no absolute security in love and it is in the nature of love not to require such absolute security. Love presupposes freedom. Love is freely bestowed and freely withheld. The lover wants the object of their love to love them, but to love them freely. The lover would not feel loved if who they loved was forced to love them. To be loved is to be freely loved. However, to love freely implies the possibility of not loving, and to be loved freely implies the possibility of not being loved. To be truly loved involves the perpetual possibility of that love being withdrawn. Love implies insecurity.

Love presupposes freedom but freedom does not presuppose love, and freedom for Sartre is in many ways a terrible thing. Indeed the layers of human interaction in which each of us is implicated accentuate our bad faith. Our being-for-others hides our freedom from ourselves, and this is as true of loving relationships as much as sadistic ones. Sartre thinks the dialectic of freedom and domination is more fundamental than the moral distinction between acts of love and acts of sadism. In the 1944 play *No Exit* (*Huis Clos*), which is set in hell, Joseph Garcin says 'l'enfer, c'est les Autres', 'Hell is other people'.

BEING AND NOTHINGNESS

Concrete relations with others

[...] since the original bond with the Other first arises in connection with the relation between my body and the Other's body, it seemed clear to us that the knowledge of the nature of the body was indispensable to any study of the particular relations of my being with that of the Other. These particular relations, in fact, on both sides presuppose facticity; that is, our existence as body in the midst of the world. Not that the body is the instrument and the cause of my relations with others. But the body constitutes their meaning and marks their limits. It is as body-in-situation that I apprehend the Other's transcendence-transcended, and it is as body-in-situation that I experience myself in my alienation for the Other's benefit. Now we can examine these concrete relations since we are cognizant of what the body is. They are not simple specifications of the fundamental relation. Although each one of them includes within it the original relation with the Other as its essential structure and its foundation, they are entirely new modes of being on the part of the for-itself. In fact they represent the various attitudes of the for-itself in a world where there are Others. Therefore each relation in its own way presents the bilateral relation: for-itself-for-others, in-itself. If then we succeed in making explicit the structures of our most primitive relations with the Other-in-the-world, we shall have completed our task. At the beginning of this work, we asked, "What are the relations of the for-itself with the in-itself?" We have learned now that our task is more complex. There is a relation of the for-itself with the in-itself *in the presence of the Other*. When we have described this concrete fact, we shall be in a position to form conclusions concerning the fundamental relations of the three modes of being, and we shall perhaps be able to attempt a metaphysical theory of being in general.

The for-itself as the nihilation of the in-itself temporalizes itself as a *flight toward*. Actually it surpasses its facticity (*i.e.*, to be either *given* or past or body) toward the in-itself which it would be if it were able to be its own foundation. This may be translated into terms already psychological—and hence inaccurate although perhaps clearer—by saying that the for-itself attempts to escape its factual existence (*i.e.*, its being there, as an in-itself for which it is in no way the foundation) and that this flight takes place toward an impossible future always pursued where the for-itself would be an in-itself-for-itself—*i.e.*, an in-itself which would be to itself its own foundation. Thus the for-itself is both a flight and a pursuit; it flees the in-itself and at the same time pursues it. The for-itself is a pursued-pursuing. But in order to lessen the danger of a psychological interpretation of the preceding remarks, let us note that the for-itself is not *first* in order to attempt *later* to attain being; in short we must not conceive of it as an existent which would be provided with tendencies as this glass is provided with certain particular qualities. This pursuing flight is not given which is added on to the being of the for-itself. The for-itself *is* this very flight. The flight is not to be distinguished from the original nihilation. To say that the for-itself is a pursued-pursuing, or that it is in the mode of having to be its being, or that it is not what it is and is what it is not—each of these statements is saying the same thing. The for-itself is not the in-itself and can not be it. But it is a relation to the in-itself. It is even the sole relation possible to the in-itself. Cut off on every side by the in-itself, the for-itself can not escape it because the for-itself is *nothing* and it is separated from the in-itself by *nothing*. The for-itself is the foundation of all negativity and of all relation. *The for-itself is relation*.

Such being the case, the upsurge of the Other touches the for-itself in its very heart. By the Other and for the Other the pursuing flight is fixed in in-itself. Already the in-itself was progressively recapturing it; already it was at once a radical negation of fact, an absolute positing of value and yet wholly paralyzed with facticity. But at least it was escaping by temporalization; at least its character as a totality detotalized conferred on it a perpetual "elsewhere." Now it is this very totality which the Other makes appear before him and which he transcends toward his own "elsewhere." It is this totality which is totalized. For the Other I am irremediably what I am, and my very freedom is a given characteristic of my being. Thus the in-self recaptures me at the threshold of the future and fixes me wholly in my very flight, which becomes a flight foreseen and contemplated, a *given* flight. But this fixed flight is never the flight which I am for myself; it is fixed *outside*. The objectivity of my flight I experience as an alienation which I can neither transcend nor know. Yet by the sole fact that I experience it and that it confers on my flight that in-itself which it flees, I must turn back toward it and assume *attitudes* with respect to it.

Such is the origin of my concrete relations with the Other; they are wholly governed by my attitudes with respect to the object which I am for the Other. And as the Other's existence reveals to me the being which I am without my being able either to appropriate that being or even to conceive it, this existence will motivate two opposed attitudes: First—The Other *looks* at me and as such he holds the secret of my being, he knows what I *am*. Thus the profound meaning of my being is outside of me, imprisoned in an absence. The Other has the advantage over me. Therefore in so far as I am fleeing the in-itself which I am without founding it, I can attempt to deny that being which is conferred on me from outside; that is, I can turn back upon the Other so as to make an object out of him in turn since the Other's object-ness destroys my object-ness for him. But on the other hand, in so far as the Other as freedom is the foundation of my being-in-itself, I can seek to recover that freedom and to possess it without removing from it its character as freedom. In fact if I could identify myself with that freedom which is the foundation of my being-in-itself, I should be to myself my own foundation. To transcend the Other's transcendence, or, on the contrary, to incorporate that transcendence within me without removing from it its character as transcendence—such are the two primitive attitudes which I assume confronting the Other. Here again we must understand the words exactly. It is not true that I first am and then later "seek" to make an object of the Other or to assimilate him; but to the extent that the upsurge of my being is an upsurge in the presence of the Other, to the extent that I am a pursuing flight and a pursued-pursuing, I am—at the very root of my being—the project of assimilating and making an object of the Other. I am the proof of the Other. That is the original fact. But this proof of the Other is in itself an attitude toward the Other; that is, I can not *be in the presence of the Other* without being that "in-the-presence" in the form of having to be it. Thus again we are describing the for-itself's structures of being although the Other's presence in the world is an absolute and self-evident fact, but a contingent fact—that is, a fact impossible to deduce from the ontological structures of the for-itself.

These two attempts which I am are opposed to one another. Each attempt is the death of the other; that is, the failure of the one motivates the adoption of the other. Thus there is no dialectic for my relations toward the Other but rather a circle—although each attempt is enriched by the failure of the other. Thus we shall study each one in turn. But it should be noted that at the very core of the one the other remains always present, precisely because neither of the two can be held without contradiction. Better yet, each of them is in the other and endangers the death of the other. Thus we can never get outside the circle. We must not forget these facts as we approach the study of these fundamental attitudes toward the Other. Since these attitudes are produced and destroyed in a circle, it is as arbitrary to begin with the one as with the other. Nevertheless since it is necessary to choose, we shall consider first the conduct in which the for-itself tries to assimilate the Other's freedom.

I. First attitude toward others: love, language, masochism

Everything which may be said of me in my relations with the Other applies to him as well. While I attempt to free myself from the hold of the Other, the Other is trying to free himself from mine; while I seek to enslave the Other, the Other seeks to enslave me. We are by no means dealing with unilateral relations with an object-in-itself, but with reciprocal and moving relations. The following descriptions of concrete behavior must therefore be envisaged within the perspective of *conflict*. Conflict is the original meaning of being-for-others.

If we start with the first revelation of the Other as a *look*, we must recognize that we experience our inapprehensible being-for-others in the form of a *possession*. I am possessed by the Other; the Other's look fashions my body in its nakedness, causes it to be born, sculptures it, produces it as it *is*, sees it as I shall never see it. The Other holds a secret—the secret of what I am. He makes me be and thereby he possess me, and this possession is nothing other than the consciousness of possessing me. I in the recognition of my object-state have proof that he has this consciousness. By virtue of consciousness the Other is for me simultaneously the one who has stolen my being from me and the one who causes "there to be" a being which is my being. Thus I have a comprehension of this ontological structure: I am responsible for my being-for-others, but I am not the foundation of it. It appears to me therefore in the form of a contingent given for which I am nevertheless responsible; the Other founds my being in so far as this being is in the form of the "there is." But he is not responsible for my being although he founds it in complete freedom—in and by means of his free transcendence. Thus to the extent that I am revealed to myself as responsible for my being, I *lay claim to* this being which I am; that is, I wish to recover it, or, more exactly, I am the project of the recovery of my being. I want to stretch out my hand and grab hold of this being which is presented to me as *my being* but at a distance—like the dinner of Tantalus; I want to found it by my very freedom. For if in one sense my being-as-object is an unbearable contingency and the pure "possession" of myself by another, still in another sense this being stands as the indication of what I should be obliged to recover and found in order to be the foundation of myself. But this is conceivable only if I assimilate the Other's freedom. Thus my project of recovering myself is fundamentally a project of absorbing the Other.

Nevertheless this project must leave the Other's nature intact. Two consequences result: (1) I do not thereby cease to assert the Other—that is, to deny concerning myself that I am the Other. Since the Other is the foundation of my being, he could not be dissolved in me without my being-for-others disappearing. Therefore if I project the realization of unity with the Other, this means that I project my assimilation of the Other's Otherness as my own possibility. In fact the problem for me is to make myself be by acquiring the possibility of taking the Other's point of view on myself. It is not a matter of acquiring a pure, abstract faculty of knowledge. It is not the pure *category* of the Other which I project appropriating to myself. This category is not conceived nor even conceivable. But on the occasion of concrete experience with the Other, an experience suffered and realized, it is this concrete Other as an absolute reality whom in his otherness I wish to incorporate into myself. (2) The Other whom I wish to assimilate is by no means the Other-as-object. Or, if you prefer, my project of incorporating the Other in no way corresponds to a recapturing of my for-itself as myself and to a surpassing of the Other's transcendence toward my own possibilities. For me it is not a question of obliterating my object-state by making an object of the Other, which would amount to *releasing* myself from my being-for-others. Quite the contrary, I want to assimilate the Other as the Other-looking-at-me, and this project of assimilation includes an augmented recognition of my being-looked-at. In short, in order to maintain before me the Other's freedom which is looking at me, I identify myself totally with my being-looked-at. And since my being-as-object is the only possible relation between me and the Other, it is this being-as-object which alone can serve me as an instrument to effect my assimilation of the *other freedom*.

Thus as a reaction to the failure of the third ekstasis, the for-itself wishes to be identified with the Other's freedom as founding its own being-in-itself. To be other to oneself—the ideal always aimed at concretely in the form of being *this Other* to oneself—is the primary value of my relations with the Other. This means that my being-for-others is haunted by the indication of an absolute-being which would he itself as other and other as itself and which by freely giving to itself its being-itself as other and its being-other as itself, would be the very being of the ontological proof—that is, God. This ideal can not be realized without my surmounting the original contingency of my relations to the Other; that is, by overcoming the fact that there is no relation of internal negativity between the negation by which the Other is made other than I and the negation by which I am made other than the Other. We have seen that this contingency is insurmountable; it is the *fact* of my relations with the Other, just as my body is the *fact* of my being-in-the-world. Unity with the Other is therefore *in fact* unrealizable. It is also unrealizable *in theory*, for the assimilation of the for-itself and the Other in a single transcendence would necessarily involve the disappearance of the characteristic of otherness in the Other. Thus the condition on which I project the identification of myself with the Other is that I persist in denying that I am the Other. Finally this project of unification is the source of *conflict* since while I experience myself as an object for the Other and while I project assimilating him in and by means of this experience, the Other apprehends me as an object in the midst of the world and does not project identifying me with himself. It would therefore be necessary—since being-for-others includes a double internal negation—to act upon the internal negation by which the Other transcends my transcendence and makes me exist for the Other; that is, *to act upon the Other's freedom*.

This unrealizable ideal which haunts my project of myself in the presence of the Other is not to be identified with love in so far as love is an enterprise; *i.e.*, an organic ensemble of projects toward my own possibilities. But it is the ideal of love, its motivation and its end, its unique value. Love as the primitive relation to the Other is the ensemble of the projects by which I aim at realizing this value.

These projects put me in direct connection with the Other's freedom. It is in this sense that love is a conflict. We have observed that the Other's freedom is the foundation of my being. But precisely because I exist by means of the Other's freedom, I have no security; I am in danger in this freedom. It moulds my being and *makes me be*, it confers values upon me and removes them from me; and my being receives from it a perpetual passive escape from self. Irresponsible and beyond reach, this protean freedom in which I have engaged myself can in turn engage me in a thousand different ways of being. My project of recovering my being can he realized only if I get hold of this freedom and reduce it to being a freedom subject to my freedom. At the same time it is the only way in which I can act on the free negation of interiority by which the Other constitutes me as an Other; that is the only way in which I can prepare the way for a future identification of the Other with me. This will be clearer perhaps if we study the problem from a purely psychological aspect. Why does the lover want to be *loved*? If Love were in fact a pure desire for physical possession, it could in many cases be easily satisfied. Proust's hero, for example, who installs his mistress in his home, who can see her and possess her at any hour of the day, who has been able to make her completely dependent on him economically, ought to be free from worry. Yet we know that he is, on the contrary, continually gnawed by anxiety. Through her consciousness Albertine escapes Marcel even when he is at her side, and that is why he knows relief only when he gazes on her while she sleeps. It is certain then that the lover wishes to capture a "consciousness." But why does he wish it? And how?

The notion of "ownership," by which love is so often explained, is not actually primary. Why should I want to appropriate the Other if it were not precisely that the Other makes me be? But this implies precisely a certain mode of appropriation; it is the Other's freedom as such that we want to get hold of. Not because of a desire for power. The tyrant scorns love, he is content with fear. If he seeks to win the love of his subjects, it is for political reasons; and if he finds a more economical way to enslave them, he adopts it immediately. On the other hand, the man who wants to be loved does not desire the enslavement of the beloved. He is not bent on becoming the object of passion which flows forth mechanically. He does not want to possess an automaton, and if we want to humiliate him, we need only try to persuade him that the beloved's passion is the result of a psychological determinism. The lover will then feel that both his love and his being are cheapened. If Tristan and Isolde fall madly in love because of a love potion, they are less interesting. The total enslavement of the beloved kills the love of the lover. The end is surpassed; if the beloved is transformed into an automaton, the lover finds himself alone. Thus the lover does not desire to possess the beloved as one possesses a thing; he demands a special type of appropriation. He wants to possess a freedom as freedom.

On the other hand, the lover can not be satisfied with that superior form of freedom which is a free and voluntary engagement. Who would be content with a love given as pure loyalty to a sworn oath? Who would be satisfied with the words, "I love you because I have freely engaged myself to love you and because I do not wish to go back on my word." Thus the lover demands a pledge, yet is irritated by a pledge. He wants to be loved by a freedom but demands that this freedom as freedom should no longer be free. He wishes that the Other's freedom should determine itself to become love—and this not only at the beginning of the affair but at each instant—and at the same time he wants this freedom to be captured *by itself*, to turn back upon itself, as in madness, as in a dream, so as to will its own captivity. This captivity must be a resignation that is both free and yet chained in our hands. In love it is not a determinism of the passions which we desire in the Other nor a freedom beyond reach; it is a freedom which *plays the role of* a determinism of the passions and which is caught in its own role. For himself the lover does not demand that he be the *cause* of this radical modification of freedom but that he be the unique and privileged occasion of it. In fact he could not want to be the cause of it without immediately submerging the beloved in the midst of the world as a tool which can be transcended. That is not the essence of love. On the contrary, in Love the Lover wants to be "the whole World" for the beloved. This means that he puts himself on the side of the world; he is the one who assumes and symbolizes the world; he is a *this* which includes all other *thises*. He is and consents to be an *object*. But on the other hand, he wants to be the object in which the Other's freedom consents to lose itself, the object in which the Other consents to find his being and his *raison d'être* as his second facticity—the object-limit of transcendence, that toward which the Other's transcendence transcends all other objects but which it can in no way transcend. And everywhere he desires the circle of the Other's freedom; that is, at each instant as the Other's freedom accepts this limit to his transcendence, this acceptance is *already* present as the motivation of the acceptance considered. It is in the capacity of an end already chosen that the lover wishes to be chosen as an end. This allows us to grasp what basically the lover demands of the beloved; he does not want to *act* on the Other's freedom but to exist *a priori* as the objective limit of this freedom; that is, to be given at one stroke along with it and in its very upsurge as the limit which the freedom must accept in order to be free. By this very fact, what he demands is a liming, a gluing down of the Other's freedom by itself; this limit of structure is in fact a *given*, and the very appearance of the given as the limit of freedom means that the freedom *makes itself exist* within the given by being its own prohibition against surpassing it. This prohibition is envisaged by the lover *simultaneously* as something lived—that is, something suffered (in a word, as a facticity) and as something freely consented to. It must be freely consented to since it must be effected only with the upsurge of a freedom which chooses itself as freedom. But it must be only what is lived since it must be an impossibility always present, a facticity which surges back to the heart of the Other's freedom. This is expressed psychologically by the demand that the free decision to love me, which the beloved formerly has taken, must slip in as a magically determining motivation *within* his present free engagement.

Now we can grasp the meaning of this demand, the facticity which is to be a factual limit for the Other in my demand to be loved and which is to result in being *his own* facticity—this is *my* facticity. It is in so far as I am the object which the Other makes come into being that I must be the inherent limit to his very transcendence. Thus the Other by his upsurge into being makes me be as unsurpassable and absolute, not as a nihilating For-itself but as a being-for-others-in-the-midst-of-the-world. Thus to want to be loved is to infect the Other with one's own facticity; it is to wish to compel him to recreate you perpetually as the condition of a freedom which submits itself and which is engaged; it is to wish both that freedom found fact and that fact have pre-eminence over freedom. If this end could be attained, it would result in the first place in my being *secure* within the Other's consciousness. First because the motive of my uneasiness and my shame is the fact that I apprehend and experience myself in my being-for-others as that which can always be surpassed towards something else, that which is the pure object of a value judgment, a pure means, a pure tool. My uneasiness stems from the fact that I assume necessarily and freely that being which another makes me be in an absolute freedom. "God knows what I am for him! God knows what he thinks of me!" This means "God knows what he makes me be." I am haunted by this being which I fear to encounter someday at the turn of a path, this being which is so strange to me and which is yet *my being* and which I know that I shall never encounter in spite of all my efforts to do so. But if the Other loves me then I become the *unsurpassable*, which means that I must be the absolute end. In this sense I am saved from *instrumentality*. My existence in the midst of the world becomes the exact correlate of my transcendence-for-myself since my independence is absolutely safeguarded. The object which the Other must make me be is an object-transcendence, an absolute center of reference around which all the instrumental-things of the world are ordered as pure *means*. At the same time, as the absolute limit of freedom—*i.e.*, of the absolute source of all values—I am protected against any eventual devalorization.

I am the absolute value. To the extent that I assume my being-for-others, I assume myself as value. Thus to want to be loved is to want to be placed beyond the whole system of values posited by the Other and to be the condition of all valorization and the objective foundation of all values. This demand is the usual theme of lovers' conversations, whether as in *La Porte Etroite*, the woman who wants to be loved identifies herself with an ascetic morality of self-surpassing and wishes to embody the ideal limit of this surpassing—or as more usually happens, the woman in love demands that the beloved in his acts should sacrifice traditional morality for her and is anxious to know whether the beloved would betray his friends for her, "would steal for her," "would kill for her," *etc.*

From this point of view, my being must escape the *look* of the beloved, or rather it must be the object of a look with another structure. I must no longer be seen on the ground of the world as a "this" among other "thises," but the world must be revealed in terms of me. In fact to the extent that the upsurge of freedom makes a world exist, I must be, as the limiting-condition of this upsurge, the very condition of the upsurge of a world. I must be the one whose function is to make trees and water exist' to make cities and fields and other men exist, in order to give them later to the Other who arranges them into a world, just as the mother in matrilineal communities receives titles and the family name not to keep them herself but to transfer them immediately to her children. In one sense if I am to be loved, I am the object through whose procuration the world will exist for the Other; in another sense I am the world. Instead of being a "this" detaching itself on the ground of the world, I am the ground-as-object on which the world detaches itself. Thus I am re-assured; the Other's look no longer paralyzes me with finitude. It no longer fixes my being in *what I am*. I can no longer be *looked at* as ugly, as small, as cowardly, since these characteristics necessarily represent a factual limitation of my being and an apprehension of my finitude as finitude. To be sure, my possibles remain transcended possibilities, dead-possibilities; but I possess all possibles. I am all the dead-possibilities in the world; hence I cease to be the being who is understood from the standpoint of other beings or of its acts. In the loving intuition which I demand, I am to be given as an absolute totality in terms of which all its peculiar acts and all beings are to be understood. One could say, slightly modifying a famous pronouncement of the Stoics, that "the beloved can fail in three ways."[1] The ideal of the sage and the ideal of the man who wants to beloved actually coincide in this that both want to be an object-as-totality accessible to a global intuition which will apprehend the beloved's or the sage's actions in the world as partial structures which are interpreted in terms of the totality. Just as wisdom is proposed as a state to be attained by an absolute metamorphosis, so the Other's freedom must be absolutely metamorphosed in order to allow me to attain the state of being loved.

Up to this point our description would fall into line with Hegel's famous description of the Master and Slave relation. What the Hegelian Master is for the Slave, the lover wants to be for the beloved. But the analogy stops here, for with Hegel the master demands the Slave's freedom only laterally and, so to speak, implicitly, while the lover wants the beloved's freedom *first and foremost*. In this sense if I am to be loved by the Other, this means that I am to be freely chosen as beloved. As we know, in the current terminology of love, the beloved is often called *the chosen one*. But this choice must not be relative and contingent. The lover is irritated and feels himself cheapened when he thinks that the beloved has chosen him *from among others*. "Then if I had not come into a certain city, if I had not visited the home of so and so, you would never have known me, you wouldn't have loved me?" This thought grieves the lover; his love becomes one love among others and is limited by the beloved's facticity and by his own facticity as well as by the contingency of encounters. It becomes *love in the world*, an object which presupposes the world and which in turn can exist for others. What he is demanding he expresses by the awkward and vitiated phrases of "fatalism." He says, "We were made for each other," or again he uses the expression "soul mate." But we must translate all this. The lover knows very well that "being made for each other" refers to an original choice. This choice can be God's, since he is the being who is absolute choice, but God here represents only the farthest possible limit of the demand for an absolute. Actually what the lover demands is that the beloved should make of him an absolute choice. This means that the beloved's being-in-the-world must be a being-as-loving. The upsurge of the beloved must be the beloved's free choice of the lover. And since the Other is the foundation of my being-as-object, I demand of him that the free upsurge of his being should have his choice of *me* as his unique and absolute end; that is, that he should choose to be for the sake of founding my object-state and my facticity.

Thus my facticity is *saved*. It is no longer this unthinkable and insurmountable given which I am fleeing; it is that for which the Other freely makes himself exist; it is as an end which he has given to himself. I have infected him with my facticity, but as it is in the form of freedom that he has been infected with it' he refers it back to me as a facticity taken up and consented to. He is the foundation of it in order that it may be his end. By means of this love I then have a different apprehension of my alienation and of my own facticity. My facticity—as for-others—is no longer a fact but a right. My existence *is* because it is *given a name.* I am because I give myself away. These beloved veins on my hands exist—beneficently. How good I am to have eyes, hair, eyebrows and to lavish them away tirelessly in an overflow of generosity to this tireless desire which the Other freely makes himself be. Whereas before being loved we were uneasy about that unjustified, unjustifiable protuberance which was our existence, whereas we felt ourselves "*de trop,*" we now feel that out existence is taken up and willed even in its tiniest details by an absolute freedom which at the same time our existence conditions and which we ourselves will with our freedom. This is the basis for the joy of love when there is joy: we feel that our existence is justified.

By the same token if the beloved can love us, he is wholly ready to be assimilated by our freedom; for this being-loved which we desire is already the ontological proof applied to our being-for-others. Our objective essense implies the existence of the Other, and conversely it is the Other's freedom which founds our essence. If we could manage to interiorize the whole system, we should be our own foundation.

Such then is the real goal of the lover in so far as his love is an enterprise—*i.e.,* a project of himself. This project is going to provoke a conflict. The beloved in fact apprehends the lover as one Other-as-object among others; that is, he perceives the lover on the ground of the world, transcends him, and utilizes him. The beloved is a *look.* He can not therefore employ his transcendence to fix an ultimate limit to his surpassings, nor can he employ his freedom to captivate itself. The beloved can not will to love. Therefore the lover must seduce the beloved, and his love can in no way be distinguished from the enterprise of seduction. In seduction I do not try to reveal my subjectivity to the Other. Moreover I could do so only by *looking at* the other; but by this look I should cause the Other's subjectivity to disappear, and it is exactly this which I want to assimilate. To seduce is to risk assuming my object-state completely for the Other; it is to put myself beneath his look and to make him look at me; it is to risk the danger of *being-seen* in order to effect a new departure and to appropriate the Other in and by means of my object-ness. I refuse to leave the level on which I make proof of my object-ness; it is on this level that I wish to engage in battle by making myself a *fascinating object.* In Part Two we defined fascination as a *state.* It is, we said, the non-thetic consciousness of being *nothing* in the presence of being. Seduction aims at producing in the Other the consciousness of his state of nothingness as he confronts the seductive object. By seduction I aim at constituting myself as a fullness of being and at making myself *recognized as such.* To accomplish this I constitute myself as a meaningful object. My acts must *point* in two directions: On the one hand, toward that which is wrongly called subjectivity and which is rather a depth of objective and hidden being; the act is not performed for itself only, but it points to an infinite, undifferentiated series of other real and possible acts which I give as constituting my objective, unperceived being. Thus I try to guide the transcendence which transcends me and to refer it to the infinity of my dead-possibilities precisely in order to be the unsurpassable and to the exact extent to which the only unsurpassable is the infinite. On the other hand, each of my acts tries to point to the great density of possible-world and must present me as bound to the vastest regions of the world. At the same time I *present* the world to the beloved, and I try to constitute myself as the necessary intermediary between her and the world; I manifest by my acts infinitely varied examples of my power over the world (money, position, "connections," etc.). In the first case I try to constitute myself as an infinity of depth, in the second case to identify myself with the world. Through these different procedures I propose myself as unsurpassable. This proposal could not be sufficient in itself; it is only a besieging of the Other. It can not take on value as fact without the consent of the Other's freedom, which I must capture by making it recognize itself as nothingness in the face of my plenitude of absolute being.

Someone may observe that these various attempts at expression *presuppose* language. We shall not disagree with this. But we shall say rather that they *are* language or, if you prefer, a fundamental mode of language. For while psychological and historical problems exist with regard to the existence, the learning and the use of *a particular* language, there is no special problem concerning what is called the discovery or invention of language. Language is not a phenomenon added on to being-for-others. It *is* originally being-for-others; that is, it is the fact that a subjectivity experiences itself as an object for the Other. In a universe of pure objects language could under no circumstances have been "invented" since it presupposes an original relation to another subject. In the intersubjectivity of the for-others, it is not necessary to invent language because it is already given in the recognition of the Other. I *am* language. By the sole fact that whatever I may do, my acts freely conceived and executed, my projects launched toward my possibilities have outside of them a meaning which escapes me and which I experience. It is in this sense—and in this sense only—that Heidegger is right in declaring that *I am what I say*.[2] Language is not an instinct of the constituted human creature, nor is it an invention of our subjectivity. But neither does it need to be referred to the pure "being-outside-of-self" of the *Dasein*. It forms part of the *human condition*; it is originally the proof which a for-itself can make of its being for-others, and finally it is the surpassing of this proof and the utilization of it toward possibilities which are my possibilities; that is, toward my possibilities of being this or that for the Other. Language is therefore not distinct from the recognition of the Other's existence. The Other's upsurge confronting me as a look makes language arise as the condition of my being. This primitive language is not necessarily seduction; we shall see other forms of it. Moreover we have noted that there is another primitive attitude confronting the Other and that the two succeed each other in a circle, each implying the other. But conversely seduction does not presuppose any earlier form of language; it is the complete realization of language. This means that language can be revealed entirely and at one stroke by seduction as a primitive mode of being of expression. Of course by language we mean all the phenomena of expression and not the articulated word, which is a derived and secondary mode whose appearance can be made the object of an historical study. Especially in seduction language does not *aim* at *giving to be known* but at causing to experience.

But in this first attempt to find a fascinating language I proceed blindly since I am guided only by the abstract and empty form of my object-state for the Other. I can not even conceive what effect my gestures and attitudes will have since they will always be taken up and founded by a freedom which will surpass them and since they can have a meaning only if this freedom confers one on them. Thus the "meaning" of my expressions always escapes me. I never know exactly if I signify what I wish to signify nor even if I *am* signifying anything. It would be necessary that at the precise instant I should read in the Other what on principle is inconceivable. For lack of knowing what I actually express for the Other, I constitute my language as an incomplete phenomenon of flight outside myself. As soon as I express myself, I can only guess at the meaning of what I express—*i.e.*, the meaning of what I am—since in this perspective to express and to be are one. The Other is always there, present and experienced as the one who gives to language its meaning. Each expression, each gesture, each word is on my side a concrete proof of the alienating reality of the Other. It is only the psychopath who can say, someone has stolen my thought"—as in cases of psychoses of influence, for example.[3] The very fact of expression is a stealing of thought since thought needs the cooperation of an alienating freedom in order to be constituted as an object. That is why this first aspect of language—in so far as it is I who employ it for the Other—is *sacred*. The sacred object is an object which is in the world and which points to a transcendence beyond the world. Language reveals to me the freedom (the transcendence) of the one who listens to me in silence.

But at the same moment I remain for the Other a meaningful object—

that which I have always been. There is no path which departing from my object-state can lead the Other to my transcendence. Attitudes, expressions, and words can only indicate to him other attitudes, other expressions, and other words. Thus language remains for him a simple property of a magical object—and this magical object itself. It is an action at a distance whose effect the Other exactly knows. Thus the word is *sacred* when I employ it and *magic* when the Other hears it. Thus I do not know my language any more than I know my body for the Other. I can not hear myself speak nor see myself smile. The problem of language is exactly parallel to the problem of bodies, and the description which is valid in one case is valid in the other.

Fascination, however, even if it were to produce a state of being-fascinated in the Other could not by itself succeed in producing love. We can be fascinated by an orator, by an actor, by a tightrope-walker, but this does not mean that we love him. To be sure we can not take our eyes off him, but he is still raised on the ground of the world, and fascination does not posit the fascinating object as the ultimate term of the transcendence. Quite the contrary, fascination *is* transcendence. When then will the beloved become in turn the lover?

The answer is easy: when the beloved projects being loved. By himself the Other-as-object never has enough strength to produce love. If love has for its ideal the appropriation of the Other qua Other (*i.e.*, as a subjectivity which is looking at an object) this ideal can be projected only in terms of my encounter with the Other-as-subject, not with the Other-as-object. If the Other tries to seduce me by means of his object-state, then seduction can bestow upon the Other only the character of a precious object "to be possessed." Seduction will perhaps determine me to risk much to conquer the Other-as-object, but this desire to appropriate an object in the midst of the world should not be confused with love. Love therefore can be born in the beloved only from the proof which he makes of his alienation and his flight toward the Other. Still the beloved, if such is the case, will be transformed into a lover only if he projects being loved; that is, if what he wishes to overcome is not a body but the Other's subjectivity as such. In fact the only way that he could conceive to realize this appropriation is to make himself be loved. Thus it seems that to love is in essence the project of making oneself be loved. Hence this new contradiction and this new conflict: each of the lovers is entirely the captive of the Other inasmuch as each wishes to make himself loved by the Other to the exclusion of anyone else; but at the same time each one demands from the other a love which is not reducible to the "project of being-loved." What he demands in fact is that the Other without originally seeking to make himself be loved should have at once a contemplative and affective intuition of his beloved as the objective limit of his freedom, as the ineluctable and chosen foundation of his transcendence, as the totality of being and the supreme value. Love thus exacted from the other could not *ask for* anything; it is a pure engagement without reciprocity. Yet this love can not exist except in the form of a demand on the part of the lover.

The lover is held captive in a wholly different way. He is the captive of his very demand since love is the demand to be loved; he is a freedom which wills itself a body and which demands an outside, hence a freedom which imitates the flight toward the Other, a freedom which qua freedom lays claim to its alienation. The lover's freedom, in his very effort to make himself be loved as an object by the Other, is alienated by slipping into the body-for-others; that is, it is brought into existence with a dimension of flight toward the Other. It is the perpetual refusal to posit itself as pure selfness, for this affirmation of self as itself would involve the collapse of the Other as a look and the upsurge of the Other-as-object—hence a state of affairs in which the very possibility of being loved disappears since the Other is reduced to the dimension of objectivity. This refusal therefore constitutes freedom as dependent on the Other; and the Other as subjectivity becomes indeed an unsurpassable limit of the freedom of the for-itself, the goal and supreme end of the for-itself since the Other holds the key to its being. Here in fact we encounter the true ideal of love's enterprise: alienated freedom. But it is the one who wants to be loved who by the mere fact of wanting someone to love him alienates his freedom.

My freedom is alienated in the presence of the Other's pure subjectivity which founds my objectivity. It can never be alienated before the Other-as-object. In this form in fact the beloved's alienation, of which the lover dreams, would be contradictory since the beloved can found the being of the lover only by transcending it on principle toward other objects of the world; therefore this transcendence can constitute the object which it surpasses both as a transcended object and as an object limit of all transcendence. Thus each one of the lovers wants to be the object for which the Other's freedom is alienated in an original intuition; but this intuition which would be love in the true sense is only a contradictory ideal of the for-itself. Each one is alienated only to the exact extent to which he demands the alienation of the other. Each one wants the other to love him but does not take into account the fact that to love is to want to be loved and that thus by wanting the other to love him, he only wants the other to want to be loved in turn. Thus love relations are a system of indefinite reference—analogous to the pure "reflection-reflected" of consciousness—under the ideal standard of the *value* "love"; that is, in a fusion of consciousnesses in which each of them would preserve his otherness in order to found the other. This state of affairs is due to the fact that consciousnesses are separated by an insurmountable nothingness, a nothingness which is both the internal negation of the one by the other and a factual nothingness between the two internal negations. Love is a contradictory effort to surmount the factual negation while preserving the internal negation. I demand that the Other love me and I do everything possible to realize my project; but if the Other loves me, he radically deceives me by his very love. I demanded of him that he should found my being as a privileged object by maintaining himself as pure subjectivity confronting me; and as soon as he loves me he experiences me as subject and is swallowed up in his objectivity confronting my subjectivity.

The problem of my being-for-others remains therefore without solution. The lovers remain each one for himself in a total subjectivity; nothing comes to relieve them of their duty to make themselves exist each one for himself; nothing comes to relieve their contingency nor to save them from facticity. At least each one has succeeded in escaping danger from the Other's freedom—but altogether differently than he expected. He escapes not because the Other makes him be as the object-limit of his transcendence but because the Other experiences him as subjectivity and wishes to experience him only as such. Again the gain is perpetually compromised. At the start, each of the consciousnesses can at any moment free itself from its chains and suddenly contemplate the other as an *object*. Then the spell is broken; the Other becomes one mean among means. He is indeed an object for-others as the lover desires but an object-as-tool, a perpetually transcended object. The illusion, the game of mirrors which makes the concrete reality of love, suddenly ceases. Later in the experience of love each consciousness seeks to shelter its being-for-others in the Other's freedom. This supposes that the Other is beyond the world as pure subjectivity, as the absolute by which the world comes into being. But it suffices that the lovers should be *looked at* together by a third person in order for each one to experience not only his own objectivation but that of the other as well. Immediately the Other is no longer for me the absolute transcendence which founds me in my being; he is a transcendence-transcended, not by me but by another. My original relation to him—*i.e.*, my relation of being the beloved for my lover, is fixed as a dead-possibility. It is no longer the experienced relation between a limiting object of all transcendence and the freedom which founds it; it is a love-as-object which is wholly alienated toward the third. Such is the true reason why lovers seek solitude. It is because the appearance of a third person, whoever he may be, is the destruction of their love. But factual solitude (*e.g.* we are alone in my room) is by no means a theoretical solitude. Even if nobody sees us, we exist for *all* consciousnesses and we are conscious of existing for all. The result is that love as a fundamental mode of being-for-others holds in its being-for-others the seed of its own destruction.

We have just defined the triple destructibility of love: in the first place it is, in essence, a deception and a reference to infinity since to love is to wish to be loved, hence to wish that the Other wish that I love him. A preontological comprehension of this deception is given in the very impulse of love—hence the lover's perpetual dissatisfaction. It does not come, as is so often said, from the unworthiness of being loved but from an implicit comprehension of the fact that the amorous intuition is as a fundamental-intuition, an ideal out of reach. The more I am loved, the more I lose my *being*, the more I am thrown back on my own responsibilities, on my own power to be. In the second place the Other's awakening is always possible; at any moment he can make me appear as an object—hence the lover's perpetual insecurity In the third place love is an absolute which is perpetually *made relative* by others. One would have to be alone in the world with the beloved in order for love to preserve its character as an absolute axis of reference—hence the lover's perpetual shame (or pride—which here amounts to the same thing).

Thus it is useless for me to have tried to lose myself in objectivity; my passion will have availed me nothing. The Other has referred me to my own unjustifiable subjectivity—either by himself or through others. This result can provoke a total despair and a new attempt to realize the identification of the Other and myself. Its ideal will then be the opposite of that which we have just described; instead of projecting the absorbing of the Other while preserving in him his otherness, I shall project causing myself to be absorbed by the Other and losing myself in his subjectivity in order to get rid of my own. This enterprise will be expressed concretely by the *masochistic* attitude. Since the Other is the foundation of my being-for-others, if I relied on the Other to make me exist, I should no longer he anything more than a being-in-itself founded in its being by a freedom. Here it is my own subjectivity which is considered as an obstacle to the primordial act by which the Other would found me in my being. It is my own subjectivity which above all must be denied by *my own freedom*. I attempt therefore to engage myself wholly in my being-as-object. I refuse to be anything more than an object. I rest upon the Other, and as I experience this being-as-object in shame, I will and I love my shame as the profound sign of my objectivity. As the Other apprehends me as object by means of *actual desire*, I wish to be desired, I make myself in shame an object of desire.

This attitude would resemble that of love if instead of seeking to exist for the Other as the object-limit of his transcendence, I did not rather insist on making myself be treated as one object among others, as an instrument to be used. Now it is *my* transcendence which is to be denied, not his. This time I do not have to project capturing his freedom; on the contrary I hope that this freedom may *be* and *will* itself to be radically free. Thus the more I shall feel myself surpassed toward other ends, the more I shall enjoy the abdication of my transcendence. Finally I project being nothing more than an *object*; that is, radically an *in-itself.* But inasmuch as a freedom which will have absorbed mine will be the foundation of this in-itself, my being will become again the foundation of itself. Masochism, like sadism, is the assumption of guilt. I am guilty due to the very fact that I am an object, I am guilty toward myself since I consent to my absolute alienation. I am guilty toward the Other, for I furnish him with the occasion of being guilty—that is, of radically missing my freedom as such. Masochism is an attempt not to fascinate the Other by means of my objectivity but to cause myself to be fascinated by my objectivity-for-others; that is, to cause myself to be constituted as an object by the Other in such a way that I non-thetically apprehend my subjectivity as a *nothing* in the presence of the in-itself which I represent to the Other's eyes. Masochism is characterized as a species of vertigo, vertigo not before a precipice of rock and earth but before the abyss of the Other's subjectivity.

But masochism is and must be itself a failure. In order to cause myself to be fascinated by my self-as-object, I should necessarily have to be able to realize the intuitive apprehension of this object such as it is *for the Other,* a thing which is on principle impossible. Thus I am far from being able to be fascinated by this alienated Me, which remains on principle inapprehensible. It is useless for the masochist to get down on his knees, to show himself in ridiculous positions, to cause himself to be used as a simple lifeless instrument. It is *for the Other* that he will be obscene or simply passive, for the Other that he will *undergo* these postures; for himself he is forever condemned to *give them to himself.* It is in and through his transcendence that he disposes of himself as a being to be transcended. The more he tries to taste his objectivity, the more he will be submerged by the consciousness of his subjectivity—hence his anguish. Even the masochist who pays a woman to whip him is treating her as an instrument and by this very fact posits himself in transcendence in relation to her.

Thus the masochist ultimately treats the Other as an object and transcends him toward his own objectivity. Recall, for example, the tribulations of Sacher Masoch, who in order to make himself scorned, insulted, reduced to a humiliating position, was obliged to make use of the great love which women bore toward him; that is, to act upon them just in so far as they experienced themselves as an object for him. Thus in every way the masochist's objectivity escapes him, and it can even happen—in fact usually does happen—that in seeking to apprehend his own objectivity he finds the Other's objectivity, which in spite of himself frees his own subjectivity. Masochism therefore is on principle a failure. This should not surprise us if we realize that masochism is a "vice" and that vice is, on principle, the love of failure. But this is not the place to describe the structures peculiar to vice. It is sufficient here to point out that masochism is a perpetual effort to *annihilate* the subject's subjectivity by causing it to be assimilated by the Other; this effort is accompanied by the exhausting and delicious consciousness of failure so that finally it is the failure itself which the subject ultimately seeks as his principal goal.

Notes

1 Literally, "can tumble three times." Tr.
2 This formulation of Heidegger's position is that of A. de Waehlens. *La philosophie de Martin Heidegger*. Louvain, 1942, p. 99. *Cf.* also Heidegger's text, which he quotes: "Diese Bezeugung meint nicht hier einen nachträglichen und bei her laufenden Ausdruck des Menschseins, sonder sie macht das Dasein des Menschen mit usw. (*Hölderlin und das Wesen der Dichtung*, p. 6.)
    ("This affirmation does not mean here an additional and supplementary expression of human existence, but it does in the process make plain the existence of man." Douglas Scott's translation. *Existence and Being*, Chicago: Henry Regnery, 1949, p. 297.)
3 Furthermore the psychosis of influence, like the majority of psychoses, is a special experience translated by myths, of a great metaphysical fact—here the fact of alienation. Even a madman in his own way realizes the human condition.

13 Psychoanalysis

The Viennese doctor Sigmund Freud (1856–1939) designed psycho-analysis as a scientific cure for neurotic disorders through the patient talking to a trained 'analyst'. It has become a *Weltanschauung* whose scientific status is controversial. Psychoanalysis entails the anti-Cartesian tenet that I may be in mental states of which I am wholly or partly unaware. My actions are the product of a power struggle between *ego*, *superego* and *id* and are the expression of *libido* and childhood trauma. Cure or explanation entails making the unconscious conscious.

Sartre invents a kind of explanation called 'existential psychoanalysis' even though he insists that the unconscious does not exist because the idea of an unconscious mental state is contradictory. Part of a state's being mental is its being conscious. How is this psychoanalysis without the unconscious possible?

To decide this, we need to examine what Sartre endorses and repudiates in classical or Freudian psychoanalysis. Sartre and Freud agree that the explanation of human action has to be holistic not atomistic. Any piece of behaviour, no matter how trivial, is revelatory and symbolic of the person as a totality, in terms of whom it has to be deciphered. A person can not be understood as an aggregate of empirical components. Nevertheless, both Sartre and Freud reject any fixed, a priori view of human nature whether biological, historical or theological. A person can not be usefully studied in abstraction from their life, including their lived situations.

Sartre's rejection of the unconscious is not so Cartesian as might appear. From the fact that my mental states are conscious it does not follow that I know what they are. Even if my attitudes towards my hopes, fears and intentions are conscious I may misunderstand or be ignorant of their contents.

Sartre replaces the Freudian concept of *libido* with his own concept of the *project*. Existential psychoanalysis entails the disclosure of a person's fundamental or original project. Sartre knows that each of us has many empirical aims, hopes and fears. Indeed, the possible projects of an individual form an infinite set. By the fundamental or original project Sartre means the unity of my deeds that fuses them into my biography. My original project does not predate my biography. Sartre denies that my actions are inwardly or mentally rehearsed before I perform them. Indeed, there is no unconscious mind or noumenal realm where this could be executed. My original project is who I am making myself through living. Sartre says the original project is the project of being. It is the desire to be. What is the desire to be?

Sartre partly means the desire to live rather than die. He also means the desire of *being-for-itself* to be someone, to be something. Ultimately, the original project is the inevitably frustrated desire of *being-for-itself* to be a synthesis of *being-for-itself* and *being-in-itself*; the desire, in fact, to be God. Existentially, it is the pattern of the uncomfortable exercise of free self-definition. If there is an a priori (but not chronologically prior) tenet of existential psychoanalysis it is the original project.

Because the being of *being-for itself* is not distinguishable from choice, existential psychoanalysis must uncover what Sartre calls 'the original choice'. In a fashion reminiscent of Hindu and Buddhist doctrines of *karma* (*kama*) Sartre holds that who I am here and now is a direct consequence of my previous subjective choices. Existential psychoanalysis explains why I am who I am through bringing to knowledge the choice original to my present condition. As in classical psychoanalysis, I can in principle psychoanalyse myself but this is difficult because it requires the detachment involved in treating oneself as another. Whether self-administered or not, existential psychoanalysis like classical analysis aims at a therapeutic self-knowledge.

Sartre deploys the techniques of existential psychoanalysis with increasing sophistication in his biographies of Baudelaire (1947), Jean Genet (1952) and Flaubert (1972). His ambition in writing the Flaubert is to totally explain another human being. *The Idiot of the Family* is a methodological culmination of Sartre's work, drawing on the phenomenology of *The Psychology of the Imagination*, the Marxist existentialism of *Search for a Method* and *Critique of Dialectical Reason* as well as the existential psychoanalysis of *Being and Nothingness*. The title is taken from Gustave Flaubert's father's judgement on his young son: 'You will be the idiot of the family'. Sartre's biography seeks to uncover Flaubert's self-constitution as a writer within his lived historical situation. Although in *Being and Nothingness* Sartre only claims to have shown the possibility of existential psychoanalysis and admits that the discipline has not yet found its Freud, Sartre thought that in the concrete case of his writing on Flaubert one person had wholly explained another.

Two extracts follow, one from *Sketch For a Theory of the Emotions,* the other from the chapter called 'Existential Psychoanalysis' from *Being and Nothingness.* In *Sketch For a Theory of the Emotions* we see the Sartre of 1939 distancing himself from classical psychoanalysis through the example of emotion. In *Being and Nothingness* Sartre argues the merits of psychoanalysis over empiricist and positivist psychology and then argues the merits of his own psychoanalysis over Freud's.

SKETCH FOR A THEORY OF THE EMOTIONS

The psychoanalytic theory

We cannot understand an emotion unless we look for its signification. And this, by its nature, is of a functional order. We are therefore led to speak of a finality of emotion. This finality we can grasp very concretely by the objective examination of emotional behaviour. Here there is no question at all of a more or less obscure theory about emotion and instinct based upon *a priori* principles or postulates. Simple consideration of the facts brings us to an empirical intuition of the finalist meaning of emotion. If we try on the other hand to fix, in a complete intuition, the essence of emotion as an interpsychological fact, we see that this finality is inherent in its structure. And all the psychologists who have rejected upon the peripheric theory of James have been more or less aware of this finalistic signification—this is what Janet, for instance, decorates with the name of "psychic"; it is this that psychologists or physiologists like Cannon and Sherrington try to reintroduce into their descriptions of the emotional facts with their hypothesis of a cerebral sensibility; it is this, again, that we find in Wallon or, more recently, among the form psychologists. This finality presupposes a synthetic organization of behaviours which could only be the "unconscious" of psychoanalysis, or consciousness. And it would be easy enough, if need be, to produce a psychoanalytic theory of emotional finality. One could show, without great difficulty, that anger or fear are means employed by unconscious urges to achieve symbolic satisfaction, to break out of a state of unbearable tension. One could thus account for this essential characteristic of emotion—that it is "suffered", that it surprises, develops of itself according to its own laws, and that conscious efforts cannot modify its course to any very appreciable extent. This dissociation between the organized character of emotion—the organizing theme being relegated to the unconscious—and its ineluctable character, which it would not have for the consciousness of the subject, would render something like the same service in the psychological domain as the Kantian distinction between the empirical and the noumenal does in the domain of metaphysic.

It is certainly true that psychoanalysis was the first to lay the emphasis upon the signification of psychic facts: that is, it was the first to insist upon the fact that every state of consciousness stands for something other than itself. For example: this clumsy theft perpetrated by a sexual-obsessive is not simply a clumsy theft. It refers to something else from the moment that we begin to consider it in the psychoanalyst's way as a phenomenon of self-punishment. Then it refers to the primary complex for which the patient is seeking to justify himself through self-punishment. We can see that a psychoanalytic theory of the emotions would be possible. Does it not already exist? There is that woman with a phobia for laurel. If she sees a clump of laurels, she faints. The psycho-analyst discovers that in her childhood there was a painful sexual incident associated with laurel bushes. What will be the corresponding emotion? A phenomenon of refusal, and of censorship. Not refusal of the *laurel* itself, but a refusal to relive the memory connected with laurels. Here the emotion is a flight from the revelation to follow, as sleep is sometimes a flight from a decision to be taken, and as the illnesses of certain young women are, according to Stekel, a flight before marriage. Naturally, emotion is not always an escape. We already have indications from the psychoanalysts of an interpretation of anger as a symbolic gratification of sexual tendencies. And certainly, none of these interpretations is to be thrust aside. That anger can *signify* sadism is in no doubt at all. That fainting away from passive fear signifies flight, the quest of a refuge, is also certain, and we shall try to show the reason for it. What is in question here is the principle itself of psychoanalytic explanation—that is what we want to envisage here.

The psychoanalytic interpretation conceives the conscious phenom-enon as the symbolic realization of a desire repressed by the censor. Note that, for consciousness, the desire is *not implicated in its symbolic realization*. In so far as it exists by and in our consciousness it is only what it gives itself out to be: emotion, desire for sleep, theft, laurel-phobia, etc. If it were otherwise, if we had any consciousness, even *only implicit*, of the real desire, we should be cheating, and that is not what the psychoanalyst means. It follows that the signification of our conscious behaviour lies wholly outside that behaviour itself or, if one prefers it so, what is signified is entirely cut off from the *signifying*. This behaviour of the subject is, in itself just what it is (if by "in itself" we mean *for itself*), but it can be deciphered by the appropriate techniques as one would decipher a given language. In a word, the conscious fact is related to what it signifies, as a thing which is the *effect* of a certain event is related to that event: as, for example, the ashes of a fire extinct upon a mountain are related to the human beings who lit the fire. Their presence is not *contained* in the remaining cinders, but connected with them by a relation causality: the relation is *external,* the ashes of the fire are *passive* considered in that causal relation, as every effect is in relation to its cause. A consciousness which had not acquired the necessary technical knowledge could not grasp these remains as *signs.* At the same time, the remains are what they are; that is, they exist in themselves, irrespective of all significant interpretation: they *are* fragments of half-calcinated wood, and that is all.

Can we admit that a fact of consciousness could be like a thing in relation to its signification—that is, receive its meaning from outside like an external quality—as, for instance, this having been burnt by men who wanted to warm themselves is a quality external to the burnt wood? It would seem, first and foremost, that the effect of such an interpretation is to make consciousness into a thing in relation to what is signified: it is to admit that consciousness can constitute itself into a meaning without being aware of the meaning that it constitutes. There is a flagrant contradiction in this, unless we are to regard consciousness as an existent of the same type as a stone, or a pond. But in that case we must finally give up the Cartesian *cogito* and treat consciousness as a secondary and passive phenomenon. In so far as a consciousness *makes itself* it is never "nothing but" what it appears to be. If, then, it has a signification, it must contain this within itself as a structure of consciousness. This does not mean that the signification must be perfectly explicit. There are many possible degrees of condensation and of clarity. It only means that we should not interrogate the consciousness from outside, as one would study the remains of the fire or the encampment, but from within; that we should look into *it* for the signification. The consciousness, if the *cogito* is to be possible, is itself the *fact,* the *signification* and what is *signified.*

Truth to tell, what makes an exhaustive refutation of psychoanalysis so difficult is that the psychoanalyst himself does not regard the signification as conferred entirely from outside the consciousness. For him, there is always an internal analogy between the conscious fact and the desire it expresses, since the *conscious fact is symbolical of the expressed complex.* And for the psychoanalyst this symbolic character is obviously not external to the fact itself, but is *constitutive* of it. Upon this point we are in full agreement with him. That the symbolization is constitutive of the symbolic consciousness can be in no doubt whatever to anyone who believes in the absolute value of the Cartesian *cogito.* But this needs to be rightly understood: if symbolization is constitutive it is legitimate to see an immanent bond of *comprehension* between the symbolization and the symbol. Only, we must agree upon this, that consciousness *constitutes itself* by symbolization. In that case there is nothing behind it, and the relation between symbol, symbolized and symbolization is an intra-structural bond of consciousness. But if we go on to say that the consciousness is symbolizing under the causal compulsion of a transcendent fact—which is the repressed desire—we are falling back upon the theory previously indicated, which treats the relation of the signified to the signifying as a causal relation. The profound contradiction in all psychoanalysis is that it presents *at the same time* a bond of causality and a bond of understanding between the phenomena that it studies. These two types of relationship are incompatible. The theorist of psychoanalysis also establishes transcendent relations of rigid causality between the facts under observation (a pincushion in a dream always *signifies* a woman's breasts, entry into a carriage signifies the sexual act), whilst the practitioner assures himself of success by studying mainly the facts of conscious understanding; that is, by flexible research into the intra-conscious relation between symbolization and symbol.

For our part, we do not reject the findings of psychoanalysis when they are obtained by the understanding. We limit ourselves to the denial that there is any value or intelligibility in its underlying theory of psychic causality. And moreover we affirm that, in so far as the psychoanalyst is making use of *understanding* to interpret consciousness, it would be better to recognize frankly that whatever is going on in consciousness can receive its explanation nowhere but from consciousness itself. And here we are brought back to our own point of departure: a theory of consciousness which attributes meaningful character to the emotive facts must look for that meaning in the consciousness itself. In other words, it is the consciousness which *makes itself* conscious, moved by the inner need for an inner signification.

And indeed, the advocates of psychoanalysis are at the same time raising a difficulty of principle. If consciousness organizes emotion as a special type of response adapted to an external situation, how does it manage to have no consciousness of this adaptation? And it must be granted that their theory renders a perfect account of this discrepancy between the signification and the consciousness—which need not astonish us since that is just what it was made for. Better still, they will say, in the majority of cases we are struggling, in our conscious spontaneity, against the development of emotional manifestations; we are trying to master our fear, to calm our anger, to restrain our weeping. Thus we have not only no consciousness of any finality of emotion, we are also rejecting emotion with all our strength and it invades us in spite of ourselves. A phenomenological description of emotion ought to resolve their contradictions.

BEING AND NOTHINGNESS

Doing and having

Existential psychoanalysis

It is not enough in fact to draw up a list of behavior patterns, of drives and inclinations, it is necessary also to *decipher* them; that is, it is necessary to know how to *question* them. This research can be conducted only according to the rules of a specific method. It is this method which we call existential psychoanalysis.

The *principle* of this psychoanalysis is that man is a totality and not a collection. Consequently he expresses himself as a whole in even his most insignificant and his most superficial behavior. In other words there is not a taste, a mannerism, or an human act which is not *revealing*.

The *goal* of psychoanalysis is to *decipher* the empirical behavior patterns of man; that is to bring out in the open the revelations which each one of them contains and to fix them conceptually.

Its *point of departure* is *experience*; its pillar of support is the fundamental, preontological comprehension which man has of the human person. Although the majority of people can well ignore the indications contained in a gesture, a word, a sign and can look with scorn on the revelation which they carry, each human individual nevertheless possesses *a priori* the *meaning* of the revelatory value of these manifestations and is capable of deciphering them, at least if he is aided and guided by a helping hand. Here as elsewhere, truth is not encountered by chance; it does not belong to a domain where one must seek it without ever having any presentiment of its location, as one can go to look for the source of the Nile or of the Niger. It belongs *a priori* to human comprehension and the essential task is an hermeneutic; that is, a deciphering, a determination, and a conceptualization.

Its *method* is comparative. Since each example of human conduct symbolizes in its own manner the fundamental choice which must be brought to light, and since at the same time each one disguises this choice under its occasional character and its historical opportunity, only the comparison of these acts of conduct can effect the emergence of the unique revelation which they all express in a different way. The first outline of this method has been furnished for us by the psychoanalysis of Freud and his disciples. For this reason it will be profitable here to indicate more specifically the points where existential psychoanalysis will be inspired by psychoanalysis proper and those where it will radically differ from it.

Both kinds of psychoanalysis consider all objectively discernible manifestations of "psychic life" as symbols maintaining symbolic relations to the fundamental, total structures which constitute the individual person. Both consider that there are no primary givens such as hereditary dispositions, character, *etc.* Existential psychoanalysis recognizes nothing *before* the original upsurge of human freedom; empirical psychoanalysis holds that the original affectivity of the individual is virgin wax *before* its history. The libido is nothing besides its concrete fixations, save for a permanent possibility of fixing anything whatsoever upon anything whatsoever. Both consider the human being as a perpetual, searching, historization. Rather than uncovering static, constant givens they discover the meaning, orientation, and adventures of this history. Due to this fact both consider man in the world and do not imagine that one can question the being of a man without taking into account all his *situation*. Psychological investigations aim at reconstituting the life of the subject from birth to the moment of the cure; they utilize all the objective documentation which they can find; letters, witnesses, intimate diaries, "social" information of every kind. What they aim at restoring is less a pure psychic event than a twofold structure: the crucial event of infancy and the psychic crystallization around this event. Here again we have to do with a *situation*. Each "historical" fact from this point of view will be considered at once as a *factor* of the psychic evolution and as a *symbol* of that evolution. For it is nothing in itself. It operates only according to the way in which it is taken and this very manner of taking it expresses symbolically the internal disposition of the individual.

Empirical psychoanalysis and existential psychoanalysis both search within an existing situation for a fundamental attitude which can not be expressed by simple, logical definitions because it is prior to all logic, and which requires reconstruction according to the laws of specific syntheses. Empirical psychoanalysis seeks to determine the *complex*, the very name of which indicates the polyvalence of all the meanings which are referred back to it. Existential psychoanalysis seeks to determine the *original choice*. This original choice operating in the face of the world and being a choice of position in the world is total like the complex; it is prior to logic like the complex. It is this which decides the attitude of the person when confronted with logic and principles; therefore there can be no possibility of questioning it in conformance to logic. It brings together in a prelogical synthesis the totality of the existent, and as such it is the center of reference for an infinity of polyvalent meanings.

Both our psychoanalyses refuse to admit that the subject is in a privileged position to proceed in these inquiries concerning himself. They equally insist on a strictly objective method, using as documentary evidence the data of reflection as well as the testimony of others. Of course the subject *can* undertake a psychoanalytic investigation of himself. But in this case he must renounce at the outset all benefit stemming from his peculiar position and must question himself exactly as if he were someone else. Empirical psychoanalysis in fact is based on the hypothesis of the existence of an unconscious psyche, which on principle escapes the intuition of the subject. Existential psychoanalysis rejects the hypothesis of the unconscious; it makes the psychic act coextensive with consciousness. But if the fundamental project is fully experienced by the subject and hence wholly conscious, that certainly does not mean that it must by the same token be *known* by him; quite the contrary. The reader will perhaps recall the care we took in the Introduction to distinguish between consciousness and knowledge. To be sure, as we have seen earlier, reflection can be considered as a quasi-knowledge. But what it grasps at each moment is not the pure project of the for-itself as it is symbolically expressed—often in several ways at once—by the concrete behavior which it apprehends. It grasps the concrete behavior itself; that is, the specific dated desire in all its characteristic network. It grasps at once symbol and symbolization. This apprehension, to be sure, is entirely constituted by a preontological comprehension of the fundamental project; better yet, in so far as reflection is almost a non-thetic consciousness of itself as reflection, it *is* this same project, as well as the non-reflective consciousness. But it does not follow that it commands the instruments and techniques necessary to isolate the choice symbolized, to fix it by concepts, and to bring it forth into the full light of day. It is penetrated by a great light without being able to express what this light is illuminating. We are not dealing with an unsolved riddle as the Freudians believe; all is there, luminous; reflection is in full possession of it, apprehends all. But this "mystery in broad daylight" is due to the fact that this possession is deprived of the means which would ordinarily permit *analysis* and *conceptualization*. It grasps everything, all at once, without shading, without relief, without connections of grandeur—not that these shades, these values, these reliefs exist somewhere and are hidden from it, but rather because they must be established by another human attitude and because they can exist only *by means of* and *for* knowledge. Reflection, unable to serve as the basis for existential psychoanalysis, will then simply furnish us with the brute materials toward which the psychoanalyst must take an objective attitude. Thus only will he be able to know what he *already understands*. The result is that complexes uprooted from the depths of the unconscious, like projects revealed by existential psychoanalysis, will be apprehended *from the point of view of the Other*. Consequently the *object* thus brought into the light will be articulated according to the structures of the transcended-transcendence; that is, its being will be the being-for-others even if the psychoanalyst and the subject of the psychoanalysis are actually the same person. Thus the project which is brought to light by either kind of psychoanalysis can be only the totality of the individual human being, the irreducible element of the transcendence with the structure of *being-for-others*. What always escapes these methods of investigation is the project as it is for itself, the complex in its own being. This project-for-itself can be experienced only as a living possession; there is an incompatibility between existence for-itself and objective existence. But the object of the two psychoanalyses has in it nonetheless the *reality of a being*; the subject's knowledge of it can in addition contribute to *clarify* reflection, and that reflection can then become a possession which will be a quasi-knowing.

At this point the similarity between the two kinds of psychoanalysis ceases. They differ fundamentally in that empirical psychoanalysis has decided upon its own irreducible instead of allowing this to make itself known in a self-evident intuition. The libido or the will to power in actuality constitutes a psycho-biological residue which is not clear in itself and which does not appear to us as *being beforehand* the irreducible limit of the investigation. Finally it is experience which establishes that the foundation of complexes is this libido or this will to power; and these results of empirical inquiry are perfectly contingent, they are not convincing. Nothing prevents our conceiving *a priori* of a "human reality" which would not be expressed by the will to power, for which the libido would not constitute the original, undifferentiated project.

On the other hand, the choice to which existential psychoanalysis will lead us, precisely because it is a choice, accounts for its original contingency, for the contingency of the choice is the reverse side of its freedom. Furthermore, inasmuch as it established on the *lack of being*, conceived as a fundamental characteristic of being, it receives its legitimacy *as a choice*, and we know that we do not have to push further. Each result then will be at once fully contingent and legitimately irreducible. Moreover it will always remain *particular*; that is, we will not achieve as the ultimate goal of our investigation and the foundation of all behavior an abstract, general term, libido for example, which would be differentiated and made concrete first in complexes and then in detailed acts of conduct, due to the action of external facts and the history of the subject. On the contrary, it will be a choice which remains unique and which is from the start absolute concreteness. Details of behavior can express or *particularize* this choice, but they can not make it more concrete than it already known in a self-evident intuition. The libido or the will to power in is. That is because the choice is nothing other than the being of each human reality; this amounts to saying that a particular partial behavior *is* or expresses the original choice of this human reality since for human reality there is no difference between existing and choosing *for* itself. From this fact we understand that existential psychoanalysis does not have to proceed from the fundamental "complex," which is exactly the choice of being, to an abstraction like the libido which would explain it. The complex is the ultimate choice, it is the choice of being and *makes itself such*. Bringing it into the light will reveal it each time as evidently irreducible. It follows necessarily that the libido and the will to power will appear to existential psychoanalysis neither as general character-istics common to all mankind nor as irreducibles. At most it will be possible after the investigation to establish that they express by virtue of particular ensembles in certain subjects a fundamental choice which can not be reduced to either one of them. We have seen in fact that desire and sexuality in general express an original effort of the for-itself to recover its being which has become estranged through contact with the Other. The will to power also originally supposes being-for-others, the comprehension of the Other, and the choice of winning its own salvation by means of the Other. The foundation of this attitude must be an original choice which would make us understand the radical identifi-cation of being-in-itself-for-itself with being-for-others.

The fact that the ultimate term of this existential inquiry must be a *choice*, distinguishes even better the psychoanalysis for which we have outlined the method and principal features. It thereby abandons the supposition that the environment acts mechanically on the subject under consideration. The environment can act on the subject only to the exact extent that he comprehends it; that is, transforms it into a situation. Hence no objective description of this environment could be of any use to us. From the start the environment conceived as a situation refers to the for-itself which is choosing, just as the for-itself refers to the environ-ment by the very fact that the for-itself is in the world. By renouncing all mechanical causation, we renounce at the same time all *general* inter-pretation of the symbolization confronted. Our goal could not be to establish empirical laws of succession, nor could we constitute a uni-versal symbolism. Rather the psychoanalyst will have to rediscover at each step a symbol functioning in the particular case which he is considering. If each being is a totality, it is not conceivable that there can exist elementary symbolic relationships (*e.g.*, the faeces = gold, or a pincushion = the breast) which preserve a constant meaning in all cases; that is, which remain unaltered when they pass from one meaningful ensemble to another ensemble. Furthermore the psychoanalyst will never lose sight of the fact that the choice is living and consequently can be *revoked* by the subject who is being studied. We have shown in the preceding chapter the importance of the *instant,* which represents abrupt changes in orientation and the assuming of a new position in the face of an unalterable past. From this moment on, we must always be ready to consider that symbols change meaning and to abandon the symbol used hitherto. Thus existential psychoanalysis will have to be completely flexible and adapt itself to the slightest observable changes in the subject. Our concern here is to understand what is *individual* and often even instantaneous. The method which has served for one subject will not necessarily be suitable to use for another subject or for the same subject at a later period.

Precisely because the goal of the inquiry must be to discover a *choice* and not a *state,* the investigator must recall on every occasion that his object is not a datum buried in the darkness of the unconscious but a free, conscious determination—which is not even resident in consciousness, but which is one with this consciousness itself. Empirical psychoanalysis, to the extent that its method is better than its principles, is often in sight of an existential discovery, but it always stops part way. When it thus approaches the fundamental choice, the resistance of the subject collapses suddenly and he *recognizes* the image of himself which is presented to him as if he were seeing himself in a mirror. This involuntary testimony of the subject is precious for the psychoanalyst; he sees there the sign that he has reached his goal; he can pass on from the investigation proper to the cure. But nothing in his principles or in his initial postulates permits him to understand or to utilize this testimony. Where could he get any such right? If the complex is really unconscious—that is, if there is a barrier separating the sign from the thing signified—how could the subject *recognize* it? Does the unconscious complex recognize itself? But haven't we been told that it lacks *understanding*? And if of necessity we granted to it the faculty of understanding the signs, would this not be to make of it by the same token a conscious unconscious? What is understanding if not to be conscious of what is understood? Shall we say on the other hand that it is the subject as conscious who recognizes the image presented? But how could he compare it with his true state since that is out of reach and since he has never had any knowledge of it? At most he will be able to judge that the psychoanalytic explanation of his case is a *probable* hypothesis, which derives its probability from the number of behavior patterns which it explains. His relation to this interpretation is that of a third party, that of the psychoanalyst himself; he has no privileged position. And if he *believes* in the probability of the psychoanalytic hypothesis, is this simple belief, which lives in the limits of his consciousness, able to effect the breakdown of the barriers which dam up the unconscious tendencies? The psychoanalyst doubtless has some obscure picture of an abrupt coincidence of conscious and unconscious. But he has removed all methods of conceiving of this coincidence in any positive sense.

Still, the enlightenment of the subject is a fact. There is an intuition here which is accompanied by evidence. The subject guided by the psychoanalyst does more and better than to give his agreement to an hypothesis; he touches it, he sees what it is. This is truly understandable only if the subject has never ceased being conscious of his deep tendencies; better yet, only if these drives are not distinguished from his conscious self. In this case as we have seen, the traditional psychoanalytic interpretation does not cause him to attain consciousness of what he is; it causes him to attain *knowledge* of what he is. It is existential psychoanalysis then which claims the final intuition of the subject as decisive.

This comparison allows us to understand better what an existential psychoanalysis must be if it is entitled to exist. It is a method destined to bring to light, in a strictly objective form, the subjective choice by which each living person makes himself a person; that is, makes known to himself what he is. Since what the method seeks is a *choice of being* at the same time as a *being*, it must reduce particular behavior patterns to fundamental relations—not of sexuality or of the will to power, but *of being*—which are expressed in this behavior. It is then guided from the start toward a comprehension of being and must not assign itself any other goal than to discover being and the mode of being of the being confronting this being. It is forbidden to stop before attaining this goal. It will utilize the comprehension of being which characterizes the investigator inasmuch as he is himself a human reality; and as it seeks to detach being from its symbolic expressions, it will have to rediscover each time on the basis of a comparative study of acts and attitudes, a symbol destined to decipher them. Its criterion of success will be the number of facts which its hypothesis permits it to explain and to unify as well as the self-evident intuition of the irreducibility of the end attained. To this criterion will be added in all cases where it is possible, the decisive testimony of the subject. The results thus achieved—that is, the ultimate ends of the individual—can then become the object of a classification, and it is by the comparison of these results that we will be able to establish general considerations about human reality as an empirical choice of its own ends. The behavior studied by this psychoanalysis will include not only dreams, failures, obsessions, and neuroses, but also and especially the thoughts of waking life, successfully adjusted acts, style, etc. This psychoanalysis has not yet found its Freud. At most we can find the foreshadowing of it in certain particularly successful biographies. We hope to be able to attempt elsewhere two examples in relation to Flaubert and Dostoevsky. But it matters little to us whether it now exists; the important thing is that it is possible.

14 Writing

Literature is the art form in which Sartre expresses his own philosophy. The novels and plays are strewn with characters in bad faith: Garcin in *No Exit*, Goetz in *The Devil and the Good Lord*, the senator in *The Respectable Prostitute*, Hugo in *Dirty Hands*, Franz in *Altona*, Lucien in the short story 'Childhood of a Leader' in *The Wall*, Daniel in *The Roads to Freedom*, Kean in the play of that name, and of course, the café waiter who features not only in *The Age of Reason*, the first volume of *The Roads to Freedom*, but in *Being and Nothingness*.

Opposed to them, but fewer in number, are the characters who in differing degrees recognise their own freedom: Mathieu in *Iron in the Soul* (but not in *The Age of Reason* and *The Reprieve*), Oreste in *The Flies*, the tortured resistance fighters in *Men Without Shadows*, Lizzie in *The Respectable Prostitute*, Roquentin in *Nausea*. Works of fiction provide a criterion for the truth of a 'humanistic' philosophy such as Sartre's existentialism.

Sartre draws a sharp distinction between literature and science: Literature is ambiguous but each sentence of science or philosophy has, or should have, one and only one meaning. Sentences of literature may have multiple meanings, or may express different propositions. This presents Sartre with a dilemma. To the extent to which the sentences making up his novels, stories and plays are ambiguous they do not serve as a vehicle for his philosophy. To the extent to which they are unambiguous, they are not literature, at least by his own criterion. This dilemma is never fully resolved in his work.

Sartre's literature, especially *Nausea*, contains putative solutions to philosophical problems. For example, in *Nausea*, some versions of the problem of induction are depicted as genuine and as at once psychologically liberating and disturbing to the central character, Antoine Roquentin. What exists exists contingently rather than necessarily, and what is is what it is contingently, not necessarily. What passes for reality is constructed by language which in turn is driven by pragmatic pre-conceptions, but these can in principle be set aside by certain unusual experiences. Existence is shown to precede essence in the case of human beings, but it is shown to coincide in naturally occurring objects such as the root of the chestnut tree, and the reverse relation obtains in the case of human artefacts such as a beer glass or the tram seat. Roquentin himself feels his existence to be pointless or without justification.

The philosophical questions to which these putative answers correspond are: Will the future resemble the past?, Could what is not be? Could what is have not been what it is? Are the ordinary objects of our experience linguistically, psychologically or pragmatically 'constructed'?, If so, could they be perceived as they are, or at least in new ways?, What is the relation between being and being something? Is it possible to be without being anything? Is it possible to be something without being? Does life have a meaning?

Roquentin, in *Nausea*, is living a philosophy. Roquentin lives Sartre's existential phenomenology. As with the characters in freedom and bad faith, to the extent to which we find Roquentin's experiences credible we should find Sartre's existential phenomenology credible.

Sartre insists that writing is an ethical and political act; an act which should be an authentic and committed (*engagé*) expression of the author's freedom. The writer should be fully committed in what they write. What is this difference between *committed* and *uncommitted* literature?

One answer is ruled out straight away. Sartre can not simply mean that the author should write what he or she believes and refrain from writing what he or she disbelieves. This ethical requirement rests upon a picture of the author which Sartre rejects: the author as a repository of beliefs or attitudes which may be externalised in writing sincerely or insincerely. Rather, writing is *a choice*: not just the choice whether to write or not, but having chosen to write, the act of writing is itself the making of choices. The literary work does not predate the writing of it. It does not already exist in the writer's mind before being written down. It comes into being by being freely composed.

The distinction between committed and uncommitted literature depends upon the distinction between authenticity and bad faith. Authenticity is the recognition of freedom, and bad faith is the denial or refusal of freedom. Committed literature is produced by authentic acts of writing; acts of writing that the author recognises as exercises of his own freedom and for which he alone accepts and has responsibility. Sartre thinks most writing is done in bad faith. We write in order to be read, in order to be needed, in order to find a substitute for immortality. This is bad faith because it is a case of 'being-for-others'; producing an image of oneself which others will judge favourably rather than exercising one's free possibilities as a writer. Sartre himself frequently insists that he writes for the present generation, not for posterity, although when interviewed he has confessed that he would not be displeased if his works were still read a hundred years from now. They no doubt will be.

Because they are written in bad faith, most literary works are would-be escapes or conquests. What is fled from is the freedom of the writer. What is conquered is the freedom of the reader. The writer is master and the reader slave but, in with Hegelian irony, the writer enslaves himself in enslaving the reader and the reader finds a new freedom in freely interpreting the writer's works in ways that undo the writer's mastery over them. *Qui perde gagne*: *loser wins*. Loser wins and winner loses.

The contingency of existence produces anguish. The writer therefore tries to make his existence necessary, indispensible, by creating something that does depend upon his own existence: a literary work. This seems successful because the work's existence does depend upon his having written it. This security is undermined, however, because what the work is is not wholly dictated by the interpretation of its author. Its essence is open to manipulation by its readers. Its existence too is contingent and not necessary. Even if it is read for thousands of years, there will no doubt come a time when it is forgotten. Its author too will be forgotten.

A literary work is the free creation of its author and readers because its existence is not causally necessitated by the prior state of the world. A writer accepting these facts evades bad faith. The role of the other in literary production is inescapable but it can either be affirmed or denied by the writer. Freedom is primordial with regard to the choice between authenticity and bad faith.

Sartre thinks the authenticity of a literary work is sufficient for its morality. *La littérature engagée* can not be immoral. He says, for example, nobody could write a good anti-semitic novel. But could not a writer recognise that their writing is the exercise of their own freedom and yet choose to write the most appalling laudits to suffering and injustice? Commitment in writing seems neither necessary nor sufficient for the morality of what is written: not necessary because something moral could be the product of bad faith, not sufficient because something immoral could be the product of authenticity. If there is freedom either good or evil can be done freely.

Sartre claims that the aesthetic imperative presupposes a moral imperative. Freedom is prior to both aesthetics and morality and freedom is the ultimate value. Committed literature not only exercises and acknowledges freedom, it provokes it, and provokes its acknowledgement. In reading committed literature the reader is a pure freedom, an unconditioned activity, and is conscious of being free. What is reading? Reading is a free dream.

Writing is a political act. For Sartre a good society is a free society. We do not know what a free society would be like, precisely because it would be one we would be free to make. There can be no blueprint for a free society – no Platonic blueprint, no Marxist blueprint, no Christian or utilitarian blueprint. There is no a priori knowledge of a free society. Committed literature dissolves the readers' bad faith and shows them their freedom, so it is the responsibility of the intellectual to be *engagé*, committed to freedom.

In the passages below from *What is Literature?* (1948) Sartre develops the idea of *la littérature engagée*. In the one from *The Family Idiot* (1972), 'Absolute-Art', he examines the possibilities of writing in the historical situation of post-romanticism in mid-nineteenth-century France.

WHAT IS LITERATURE?

Why write?

Each has his reasons: for one, art is a flight; for another a means of conquering. But one can flee into a hermitage, into madness, into death. One can conquer by arms. Why does it have to be *writing*, why does one have to manage one's escapes and conquests by *writing?* Because, behind the various aims of authors, there is a deeper and more immediate choice which is common to all of us. We shall try to elucidate this choice, and we shall see whether it is not in the name of this very choice of writing that the self-commitment of writers must be required.

Each of our perceptions is accompanied by the consciousness that human reality is a "revealer", that is, it is through human reality that "there is" being, or, to put it differently, that man is the means by which things are manifested. It is our presence in the world which multiplies relations. It is we who set up a relationship between this tree and that bit of sky. Thanks to us, that star which has been dead for millennia, that quarter moon, and that dark river are disclosed in the unity of a landscape. It is the speed of our car and our aeroplane which organizes the great masses of the earth. With each of our acts, the world reveals to us a new face. But, if we know that we are directors of being, we also know that we are not its producers. If we turn away from this landscape, it will sink back into its dark permanence. At least, it will sink back; there is no one mad enough to think that it is going to be annihilated. It is we who shall be annihilated, and the earth will remain in its lethargy until another consciousness comes along to awaken it. Thus, to our inner certainty of being "revealers" is added that of being inessential in relation to the thing revealed.

One of the chief motives of artistic creation is certainly the need of feeling that we are essential in relationship to the world. If I fix on canvas or in writing a certain aspect of the fields or the sea or a look on someone's face which I have disclosed, I am conscious of having produced them by condensing relationships, by introducing order where there was none, by imposing the unity of mind on the diversity of things. That is, I feel myself essential in relation to my creation. But this time it is the created object which escapes me; I cannot reveal and produce at the same time. The creation becomes inessential in relation to the creative activity. First of all, even if it appears finished to others, the created object always seems to us in a state of suspension; we can always change this line, that shade, that word. Thus, it never *forces itself*. A novice painter asked his teacher, "When should I consider my painting finished?" And the teacher answered, "When you can look at it in amazement and say to yourself '*I'm* the one who did *that!*'"

Which amounts to saying "never". For it is virtually considering one's work with someone else's eyes and revealing what one has created. But it is self-evident that we are proportionally less conscious of the thing produced and more conscious of our productive activity. When it is a matter of pottery or carpentry, we work according to traditional patterns, with tools whose usage is codified; it is Heidegger's famous "they" who are working with our hands. In this case, the result can seem to us sufficiently strange to preserve its objectivity in our eyes. But if we ourselves produce the rules of production, the measures, the criteria, and if our creative drive comes from the very depths of our heart, then we never find anything but ourselves in our work. It is we who have invented the laws by which we judge it. It is our history, our love, our gaiety that we recognize in it. Even if we should look at it without touching it any further, we never *receive* from it that gaiety or love. We put them into it. The results which we have obtained on canvas or paper never seem to us *objective*. We are too familiar with the processes of which they are the effects. These processes remain a subjective discovery; they are ourselves, our inspiration, our trick, and when we seek to *perceive* our work, we create it again, we repeat mentally the operations which produced it; each of its aspects appears as a result. Thus, in the perception, the object is given as the essential thing and the subject as the inessential. The latter seeks essentiality in the creation and obtains it, but then it is the object which becomes the inessential.

This dialectic is nowhere more apparent than in the art of writing, for the literary object is a peculiar top which exists only in movement. To make it come into view a concrete act called reading is necessary, and it lasts only as long as this act can last. Beyond that, there are only black marks on paper. Now, the writer cannot read what he writes, whereas the shoemaker can put on the shoes he has just made if they are his size, and the architect can live in the house he has built. In reading, one foresees; one waits. One foresees the end of the sentence, the following sentence, the next page. One waits for them to confirm or disappoint one's foresights. The reading is composed of a host of hypotheses, of dreams followed by awakenings, of hopes and deceptions. Readers are always ahead of the sentence they are reading in a merely probable future which partly collapses and partly comes together in proportion as they progress, which withdraws from one page to the next and forms the moving horizon of the literary object. Without waiting, without a future, without ignorance, there is no objectivity.

Now the operation of writing involves an implicit quasi-reading which makes real reading impossible. When the words form under his pen, the author doubtless sees them, but he does not see them as the reader does, since he knows them before writing them down. The function of his gaze is not to reveal, by brushing against them, the sleeping words which are waiting to be read, but to control the sketching of the signs. In short, it is a purely regulating mission, and the view before him reveals nothing except for slight slips of the pen. The writer neither foresees nor conjectures; he *projects*. It often happens that he awaits, as they say, the inspiration. But one does not wait for oneself the way one waits for others. If he hesitates, he knows that the future is not made, that he himself is going to make it, and if he still does not know what is going to happen to his hero, that simply means that he has not thought about it, that he has not decided upon anything. The future is then a blank page, whereas the future of the reader is two hundred pages filled with words which separate him from the end. Thus, the writer meets everywhere only *his* knowledge, *his* will, *his* plans, in short, himself. He touches only his own subjectivity; the object he creates is out of reach; he does not create it *for himself*. If he re-reads himself, it is already too late. The sentence will never quite be a thing in his eyes. He goes to the very limits of the subjective but without crossing it. He appreciates the effect of a touch, of an epigram, of a well-placed adjective, but it is the effect they will have on others. He can judge it, not feel it. Proust never discovered the homosexuality of Charlus, since he had decided upon it even before starting on his book. And if a day comes when the book takes on for its author a semblance of objectivity, it is because years have passed, because he has forgotten it, because its spirit is quite foreign to him, and doubtless he is no longer capable of writing it. This was the case with Rousseau when he re-read the *Social Contract* at the end of his life.

Thus, it is not true that one writes for oneself. That would be the worst blow. In projecting one's emotions on paper, one barely manages to give them a languid extension. The creative act is only an incomplete and abstract moment in the production of a work. If the author existed alone he would be able to write as much as he liked; the work as *object* would never see the light of day and he would either have to put down his pen or despair. But the operation of writing implies that of reading as its dialectical correlative and these two connected acts necessitate two distinct agents. It is the joint effort of author and reader which brings upon the scene that concrete and imaginary object which is the work of the mind. There is no art except for and by others.

Reading seems, in fact, to be the synthesis of perception and creation.[1] It supposes the essentiality of both the subject and the object. The object is essential because it is strictly transcendent, because it imposes its own structures, and because one must wait for it and observe it; but the subject is also essential because it is required not only to disclose the object (that is, to make it possible for there to *be* an object) but also so that this object might exist absolutely (that is, to produce it). In a word, the reader is conscious of disclosing in creating, of creating by disclosing. In reality, it is not necessary to believe that reading is a mechanical operation and that signs make an impression upon him as light does on a photographic plate. If he is inattentive, tired, stupid, or thoughtless, most of the relations will escape him. He will never manage to "catch on" to the object (in the sense in which we see that fire "catches" or "doesn't catch"). He will draw some phrases out of the shadow, but they will seem to appear as random strokes. If he is at his best, he will project beyond the words a synthetic form, each phrase of which will be no more than a partial function: the "theme", the "subject", or the "meaning". Thus, from the very beginning, the meaning is no longer contained in the words, since it is he, on the contrary, who allows the significance of each of them to be understood; and the literary object, though realized *through* language, is never given *in* language. On the contrary, it is by nature a silence and an opponent of the word. In addition, the hundred thousand words aligned in a book can be read one by one so that the meaning of the work does not emerge. Nothing is accomplished if the reader does not put himself from the very beginning and almost without a guide at the height of this silence; if, in short, he does not invent it and does not then place there, and hold on to, the words and sentences which he awakens. And if I am told that it would be more fitting to call this operation a re-invention or a discovery, I shall answer that, first, such a re-invention would be as new and as original an act as the first invention. And, especially, when an object has never existed before, there can be no question of re-inventing it or discovering it. For if the silence about which I am speaking is really the goal at which the author is aiming, he has, at least, never been familiar with it; his silence is subjective and anterior to language. It is the absence of words, the undifferentiated and lived silence of inspiration, which the word will then particularize, whereas the silence produced by the reader is an object. And at the very interior of this object there are more silences—which the author does not mention. It is a question of silences which are so particular that they could not retain any meaning outside the object which the reading causes to appear. However, it is these which give it its density and its particular face.

To say that they are unexpressed is hardly the word; for they are precisely the inexpressible. And that is why one does not come upon them at any definite moment in the reading; they are everywhere and nowhere. The quality of the marvellous in *Le Grand Meaulnes,* the grandioseness of *Armance,* the degree of realism and truth of Kafka's mythology, these are never given. The reader must invent them all in a continual exceeding of the written thing. To be sure, the author guides him, but all he does is guide him. The landmarks he sets up are separated by the void. The reader must unite them; he must go beyond them. In short, reading is directed creation.

On the one hand, the literary object has no other substance than the reader's subjectivity; Raskolnikov's waiting is *my* waiting which I lend him. Without this impatience of the reader he would remain only a collection of signs. His hatred of the police magistrate who questions him is my hatred which has been solicited and wheedled out of me by signs, and the police magistrate himself would not exist without the hatred I have for him via Raskolnikov. That is what animates him, it is his very flesh.

But on the other hand, the words are there like traps to arouse our feelings and to reflect them towards us. Each word is a path of transcendence; it shapes our feelings, names them, and attributes them to an imaginary personage who takes it upon himself to live them for us and who has no other substance than these borrowed passions; he confers objects, perspectives, and a horizon upon them.

Thus, for the reader, all is to do and all is already done; the work exists only at the exact level of his capacities; while he reads and creates, he knows that he can always go further in his reading, can always create more profoundly, and thus the work seems to him as inexhaustible and opaque as things. We would readily reconcile that "rational intuition" which Kant reserved to divine Reason with this absolute production of qualities, which, to the extent that they emanate from our subjectivity, congeal before our eyes into impenetrable objectivities.

Since the creation can find its fulfilment only in reading, since the artist must entrust to another the job of carrying out what he has begun, since it is only through the consciousness of the reader that he can regard himself as essential to his work, all literary work is an appeal. To write is to make an appeal to the reader that he lead into objective existence the revelation which I have undertaken by means of language. And if it should be asked *to what* the writer is appealing, the answer is simple. As the sufficient reason for the appearance of the aesthetic object is never found either in the book (where we find merely solicitations to produce the object) or in the author's mind, and as his subjectivity, which he cannot get away from, cannot give a reason for the act of leading into objectivity, the appearance of the work of art is a new event which cannot *be explained* by anterior data. And since this directed creation is an absolute beginning, it is therefore brought about by the freedom of the reader, and by what is purest in that freedom. Thus, the writer appeals to the reader's freedom to collaborate in the production of his work.

It will doubtless be said that all tools address themselves to our freedom since they are the instruments of a possible action, and that the work of art is not unique in that. And it is true that the tool is the congealed outline of an operation. But it remains on the level of the hypothetical imperative. I may use a hammer to nail up a case or to hit my neighbour over the head. In so far as I consider it in itself, it is not an appeal to my freedom; it does not put me face to face with it; rather, it aims at using it by substituting a set succession of traditional procedures for the free invention of means. The book does not serve my freedom; it requires it. Indeed, one cannot address oneself to freedom as such by means of constraint, fascination, or entreaties. There is only one way of attaining it; first, by recognizing it, then, having confidence in it, and finally, requiring of it an act, an act in its own name, that is, in the name of the confidence that one brings to it.

Thus, the book is not, like the tool, a means for any end whatever; the end to which it offers itself is the reader's freedom. And the Kantian expression "finality without end" seems to me quite inappropriate for designating the work of art. In fact, it implies that the aesthetic object presents only the appearance of a finality and is limited to soliciting the free and ordered play of the imagination. It forgets that the imagination of the spectator has not only a regulating function, but a constitutive one. It does not play; it is called upon to recompose the beautiful object beyond the traces left by the artist. The imagination cannot revel in itself any more than can the other functions of the mind; it is always on the outside, always engaged in an enterprise. There would be finality without end if some object offered such a well-arranged composition that it would lead us to suppose that it has an end even though we cannot ascribe one to it. By defining the beautiful in this way one can—and this is Kant's aim—liken the beauty of art to natural beauty, since a flower, for example, presents so much symmetry, such harmonious colours, and such regular curves, that one is immediately tempted to seek a finalist explanation for all these properties and to see them as just so many means at the disposal of an unknown end. But that is exactly the error. The beauty of nature is in no way comparable to that of art. The work of art *does not have* an end; there we agree with Kant. But the reason is that it is an end. The Kantian formula does not account for the appeal which resounds at the basis of each painting, each statue, each book. Kant believes that the work of art first exists as fact and that it is then seen. Whereas) it exists only if one *looks* at it and if it is first pure appeal, pure exigence to exist. It is not an instrument whose existence is manifest and whose end is undetermined. It presents itself as a task to be discharged; from the very beginning it places itself on the level of the categorical imperative. You are perfectly free to leave that book on the table. But if you open it, you assume responsibility for it. For freedom is not experienced by its enjoying its free subjective functioning, but in a creative act required by an imperative. This absolute end, this imperative which is transcendent yet acquiesced in, which freedom itself adopts as its own, is what we call a value. The work of art is a value because it is an appeal.

If I appeal to my readers so that we may carry the enterprise which I have begun to a successful conclusion, it is self-evident that I consider him as a pure freedom, as an unconditioned activity; thus, in no case can I address myself to his passiveness, that is, try to *affect* him, to communicate to him, from the very first, emotions of fear, desire, or anger. There are, doubtless, authors who concern themselves solely with arousing these emotions because they are foreseeable, manageable, and because they have at their disposal sure-fire means for provoking them. But it is also true that they are reproached for this kind of thing, as Euripides has been since antiquity because he had children appear on the stage. Freedom is alienated in the state of passion; it is abruptly engaged in partial enterprises; it loses sight of its task, which is to produce an absolute end. And the book is no longer anything but a means for feeding hate or desire. The writer should not seek to *overwhelm;* otherwise he is in contradiction with himself; if he wishes to *make demands* he must propose only the task to be fulfilled. Hence, the character of pure presentation which appears essential to the work of art. The reader must be able to make a certain aesthetic withdrawal. This is what Gautier foolishly confused with "art for art's sake" and the Parnassians with the imperturbability of the artist. It is simply a matter of precaution, and Genet more justly calls it the author's politeness towards the reader. But that does not mean that the writer makes an appeal to some sort of abstract and conceptual freedom. One certainly creates the aesthetic object with feelings; if it is touching, it appears through our tears; if it is comic, it will be recognized by laughter. However, these feelings are of a particular kind. They have their origin in freedom; they are loaned. The belief which I accord the tale is freely assented to. It is a Passion, in the Christian sense of the word, that is, a freedom which resolutely puts itself into a state of passiveness to obtain a certain transcendent effect by this sacrifice. The reader renders himself credulous; he descends into credulity which, though it ends by enclosing him like a dream, is at every moment conscious of being free. An effort is sometimes made to force the writer into this dilemma: "Either one believes in your story, and it is intolerable, or one does not believe in it, and it is ridiculous". But the argument is absurd because the characteristic of aesthetic consciousness is to be a belief by means of commitment, by oath, a belief sustained by fidelity to one's self and to the author, a perpetually renewed choice to believe. I can awaken at every moment, and I know it; but I do not want to; reading is a free dream. So that all feelings which are exacted on the basis of this imaginary belief are like particular modulations of my freedom. Far from absorbing or masking it, they are so many different ways it has chosen to reveal itself to itself. Raskolnikov, as I have said, would only be a shadow, without the mixture of repulsion and friendship which I feel for him and which makes him live. But, by a reversal which is the characteristic of the imaginary object, it is not his behaviour which excites my indignation or esteem, but my indignation and esteem which give consistency and objectivity to his behaviour. Thus, the reader's feelings are never dominated by the object, and as no external reality can condition them, they have their permanent source in freedom; that is, they are all generous—for I call a feeling generous which has its origin and its end in freedom. Thus, reading is an exercise in generosity, and what the writer requires of the reader is not the application of an abstract freedom but the gift of his whole person, with his passions, his prepossessions, his sympathies, his sexual temperament, and his scale of values. Only this person will give himself generously; freedom goes through and through him and comes to transform the darkest masses of his sensibility. And as activity has rendered itself passive in order for it better to create the object, vice versa, passiveness becomes an act; the man who is reading has raised himself to the highest degree. That is why we see people who are known for their toughness shed tears at the recital of imaginary misfortunes; for the moment they have become what they would have been if they had not spent their lives hiding their freedom from themselves.

Thus, the author writes in order to address himself to the freedom of readers, and he requires it in order to make his work exist. But he does not stop there; he also requires that they return this confidence which he has given them, that they recognize his creative freedom, and that they in turn solicit it by a symmetrical and inverse appeal. Here there appears the other dialectical paradox of reading; the more we experience our freedom, the more we recognize that of the other; the more he demands of us, the more we demand of him.

When I am enchanted with a landscape, I know very well that it is not I who create it, but I also know that without me the relations which are established before my eyes among the trees, the foliage, the earth, and the grass would not exist at all. I know that I can give no reason for the appearance of finality which I discover in the assortment of hues and in the harmony of the forms and movements created by the wind. Yet, it exists; there it is before my eyes, and I can make something more out of what is already there. But even if I believe in God, I cannot establish any passage, unless it be purely verbal, between the divine, universal solicitude and the particular spectacle which I am considering. To say that He made the landscape in order to charm me or that He made me the kind of person who is pleased by it is to take a question for an answer. Is the marriage of this blue and that green deliberate? How can I know? The idea of a universal providence is no guarantee of any particular intention, especially in the case under consideration, since the green of the grass is explained by biological laws, specific constants, and geographical determinism, while the reason for the blue of the water is accounted for by the depth of the river, the nature of the soil and the swiftness of the current. The assorting of the shades, if it is willed, can only be something *thrown into the bargain*; it is the meeting of two causal series, that is to say, at first sight, a fact of chance. At best, the finality remains problematic. All the relations we establish remain hypotheses; no end is proposed to us in the manner of an imperative, since none is expressly revealed as having been willed by a creator. Thus, our freedom is never *called forth* by natural beauty. Or rather, there is an appearance of order in the whole which includes the foliage, the forms, and the movements, hence, the illusion of a calling forth which seems to solicit this freedom and which disappears immediately when one looks at it. Hardly have we begun to run our eyes over this arrangement, than the appeal disappears; we remain alone, free to tie up one colour with another or with a third, to set up a relationship between the tree and the water or the tree and the sky, or the tree, the water and the sky. My freedom becomes caprice. To the extent that I establish new relationships, I remove myself further from the illusory objectivity which solicits me. I *muse* about certain motifs which are vaguely outlined by the things; the natural reality is no longer anything but a pretext for musing. Or, in that case, because I have deeply regretted that this arrangement which was momentarily perceived was not offered to me by somebody and consequently is not *real*, the result is that I fix my dream, that I transpose it to canvas or in writing. Thus, I interpose myself between the finality without end which appears in the natural spectacles and the gaze of other men. I transmit it to them. It becomes human by this transmission. Art here is a ceremony of the *gift* and the gift alone brings about the metamorphosis. It is something like the transmission of titles and powers in the matriarchate where the mother does not possess the names, but is the indispensable intermediary between uncle and nephew. Since I have captured this illusion in flight, since I lay it out for other men and have disentangled it and rethought it for them, they can consider it with confidence. It has become intentional. As for me, I remain, to be sure, at the border of the subjective and the objective without ever being able to contemplate the objective arrangement which I transmit.

The reader, on the contrary, progresses in security. However far he may go, the author has gone further. Whatever connections he may establish among the different parts of the book—among the chapters or the words—he has a guarantee, namely, that they have been expressly willed. As Descartes says, he can even pretend that there is a secret order among parts which seem to have no connection. The creator has preceded him along the way, and the most beautiful disorders are effects of art, that is, again order. Reading is induction, interpolation, extrapolation, and the basis of these activities rests on the reader's will, as for a long time it was believed that that of scientific induction rested on the divine will. A gentle force accompanies us and supports us from the first page to the last. That does not mean that we fathom the artist's intentions easily. They constitute, as we have said, the object of conjectures, and there is an *experience of* the reader; but these conjectures are supported by the great certainty we have that the beauties which appear in the book are never accidental. In nature, the tree and the sky harmonize only by chance; if, on the contrary, in the novel, the protagonists find themselves in a *certain* tower, in a *certain* prison, if they stroll in a *certain* garden, it is a matter both of the restitution of independent causal series (the character had a certain state of mind which was due to a succession of psychological and social events; on the other hand, he betook himself to a determined place and the layout of the city required him to cross a certain park) and of the expression of a deeper finality, for the park came into existence only *in order to* harmonize with a certain state of mind, to express it by means of things or to put it into relief by a vivid contrast, and the state of mind itself was conceived in connection with the landscape. Here it is causality which is appearance and which might be called "causality without cause", and it is the finality which is the profound reality. But if I can thus in all confidence put the order of ends under the order of causes, it is because by opening the book I am asserting that the object has its source in human freedom.

If I were to suspect the artist of having written out of passion and in passion, my confidence would immediately vanish, for it would serve no purpose to have supported the order of causes by the order of ends. The latter would be supported in its turn by a psychic causality and the work of art would end by re-entering the chain of determinism. Certainly I do not deny when I am reading that the author may be impassioned, nor even that he might have conceived the first plan of his work under the sway of passion. But his decision to write supposes that he withdraws somewhat from his feelings, in short, that he has transformed his emotions into free emotions as I do mine while reading him, that is, that he is in an attitude of generosity.

Thus, reading is a pact of generosity between author and reader. Each one trusts the other; each one counts on the other, demands of the other as much as he demands of himself. For this confidence is itself generosity. Nothing can force the author to believe that his reader will use his freedom; nothing can force the reader to believe that the author has used his. Both of them make a free decision. There is then established a dialectical going-and-coming; when I read, I make demands; if my demands are met, what I am then reading provokes me to demand more of the author, which means to demand of the author that he demand more of me. And, vice versa, the author's demand is that I carry my demands to the highest pitch. Thus, my freedom, by revealing itself, reveals the freedom of the other.

It matters little whether the aesthetic object is the product of "realistic" art (or supposedly such) or "formal" art. At any rate, the natural relations are inverted; that tree on the first plane of the Cézanne painting first appears as the product of a causal chain. But the causality is an illusion; it will doubtless remain as a proposition as long as we look at the painting, but it will be supported by a deep finality; if the tree is placed in such a way it is because the rest of the painting *requires* that this form and those colours be placed on the first plane. Thus, through the phenomenal causality, our gaze attains finality as the deep structure of the object, and, beyond finality, it attains human freedom as its source and original basis. Vermeer's realism is carried so far that at first it might be thought to be photographic. But if one considers the splendour of his texture, the pink and velvety glory of his little brick walls, the blue thickness of a branch of woodbine, the glazed darkness of his vestibules, the orange coloured flesh of his faces, which are as polished as the stone of holy-water basins, one suddenly feels, in the pleasure that he experiences, that the finality is not so much in the forms or colours as in his material imagination. It is the very substance and temper of the things which here give the forms their reason for being. With this realist we are perhaps closest to absolute creation, since it is in the very passiveness of the matter that we meet the unfathomable freedom of man.

The work is never limited to the painted, sculpted, or narrated object. Just as one perceives things only against the background of the world, so the objects represented by art appear against the background of the universe. On the background of the adventures of Fabrice are the Italy of 1820, Austria, France, the sky and stars which the Abbé Blanis consults, and finally the whole earth. If the painter presents us with a field or a vase of flowers, his paintings are windows which are open on the whole world. We follow the red path which is buried among the wheat much farther than Van Gogh has painted it, among other wheat fields, under other clouds, to the river which empties into the sea, and we extend to infinity, to the other end of the world, the deep finality which supports the existence of the field and the earth. So that, through the various objects which it produces or reproduces, the creative act aims at a total renewal of the world. Each painting, each book, is a recovery of the totality of being. Each of them presents this totality to the freedom of the spectator. For this is quite the final goal of art: to recover this world by giving it to be seen as it is, but as if it had its source in human freedom. But, since what the author creates takes on objective reality only in the eyes of the spectator, this recovery is consecrated by the ceremony of the spectacle—and particularly of reading. We are already in a better position to answer the question we raised a while ago: the writer chooses to appeal to the freedom of other men so that, by the reciprocal implications of their demands, they may re-adapt the totality of being to man and may again enclose the universe within man.

If we wish to go still further, we must bear in mind that the writer, like all other artists, aims at giving his reader a certain feeling that is customarily called aesthetic pleasure, and which I would very much rather call aesthetic joy, and that this feeling, when it appears, is a sign that the work is achieved. It is therefore fining to examine it in the light of the preceding considerations. In effect, this joy, which is denied to the creator, in so far as he creates, becomes one with the aesthetic consciousness of the spectator, that is, in the case under consideration, of the reader. It is a complex feeling but one whose structures and condition are inseparable from one another. It is identical, at first, with the recognition of a transcendent and absolute end which, for a moment, suspends the utilitarian round of ends-means and means-ends,[2] that is, of an appeal or, what amounts to the same thing, of a value. And the positional consciousness which I take of this value is necessarily accompanied by the non-positional consciousness of my freedom, since my freedom is manifested to itself by a transcendent exigency. The recognition of freedom by itself is joy, but this structure of non-thetical consciousness implies another: since, in effect, reading is creation, my freedom does not only appear to itself as pure autonomy but as creative activity, that is, it is not limited to giving itself its own law but perceives itself as being constitutive of the object. It is on this level that the phenomenon specifically is manifested, that is, a creation wherein the created object is given *as object* to its creator. It is the sole case in which the creator gets any enjoyment out of the object he creates. And the word enjoyment which is applied to the positional consciousness of the work read indicates sufficiently that we are in the presence of an essential structure of aesthetic joy. This positional enjoyment is accompanied by the non-positional consciousness of being essential in relation to an object perceived as essential. I shall call this aspect of aesthetic consciousness the feeling of security; it is this which stamps the strongest aesthetic emotions with a sovereign calm. It has its origin in the authentication of a strict harmony between subjectivity and objectivity. As, on the other hand, the aesthetic object is properly the world in so far as it is aimed at through the imaginary, aesthetic joy accompanies the positional consciousness that the world is a value, that is, a task proposed to human freedom. I shall call this the aesthetic modification of the human project, for, as usual, the world appears as the horizon of our situation, as the infinite distance which separates us from ourselves, as the synthetic totality of the given, as the undifferentiated whole of obstacles and implements—but never as a demand addressed to our freedom. Thus, aesthetic joy proceeds to this level of the consciousness which I take of recovering and internalizing that which is non-ego *par excellence*, since I transform the given into an imperative and the fact into a value. The world is *my task*, that is, the essential and freely accepted function of my freedom is to make that unique and absolute object which is the universe come into being in an unconditioned movement. And, thirdly, the preceding structures imply a pact between human freedoms, for, on the one hand, reading is a confident and exacting recognition of the freedom of the writer, and, on the other hand, aesthetic pleasure, as it is itself experienced in the form of a value, involves an absolute exigence in regard to others; every man, in so far as he is a freedom, feels the same pleasure in reading the same work. Thus, all mankind is present in its highest freedom; it sustains the being of a world which is both *its* world and the "external" world. In aesthetic joy the positional consciousness is an *image-making* consciousness of the world in its totality both as being and having to be, both as totally ours and totally foreign, and the more ours as it is the more foreign. The nonpositional consciousness *really* envelops the harmonious totality of human freedoms in so far as it makes the object of a universal confidence and exigency.

To write is thus both to disclose the world and to offer it as a task to the generosity of the reader. It is to have recourse to the consciousness of others in order to make one's self be recognized as *essential* to the totality of being; it is to wish to live this essentiality by means of interposed persons; but, on the other hand, as the real world is revealed only by action, as one can feel oneself in it only by exceeding it in order to change it, the novelist's universe would lack depth if it were not discovered in a movement to transcend it. It has often been observed that an object in a story does not derive its density of existence from the number and length of the descriptions devoted to it, but from the complexity of its connections with the different characters. The more often the characters handle it, take it up, and put it down, in short, go beyond it towards their own ends, the more real will it appear. Thus, of the world of the novel, that is, the totality of men and things, we may say that in order for it to offer its maximum density the disclosure-creation by which the reader discovers it must also be an imaginary participation in the action; in other words, the more disposed one is to change it, the more alive it will be. The error of realism has been to believe that the real reveals itself to contemplation, and that consequently one could draw an impartial picture of it. How could that be possible, since the very perception is partial, since by itself the naming is already a modification of the object? And how could the writer, who wants himself to be essential to this universe, want to be essential to the injustice which this universe comprehends? Yet, he must be; but if he accepts being the creator of injustices, it is in a movement which goes beyond them towards their abolition. As for me who read, if I create and keep alive an unjust world, I cannot help making myself responsible for it. And the author's whole art is bent on obliging me to *create* what he *discloses*, therefore to compromise myself. So both of us bear the responsibility for the universe. And precisely because this universe is supported by the joint effort of our two freedoms, and because the author, with me as medium, has attempted to integrate it into the human, it must appear truly *in itself* in its very marrow, as being shot through and through with a freedom which has taken human freedom as its end, and if it is not really the city of ends that it ought to be, it must at least be a stage along the way; in a word, it must be a becoming and it must always be considered and presented not as a crushing mass which weighs us down, but from the point of view of its going beyond towards that city of ends. However bad and hopeless the humanity which it paints may be, the work must have an air of generosity. Not, of course, that this generosity is to be expressed by means of edifying discourses and virtuous characters; it must not even be premeditated, and it is quite true that fine sentiments do not make fine books. But it must be the very warp and woof of the book, the stuff out of which the people and things are cut; whatever the subject, a sort of essential lightness must appear everywhere and remind us that the work is never a natural datum, but an *exigence* and a *gift*. And if I am given this world with its injustices, it is not so that I may contemplate them coldly, but that I may animate them with my indignation, that I may disclose them and create them with their nature as injustices, that is, as abuses to be suppressed. Thus, the writer's universe will only reveal itself in all its depth to the examination, the admiration, and the indignation of the reader; and the generous love is a promise to maintain, and the generous indignation is a promise to change, and the admiration a promise to imitate; although literature is one thing and morality a quite different one, at the heart of the aesthetic imperative we discern the moral imperative. For, since the one who writes recognizes, by the very fact that he takes the trouble to write, the freedom of his readers, and since the one who reads, by the mere fact of his opening the book, recognizes the freedom of the writer, the work of art, from whichever side you approach it, is an act of confidence in the freedom of men, And since readers, like the author, recognize this freedom only to demand that it manifest itself, the work can be defined as an imaginary presentation of the world in so far as it demands human freedom. The result of which is that there is no "gloomy literature", since, however dark may be the colours in which one paints the world, one paints it only so that free men may feel their freedom as they face it. Thus, there are only good and bad novels. The bad novel aims to please by flattering, whereas the good one is an exigence and an act of faith. But above all, the unique point of view from which the author can present the world to those freedoms whose concurrence he wishes to bring about is that of a world to be impregnated always with more freedom. It would be inconceivable that this unleashing of generosity provoked by the writer could be used to authorize an injustice, and that the reader could enjoy his freedom while reading a work which approves or accepts or simply abstains from condemning the subjection of man by man. One can imagine a good novel being written by an American negro even if hatred of the whites were spread all over it, because it is the freedom of his race that he demands through this hatred. And, as he invites me to assume the attitude of generosity, the moment I feel myself a pure freedom I cannot bear to identify myself with a race of oppressors. Thus, I require of all freedoms that they demand the liberation of coloured people against the white race and against myself in so far as I am a part of it, but nobody can suppose for a moment that it is possible to write a good novel in praise of anti-Semitism.[3] For, the moment I feel that my freedom is indissolubly linked with that of all other men, it cannot be demanded of me that I use it to approve the enslavement of a part of these men. Thus, whether he is an essayist, a pamphleteer, a satirist, or a novelist, whether he speaks only of individual passions or whether he attacks the social order, the writer, a free man addressing free men, has only one subject—freedom.

Hence, any attempt to enslave his readers threatens him in his very art. A blacksmith can be affected by fascism in his life as a man, but not necessarily in his craft; a writer will be affected in both, and even more in his craft than in his life. I have seen writers, who before the war called for fascism with all their hearts, smitten with sterility at the very moment when the Nazis were loading them with honours. I am thinking of Drieu la Rochelle in particular; he was mistaken, but he was sincere. He proved it. He had agreed to direct a Nazi-inspired review. The first few months he reprimanded, rebuked, and lectured his countrymen. No one answered him because no one was free to do so. He became irritated; he no longer *felt* his readers. He became more insistent, but no sign appeared to prove that he had been understood. No sign of hatred, nor of anger either; nothing. He seemed to have lost his bearings, the victim of a growing distress. He complained bitterly to the Germans. His articles had been superb; they became shrill. The moment arrived when he struck his breast; no echo, except among the bought journalists whom he despised. He handed in his resignation, withdrew it, again spoke, still in the desert. Finally, he said nothing, gagged by the silence of others. He had demanded the enslavement of others, but in his crazy mind he must have imagined that it was voluntary, that it was still free. It came; the man in him congratulated himself mightily, but the writer could not bear it. While this was going on, others, who, happily, were in the majority, understood that the freedom of writing implies the freedom of the citizen. One does not write for slaves. The art of prose is bound up with the only régime in which prose has meaning, democracy. When one is threatened, the other is too. And it is not enough to defend them with the pen. A day comes when the pen is forced to stop, and the writer must then take up arms. Thus, however you might have come to it, whatever the opinions you might have professed, literature throws you into battle. Writing is a certain way of wanting freedom; once you have begun, you are committed, willy-nilly.

Committed to what? Defending freedom? That's easy to say. Is it a matter of acting as a guardian of ideal values like Benda's "clerk" before the betrayal,[4] or is it concrete everyday freedom which must be protected by our taking sides in political and social struggles? The question is tied up with another one, one very simple in appearance but which nobody ever asks himself: "For whom does one write?"

THE FAMILY IDIOT

The post-Romantic apprentice author

Absolute-Art

Throughout the works of the eighteenth century, autonomy seems to be an objective status of literature. A class literature, to be sure, but as that class is combatant, autonomy here represents a pure, combative negativity; it asserts itself as an institutional imperative, inseparable from analytic reason, the chief weapon of the bourgeoisie, whose ultimate outcome must be mechanism, that is, dissolution taken to its logical conclusion.

The same notion, after a period of eclipse, reappears in Romantic literature. But its function is no longer the same and its meaning has changed; it is now merely the obligation of aristocratic writers to impose the ideology of their class. Beneath the positive idea of synthetic totality, of creation, that ideology conceals two negations—one compensatory, the victory-failure of the nobility, the other fixed and absolute, the radical condemnation of the bourgeoisie.

These two imperatives, reanimated by reading, are intertwined and give literary autonomy an instable and circular content; for that autonomy is based on analysis, whose function is to reduce everything to its elements, and on the aristocratic synthesis that establishes totalitarian unities on the unity of the creating fiat. Thus the project imposed on the future writer is forever to depict the creation in his work as the production of a harmonious whole, and forever to eat away at it with the worm of analysis, whose self-imposed task must be to reduce it to mechanistic dispersal. But this final term of the dissection is not the ultimate theme of the work, though the analysis cannot be carried further; indeed, through the coexistence of the two imperatives, neither of which destroys the other, the totality is no sooner atomized than it is revived and once again subjected to analytic diastasis. So this double, contradictory autonomy somehow demands of the young bourgeois would-be writer the *literary* disclosure of the nothingness of being and the being of nothingness—which reflects, with the *hysteresis* proper to cultural works, the antagonism of two classes, one of which is on the way to its demise. The general theme suggested by literature-to-be-written is the reduction of the world as totality to nothingness, and the reestablishment of that totality as appearance. Behind this perpetual movement, however, a third term is concealed, for totality, an optimistic but mortal instrument of the aristocracy, is realized on the literary suppression of the bourgeoisie; thus totalization by the master, while devoured by servile negativity, destroys the slave and his labor by a fixed, total, irreducible negation. No literary works after 1850 are without the skeletal structure of this triple antagonism. Revealing it, as I have just done, we can say that it *offers no meaning*: the slave denies the master, who does away with him, that's all; or, if you like, the creation is reduced to mechanism, which is reduced to the absolute void from which the creation is reborn. Meaning cannot come from these contradictions, which coexist only because their spatial contiguity as *practico-inert* determinations has effaced the historical temporalization that produced them *successively*. A meaning *must* emerge from these antagonisms, and the future author is bidden to provide it through his work. He is free to choose it, provided that he integrates all contradictions in the aesthetic unity of the object produced.

The freedom to choose, without ever being entirely suppressed, is nonetheless singularly reduced by imperatives *exterior* to the first. Other historical circumstances have in effect produced new determinations of the Objective Spirit which, in the trinity comprised of totality, negativity, and negation, tend to demand the predominance of absolute negation. For these young bourgeois, the autonomy of literature is the fundamental requirement of that cultural sector and the primary reason for their choice to write; and yet at the moment when their class triumphs and demands positive books, that autonomy seems to them merely a way of gilding its utilitarian morality with a little idealism. As a result, these future authors have broken with the readership of their own class even before they have written, meaning that by 1840, they have broken with the public pure and simple. Consequently, negativity and the spirit of analysis, instruments that were so effective in the previous century, seem suspect to them; when they yearn to make use of them, they run up against objective resistances arising from the fact that these are the tools proper to their class, and they will not appropriate them without being appropriated in turn. As a result, the human subject of their books—if there is one—will no longer be the man depicted by Voltaire, Diderot, or Rousseau himself; he will no longer contain that "human nature" defined by analysis thanks to social and psychological atomism. But the young writer offers no substitute; in any case, nothing new occurs to these young minds spoiled by analysis. Romantic man, in effect, could not seduce them for long. In 1840, Romanticism is dead, as witness the failure of *Les Burgraves*; for Romantic man represents a synthetic totality, and as good bourgeois they could not refrain from dismantling him despite themselves. Yet by vanishing, the hero made them ashamed of themselves, of their class of origin. The aristocratic authors' contempt remains in them as the great mute negation hidden behind Romantic frenzy. They have contempt for themselves without knowing why. And this contempt becomes their sole greatness since it raises them above themselves. This contorted attitude, the internalization of absolute negation, must be held without respite. But which do they scorn in Others and themselves, the bourgeois or the man? First, surely, the bourgeois. These unhappy young men have internalized the contested but ubiquitous and scornful gaze of another, nearly moribund class; they are cut off from themselves by this gaze of failure and death that reveals only bourgeois utilitarianism and the spirit of analysis—ethical and epistemological norms *already familiar* to them. But the bourgeoisie rejects the "people," that vast national unity invented by the monarchy in the interest of propaganda. It knows the working classes, which it exploits, fears, and dislikes, and which its resident thinkers attempt to reduce to the swarmings of individuals; it takes itself for the universal class and now proclaims that classes are abolished. Consequently, its younger sons see *bourgeois man* everywhere; for it means to impose bourgeois *nature*, on the ethical and psychological level, on the individuals who each day, constrained by the wretched poverty spawned by industrialization, make "free" individual contracts with it. The bourgeoisie teaches them, it teaches its own children that this "nature" is truly the essence of the species, that like good bourgeois, the workers, too, seek their interest, competing with each other for employment just like businessmen or entrepreneurs, and that—like bourgeois, maybe more so—they are individually *envious* of the prosperity of others. The fact is that human nature is bad; it must be restrained by rigorous institutions and its weaknesses supported by real property. Raised in these principles—without much questioning them—the young bourgeois have no difficulty extending their contempt to the universe. This is made even easier by the fact that the world is bourgeois—or at least it is expressed only by bourgeois voices—from 1830 on. If man is bourgeois, these children have contempt for the bourgeois in themselves as the definition of mankind. And that contempt, despairing at its lack of support, extending from their class of origin to their race and back again to their class, having acquired a sufficient degree of mystification to follow the path to the universal, will be called *dissatisfaction* by the most realistic. On the one hand it is the verification of what exists and could not be otherwise (In whose name would they contest this nature, these natural laws, and the society that issues from it?); on the other hand it is the global and harmless negation they inherited from Romanticism, defeated in advance, without principle or privilege in this real domain. Nothing else is even declared possible—How would they dare to affirm such a thing when they were raised in unbelief, in agnosticism, or in a superficial religion practiced to give the poor a reason to live and subjected by the lycée student as a matter of major concern to triumphant bourgeois analysis? They may even think, like Laplace, that everything had to be this way from all eternity. In short, they say nothing; they simply live out an impotent denial of the whole world, whose meaning is: I *am not* part of it, I do not *recognize* myself in it. These boys in no way consider themselves fallen gods who remember the heavens; they remember nothing at all. They deny that being, such as it is, *represents* them (in their eyes, in the eyes of others); they claim not to be incarnate in it, not to be objectified in it as bourgeois or as men through work. And this claim, which by itself would be consciously futile, assumes in their eyes the substance of an imperative because it is contiguous in them with autonomy as the rigorous requirement of literature and gives it, ultimately, its content.

Autonomy, the necessary means of writing in 1850, the arrogant exercise of the privileged aristocratic gaze in 1830, appears *in any case* to the new generation as art for its own sake. This *obvious* characteristic of literature-to-be-written represents to them the eternal imperative that their fathers and grandfathers misunderstood *and* originality, since it will be *their* task to obey it. Yet if art has no end but itself, if it disappears from the work when asked to serve, if its major imperative condemns utilitarianism—without even referring to it—and along with it all human ends, then this calm and thorough negation, this perfect inhumanity, can be revealed only to the dissatisfied, who exhaust themselves condemning the world but lack the power to leave it. In other words, in this period as in any other, art defines its artist. No one can accede to it who is not first discontent with everything; indeed, if he has made the slightest accommodation to real society, he will not even think of tearing himself away and will attempt to make a place for himself in it, to objectify himself through productive work. Conversely, absolute negation as perpetual dissatisfaction will be merely an insubstantial whim and will not be raised to ontological dignity insofar as it will not be incarnate in a work whose absolute nihilism—without being the overriding goal[5]—is its immediate and necessary condition. Thus, while the subject of a literature that is posed as its own end is yet undetermined, one thing is certain: its autonomy is not experienced at this time as the necessary status of a social activity, nor even as the result of the writer's permanent struggle against the powers that be; it is an affirmation of art as the *only absolute*, hence the condemnation of all *practical* enterprise—aiming at any objective, at a given date, in a given society. Absolute-art produces its own temporality—as an inner temporalization imposed by the work on the public. But the refusal to serve, sustained by the young authors' internalized, aristocratic disgust for bourgeois activities, immediately rises above practical temporality. In other words, there are only eternal works, and those that are not eternal *at their inception*, even if distinguished by some purely aesthetic quality, can *in no way* be called works of art.

But while this notion of absolute-art is generated by the interference of the aristocratic imperative with several other imperatives we have enumerated, while it is based indirectly on contempt, or perhaps because it is, the work-to-be-written does not seem a gift to the new generation and does not demand any generosity of the artist. Absolute negation in these youngsters comes, in fact, from the bourgeois certainty that generosity is a mirage, a booby trap invented by the nobility for its conquerors; they looked for and found interested motives behind generous actions. Besides, to whom would the work be given? The only *real* public is the bourgeoisie, who want a class literature. To be *given* a disinterested work, they would at least have to imagine accepting it, which is by definition impossible. And why give anything to men when you have contempt for them all, and when the novel or poem expresses absolute negation, its author's regret at belonging to humanity?

The fact is that the work is not a *donation,* it is not addressed to anyone, and when Musset *gives* his sufferings to readers, these young puritans are horrified by his striptease. This is the same literary current that will soon account for the success of the idea, now outdated, that literature is a form of prostitution. At that moment, turning its negation against itself, literature would condemn itself because it would eventually be read. No, the author is not generous; what he seeks in art, and in the rigorous impersonality of the work, is his *personal* salvation. His refusal to be man will become objectified in the inhumanity of absolute-art: the inaccessible beauty of his product will turn the negative into something positive.

Thus the notion of the panoramic *overview* takes on a third meaning generated by the other two. In the eighteenth century, the writer must survey society because—in his own eyes—he escapes class determinations and finds himself thereby representing human nature "without foreign additives"; through the Romantic overview, the writers of 1830 reaffirm the superiority of the aristocratic, and the lofty gaze they level on other classes restores the hierarchical society in which by divine right they occupy the highest rung. The former believe they are surveying society and declare their solidarity with all men; the latter are and want to be inside it but in first place; in solidarity with their class and with it alone, they protest that exemplary man exists only as an aristocrat, and that the other ranks are merely rough drafts of humanity. In both cases, such a panoramic overview does not dehumanize; on the contrary, it allows the author—though in rather different ways—to express the human in its plenitude. Man of the eighteenth century is simply by definition what Romantic man rejects; in 1840 this internalized contradiction produces uncertainty and disgust in the young men who are ready to go on duty; consequently, the panoramic overview becomes a metaphysical rupture of the writer with his race. Denying human nature in himself, he takes an artist's overview of the world, that apparent totality which breaks up into molecules, and of man, that stranger who inhabits it. What he discovers, we surmise, is universal nothingness—as the noetic counterpart of his attitude of absolute negation. The contradiction of this attitude is that he claims simultaneously to make himself an aristocrat (therefore the best of men)—a notion borrowed from the Romantics—and to sever his ties with humanity. And this contradiction is attributable not to subjective motives but to the coexistence in the practico-inert of two determinations of the Objective Spirit that are internalized through reading in the same mind in which they are united, opposing each other through bonds of interiority. As if the young reader had concluded that in order to *make himself* aristocratic, he had no choice but to escape from his own nature through absolute-art. As a consequence, absolute-art expresses the point of view of the absolute on the world. A point of view that is resumed in the absolute of negation.

Yet the most basic requirement of the new art is impossible to satisfy. In the first place, the idea of absolute negation is a contradiction *in adjecto*. The existence of an object or a quality in a determined sector of being, and in relation to another object or another sector, is denied. Moreover, negation is merely the formal and judicial aspect of negativity, which is praxis, destructive work. It is logically admissible, for example, that one class can deny the privileges of another class or its rights. And this is precisely the source of negation as an attitude: the writer-aristocrats, by their contempt and the positive aspect of their ideology, deny the humanism and humanity of the bourgeois. But transposed to the young men of 1840, pushed to the limit and decreed a priori a literary requirement without the support of a social class, or at least a social stratum, negation becomes absolute at the moment it ceases to express an external view of the object, and it no longer signifies anything but the subjective effort of those young malcontents to take their distance in relation to the class that produced and sustained them. A futile effort, obviously, and one that leads to the denial of *everything* in the name of nothing. Indeed, the Postromantics' condemnation extends to the totality of the world: they want to expose it, beneath the mosaic of appearances, as nothingness. But *in relation to what* can this world, which in any case exists, be regarded as a lesser being and finally as that nothingness, vanity of vanities, which must be its ultimate secret? If it were in relation to God, who represents the total plenitude of being, that negation would be conceivable; but precisely for that reason a Christian would ascribe to it only a *relative* meaning: *in relation* to God, the world is nothingness; but in itself, and to the extent that it was the object of the Almighty's creative act, it is impossible to deny it a certain reality. If, on the other hand, God is not at issue, and if nihilism is applied to the world in itself, negation becomes absolute but now signifies nothing; and, as we know, those young agnostics no more claim to compare the world to a Creator than to judge the bourgeoisie through the eyes of the real aristocracy. The purpose of a work of art, according to them, is to manifest the inconceivable. Nothingness is not only the disintegration of the totality into molecules whose movements are governed from the outside by laws of exteriority; it is at the same time the condemnation of mechanism in the name of that impossible totality. Thesis, in effect, would be merely the application of bourgeois thought to the mendacious syntheses of history and religion. But if antithesis were reformulated and now defined mechanism itself as nothingness (a *nothing* without unity) even while destroying it, the writer would attempt to retain in himself that *arrested* double movement and present it as the world's negation of itself. Art, then, sets itself an unrealizable task: it will have to hide the real antinomy of thesis and antithesis and give it its purely fictive solution in beauty—in this case in the flaunted cult of appearance, of that which denounces its own lack of reality.

These young writers, when they aspire to that overview, have never meant it to be a real activity. In any event, overview is impossible, as we know, since we are fixed in space. But they know it as well. They have never dreamed, like philosophical dogmatists, of acquiring by that "distancing" an absolute knowledge of being. And although they like to speak of mystical ecstasies, they have not tried to envisage distancing as a real transcendence, a real ascent toward that absolute term, the God of believers. Their scientism, the sad fruit of the surprising progress of science, deters them from regarding philosophy as a rigorous discipline; rather, they have seen it as an auxiliary of art. The free play of ideas gave a broader foundation and some guiding schemes to the free play of imagination. And as for mysticism$_1$ apart from the fact that they lacked faith—the result above all of the progressive laicization of all sectors of human activity—they could not espouse the elevation of the mystic *in any case*. Indeed, if the mystic in his dark night has the feeling of progressively shedding the mundane determinations of his finitude, passions, language, and even imagination, it is because his enterprise has only one purpose: to offer himself to God so that He might penetrate him and suffuse him with ecstasy. He isn't the least concerned with leaning over and looking down to contemplate terrestrial nothingness from above. The negative is merely a means of ascesis; the end is pure positivity. And if, on the contrary, he returns to our world, he does so in order to regard it with the utmost seriousness and to help his brothers, as did John of the Cross and Theresa of Avila. Instead, our young men, caught between negativity and nothingness, frustrated by faith, convinced of the truth of scientism but hardly attracted by its austere theories, elevate themselves only to take their distance from the world and to embrace it in a single negative view. Having taken up literature in order to escape their fathers, naively persuaded that it could treat only lofty sentiments, they have seen those sentiments disappear and have understood in their disappointment that literary art was the terrain dreamed of for the totalization of their rancor and the assuaging of that hatred of man provoked by the Objective Spirit. But since they must elevate themselves without any source of support or lifeline, and without any real destination, they cannot help knowing that their ascension is fictive, or, rather, that they are embarking upon it without considering its strict impossibility, and even *against* it. And this is precisely why they define the imaginary as a permanent recourse against the impossible.

For these young men, literature opens an emergency exit; the imaginary being beyond the impossible but without its own consistency, its objectivization in the work will give it the consistency it lacks. In view of the work, and by virtue of it, they insist on their unconditional condemnation of the real by absolute negation as an unreal negation whose virulence comes, in fact, from *their choice of unreality*. In other words, literature imposes itself on them through the Objective Spirit as having no domain but the antireal, or pure unreality, pitting itself against the palpable world. Only in this way can they give a certain efficacy to the various ruptures imposed on them by their situation and the determinations of the Objective Spirit. In the name of autonomy they had to break with the public just when contrary imperatives were compelling them to break with man, then with the world. In short, with the totality of the real. And yet they remained what they were: young bourgeois of the middle class, supported by their family or practicing a "liberal" profession. So they had to choose: either nothing had been produced—because nothing could be produced—except in dreams; and so literature, insofar as it demanded these ruptures, had become *impossible.* Or the choice of the imaginary, insofar as it represented the common signification of that behavior, was an effective and revolutionary step. The Postromantics chose the imaginary *so as to be able* to write.

But the necessity of this choice represents in itself an element of objective neurosis. Let us examine what it means. In the first place, rupture with the real—which is equivalent to condemning it—cannot be lived except as a permanent refusal to adapt; the artist must deny the aims of the race and society in himself and others as much as possible. And as he does not always manage to do so, the refusal must be imaginary. Similarly, he is required to lose the ordinary comprehension of objects, acts, and words to the same extent that absolute negation compels him no longer to share common aims. But this incomprehension does not come—as with the philosophers of the Platonic cave—from a superior knowledge that would in itself degrade the superficial activities of men in the name of their underlying essence and the essential goals of humanity, or even from a demand for deeper knowledge of them. Outside this incomprehension there is nothing: it confines itself to manifesting things in a state of estrangement precisely because of the refusal to integrate them into a real system. The point, in short, is to live in a permanent state of slight depersonalization, sometimes sincerely felt, sometimes maintained in the form of a *role.* In this state, if it can be sustained by external assistance, the writer must put himself and the world between parentheses; he does not intervene, he abstains. Consequently, things lose their weight of reality and sensation loses its "seriousness"; this is a subtle way of "realizing" absolute negation by reducing the universe to a series of apparitions untested by praxis and which—by their nothingness of being, the total absence of any co-efficient of instrumentality or adversity—are finally equal to *appearances.* Since art must be the supreme negation, the content of the work will be that desubstantialized, invisible universe of the imaginary. And in order to obtain the suppression of being in the interest of the pure, unreal apparition, the artist will have to receive his impressions *as if he were imagining them.* This is called the *aesthetic attitude,* the rigorous requirement of a literature that claims its full autonomy just when the bourgeoisie wants a class literature. With this attitude the artist un-realizes himself and at the same time derealizes the world. And as art is posited for its own sake through him, these strategies must in themselves imply a reversal of the usual set of values, making appearances worth more than realities and any apparition valued in proportion to its quantity of nonbeing. Thus the autonomy of art in 1850 can be obtained only through the nonreality of the artist and the content of the work, since these show us the nonreality of the world or the subordination of being to appearance. This may mean that the techniques of art are used to destroy the real, to present it in the work as it appears to the aesthetic attitude. Or it may mean that the artist can turn his back on reality, a strategy particularly favored in the Symbolist period for the purpose of choosing the imaginary and even attempting an oneiric literature. The chief thing, in one form or another, is the valorization of nonbeing. Around this time, the reason for writing is to resurrect vanished civiliza-tions, to contest quotidian banality by an exoticism often entirely fabricated in Paris. Everything that is no longer there, that is not there, that is fixed in a permanent absence, is good provided one has access to the resurrected object solely through imagination. There is nothing accidental in the widespread vogue of Orientalism, the translation of sacred Indian songs, the recurrent presence of antique Greece—works on Greek history and art proliferate—but it is more dead and distant than ever. Writers thus hoped to escape their element and wanted that ancient, exotic culture to remain savage and inaccessible, its un-assimilable originality revealing itself in the very heart of reading to be an image beyond all images, making palpable the nothingness at the very heart of imagination as the limit imposed on it by absence and death.

Absolute-art, an objective determination of literature-to-be-written, imposes the rupture with being on its future ministers from the outset. They cannot write without a metamorphosis which, unable to call itself by name without exposing its neurotic nature, announces itself *object-ively* as an *ordination.* But the comparison is misleading: a religious order is an institution that sustains the vocation of the neophyte against the exterior and often against himself; in addition, for a believer, and above all in eras when faith is a positive bond between men, a young man *leaving the world,* in what is actually a negative moment, believes he is turning toward the full positivity of being. But when literature makes itself the absolute, that absolute can be only an absolute of negation. Thus the *vows* of the writer commit him only to himself and are posited by themselves as always revocable. In other words, they will be irrevocable—which is a necessity—only if the artist is unable to revoke them. The fact is that his first negation or renunciation of the world is not supported by any community and, far from being a source of integration, reveals exile and solitude as his imperative lot; on the other hand, this negation is not transformed into negativity—or the patient and joyous work of undermining—or into the gateway to positivity (the neophyte's access to the primary truths of the supernatural plenitude of real being). It must remain radical negation. And the supreme dignity of the work—a false positivity—lies in its vampirization of being (and primordially language); its fabric is, and must remain, *imaginary*. Therefore the artist can choose to show our world or a possible world in the brightest colors; the imperative simply demands that those colors, in one way or another, denounce their own nonbeing and that of the depicted object. In other words, absolute-art demands a suicide swiftly followed by genocide. And together these operations—one subjective, the other objective—can only be *imaginary*. Absolute-art requires *entrance-into-literature* the way in certain times and places *people entered into religion*. But as this conduct is purely fictive for the writer, it could be called his *entrance-into-the-imaginary-realm*. The Objective Spirit demands that he choose unreality as a rigorous refusal of the real (which he may subsequently depict, but as the real refused); but since this option *is itself imaginary*, its precariousness is evident to the author and denounces him as a traitor to art, possibly forever, indeed as a traitor to himself *unless* that precariousness has the consistency and irreducibility of a neurosis, or a suffered option. Of course neurosis as a *solution*, as the only possible support for the vow of unreality, is not imposed by the imperatives of 1850; those demand simply that the artist become *other than man*, that he attain this state through an ascesis and maintain himself there. But in this impossibility born of contradictory demands, neurosis emerges as a possible solution. And it amounts to this fascinating suggestion: let us behave as if all those insurmountable difficulties were resolved; let us, indeed, start from this solution, leaving to our bodies the task of finding and living it; let us write *beyond* the negative convulsions of our decrepitude.

Notes

1   The same is true in different degrees regarding the spectator's attitude before other works of art (paintings, symphonies, statues, etc.).

2   In *practical life* a means may be taken for an end as soon as one searches for it, and each end is revealed as a means of attaining another end.

3   This last remark may arouse some readers. If so, I'd like to know a single good novel whose express purpose was to serve oppression, a single good novel which has been written against Jews, negroes, workers, or colonial people. "But if there isn't any, that's no reason why someone may not write one some day." But you then admit that you are an abstract theoretician. You, not I. For it is in the name of your abstract conception of art that you assert the possibility of a fact which has never come into being, whereas I limit myself to proposing an explanation for a recognized fact.

4   The reference here is to Benda's *La Trahison des clercs*, translated into English as *The Great Betrayal.—Translator.*

5   To pursue in a work of art a direct enterprise of radical negation, to make it the *goal* of art, is to give it an end other than itself. But if art is pursued *for art's sake*, the affirmation of the beautiful implies negation of the real.

15 The work of art

The conclusion of *The Psychology of the Imagination* includes a discussion of the work of art, reproduced below. Here I discuss Sartre's views on music and painting.

Although music meant a great deal to Sartre personally, he wrote very little about it. What he does say, in *The Psychology of the Imagination*, in *What is Literature?* and in *Situations* is of considerable philosophical interest.

Sartre thinks that what is expressed or communicated through music can not be wholly expressed or communicated in words. Words can not substitute for music. (If they could, music would be in a sense redundant. Music would be, perhaps, an abbreviation of verbal language.) Sartre says of music it will always be over and above anything you can say about it. No matter how thorough the attempt to characterise in words what is expressed in music something remains uncaptured. Music says more than we can say that it says. Music as heard can not be verbally described, even though musical notation is an abstract description of music, and the language of physics or aesthetic appreciation includes true assertions about music.

Sartre thinks music does not take on meaning by referring to non-musical reality. The 'significance' of a melody is nothing outside the melody itself. If what music signifies is music then the significance of music can not be found in non-musical reality. It does not follow that words can not express what music expresses but it is inconsistent with the existence of any non-musical source of musical significance that could be accessed either verbally or musically. Language expresses non-linguistic reality but music does not express non-musical reality. This does not soundly refute the possibility of the verbal expression of the musical but it is inconsistent with one picture of that putative possibility.

What is music? What is a musical work of art? Sartre does not address these questions directly but, perhaps surprisingly, he says of Beethoven's

7th Symphony 'I do not hear it actually'. He says 'I listen to it in the imaginary'. If we draw a distinction between a symphony and the performance of that symphony then it makes more sense to speak of listening to the performance than listening to the symphony. If one is listening to a performance then, at any one time ('actually'), one is hearing only part of the performance although, in another sense, one is thereby hearing all of it.

In order to hear part of a performance of a symphony as part of the performance of that symphony certain psychological facts have to obtain. Sartre largely endorses the distinction Husserl draws between *protention* and *retention* in *Lectures on the Phenomenology of Internal Time Consciousness* (1905). Protentions are tacit anticipations about the course of one's future experience. Retentions are memory-like traces of the past course of one's experience. Both protentions and retentions are 'read into' the present content of one's experience to make it the kind of experience it is. For example, a note that is part of Beethoven's 7th is heard as such if and only if it is located as such through protention and retention. It has to be heard as a *continuation* of as much of the performance has elapsed and as the *initiation* of the remainder of the performance. Hearing the performance as a performance, and as a performance of Beethoven's 7th, requires imagination. We see here a preliminary plausibility in Sartre's claim that 'I listen to it in the imaginary'.

Sartre is claiming that the performance is heard in the concert auditorium but *the symphony it is a performance of* is heard in the imagination. A performance is an audible and datable occurrence and numerically distinct performances may exist at different times and in different places. A symphony is not that. A symphony is what a performance is a performance of. A symphony not only does not exist at different times in different places, a symphony could exist even if there were no performances of it. There could be and are unperformed symphonies.

Sartre refuses to identify the symphony with its performance because it is beyond the real. The real is what exists in the past, present or future. The symphony does not exist in past, present or future so the symphony does not exist in the real.

Sartre's concept of painting is also ontologically controversial. He does not provide us with necessary and sufficient conditions for something's being a painting, but he does try to explain how it is possible to see something as a painting. He also claims that a painting may effect peculiar ontological syntheses. For example, he says in *What is Literature?* that 'Tintoretto did not choose that yellow rift in the sky above Golgotha to signify anguish or to provoke it. It is anguish and yellow sky at the same time. Not sky of anguish or anguished sky: it is an anguish become thing, an anguish that has turned into yellow rift of sky' (p. 3). It is doubtful whether Sartre knows Tintoretto's intentions, and doubtful whether they affect the truth of the crucial identification of anguish with the yellow sky. Anguish is an emotion, something intrinsically unobservable but undergone. A painted rift in the sky is observable and it lacks literal sense to say it is undergone, even though I might undergo something on observing it. However, if we could see anguish it might look like Tintoretto's yellow sky. Anguish and his sky have something in common which is more aesthetically conspicuous than the differences between them. The yellow sky could be an expression of anguish. It could be anguish made outward in paint, rather perhaps, as speech is the expression of thought. Speech is thought made outward in sound. Can you hear thinking? Perhaps listening to speech is the nearest possibility.

Rather as a piece of music is neither its performance nor its score, a painting is not a distribution of paint on canvas even though to destroy an intentionally painted canvas is enough to destroy a painting, and to intentionally put paint on canvas is enough to bring a painting into existence. A painting is not identical with what is necessary and sufficient for its existence. The painted canvas is only the distribution of paint molecules on a surface, or a grouping of phenomenological colours. Something makes the canvas, wood and paint count as, say, a painting of Charles VIII. A painting is not what a painting is a painting of (excluding certain ambitiously self-reflexive paintings). A painting of Charles VIII is not Charles VIII. A painting is something 'between' the canvas and what it is a painting of. It is neither but it depends on both.

Sartre says a painting is an 'unreality', and an 'aesthetic object'. It is a product of the special kind of consciousness he calls 'imaginative consciousness'. Rather dramatically, imaginative consciousness negates the world and freely generates its own substitute unrealities. Visually confronted with the physical object that is wood, canvas and paint imaginative consciousness sees this as a painting of Charles VIII. The content of this act of imagination is not an image. Sartre is not claiming that an image of Charles VIII psychologically accompanies the visual presentation of the painted canvas. It is not the case that two things are presented simultaneously: the painted canvas and the image. Rather, that painted canvas is seen in a special way, as something phenomenologically similar to the visual appearance of Charles VIII.

Sartre tries to draw a distinction between cinema and theatre when he says 'A tree for a cinema-goer is a real tree, while a tree on the stage is obviously synthetic' but this provides us at best with an inductive generalisation about some films and some plays. Mid-twentieth-century black and white films frequently include artificial scenery and a theatre play might deploy real trees or plants. Sartre misses the point that in watching a play we see real people but in watching a film we see pictures of people, and each showing of a play is a performance of that play but each showing of a film is not a performance of that film.

Sartre claims 'It is not the character who becomes real in the actor, it is the actor who becomes unreal in his character'. Hamlet never becomes non-fictional in a performance or film showing of *Hamlet* but the living psycho-physical whole human being who is the actor who plays Hamlet is negated or ignored by an act of imagination by the audience. The audience sees the actor as Hamlet but they do not mix him up with a real prince of Denmark.

Although Sartre never published any poetry, it is clear that he regards poetry as a radical art form. He says in *What is Literature?*: 'the poet is outside language' (p. 6). Sartre takes the neo-Hegelian view that language is the 'element' in which human beings exist, rather, perhaps as fish exist in water. With the exception of rare individuals such as *Nausea*'s Roquentin human reality is mediated by language. The world appears to us through our language. Poets are capable of escaping this linguistic prison and perceive things in their bare particularity. With unscientific detachment they concatenate words in original forms to present us with new phenomenologies of things. Sartre says of the poet 'He sees words inside out'.

A work of art involves an image and what Sartre calls an 'analogue'. The analogue of a work of art is its material vehicle. The analogue of a poem or a novel is the ink distributed over the page, the analogue of a painting is the wood, canvas and paint, the analogue of a character in a play is the actor who plays that character. The existence of the analogue is a necessary condition for the existence of the work of art, at least as a publically available object.

Does the work of art as aesthetic object have an ethereal or abstract ontological status in Sartre's philosophy? It is not spatio-temporally located. It is not identical with its material vehicle. It is not an image in the consciousness of the artist or the audience. It is *unreal*. Despite all this, the work of art exists. What is it then? Sartre's answer in *What is Literature?* dispels any Platonic construal: 'the aesthetic object is properly the world in so far as it is aimed at through the imaginary' (p. 42).

If the world is what is, then in watching a play or looking at a painting, we are grasping what is in a new way. The work of art does not exist in its own world. We are imaginatively presented with a transformed world.

THE PSYCHOLOGY OF THE IMAGINATION

The work of art

It is not our intention to deal here with the problem of the work of art in its entirety. Closely related as this problem is to the question of the Imaginary, its treatment calls for a special work in itself. But it is time we drew some conclusions from the long investigations in which we used a statue or the portrait of Charles VIII or a novel as an example. The following comments will be concerned essentially with the existential category of the work of art. And we can at once formulate the law that the work of art is an unreality.

This appeared to us clearly from the moment we took for our example, in an entirely different connection, the portrait of Charles VIII. We understood at the very outset that this Charles VIII was an object. But obviously this is not the same object as is the painting, the canvas, which are the real objects of which the painting is composed. As long as we observe the canvas and the frame for themselves the aesthetic object "Charles VIII" will not appear. It is not that it is hidden by the picture, but that it cannot present itself to a realizing consciousness. It will appear at the moment when consciousness, undergoing a radical change in which the world is negated, itself becomes imaginative. The situation here is like that of the cubes which can be seen at will to be five or six in number. It will not do to say that when they are seen as five it is because at that time the aspect of the drawing in which they are six is *concealed.* The intentional act that apprehends them as five is complete in itself and *exclusive* of the act which grasps them as six. And so it is with the apprehension of Charles VIII as an image which is depicted on the picture. This Charles VIII on the canvas is necessarily the correlative of the intentional act of an imaginative consciousness. And since this Charles VIII, who is an unreality so long as he is grasped on the canvas, is precisely the object of our aesthetic appreciations (it is he who "moves" us, who is "painted with intelligence, power, and grace", etc.), we are led to recognize that, in a picture, the aesthetic object is something *unreal.* This is of great enough importance once we remind ourselves of the way in which we ordinarily confuse the real and the imaginary in a work of art. We often hear it said, in fact, that the artist first has an idea in the form of an image which he then *realizes* on canvas. This mistaken notion arises from the fact that the painter can begin with a mental image which is, as such, incommunicable, and from the fact that at the end of his labours he presents the public with an object which anyone can observe. This leads us to believe that there occurred a transition from the imaginary to the real. But this is in no way true. That which is real, we must not fail to note, are the results of the brush strokes, the stickiness of the canvas, its grain, the varnish spread over the colours. But all this does not constitute the object of aesthetic appreciation. What is "beautiful" is something which cannot be experienced as a perception and which, by its very nature, is out of the world. We have just shown that it cannot be *brightened,* by projecting a light beam on the canvas for instance: it is the canvas that is brightened and not the painting. The fact of the matter is that the painter did not *realize* his mental image at all: he has simply constructed a material analogue of such a kind that everyone can grasp the image provided he looks at the analogue. But the image thus provided with an external analogue remains an image. There is no realization of the imaginary, nor can we speak of its *objectification.* Each stroke of the brush was not made *for itself* nor even for the constructing of a coherent real whole (in the sense in which it can be said that a certain lever in a machine was conceived in the interest of the whole and not for itself). It was given together with an unreal synthetic whole and the aim of the artist was to construct a whole of *real* colours which enable this unreal to manifest itself. The painting should then be conceived as a material thing visited from time to time (every time that the spectator assumes the imaginative attitude) by an unreal which is precisely the *painted object.* What deceives us here is the real and sensuous pleasure which certain real colours on the canvas give us. Some reds of Matisse, for instance, produce a sensuous enjoyment in those who see them. But we must understand that this sensuous enjoyment, if thought of in isolation—for instance, if aroused by a colour in nature—has nothing of the aesthetic. It is purely and simply a pleasure of sense. But when the red of the painting is grasped, it is grasped, in spite of everything, as a part of an unreal whole and it is in this whole that it is beautiful. For instance, it is the red of a rug by a table. There is, in fact, no such thing as pure colour. Even if the artist is concerned solely with the sensory relationships between forms and colours, he chooses a rug for that very reason in order to increase the sensory value of the red: tactile elements, for instance, must be intended through the red, it is a *fleecy* red, because the rug is of a fleecy material. Without this "fleeciness" of the colour something would be lost. And surely the rug is painted there *for the red* it justifies and not the red for the rug. If Matisse chose a rug rather than a sheet of dry and glossy paper it is because of the voluptuous mixture of the colour, the density and the tactile quality of the wool. Consequently the red can be truly enjoyed only in grasping it as the *red of the rug,* and therefore unreal. And he would have lost his strongest contrast with the green of the wall if the green were not rigid and cold, because it is the green of a wall tapestry. It is therefore in the unreal that the relationship of colours and forms takes on its real meaning. And even when drawn objects have their usual meaning reduced to a minimum, as in the painting of the cubists, the painting is at least not flat. The forms we see are certainly not the forms of a rug, a table nor anything else we see in the world. They nevertheless do have a density, a material, a depth, they bear a relationship of perspective towards each other. They are *things*. And it is precisely in the measure in which they are things that they are unreal. Cubism has introduced the fashion of claiming that a painting should not *represent* or *imitate* reality but should constitute an object in itself. As an aesthetic doctrine such a programme is perfectly defensible and we owe many masterpieces to it. But it needs to be understood. To maintain that the painting, although altogether devoid of meaning, is nevertheless a *real* object, would be a grave mistake. It is certainly not an object of nature. The real object no longer functions as an analogue of a bouquet of flowers or a glade. But when I "contemplate" it, I nevertheless am not in a realistic attitude. The painting is still an *analogue*. Only what manifests itself through it is an unreal collection of *new things*, of objects I have never seen and never will see, but which are not less unreal because of it; objects which do not exist *in the painting*, nor anywhere in the world, but which manifest themselves by means of the canvas, and which have got hold of it by some sort of possession. And it is the configuration of these unreal objects that I designate as *beautiful*. The aesthetic enjoyment is real but it is not grasped for itself, as if produced by a real colour: it is but a manner of apprehending the unreal object and, far from being directed onto the real painting, it serves to constitute the imaginary object through the real canvas. This is the source of the celebrated disinterestedness of aesthetic experience. This is why Kant was able to say that it does not matter whether the object of beauty, when experienced as beautiful, is or is not objectively real; why Schopenhauer was able to speak of a sort of Suspension of the Will. This does not come from some mysterious way of apprehending the real which we are able to use occasionally. What happens is that the aesthetic object is constituted and apprehended by an imaginative consciousness which posits it as unreal.

What we have just shown regarding painting is readily applied to the art of fiction, poetry and drama as well. It is self-evident that the novelist, the poet and the dramatist construct an unreal object by means of verbal analogues; it is also self-evident that the actor who plays Hamlet makes use of himself, of his whole body, as an analogue of the imaginary person. Even the famous dispute about the paradox of the comedian is enlightened by the view here presented. It is well known that certain amateurs proclaim that the actor *does not believe* in the character he portrays. Others, leaning on many witnesses, claim that the actor becomes identified in some way with the character he is enacting. To us these two views are not exclusive of each other; if by "belief" is meant actually real it is obvious that the actor does not actually consider himself to be Hamlet. But this does not mean that he does not "mobilize" all his powers to make Hamlet real. He uses all his feelings, all his strength, all his gestures as analogues of the feelings and conduct of Hamlet. But by this very fact he takes the reality away from them. *He lives completely in an unreal way.* And it matters little that he is *actually* weeping in enacting the role. He himself experiences these tears (whose origin we explained above, see Chapter 2, 2: Affectivity) as the tears of Hamlet, that is, as the analogue of unreal tears—and so does the audience. "be transformation that occurs here is like that which we discussed in the dream: the actor is completely caught up, inspired, by the unreal. It is not the character who becomes real in the actor, it is the actor who *becomes unreal* in his character.[1]

But are there not some arts whose objects seem to escape unreality by their very nature? A melody, for instance, refers to nothing but itself. Is a cathedral anything more than a mass of *real* stone which dominates the surrounding house tops? But let us look at this matter more closely. For instance, I listen to a symphony orchestra playing Beethoven's Seventh Symphony. Let us disregard exceptional cases—which are besides on the margin of aesthetic contemplation—as when I go mainly "to hear Toscanini" interpret Beethoven in his own way. As a general rule what draws me to the concert is the desire "to hear the Seventh Symphony". Of course I have some objection to hearing an amateur orchestra, and prefer this or that well-known musical organization. But this is due to my desire to hear the symphony "played perfectly", because the symphony will then be *perfectly itself*. The shortcomings of a poor orchestra which plays "too fast" or "too slow", "in the wrong tempo", etc., seem to me to rob, to "betray" the work it is playing. At most the orchestra effaces itself before the work it performs and, provided I have reason to trust the performers and their conductor, I am confronted by the symphony itself. This everyone will grant me. But now, what is the Seventh Symphony itself? Obviously it is a *thing,* that is something which is before me, which endures, which lasts. Naturally there is no need to show that that thing is a synthetic whole, which does not consist of tones but of a thematic configuration. But is that "thing" real or unreal? Let us first bear in mind that I am listening to the Seventh Symphony. For me that "Seventh Symphony" does not exist in time, I do not grasp it as a dated event, as an artistic manifestation which is unrolling itself in the Châtelet auditorium on the 17th of November, 1938. If tomorrow or eight days later I hear Furtwaengler conduct another orchestra performing the same symphony, I am in the presence of the same symphony once more. Only it is being played either better or worse. Let us now see *how* I hear the symphony: some persons shut their eyes. In this case they detach themselves from the *visual* and dated event of this particular interpretation: they give themselves up to the pure sounds. Others watch the orchestra or the conductor's back But they do not see what they are looking at. This is what Revault d'Allonnes calls reflection with auxiliary fascination. The auditorium, the conductor and even the orchestra have disappeared. I am therefore confronted by the Seventh Symphony, but on the express condition that I understand *nothing about it*, that I do not think of the event as an actuality and dated, and that I listen to the succession of themes as an absolute succession and not as a real succession which is unfolding itself on a particular occasion. In the degree to which I hear the symphony it is *not here*, between these walls, at the tip of the violin bows. Nor is it "in the past" as if I thought: this is the work that matured in the mind of Beethoven on such a date. It is completely beyond the real. It has its own time, that is, it possesses an inner time which runs from the first tone of the allegro to the last tone of the finale, but this time is not a succession of a preceding time which it continues and which happened "before" the beginning of the allegro; nor is it followed by a time which will come "after" the finale. The Seventh Symphony is in no way *in time*. It is therefore in no way real. It occurs *by itself*, but as absent, as being out of reach. I cannot act upon it, change a single note of it, or slow down its movement. But it depends on the real for its appearance: that the conductor does not faint away, that a fire in the hall does not put an end to the performance. From this we cannot conclude that *the* Seventh Symphony has come to an end. No, we only think that the *performance* of the symphony has ceased. Does this not show clearly that the performance of the symphony is its *analogue?* It can manifest itself only through analogues which are dated and which unroll in our time. But to experience it on these analogues the imaginative reduction must be functioning, that is, the real sounds must be apprehended as analogues. It therefore occurs as a perpetual elsewhere, a perpetual absence. We must not picture it (as does Spandrell in *Point Counterpoint* by Huxley—as so many platonisms) as existing in another world, in an intelligible heaven. It is not only outside time and space—as are essences, for instance—it is outside the real, outside existence. I do not hear it actually, I listen to it in the imaginary. Here we find the explanation for the considerable difficulty we always experience in passing from the world of the theatre or of music into that of our daily affairs. There is in fact no passing from one world into the other, but only a passing from the imaginative attitude to that of reality. Aesthetic contemplation is an induced dream and the passing into the real is an actual waking up. We often speak of the "deception" experienced on returning to reality. But this does not explain why this discomfort also exists after having witnessed a realistic and cruel play, for instance, in which case reality should be experienced as comforting. This discomfort is simply that of the dreamer on awakening; an entranced consciousness, engulfed in the imaginary, is suddenly freed by the sudden ending of the play, of the symphony, and comes suddenly in contact with existence. Nothing more is needed to arouse the nauseating disgust that characterizes the consciousness of reality.

From these few observations we can already conclude that the real is never beautiful. Beauty is a value applicable only to the imaginary and which means the negation of the world in its essential structure. This is why it is stupid to confuse the moral with the aesthetic. The values of the Good presume being-in-the-world, they concern action in the real and are subject from the outset to the basic absurdity of existence. To say that we "assume" an aesthetic attitude to life is to confuse the real and the imaginary. It does happen, however, that we do assume the attitude of aesthetic contemplation towards real events or objects. But in such cases every one of us can feel in himself a sort of recoil in relation to the object contemplated which slips into nothingness so that, from this moment on, it is no longer *perceived*; it functions as an *analogue of* itself, that is, an unreal image of what it is appears to us through its actual presence. This image can be purely and simply the object "itself" neutralized, annihilated, as when I contemplate a beautiful woman or death at a bull fight; it can also be the imperfect and confused appearance of *what it could be* through what it is, as when the painter grasps the harmony of two colours as being greater, more vivid, *through* the real blots he finds on a wall. The object at once appears to be *behind* itself, becomes *untouchable,* it is beyond our reach; and hence arises a sort of sad disinterest in it. It is in this sense that we may say that great beauty in a woman kills the desire for her. In fact, when this unreal "herself" which we admire appears, we cannot simultaneously place ourselves on the plane of the aesthetic and on the realistic plane of physical possession. To desire her we must forget she is beautiful, because desire is a plunge into the heart of existence, into what is most contingent and most absurd. Aesthetic contemplation of *real* objects is of the same structure as paramnesia, in which the real object functions as analogue of itself in the past. But in one of the cases there is a negating and in the other a placing of the thing in the past. Paramnesia differs from the aesthetic attitude as memory differs from imagination.

Note

1 It is in this sense that a beginner in the theatre can say that stage-fright served her to represent the timidity of Ophelia. If it did so, it is because she suddenly turned it into an unreality, that is, that she ceased to apprehend it for itself and that she grasped it as *analogue* for the timidity of Ophelia.

16 Politics

Sartre's massive and complex 1960 work *Critique of Dialectical Reason* and its preface *Questions of Method* are a putative synthesis of existentialism and Marxism.

On the face of it, existentialism and Marxism are mutually inconsistent philosophies. Existentialism entails libertarianism, the doctrine that human beings have freedom of choice, but classical Marxism is deterministic. Marx and Engels thought that the economic organisation of a society causally determines all other facts about that society. In particular, the ideological 'superstructure', the laws, religions, social mores and the behaviour of individuals, is caused by the 'infrastructure' or 'economic base'.

Marxism is also a kind of materialism, but Sartre's existentialism places an enormous emphasis on the existence of consciousness. Marxist materialism is not the eliminative thesis that everything is only physical. However, it is the thesis that unless there were physical things there could be nothing non-physical. In particular, social, abstract and mental change depends on physical change. Sartre, however, frequently speaks as though each person's consciousness were a quasi-Kantian 'spontaneity'; a repository of free acts that has no physical prerequisite.

Marxism entails a theory of history but existentialism emphasises the lived reality of the present time. Despite the occasional allusions to the revolutions of 1789 and 1848 in *Being and Nothingness*, Sartre, the existential phenomenologist, has little to say about history. Marxism, in contrast, includes an account of how one form of socio-economic organisation supplants another through class-struggle. In *The German Ideology* (1846) Marx and Engels claim that nomadic societies are replaced by settled agriculture over which feudal relations of land tenure are established. Feudalism is eventually destroyed by an emergent monied, merchantile, professional and capital-owning parliamentary class. This capitalist class or bourgeoisie will eventually be overthrown by the proletariat or working class whose labour they exploit for profit. After a short but severe 'dictatorship of the proletariat' in which the capitalist class and its state is destroyed a classless communist society is established. This historicist account and the socio-economic models it entails are essential to Marxism but existentialism contains nothing like it.

Marxism is a social theory. Existentialism is an extreme form of individualism. If we ask the question 'who acts?' existentialism and Marxism provide radically different answers. For the Marxist it is the group, paradigmatically the socio-economic class, that acts. Individuals only act as members of a class. For the existentialist it is quite the reverse: groups only act is so far as their individual members act. The agent is the individual human being.

If we draw a distinction between self and other, between being a human being, (the one that is), and human beings as observed (all those one is not), then existentialism is a philosophy of the self. Marxism is a philosophy of the other. Sartre's existentialism contains a phenomenological obsession with what it is like to be someone. Marxism depicts people in the abstract with an almost Newtonian anonymity. To understand existentialism it is necessary to think of a human being on the model of oneself. To understand Marxism it is necessary to think of human beings on the model of others.

Finally, if despite all his disavowals Sartre's existentialism is a pessimistic philosophy, then Marxism is its opposite in this sense too. Even though Marx criticised nineteenth-century socialists, for example the French anarchist Pierre-Joseph Proudhon (1809–65), for what he saw as their unrealistic utopianism, Marxism remains profoundly optimistic. History concludes with the revolutionary overthrow of exploitation and unfair inequality and its replacement with an ideal classless society without the state. Sartre's existentialism, on the other hand, includes no political solution to human anxiety in the face of loneliness, freedom and death. Humanity is condemned to the impossible project of being both in-itself and for-itself. Man wants to be God, but in Sartre's existentialism there is no metaphysical heaven and no heaven on earth either.

It follows that existentialism is an individualistic libertarian philosophy of consciousness, subjectivity and the present which offers mankind no grounds for political or metaphysical optimism. Marxism, on the other hand, is a deterministic social and historical theory that is essentially materialist in content and holds out the promise of a future utopia in which scarcity and exploitation will be overcome. It seems that Sartre faces an insurmountable task in reconciling these two philosophies into a homogeneous world-picture.

The problems Sartre faces are some of the central problems of philosophy: freedom and determinism, the mind–body problem, the existence of past, present and future, relations between individual and social, self and other. Metaphysics is an obstacle to politics. How is this synthesis to be effected?

Sartre's existentialist thesis that an individual freely chooses in a situation is now located in the Marxist doctrine that humanity is self-determining in history. 'Situation' now conspicuously includes class location. In a dialectical unity of freedom and necessity humans constitute their environment and the constituted environment constitutes humanity. This is a fusion of existentialist *being-in-the-world* and Marxist *praxis*.

'Praxis' is the Greek word for 'action' used in Marxist theory to denote the transformation of the natural material world by human beings. It subsumes Sartre's idea of *the project* because the future-orientated choice of the individual is included in the historical *praxis* of the class. Marxist dialectic without the Sartrean *project* is not thoroughly dialectical because it does not recognise the historical role of the individual. For example, Sartre says that although Paul Valéry is a petty bourgeois intellectual, not every petty bourgeois intellectual is Paul Valéry. The originality and spontaneity of Valéry the poet are not entailed by his being 'bourgeois' even though his being Valéry entails his being 'bourgeois'. According to Sartre's 'progressive–regressive' method it is necessary to refer to society to understand the individual and to the individual to understand the society.

Sartre thinks there are three fundamental forms of social organisation: *the series, the group,* and *the class.* A series is based on competition, a group on cooperation and a class on economics. A class may be a series or a group or exhibit features of both. A series or a group is not necessarily a class.

The members of a series have no common, internal or collective purpose as members of that series. A series is, as Sartre puts it, a plurality of solitudes. Nor does an individual have to be conscious of being in competition with other individuals to belong to the same series as those individuals. Being in a series does not presuppose being conscious of being in a series. The members of a series are paradigmatically individuals living under capitalism. They compete over material wealth, status, education, health care, sex and political power. The bourgeoisie, or capital-owning class, is essentially a series but the proletariat also exhibits seriality to the extent to which its members are compelled to engage in competition.

The series is defined by competition but the group is defined by cooperation. The members of a group have to have some common, internal or collective purpose. Being conscious of being in the group is a necessary condition for being in the group. The group is essentially characterised by solidarity or fraternity because each member knows that his or her actions partly depend upon the actions and omissions of other members for their success. Paradigmatically, the members of a group are individuals living in a socialist society. Such individuals freely cooperate in meeting their collective needs and do not compete. In the group, according to Sartre, the individual converts his own *praxis* into social *praxis*. Social *praxis* differs from individual *praxis* in two respects. It is a joint consequence and it has joint consequences. It is a kind of action that can not be executed by one individual without others. It is a kind of action that benefits more than one individual.

The kind of *praxis* exercised by the group is morally and metaphysically 'higher' than that exercised by the series. *Praxis* has a biological origin. *Praxis* exists because the organism tries to sustain itself so the primordial practical relation is between humanity and nature. Unless humanity were related to nature by struggle, humanity would not be related to itself in series and groups. Matter is manipulated through *praxis* because humans need food, shelter and warmth. Some human needs do not require *praxis*. For example, humans need oxygen but do not need to actively mould the world to breathe it. However, agriculture and industry, towns and communication systems imply *praxis*. These human organisations exist to overcome scarcity, whether real or perceived, global or local. *Praxis*, as Sartre puts it, is born of need.

Historically and dialectically, biological need is prior to individual *praxis*, individual *praxis* is prior to serial *praxis*, and serial *praxis* is prior to group *praxis*. Serial *praxis* is morally inferior to group *praxis* because it sacrifices the needs of one individual to those of another. In these dialectical dependencies and their moralistic culmination we are able to discern the Marxist historical transitions from nomadic society through feudalism and mercantile captitalism to the overthrow of capitalism by socialism. Sartre's individual is at the heart of this process. His free project is human *praxis*.

In political reality the difference between a series and a group is frequently one of degree. Cooperation may be discerned between individuals in competition and competition may be discerned between individuals in cooperation. Also, groups and series may become one another. In a socialist revolution the series that was the proletariat under capitalism becomes a group. Crucially however, according to Sartre any group is in danger of lapsing into seriality. It follows that socialism is in danger of lapsing into capitalism and the most severe political measures are needed.

Sartre distinguishes between 'the pledge', 'violence' and 'terror' all of which contribute to halting the regress of the group into seriality. The pledge is a social contract between members of the group to further their collective interests, and refrain from furthering their individual self-interest at the expense of those collective interests. Violence is the infliction of pain or death on bodies exterior to the group that threaten to convert the group into a series. Terror is pain and death exerted by the group on the group to eliminate the same threat. Terror is internalised violence.

Terror is dialectically related to the pledge, because whoever makes the pledge further agrees to submit to terror. Indeed, he agrees to submit himself to terror because in terror the individuals in the group are both the subjects and the objects of terror.

Although *Critique of Dialectical Reason* is designed as a synthesis of existentialism and Marxism, it admits of another reading; one which would have appalled Sartre and one he certainly did not intend. The *Critique* may be read as an unconscious synthesis of capitalism and socialism: the missing synthesis of the twentieth century. Arguably, the tenets of existentialism: the emphasis on the individual not society, freedom of choice not economic determinism, the present projected into the future, not the burden of history, are all presuppositions of capitalism. We should not be wholly surprised by this if existentialism is a product of capitalism, if, for example, it is a dimension of alienation. To allow this reading of the *Critique* we have to accept the lesson of *What is Literature?* that an author does not have a monopoly over the interpretation of his own work.

The extracts below are from *Questions of Method* and *The Critique of Dialectical Reason I*.

SEARCH FOR A METHOD

The progressive–regressive method

I have said that we accept without reservation the thesis set forth by Engels in his letter to Marx: "Men themselves make their history but in a given environment which conditions them." However, this text is not one of the clearest, and it remains open to numerous interpretations. How are we to understand that man makes History if at the same time it is History which makes him? Idealist Marxism seems to have chosen the easiest interpretation: entirely determined by prior circumstances—that is, in the final analysis, by economic conditions—man is a passive product, a sum of conditioned reflexes. Being inserted in the social world amidst other equally conditioned inertias, this inert object, with the nature which it has received, contributes to precipitate or to check the "course of the world." It changes society in the way that a bomb, without ceasing to obey the principle of inertia, can destroy a building. In this case there would be no difference between the human agent and the machine. Marx wrote, in fact: "The invention of a new military weapon, the firearm, of necessity modified the whole inner organization of the army, the relationships inside the cadre on the basis of which individuals form an army and which make of the army an organized whole, and finally, the relations between different armies." In short, the advantage, here seems to be on the side of the weapon or the tool, their simple appearance overturns everything.

This conception can be summed up by a statement which appeared in the *Courrier européen* (in Saint Petersburg): "Marx considers social evolution to be a natural process governed by laws which do not depend upon the will, the consciousness, or the intention of men, but which, on the contrary, determine them." Marx quotes this passage in the second preface to *Capital*. Does he really accept it as a fair appraisal of his position? It is difficult to say. He compliments the critic for having excellently described *his* method and points out to him that the real problem concerns *the* dialectical method. But he does not comment on the article in detail, and he concludes by noting that the practical bourgeois *is very clearly conscious* of the contradictions in capitalist society, a remark which seems to be the counterpart of his statement in 1860: "[The workers' movement represents] the conscious participation in the historical process which is overturning society." Now one will observe that the statements in the *Courrier européen* contradict not only the passage quoted earlier from *Herr Vogt* but also the famous third thesis of Feuerbach. "The materialist doctrine according to which men are a product of circumstances and of education . . . does not take into account the fact that circumstances are modified precisely by men and that the educator must be himself educated." Either this is a mere tautology, and we are simply to understand that the educator himself is a product of circumstances and of education—which would render the sentence useless and absurd; or else it is the decisive affirmation of the irreducibility of human *praxis*. The educator must be educated; this means that education must be an enterprise.[1]

If one wants to grant to Marxist thought its fall complexity, one would have to say that man in a period of exploitation is *at once both* the product of his own product and a historical agent who can under no circumstances be taken as a product. This contradiction is not fixed; it must be grasped in the very movement of *praxis*. Then it will clarify Engels's statement: men make their history on the basis of real, prior conditions (among which we would include acquired characteristics, distortions imposed by the mode of work and of life, alienation, etc.), but it is *the men* who make it and not the prior conditions. Otherwise men would be merely the vehieles of inhuman forces which through them would govern the social world. To be sure these conditions exist, and it is they, they alone, which can furnish a direction and a material reality to the changes which are in preparation; but the movement of human *praxis* goes beyond them while conserving them.

Certainly men do not grasp the real measure of what they do—at least its full import must escape them so long as the Proletariat, the subject of History, will not in a single movement realize its unity and become conscious of its historical role. But if History escapes me, this is not because I do not make it; it is because the other is making it as well. Engels—who has left us many hardly compatible statements on this subject—has shown in *The War of the Peasants*, at any rate, the meaning which he attached to this contradiction. After emphasizing the courage and passion of the German peasants, the justice of their demands, the genius of certain of their leaders (especially Münzer), the intelligence and competence of the revolutionary elite, he concludes: "In the War of the Peasants, only the princes had anything to gain; therefore this was its result. They won not only relatively, since their rivals (the clergy, the nobility, the city) found themselves weakened, but also absolutely, since they carried off the best spoils from the other orders." What was it then which *stole* the *praxis* of the rebels? Simply their separation, which had as its source a definite historical condition—the division of Germany. The existence of numerous provincial movements which never succeeded in uniting with one another, where each one, *other* than the others, acted differently—this was enough to make each group lose the real meaning of its enterprise. This does not mean that the enterprise *as a real action of man upon history* does not exist, but only that the result achieved, when it is placed in the totalizing movement, is radically different from the way it appears locally—*even when the result conforms with the objective proposed.* Finally, the division of the country caused the war to fail, and the war resulted only in aggravating and consolidating this division.

Thus man makes History; this means that he objectifies himself in it and is alienated in it. In this sense History, which is the proper work of *all* activity and of *all* men, appears to men as a foreign force exactly insofar as they do not recognise the meaning of their enterprise (even when locally successful) in the total, objective result. By making a separate peace, the peasants of a certain province won—*so far as they were concerned*. But they weakened their class, and its defeat was to be turned back against them when the landholders, sure of their strength, would deny their pledges. Marxism in the nineteenth century is a gigantic attempt not only to make History but to get a grip on it, practically and theoretically, by uniting the workers' movement and by clarifying the Proletariat's action through an understanding both of the capitalist process and of the workers' objective reality. At the end of this effort, by the unification of the exploited and by the progressive reduction of the number of classes in the struggle, History was finally to have a meaning for man. By becoming conscious of itself, the Proletariat becomes the subject of History; that is, it must recognize itself in History. Even in the everyday struggle the working class must obtain results conforming to the objective aimed at, the consequences of which will at least never be turned back against it.

We are not at this point yet. There is more than one Proletariat, simply because there are national production groups which have developed differently. Not to recognize the solidarity of these Proletariats would be as absurd as to underestimate their *separation*. It is true that the violent divisions and their theoretical consequences (the decay of bourgeois ideology, the temporary arrest of Marxism) force our period to make itself without knowing itself. On the other hand, although we are more than ever subject to these limitations, it is not true that History appears to us as an entirely alien force. Each day with our hands we make it something other than what we believe we are making it. And History, backfiring, makes us other than we believe ourselves to be or to become. Yet it is less opaque than it was. The Proletariat has discovered and released "its secret"; the capitalist movement is conscious of itself, both as the result of the capitalists' own self-study and through the research carried on by theoreticians in the workers' movement. For each one, the multiplicity of groups, their contradictions and their separations, appear *situated* within more profound unifications. Civil war, colonial war, foreign war, are manifested to all, under cover of the usual mythologies, as different and complementary forms of a single class struggle. It is true that the majority of socialist countries *do not know themselves*; and yet de-Stalinization—as the example of Poland shows— is *also* a progress toward the attainment of awareness. Thus the plurality of *the meanings* of History can be discovered and posited for itself only upon the ground of a future totalization—in terms of the future totalization and in contradiction with it. It is our theoretical and practical duty to bring this totalization closer every day. All is still obscure, and yet everything is in full light. To tackle the theoretical aspect, we have the instruments; we can establish the method. Our historical task, at the heart of this polyvalent world, is to bring closer the moment when History will have *only one meaning*, when it will tend to be dissolved in the concrete men who will make it in common.[2]

The project

Thus alienation can modify the *results* of an action but not its profound reality. We refuse to confuse the alienated man with a thing or alienation with the physical laws governing external conditions. We affirm the specificity of the human act, which cuts across the social milieu while still holding on to its determinations, and which transforms the world on the basis of given conditions. For us man is characterized above all by his going beyond a situation, and by what he succeeds in making of what he has been made—even if he never recognizes himself in his objectification. This going beyond we find at the very root of the human—in *need*. It is need which, for example, links the scarcity of women in the Marquesas, as a structural fact of the group, and polyandry as a matrimonial institution. For this scarcity is not a simple lack; in its most naked form it expresses a situation in society and contains already an effort to go beyond it. The most rudimentary behavior must be determined both in relation to the real and present factors which condition it and in relation to a certain object, still to come, which it is trying to bring into being.[3] This is what we call *the project*.

Starting with the project, we define a double simultaneous relationship. In relation to the given, the *praxis* is negativity; but what is always involved is the negation of a negation. In relation to the object aimed at, *praxis* is positivity, but this positivity opens onto the "non-existent," to what has *not yet* been. A flight and a leap ahead, at once a refusal and a realization, the project retains and unveils the surpassed reality which is refused by the very movement which surpassed it. Thus knowing is a moment of *praxis*, even its most fundamental one; but this knowing does not partake of an absolute Knowledge. Defined by the negation of the refused reality in the name of the reality to be produced, it remains the captive of the action which it clarifies, and disappears along with it. Therefore it is perfectly accurate to say that man is the product of his product. The structures of a society which is created by human work define for each man an objective situation as a starting point; the truth of a man is the nature of his work, and it is his wages. But this truth defines him just insofar as he constantly goes beyond it in his practical activity. (In a popular democracy this may be, for example, by working a double shift or by becoming an "activist" or by secretly resisting the raising of work quotas. In a capitalist society it may be by joining a union, by voting to go on strike, etc.) Now this surpassing is conceivable only as a relation of the existent to its possibles. Furthermore, to say what man "is" is also to say what he can be—and vice versa. The material conditions of his existence circumscribe the field of his possibilities (his work is too hard, he is too tired to show any interest in union or political activity). Thus the field of possibles is the goal toward which the agent surpasses his objective situation. And this field in turn depends strictly on the social, historical reality. For example, in a society where everything is bought, the possibilities of culture are practically eliminated for the workers if food absorbs 50 per cent or more of their budget. The freedom of the bourgeois, on the contrary, consists in the possibility of his allotting an always increasing part of his income to a great variety of expenditures. Yet the field of possibles, however reduced it may be, always exists, and we must not think of it as a zone of indetermination, but rather as a strongly structured region which depends upon all of History and which includes its own contradictions. It is by transcending the given toward the field of possibles and by realizing one possibility from among all the others that the individual objectifies himself and contributes to making History. The project then takes on a reality which the agent himself may not know, one which, through the conflicts it manifests and engenders, influences the course of events.

Therefore we must conceive of the possibility as doubly determined. On the one side, it is at the very heart of the particular action, the presence of the future as *that which is lacking* and that which, by its very absence, reveals reality. On the other hand, it is the real and permanent future which the collectivity forever maintains and transforms. When common needs bring about the creation of new offices (for example, the multiplication of physicians in a society which is becoming industrial-ized), these offices, not yet filled—or vacant as the result of retirement or death—constitute for certain people a real, concrete, and *possible* future. These persons *can* go into medicine. This career is not closed to them; at this moment their life lies open before them until death. All things being equal, the professions of army doctor, country doctor, colonial doctor, etc., are characterized by certain advantages and certain obligations which they will quickly know. This future, to be sure, is only partly true; it presupposes a *status quo* and a minimum of order (barring accidents) which is contradicted precisely by the fact that our societies are in constant process of making history. But neither is it false, since it is this—in other words, the interests of the profession, of class, etc., the ever-increasing division of labor, etc.—which first manifests the present contradictions of society. The future is presented, then, as a schematic, always open possibility and as an immediate action on the present.

Conversely, this future defines the individual in his present reality; the conditions which the medical students must fulfill in a bourgeois society *at the same time* reveal the society, the profession, and the social situa-tion of the one who will meet these conditions. If it is still necessary for parents to be well-off, if the practice of giving scholarships is not widespread, then the future doctor appears in his own eyes as a member of the moneyed classes. In turn, he becomes aware of his class by means of the future which it makes possible for him; that is, through his chosen profession. In contrast, for the man who does not meet the required conditions, medicine becomes his *lack*, his *non-humanity* (all the more so as many other careers are "closed" to him at the same time). It is from this point of view, perhaps, that we ought to approach the problem of relative pauperism. Every man is defined negatively by the sum total of possibles which are impossible for him; that is, by a future more or less blocked off. For the under-privileged classes, each cultural, technical, or material enrichment of society represents a diminution, an impoverishment; the future is almost entirely barred. Thus, both positively and negatively, the social possibles are lived as schematic determinations of the individual future. And the most individual possible is only the internalization and enrichment of a social possible.

A member of the ground crew at an air base on the outskirts of London took a plane and, with no experience as a pilot, flew it across the Channel. He is colored; he is prevented from becoming a member of the flying personnal. This prohibition becomes for him a *subjective* impoverishment, but he immediately goes beyond the subjective to the objective. This denied future reflects to him the fate of his "race" and the racism of the English. The *general* revolt on the part of colored men against colonialists is expressed *in him* by his particular refusal of this prohibition. He affirms that a future *possible for whites* is *possible for everyone*. This political position, of which he doubtless has no clear awareness, he lives as a personal obsession; aviation becomes *his* possibility as a *clandestine future*. In fact he chooses a possibility *already recognized* by the colonialists as existing in the colonized (simply because they cannot rule it out at the start)—the possibility of rebellion, of risk, of scandal, of repression. This choice allows us to understand at the same time his individual project and the present stage of the struggle of the colonized against the colonialists (the colored have gone beyond the moment of passive, dignified resistance, but the group of which this man is a part does not yet have the means of going beyond individual revolt and terrorism). This young rebel is all the more *individual* and *unique* in that the struggle in his country demands, for the time being, individual acts. Thus the unique particularity of this person is the internalization of a double future—that of the whites and that of his brothers; the contradiction is cloaked and surmounted in a project which launches it toward a brief, dazzling future, *his* future, shattered immediately by prison or by accidental death.

What makes American culturism and Kardiner's theory appear mechanistic and outmoded is the fact they never conceive of cultural behavior and basic attitudes (or roles, etc.) within the true, living perspective, which is temporal, but rather conceive of them as past determinations ruling men in the way that a cause rules its effects. Everything changes if one considers that society is presented to each man as *a perspective of the future* and that this future penetrates to the heart of each one as a motivation for his behavior. That the Marxists allow themselves to be duped by mechanistic materialism is inexcusable. since they know and approve of large-scale socialist planning. For a man in China the future is more true than the present. So long as one has not studied the structures of the future in a defined society, one necessarily runs the risk of not understanding anything whatsoever about the social.

I cannot describe here the true dialectic of the subjective and the objective. One would have to demonstrate the joint necessity of "the internalization of the external" and "the externalization of the internal." *Praxis,* indeed, is a passage from objective to objective through internalization. The project, as the subjective surpassing of objectivity toward objectivity, and stretched between the objective conditions of the environment and the objective structures of the field of possibles, represents *in itself* the moving unity of subjectivity and objectivity, those cardinal determinants of activity. The subjective appears then as a necessary moment in the objective process. If the material conditions which govern human relations are to become real conditions of *praxis*, they must be lived in the particularity of particular situations. The diminution of buying power would never provoke the workers to make economic demands if they did not feel the diminution in their flesh in the form of a need or of a fear based on bitter experiences. The practice of union action can increase the importance and the efficacy of objective significations among the experienced party militants; the wage scale and the price index can by themselves clarify or motivate their action. But all this objectivity refers ultimately to a lived reality. The worker knows what he has resented and what others will resent. Now, to resent is already to go beyond, to move toward the possibility of an objective transformation. In the *lived experience*, the subjectivity turns back upon itself and wrenches itself from despair by means of *objectification.* Thus the subjective contains within itself the objective, which it denies and which it surpasses toward a new objectivity; and this new objectivity by virtue of *objectification* externalizes the internality of the project as an objectified subjectivity. This means *both* that the lived as such finds its place in the result and that the projected meaning of the action appears in the reality of the world that it may get its truth in the process of totalization.[4]

Only the project, as a mediation between two moments of objectivity, can account for history; that is, for human *creativity*. It is necessary to choose. In effect: either we reduce everything to identity (which amounts to substituting a mechanistic materialism for dialectical materialism)—or we make of dialectic a celestial law which imposes itself on the Universe, a metaphysical force which, by itself engenders the historical process (and this is to fall back into Hegelian idealism)—or we restore to the individual man his power to go beyond his situation by means of work and action. This solution alone enables us to base the movement of totalization *upon the real*. We must look for dialectic in the relation of men with nature, with "the starting conditions," and in the relation of men with one another. There is where it gets its start, *resulting* from the confrontation of projects. The characteristics of the human project alone enable us to understand that this result is a new reality provided with its own signification instead of remaining simply a statistical mean.[5] It is impossible to develop these considerations here. They will be the subject of Part Two of *Critique of Dialectical Reason*.

CRITIQUE OF DIALECTICAL REASON, VOL. I

Collectives

Series: the queue

Let us illustrate these notions by a superficial everyday example. Take a grouping of people in the Place Saint-Germain. They are waiting for a bus at a bus stop in front of the church. I use the word "grouping" here in a neutral sense: we do not yet know whether this gathering is, as such, the inert effect of separate activities, or whether it is a common reality, regulating everyone's actions, or whether it is a conventional or contractual organisation. These people—who may differ greatly in age, sex, class, and social milieu—realise, within the ordinariness of everyday life, the relation of isolation, of reciprocity and of unification (and massification) from outside which is characteristic of, for example, the residents of a big city in so far as they are united though not integrated through work, through struggle or through any other activity in an organised group common to them all. To begin with, it should be noted that we are concerned here with a plurality of isolations: these people do not care about or speak to each other and, in general, they do not look at one another; they exist side by side alongside a bus stop. At this level, it is worth noting that their isolation is not an inert statute (or the simple reciprocal exteriority of organisms); rather, it is *actually* lived in everyone's project as its negative structure. In other words, the isolation of the organism, as the impossibility of uniting with Others in an organic totality, is revealed through the isolation which everyone lives as the provisional negation of their reciprocal relations with Others. This man is isolated not only by his body as such, but also by the fact that he turns his back on his neighbour—who, moreover, has not even noticed him (or has encountered him in his practical field as a general individual defined by waiting for the bus). The practical conditions of this attitude of semi-unawareness are, first, his real membership of other groups (it is morning, he has just got up and left his home; he is still thinking of his children, who are ill, etc.; furthermore, he is going to his office; he has an oral report to make to his superior; he is worrying about its phrasing, rehearsing it under his breath, etc.); and secondly, his being-in-the-inert (that is to say, his interest). This plurality of separations can, therefore, in a way, be expressed as the negative side of individual integration into separate groups (or into groups that are separate at *this time* and *at this level*); and, through this, as the negative side of everyone's projects in so far as they determine the social field on the basis of given conditions. On the other hand, if the question is examined from the point of view of groups, interests, etc.—in short, of social structures in so far as they express the fundamental social order (mode of production, relations of production, etc.)—then one can define each isolation in terms of the forces of disintegration which the social group exerts on individuals. (These forces, of course, are correlatives of forces of integration, which we shall discuss soon.)

In other words, the intensity of isolation, as a relation of exteriority between the members of a temporary and contingent gathering, expresses *the degree of massification* of the social ensemble, in so far as it is produced on the basis of given conditions.[6]

At this level, reciprocal isolations, as the negation of reciprocity, signify the integration of individuals into one society and, *in this sense*, can be defined as a particular way of living (conditioned by the developing totalisation), in interiority and as reciprocity within the social, the exteriorised negation of all interiority ("No one helps anyone, it's everyone for himself") or, on the other hand, in sympathy (as in Proust's "Every person is very much alone"). Finally, in our example, isolation becomes, for and through everyone, for him and for others, the real, social product of cities. For each member of the group waiting for the bus, the city is in fact present (as I have shown in *The Problem of Method*) as the practico-inert ensemble within which there is a movement towards the interchangeability of men and of the instrumental ensemble; it has been there since morning, as exigency, as instrumentality, as milieu, etc. And, through the medium of the city, there are given the millions of people who are the city, and whose completely invisible presence makes of everyone *both* a polyvalent isolation (with millions of facets), *and* an *integrated* member of the city (the *"vieux Parisien"*, the *"Parisien de Paris"*, etc.). Let me add that the mode of life occasions *isolated behaviour* in everyone—buying the paper as you leave the house, reading it on the bus, etc. These are often *operations* for making the transition from one group to another (from the intimacy of the family to the public life of the office). Thus isolation is a project. And as such it is relative to particular individuals and moments: to isolate oneself by reading the paper is to make use of the national collectivity and, ultimately, the totality of living human beings, in so far as one is one of them and dependent on all of them, in order to separate oneself from the hundred people who are waiting for or using the same vehicle. Organic isolation, suffered isolation, lived isolation, isolation as a mode of behaviour, isolation as a social statute of the individual, isolation as the exteriority of groups conditioning the exteriority of individuals, isolation as the reciprocity of isolations in a society which creates *masses:* all these forms, all these oppositions co-exist in the little group we are considering, in so far as isolation is a historical and social form of human behaviour in human gatherings.

But, at the same time, the relation of reciprocity remains in the gathering itself; and among its members; the negation of isolation by *praxis* preserves it as negated: it is, in fact, quite simply, the practical existence of men among men. Not only is there a lived reality—for everyone, even if he turns his back on the Others, and is unaware of their number and their appearance, knows that they exist as a finite and indeterminate plurality *of which* he is *a part*—but also, even outside everyone's real relation to the Others, the ensemble of *isolated* behaviour, in so far as it is conditioned by historical totalisation, presupposes a structure of reciprocity at every level. This reciprocity must be the most constant possibility and the most immediate reality, for otherwise the social models in currency (clothes, hair style, bearing, etc.) would not be adopted by everyone (although of course this is *not sufficient),* and neither would everyone hasten to repair anything wrong with their dress as soon as they notice it, and if possible in secret. This shows that isolation does not remove one from the visual and practical field of the Other, and that it realises itself objectively in this field.

At this level, we recognise the same society (which we just saw as an agent of massification), in so far as its practico-inert being serves as a medium conducive to inter-individual reciprocities: for these separate people form a group, *in so far* as they are all standing on the same pavement, which protects them from the traffic crossing the square, *in so far as* they are grouped around the same bus stop, etc. Above all, these individuals form a group to the extent that they have a *common interest*, so that, though separated as organic individuals, they share a structure of their practico-inert being, and it unites them from outside. They are all, or nearly all, workers, and regular users of the bus service; they know the time-table and frequency of the buses; and consequently they all wait for the *same* bus: say, the 7.49. This object, in so far as they are dependent upon it (breakdowns, failures, accidents), *is their present interest*. But this present interest—since they all live in the district—refers back to fuller and deeper structures of their general interest: improvement of public transport, freezing of fares, etc. The bus they wait for unites them, being their interest as individuals who *this morning* have business on the *rive droite*; but, as the 7.49, it is *their interest as commuters*; everything is temporalised: the traveller recognises himself as a *resident* (that is to say, he is referred to the five or ten previous years), and then the bus becomes characterised by its daily eternal return (it is actually *the very same* bus, with the same driver and conductor). The object takes on a structure which overflows its pure inert existence; as such it is provided with a passive future and past, and these make it appear to the passengers as a fragment (an insignificant one) of their destiny.

However, to the extent that the bus designates the present commuters, it constitutes them in their *interchangeability*: each of them is effectively produced by the social ensemble as united with his neighbours, in so far as he is strictly identical with them. In other words, their being-outside (that is to say, their interest as regular users of the bus service) is unified, in that it is a pure and indivisible abstraction, rather than a rich, differentiated synthesis; it is a simple identity, designating the commuter as an abstract generality by means of a particular *praxis* (signalling the bus, getting on it, finding a seat, paying the fare), in the development of a broad, synthetic *praxis* (the undertaking which unites the driver and conductor every morning, in the temporalisation which is *one* particular route through Paris at a particular time). At this moment of the investigation, the unit-being *(être-unique)* of the group lies outside itself; in a future object, and everyone, in so far as he is determined by the common interest, differentiates himself from everyone else only by the simple materiality of the organism. And already, if they are characterised in their temporalisation as awaiting their being as the being of all, the abstract unity of their common tuture being manifests itself as *other-being* in relation to the organism which *it is in person* (or, to put it another way, which it *exists*). This moment cannot be one of conflict, but it is no longer one of reciprocity; it must simply be seen as the abstract stage of identity. In so far as *they have the same objective reality* in the future (a minute later, the same for everyone, and the bus will come round the corner of the boulevard), the *unjustified* separation of these organisms (in so far as it arises from other conditions and another region of being) determines itself as *identity*. There is *identity* when the *common* interest (as the determination of generality by the unity of an object in the context of particular practices) is made manifest, and when the plurality is defined just *in relation to this interest*. In that moment, in fact, it matters little if the commuters are biologically or socially differentiated; in so far as they are united by an abstract generality, they are identical as separate individuals. Their identity is their future practico-inert unity, in so far as it determines itself at the present time as *meaningless separation*. And, since all the lived characteristics which might allow some interior differentiation lie outside this determination, everyone's identity with every Other is their unity elsewhere, as other-being; here and now, it is their common alterity. Everyone is the same as the Others in so far as he is Other than himself. And identity as alterity is *exterior separation*; in other words, it is the impossibility of realising, through the body, the transcendent unity to come, in so far as this unity is experienced as an irrational necessity.[7]

   It is at precisely this level that material objects will be found to determine the serial order as the social reason for the separation of individuals. The practico-inert exigency, here, derives from scarcity: *there are not enough places for everyone*. But, apart from scarcity as the contingent but fundamental relation of man to Nature, which remains the context of the whole investigation, *this* particular scarcity is an aspect of material inertia. Whatever the demands, the object remains passively what it is: there is no reason to believe that material exigency must be a special, directly experienced scarcity: we shall find different practico-inert structures of the object as an *individuated being of generality* conditioning different serial relations. I take this example for its simplicity. Thus the specific scarcity—the number of people in relation to the number of places—in the absence of any particular practice, would designate every individual as dispensable; the Other would be the rival of the Other because of their identity; separation would turn into contradiction. But, except in cases of panic—where, in effect, everyone fights *himself in the Other*, in the whirling madness of an abstract unity and a concrete but unthinkable individuality—the relation of reciprocity, emerging or re-emerging in the exteriority of identity, establishes interchangeability as the impossibility of deciding, *a priori*, which individuals are dispensable; and it occasions some practice whose sole purpose is to avoid conflicts and arbitrariness by creating an order.

The travellers waiting for the bus take tickets indicating the order of their arrival. This means that they accept *the impossibility of deciding which individuals are dispensable in terms of the intrinsic qualities of the individual*; in other words, that they remain on the terrain of common interest, and of the identity of separation as meaningless negation; positively, this means that they try to differentiate every Other from Others without adding anything to his characteristic *as Other* as the sole social determination of his existence. *Serial unity*, as common interest, therefore imposes itself as exigency and destroys all opposition. The ticket no doubt refers to a temporal determination. But this is precisely why it is *arbitrary*: the time in question is not a practical temporalisation, but a homogeneous medium of repetition. Taking his ticket as he arrives, everyone does the same as the Other. He realises a practico-inert *exigency* of the ensemble; and, since they are going to different jobs and have different objectives, the fact of having arrived first does not give *any distinctive characteristic*, but simply the right to get on the bus first. The material justifications for the order have meaning, in fact, only after the event: being the first to arrive is no virtue; having waited longest confers no right. (Indeed, one can imagine fairer classifications —waiting means nothing to a young man, but it is very tiring for an old woman. Besides, war wounded have priority in any case, etc.) The really important transformation is that alterity as such, pure alterity, is no longer *either* the simple relation to common unity, *or* the shifting identity of organisms. As an ordering, it becomes a negative principle of unity and of determining everyone's fate as Other *by every Other as Other*. It matters a lot to me, in effect, that I have the tenth number rather than the twentieth. But I am tenth *through Others* in so far as they are Other than themselves, that is to say, in so far as the Reason for their number does not lie in themselves. If I am after my neighbour, this may be because he did not buy his newspaper this morning, or because I was late leaving the house. And if we have numbers 9 and 10, this depends on both of us and also on all the Others, both before and after.

On this basis, it is possible to grasp our relations to the object in their complexity. On the one hand, we have effectively remained general individuals (in so far as we form part of this gathering, of course). Therefore the unity of the collection of commuters lies in the bus they are waiting for; in fact it *is* the bus, as a simple possibility of transport (not for transporting *all* of us, for we do not act together, but for transporting each of us). Thus, as an appearance and a first abstraction, a structure of universality really exists in the grouping; indeed, everyone is identical with the Other in so far as they are waiting for the bus. However, their acts of waiting are not a communal fact, but are lived separately as identical instances of the same act. From this point of view, the group is not structured; it is a gathering and the number of individuals in it is contingent. This means that any other number was *possible* (to the extent that the individuals are considered as arbitrary particles and that they have not collected together as a result of any common dialectical process). This is the level where conceptualisation has its place; that is to say, concepts are based on the molecular appearance of organisms and on the transcendent unity of the group (common interest).

But this generality, as the fluid homogeneity of the gathering (in so far as its unity lies outside it), is just an abstract appearance, for it is actually constituted in its very multiplicity by its transcendent unity as a structured multiplicity. With a concept, in effect, everyone is the same as the Others in so far as he is himself. In the series, however, everyone becomes himself (*as Other than self*) in so far as he is other than the Others, and so, in so far as the Others are other than him. There can be no *concept* of a series, for every member is serial by virtue of his place in the order, and therefore by virtue of his alterity in so far as it is posited as irreducible. In arithmetic, this can be demonstrated by reference to numbers, both as concepts and as serial entities. All whole numbers, or integers, can be the object of the same concept, in so far as they all share the same characteristics; in particular, any whole number can be represented by the symbol $n + 1$ (if we take $n = 0$ for the number one). But *for just this reason*, the arithmetical series of integers, in so far as all of them are constituted by adding one to the preceding number, is a practical and material reality, constituted by an infinite series of unique entities; and the uniqueness of each number is due to the fact that it stands in the same relation to the one that precedes it as this one does to the one preceding it. In the case of ordinals, alterity also changes its meaning: it manifests itself in the concept as common to all, and it designates everyone as a molecule identical with all the others; but, in the series, it becomes a rule of differentiation. And whatever ordering procedure is used, seriality derives from practico-inert matter, that is to say, from the future as an ensemble of inert, equivalent possibilities (equivalent, in this case, because no means of forecasting them is given): there is the possibility that there will be one place, that there will be two, or three, etc. These rigid possibilities are inorganic matter itself in so far as it is non-adaptability. They retain their rigidity by passing into the serial order of separate organisms: for everyone, as a holder of a numbered ticket, they become a complex of possibilities peculiar to him (he will get a place if there is room for ten or more people on the bus; he will not do so if there is only room for nine, but then he will be the first for the next bus). And it is these possibilities and these alone which, within the group, constitute *the real content* of his alterity.

But it should be noticed that this constituent alterity must depend both on all the Others, and on the particular possibility which is actualised, and therefore that the Other has his essence in all the Others, in so far as he differs from them.[8] Moreover, this alterity, as a principle of ordering, naturally produces itself as a *link*. Now this link between men is of an entirely different kind from those already examined. On the one hand, it cannot be explained in terms of reciprocity, since the serial movement in our example excludes the relation of reciprocity: everyone is the Reason for the Other-Being of the Other in so far as an Other is the reason for his being. In a sense, we are back with material exteriority, which should come as no surprise since the series is determined by inorganic matter. On the other hand, to the extent that the ordering was performed *by some practice*, and that this practice included reciprocity within it, it contains a *real interiority*: for it is *in his real being*, and as an integral part of a totality which has totalised itself outside, that each is dependent on the Other in his reality. To put it another way: reciprocity in the milieu of identity becomes a false reciprocity of relations: what a is to b (the reason for his being other), b is to c, b and the entire series are to a. Through this opposition between the Other and the same in the milieu of the Other, alterity becomes this paradoxical structure: the identity of everyone as everyone's action of serial interiority on the Other. In the same way, *identity* (as the sheer absurdity of meaningless dispersal) becomes synthetic: everyone is identical with the Other in so far as the others make him an Other acting on the Others; the formal, universal structure of alterity produces the *formula of the series* (*la Raison de la série*).

In the formal, strictly *practical*, and limited case that we have been examining, the adoption of the serial mode remains a mere convenience, with no special influence on the individuals. But this simple example has the advantage of showing the emergence of new pratico-inert characteristics: it reveals two characteristics *of the inactive human gathering*. The visible unity, in this case, in the time of the gathering (the totalised reality which they comprise for someone who sees them from a window or from the pavement opposite), is only an *appearance*; its origin for every observer to whom this totality is revealed, is integral *praxis* in so far as it is a perpetual organisation of *its* own dialectical field and, in practico-inert objectivity, the general, inert link between all the people in a field which is limited by its instrumentality, in so far as it is social—

that is to say, in so far as its inert, instrumental materiality ultimately refers back to the order of historical movement—combined with their true being-outside-themselves in a particular practical object which, far from being a symbol, is a material being which produces their unity within itself and imposes it on them through the inert practices of the practico-inert field.

In short, the visible unity of a gathering is produced *partly* by accidental factors (accidental at this level of the investigation—their unity will be restored in a broader movement of totalisation), and *partly* by the *real* but *transcendent* unity of a practico-inert object, in so far as this unity, in the development of a directed process, *produces itself* as the real material unity of the individuals in a given multiplicity, which it itself defines and limits. I have already said that this unity is *not* symbolic; it is now possible to see why. It is because it has nothing to symbolise; *it* is what unites everything. And if, in special circumstances, it is possible to see a symbolic relation between the gathering, as a visible assembly of discrete particles (where it presents itself in a visible form), and its objective unity, this is to be found in the small visible crowd which, by its presence as a gathering, *becomes a symbol* of the practical unity of its *interest* or of some other object which is produced as its inert synthesis. This unity itself, in so far as it is practico-inert, may present itself to individuals through a larger *praxis* of which they are either the inert means, the ends or the objects, or a combination of these, and which constitutes the true synthetic field of their gathering and which produces them in the object with their new laws of unified multiplicity. This *praxis* unifies them by producing the object in which they are already inscribed, in which their forms are negatively determined, and, in so far as it is already other (affected by the entire inertia of matter), it is this *praxis* which produces them in common in other unity.

The second point to be made is that the apparent absence of structure in the gathering (or its apparent structures) does not correspond to objective reality: if they were all unaware of each other and if they carried their social isolation behaviour to the limit, the passive unity of the gathering *in the object* would both require and produce an *ordinal* structure from the multiplicity of the organisms. In other words, what presents itself to perception either as a sort of organised totality (men huddled together, waiting) or as a dispersal, possesses, as a collecting together of men by the object, a completely different basic structure which, by means of serial ordering, transcends the conflict between exterior and interior, between unity and identity. From the point of view of the activity-institution (the exact meaning of these terms will be clarified later), which is represented in Paris by the RATP (the public transport authority), the small gathering which slowly forms around the bus stop, apparently by a process of mere aggregation, *already has* a serial structure. It was produced *in advance* as the structure of some unknown group by the ticket machine attached to the bus stop. Everyone realises it for himself and confirms it for Others through his own individual *praxis* and his own ends. This does *not* mean that he helps to create an active group by freely determining, with other individuals, the end, the means, and the division of tasks; it means that he *actualises* his being-outside-himself as a reality shared by several people and *which already exists, and awaits him*, by means of an inert practice, denoted by instrumentality, whose meaning is that it integrates him into an ordered multiplicity by assigning him a place in a prefabricated seriality.

In this sense, the indifferentiation of beings-outside-themselves in the passive unity of an object exists between them as a serial order, as separation-unity in the practico-inert milieu of the Other. In other words, there is an objective, fundamental connection between collective unity as a transcendence which is *given to the gathering* by the future (and the past), and seriality as everyone's practico-inert actualisation of a relation with Others in so far as this relation determines him in his being *and already awaits him*. The thing as *common being* produces seriality as its own practico-inert being-outside-itself in the plurality of practical organisms; everyone realises himself outside himself in the objective unity of interpenetration in so far as he constitutes himself in the gathering as an objective element of a series. Or again, as we shall see more clearly later, whatever it may be, and whatever the circumstances, the series constitutes itself on the basis of the unity-object and, conversely, it is in the serial milieu and through serial behaviour that the individual achieves practical and theoretical participation in common being.

There are serial behaviour, serial feelings and serial thoughts; in other words a *series is a mode of being for individuals both in relation to one another and in relation to their common being* and this mode of being transforms all their structures. In this way, it is useful to distinguish serial *praxis* (as the *praxis* of the individual in so far as he is a member of the series and as the *praxis* of the whole series, or of the series totalised through individuals) both from common *praxis* (group action) and from individual, constituent *praxis*. Conversely, in every non-serial *praxis*, a serial *praxis* will be found, as the practico-inert structure of the *praxis* in so far as it is social. And, just as there is a *logic* of the practico-inert layer, there are *also* structures proper to the thought which is produced at this social level of activity; in other words, there is *a rationality* of the theoretical and practical behaviour of an agent as a member of a series. Lastly, to the extent that *the series* represents the use of alterity as a bond between men under the passive action of an object, and as this passive action defines the general type of alterity which serves as a bond, alterity is, ultimately, the practico-inert object itself in so far as it produces itself in the milieu of multiplicity with its own particular exigencies. Indeed, every Other is both Other than himself and Other than Others, in so far as their relations constitute both him and Others in accordance with an objective, practical, inert rule of alterity (in the formal particularisation of this alterity).

Thus this rule—the *formula of the series*—is common to all precisely to the extent that they differentiate themselves. I say common, but not identical: for identity is separation, whereas the *formula of the series* is a dynamic scheme which determines each through all and all through each. *The Other,* as formula of the series and as a factor in every particular case of alterity, therefore becomes, beyond its structure of identity and its structure of alterity, a being common to all (as negated and preserved interchangeability). At this level, beyond the concept and the rule, the Other is me in every Other and every Other in me and everyone as Other in all the Others; finally, it is the passive Unity of the multiplicity in so far as it exists in itself; it is the reinteriorisation of exteriority by the human ensemble, it is the being-one of the organisms in so far as it corresponds to the unity of their being-in-themselves in the object. But, in so far as everyone's unity with the Other and with all Others is never given in him and the Other in a true relation based on reciprocity, and in so far as this *interior* unity of all is always and for everyone in all the Others, in so far as they are others and never *in him* except *for Others*, and in so far as he is other than them, this unity, which is *ever present but always elsewhere*, again becomes interiority lived in the milieu of exteriority. It no longer has any connection with molecularity: *it is genuinely a unity,* but the unity of a flight.

This can best be understood in the light of the fact that in an active, contractual and differentiated group, everyone can regard himself both as subordinate to the whole and as essential, as the practical local presence of the whole, in his own particular action. In the case of the bond of alterity, however, the whole is a totalisation of flight; Being as material reality is the totalised series of *not-being*; it is what everyone causes the other to become, as his double, out of reach, incapable of acting on him directly, and, simply in its transformation, subject to the action of an Other. Alterity, as the unity of identities, must always be elsewhere. *Elsewhere* there is only an Other, always other than self and which seems, from the point of view of idealist thought concerning other real beings, to engender them by logical scissiparity, that is to say, to produce the Others as indefinite moments of its alterity (whereas, in reality, exactly the opposite occurs). Ought we to say that this hypostas-ised serial reason simply refers us back to the *practico-inert object* as the unity outside themselves of individuals? On the contrary, for it engenders it as a particular practical interiorisation of being-outside through multiplicity. In this case, must we treat it as an Idea, that is to say, *an ideal label*? Surely not.

The Jew (as the internal, serial unity of Jewish multiplicities), or *the* colonialist, or *the* professional soldier, etc., are not ideas, any more than *the* militant or, as we shall see, *the* petty bourgeois, or *the* manual worker. The theoretical error (it is not a practical one, because *praxis* really does constitute them in alterity) was to conceive of these beings as concepts, whereas—as the fundamental basis of extremely complex relations—they are *primarily* serial unities. In fact, the being-Jewish of every Jew in a hostile society which persecutes and insults them, and opens itself to them only to reject them again, cannot be the only relation between the individual Jew and the anti-semitic, racist society which surrounds him; it is this relation in so far as it is lived by every Jew in his direct or indirect relations with all the other Jews, and in so far as it constitutes him, through them all, as Other and threatens him in and through the Others. To the extent that, for the conscious, lucid Jew, being-Jewish (which is his statute *for non-Jews*) is interiorised as his responsibility in relation to all other Jews and his being-in-danger, out there, owing to some possible carelessness caused by Others who mean nothing to him, over whom he has no power and every one of whom is himself like Others (in so far as he makes them exist as such in spite of himself), *the* Jew, far from being *the type* common to each separate instance, represents *on the contrary* the perpetual *being-outside-themselves-in-the-other* of the members of this practico-inert grouping. (I call it this *because* it exists within societies which have a non-Jewish majority and because every child even if he subsequently adopts it with pride and by a deliberate practice—must begin by *submitting to* his statute.)

Thus, for example, if there is an outbreak of anti-semitism, and Jewish members of society are beginning to be accused of "getting all the best jobs", then for every Jewish doctor or teacher or banker, every other banker, doctor or teacher will constitute him as dispensable (and conversely). Indeed it is easy to see why this should be so: alterity as everyone's interiorisation of his common-being-outside-himself in the unifying object can be conceived as the unity of all only in the form of common-being-outside-oneself-in-the-other. This is because totalisation as an *organised form of social relations* actually presupposes (in the abstract and in extreme cases, of course) an original synthetic *praxis* whose aim is the human production of unity as its objectification in and through men. This totalisation—which will be described below—comes to men through themselves. But the totality of the gathering is only the passive action of a practico-inert object on a dispersal. The limitation of the gathering to *these* particular individuals is only an accidental negation (since, in principle, as *identities*, their number is not determined). Transformation into a totality is never the aim of a *praxis*; it reveals itself in so far as men's relations are governed by object-relations, that is to say, in so far as it comes to them as a practico-inert structure whose sealed exteriority is revealed as the interiority of real relations. On this basis, and in the context of *exigency* as an objectivity to be realised, plurality becomes unity, alterity becomes my own spontaneity in the Other and that of everyone in me, and the reciprocity of flights (as a pseudo-reciprocity) becomes a human relation of reciprocity. I have taken the simple and unimportant example of the passengers on the bus only in order to show serial structure as the being of the most ordinary, everyday gatherings: as a fundamental constitution of sociality, this structure does in fact tend to be neglected by sociologists. Marxists are aware of it, but they seldom mention it and generally prefer to trace the difficulties in the *praxis* of emancipation and agitation to organised forces rather than to seriality as the material resistance of gatherings and masses to the action of groups (and even to the action of practico-inert factors).

If we are to encompass the world of seriality, if only in one glance, or to note the importance of its structures and practices—in so far as they ultimately constitute the foundation of all seriality, even that which aims to bring man back to the Other through the organisation *of praxis*—we must abandon the example we have been using and consider what occurs in a domain where this basic reality discloses to our investigation its true nature and efficacity. I call the two-way relation between a material, inorganic, worked object and a multiplicity which finds its unity of exteriority in it *collective*. It defines *a social object;* it is a two-way relation (false reciprocity) because it is possible not only to conceive the inorganic object as materiality eroded by serial flight, but also to conceive the totalised plurality as materialised outside itself as common exigency in the object. Conversely, one can start either from material unity as exteriority, moving towards serial flight as a determinant of the behaviour which marks the social and material milieu with the original seal of seriality, or from serial unity, defining its reactions (as the practico-inert unity of a multiplicity) to the common object (that is to say, the transformations they bring about in the object). Indeed, from this point of view the false reciprocity between the common object and the totalised multiplicity can be seen as an interchangeability of two material statutes in the practico-inert field; but at the same time it must be regarded as a developing transformation of every one of the practico-inert materialities by the Other. In any case, we can now elucidate the meaning of serial structure and the possibility of applying this knowledge to the study of the dialectical intelligibility of the social.

[...]

The fused group

The group—the equivalence of freedom as necessity and of necessity as freedom—the scope and limits of any realist dialectic.

The genesis of groups

As we have seen, the necessity of the group is not present *a priori* in a gathering. But we have also seen that through its serial unity (in so far as the negative unity of the series can, as abstract negation, oppose seriality) the gathering furnishes the elementary conditions of the *possibility* that its members should constitute a group. But this remains abstract. Obviously everything would be simpler in a transcendental, idealist dialectic: the movement of integration by which every organism contains and dominates its inorganic pluralities would be presented as transforming itself, at the level of social plurality, into an integration of individuals into an organic totality. Thus the group would function as a hyper-organism in relation to individual organisms. This organicist idealism is often to be seen re-emerging as a social model of conservative thought (under the Restoration, it was opposed to liberal atomism; after 1860, it tried to dissolve class formations into a national solidarity). But it would be a mistake to reduce the organicist illusion to the role of a reactionary theory. Indeed, it is obvious that the *organic* character of the group—its *biological* unity—reveals itself as a particular moment of the investigation. As we approach the third stage of the dialectical investigation, we can describe the organic structure as *above all* the illusory, immediate appearance of the group as it produces itself in and against the practico-inert field.

In two remarkable works[9] Marc Bloch has shown how, in and even before the twelfth century, the nobility, the bourgeoisie and the serfs— to mention only these three classes—existed *de facto* if not *de jure*. In our terminology we would describe them as collectives. But the repeated efforts of rich bourgeois, as *individuals,* to integrate themselves into the noble class caused this class to close up: it moved from a *de facto* statute to a *de jure* one. Through a common undertaking, it imposed draconian conditions on anyone wishing to enter *knighthood*, with the result that this mediating institution between the generations became a selective organ. But this also conditioned the class consciousness of the serfs. Prior to the juridical unification of the nobility, every serf had regarded his situation as an individual destiny, and lived it as an ensemble of human relations with a family of landowners, in other words, as an accident. But by positing itself for itself; the nobility *ipso facto* constituted serfdom as a juridical institution and showed the serfs their interchangeability, their common impotence and their common interests. This revelation was one of the factors of peasant revolts in later centuries.

The point of this example is simply to show how, in the movement of History, an exploiting class, by tightening its bonds against an enemy and by becoming aware of itself as a unity of individuals *in solidarity*, shows the exploited classes their material being as a collective and as a point of departure for a constant effort to establish lived bonds of solidarity between its members. There is nothing surprising about this: in this inert quasi-totality, constantly swept by great movements of counter-finality, the historical collectivity, the dialectical law, is at work: the constitution of a group (on the basis, of course, of real, material conditions) as an ensemble of solidarities has the dialectical consequence of making it the negation of the rest of the social field, and, as a result, of occasioning, in this field in so far as it is defined as *non-grouped*, the conditions for an antagonistic grouping *(on the basis* of scarcity and in divided social systems).

But the most important point here is that the non-grouped, on the outside, behave towards the group by positing it through their very *praxis* as *an organic totality*. Thus every new collective organisation can find its archetype in any other older one, because *praxis* as the unification of the practical field objectively tightens the bonds of the object-group. It is striking that our most elementary patterns of behaviour relate to *external collectives* as if they were organisms. The structure of *scandal*, for example, is, for everyone, that of a collective taken as a totality: in a theatre, everyone, in confronting each speech of a scene which he finds outrageous, is in fact conditioned by the serial reaction of his neighbours. Scandal is the Other as the formula of a series. *But as soon as* the first manifestations of scandal have occurred (that is to say, the first acts of someone acting for the Others in so far as he is Other than himself), they create the living unity of the audience against the author, simply because the first protester, through his unity as an individual, *realises this unity* for everyone in transcendence (*la transcendance*). Moreover, it will remain a profound contradiction in everyone, because this unity is that of all the Others (including himself) as Others and by an Other: the protester was not revealing or expressing popular opinion; rather, he was expressing, in the objective unity of a direct action (shouts, insults, etc.), what still existed for everyone only as the opinion of the Others, that is to say, as their shifting, serial unity. But once the scandal has been reported and discussed, it becomes, in the eyes of those who did not witness it, a synthetic event which gave the audience which saw the play that night a temporary unity as an organism. Everything becomes clear if we *situate* the non-grouped who discover themselves to be a collective through their impotence in relation to the group which they reveal. To the extent that, through the unity of its *praxis,* the group determines them in their inorganic inertia, they conceive its ends and its unity through the free unifying unity of their own individual *praxis* and on the model of the free synthesis which is fundamentally the practical temporalisation of the organism. Indeed, in the practical field, all exterior multiplicity becomes, for every agent, the object of a unifying synthesis (and, as we have already seen, the result of this synthesis is that the serial structure of gatherings is concealed). But the group which I unify in the practical field produces itself, as a group, as already unified, that is to say, as structured by a unity which in principle eludes my unification and negates it (in so far as it is *praxis relegating me to impotence*). This free active unity which eludes me appears as the substance of a reality of which I myself, in my practical and perceptual field, have unified only its multiplicity as the pure materiality of appearance; or, to put it another way, I do not attribute inertia—which must constitute the real foundation of the group (as inertia which has been transcended and preserved)—to the active community; on the contrary, it is my *praxis* which, in its unificatory movement takes responsibility for it. And the common action, which eludes me, becomes the *reality* of this appearance, that is to say, the practical, synthetic substance, the totality controlling its parts, entelechy, life; or, at another level of perception and for other groups, a *Gestalt.* We shall encounter this naive organicism both as an immediate relation of the individual to the group and as an ideal of absolute integration. But we must reject organicism *in every form.* The relation of the group, as the determination of a collective and as a perpetual threat of relapsing into a collective, to its inertia as a multiplicity can never in any way be assimilated to the relation of the organism to the inorganic substances which compose it.

But if there is no dialectical process through which the moment of the anti-dialectic can become by itself a mediation between the multiple dialectics of the practical field and the constituted dialectic as common *praxis,* does the emergence of the group contain its own intelligibility? Following the same method as we have used so far, we shall now attempt to find in our investigation the characteristics and moments of a particular process of grouping from the point of view of the purely *critical* aim of determining its rationality. In our investigation we shall therefore have to study successively the genesis of groups, and the structures of their *praxis*—in other words, the dialectical rationality of collective action—and, finally, the group as *passion*, that is to say, in so far as it struggles in itself against *the practical inertia* by which it is affected.

I will begin with two preliminary observations. First, I have claimed that the inert gathering with its structure of seriality is the basic type of sociality. But I have not meant this in a historical sense, and the term "fundamental" here does not imply temporal priority. Who could claim that collectives come before groups? No one is in a position to advance any hypothesis on this subject; or rather—despite the data of pre-history and ethnography—no such hypothesis has any meaning. Besides, the constant metamorphosis of gatherings into groups and of groups into gatherings would make it quite impossible to know *a priori* whether a particular gathering was a primary historical reality or whether it was the remains of a group which had been reabsorbed by the field of passivity: in either case, only the study of earlier structures and conditions can answer the question—if anything can. Our reason for positing the logical anteriority of collectives is simply that according to what History teaches us, groups constitute themselves as determinations and negations of collectives. In other words, they transcend and preserve them. Collectives, on the other hand, even when they result from the disintegration of active groups, preserve nothing of themselves *as collectives,* except for dead, ossified structures which scarcely conceal the flight of seriality. Similarly, the group, whatever it may be, *contains in itself* its reasons for relapsing into the inert being of the gathering: thus the disintegration of a group, as we shall see, has an *a priori* intelligibility. But the collective— as such and apart from the action of the factors we are about to study— contains *at most* the mere possibility of a synthetic union of its members. Lastly, regardless of *pre-history*, the important thing here, in a *history* conditioned by class struggle, is to explain the transition of oppressed classes from the state of being collectives to revolutionary group *praxis.* This is particularly important because such a transition has *really* occurred in each case.

But having mentioned class relations, I will make a second observation: that it would be premature to regard these classes as also being groups. In order to determine the conditions of their intelligibility, I shall, as with collectives, take and discuss ephemeral, superficial groups, which form and disintegrate rapidly, and approach the basic groups of society progressively.

The upheaval which destroys the collective by the flash of a common *praxis* obviously originates in a synthetic, and therefore material, transformation, which occurs in the context of scarcity and of existing structures. For organisms whose risks and practical movement, as well as their suffering, reside in need, the driving-force is either danger, at every level of materiality (whether it be hunger, or the bankruptcy *whose meaning* is hunger, etc.), or transformations of instrumentality (the exigencies and scarcity of the tool replacing the scarcity of the immediate object of need; or the modifications of the tool, seen in their ascending signification, as necessary modifications of the collective). In other words, without the original tension of need as a relation of interiority with Nature, there would be no change; and, conversely, there is no common *praxis* at any level whose regressive or descending signification is not directly or indirectly related to this original tension. It must therefore be understood *at the outset* that the origin of any restructuration of a collective into a group is a complex event which takes place *simultaneously* at every level of materiality, but is transcended into organising *praxis* at the level of serial unity.

But however universal the event may be, it cannot be lived as its own transcendence towards the unity of all, unless its universality is objective *for everyone*, or unless it creates in everyone a structure of unifying objectivity. Up to this point, in fact—in the dimension of the collective—the real has defined itself by its impossibility. Indeed, what is called the *meaning of realities* is precisely the meaning of that which, in principle, is forbidden. The transformation therefore occurs when impossibility itself becomes impossible, or when the synthetic event reveals that the impossibility of change is an impossibility of life.[10] The direct result of this is to make *the impossibility of change* the very object which has to be transcended if life is to continue. In other words, we have come to a vicious circle: the group constitutes itself on the basis of a need or common danger and defines itself by the common objective which determines its common *praxis*. Yet neither common need, nor common praxis, nor common objectives can define a community unless it makes itself into a community by feeling individual need as common need, and by projecting itself, in the internal unification of a common integration, towards objectives which it produces as common. Without famine, this group would not have constituted itself: but why does it define itself as common struggle against common need? Why is it that, as sometimes happens, individuals in a given case do not quarrel over food like dogs? That is the same as asking how a synthesis can take place when the power of synthetic unity is both everywhere (in all individuals as a free unification of the field) and nowhere (in that it would be a free transcendent (*transcendante*) unification of the plurality of individual unifications). Indeed, let us not forget that the *common object*, as the unity of the multiple outside itself, is above all the producer of serial unity and that it is on the basis of this double determination that the anti-dialectical structure of the collectivity, or *alterity*, constitutes itself.

But this last observation may help us. If the object really produces itself as the bond of alterity between the individuals of a collective, then the serial structure of multiplicity depends, basically, on the fundamental characteristics of the object itself and on its original relation with each and all. This is how the set of means of production, in so far as they are the property of *Others*, gives the proletariat an original structure of seriaiity because it produces itself as an indefinite ensemble of objects whose exigencies themselves reflect the *demand* of the bourgeois class as the seriality of the Other. Conversely, however, it is possible for the investigation to consider the common objects which constitute by themselves, and in the *practico-inert field*, an approximation to a totality (as the totalisation of the multiple by the Other through matter) and to try to discover whether they too must constitute the multiple in question as seriality.

Notes

1 Marx has stated this thought specifically: to act upon the educator, it is necessary to act upon the factors which condition him. Thus the qualities of external determination and those of that synthetic, progressive unity which is human *praxis* are found inseparably connected in Marxist thought. Perhaps we should maintain that wish to transcend the oppositions of externality and internality, of multiplicity and unity, of analysis and synthesis, of nature and anti-nature, is actually the most profound theoretical contribution of Marxism. But these are suggestions to be developed, the mistake would be to think that the task is an easy one.

2 It is relatively easy to foresee to what extent every attempt (even that of a *group*) will be posited as a particular determination at the heart of the totalizing movement and thereby will achieve results opposed to those which it sought: this will be *a* method, *a* theory, etc. But one can also foresee how its partial aspect will later be broken down by a new generation and how, within the Marxist philosophy, it will be integrated in a wider totality. To this extent even, one may say that the rising generations are more capable of *knowing* (*savoir*)—at least formally—what they are doing than the generations which have preceded us.

3 Failing to develop by real investigations, Marxism makes use of an arrested dialectic. Indeed, it achieves the totalization of human activities within a

homogeneous and infinitely divisible continuum which is nothing other than the "time" of Cartesian rationalism. This temporal environment is not unduly confining when the problem is to examine the process of capitalism, because it is exactly that temporality which capitalist economy produces as the signification of production, of monetary circulation, of the redistribution of property, of credit, of "compound interest." Thus it can be considered a product of the system. But the description of this universal container as a phase of social development is one thing and the dialectical determination of *real* temporality (that is, of the true relation of men to their past and their future) is another. Dialectic as a movement of reality collapses if time is not dialectic; that is, if we refuse to recognize a certain action of the future as such. It would be too long to study here the dialectical temporality of history. For the moment, I have wanted only to indicate the difficulties and to formulate the problem. One must understand that neither men nor their activities are *in time*, but that time, as a concrete quality of history, is made by men on the basis of their original temporalization. Marxism caught a glimpse of true temporality when it criticized and destroyed the bourgeois notion of "progress"—which necessarily implies a homogeneous milieu and coordinates which would allow us to situate the point of departure and the point of arrival. But—without ever having said so—Marxism has renounced these studies and preferred to make use of "progress" again for its own benefit.

4 I add these observations: (1) That this objective truth of the objectified subjective must be considered as the only truth of the subjective. Since the latter exists only in order to be objectified, it is on the basis of the objectification—that is, on the realization—that it must be judged in itself and in the world. An action cannot be judged by the intention behind it. (2) That this truth will allow us to evaluate the *objectified project* in the total picture. An action, such as it appears in the light of contemporary history and of a particular set of circumstances, may be shown to be ill-fated from the start—for the group which supports it (or for some wider formation, a class or a fragment of a class, of which this group forms a part). And at the same time its unique objective characteristic may reveal it to be *an enterprise in good faith*. When one considers an action harmful to the establishing of socialism, it may be so only in relation to this particular aim. To characterize it as harmful can *in no case* prejudice what the action is in itself; that is, considered on another level of objectivity and related to particular circumstances and to the conditioning of the individual environment. People often set up a dangerous distinction: an act may be objectively *blameworthy* (by the Party, by the Cominform, etc.) while remaining *subjectively acceptable*. A person could be subjectively of good will, objectively a traitor. This distinction testifies to an advanced disintegration in Stalinist thought; that is, in voluntaristic idealism. It is easy to see that it goes back to that "petit bourgeois" distinction between the good intentions with which "hell is paved," etc., and their real consequences. In fact, the general import of the action considered and its individual signification are equally *objective* characteristics (since they are interpreted within an objectivity), and they both engage subjectivity (since they are its objectification) whether within the total movement which discovers it as it is *from the point of view of the totalization* or within a particular synthesis. Furthermore, an act has many other levels of truth, and these levels do not represent a dull hierarchy, but a

complex movement of contradictions which are posited and surpassed; for example, the totalization which appraises the act in its relation to historical *praxis* and to the conjuncture of circumstances is itself denounced as an abstract, incomplete totalization (a *practical* totalization) insofar as it has not turned back to the action to reintegrate it *also* as a uniquely individual attempt. The condemnation of the insurgents at Kronstadt was perhaps inevitable; it was perhaps the judgment of history on this tragic attempt. But at the same time this practical judgment (the only real one) will remain that of an enslaved history so long as it does not include the free interpretation of the revolt in terms of the insurgents themselves and of the contradictions of the moment. This free interpretation, someone may say, is in no way *practical* since the insurgents, as well as their judges, are dead. But that is not true. The historian, by consenting to study facts at all levels of reality, liberates future history. This liberation can come about, as a visible and efficacious action, only within the compass of the general movement of democratization; but conversely it cannot fail to accelerate this movement. (3) In the world of alienation, the historical agent never entirely recognizes himself in his act. This does not mean that historians should not recognize him in it precisely *as* an alienated man. However this may be, alienation is at the base and at the summit; and the agent never undertakes anything which is not the negation of alienation and which does not fall back into an alienated world. But the alienation of the objectified result is not the same as the alienation at the point of departure. It is the passage from the one to the other which defines the person.

5   On exactly this point Engels's thought seems to have wavered. We know the unfortunate use which he sometimes makes of this idea of a *mean*. His evident purpose is to remove from dialectic its a priori character as an unconditioned force. But then dialectic promptly disappears. It is impossible to conceive of the appearance of systematic processes such as capitalism or colonialism if we consider the resultants of antagonistic forces to be means. We must understand that individuals do not collide like molecules, but that, upon the basis of given conditions and divergent and opposed interests, each one understands and surpasses the project of the other. It is by these surpassings and surpassings of surpassings that a social object may be constituted which, taken as a whole, is a reality *provided with meaning and something* in which nobody can completely recognize himself; in short, *a human work without an author. Means*, as Engels and statisticians conceive of them, suppress the author, but by the same stroke they suppress the work and its "humanity." We shall have the opportunity to develop this idea in Part Two of the *Critique*.

6   When I say that the intensity of isolation *expresses* the degree of massification, I mean that it does this in a purely *indicative* way.

7   It becomes perfectly rational when the stages of the entire process are reconstructed. All the same, the conflict between interchangeability and existence (as unique, lived *praxis*) must be lived at some level as a *scandalous absurdity*.

8   In so far as he is *the same*, he is simply and formally *an other*.

9   Marc Bloch, *Feudal Society*, two volumes (1939–40). English translation by L. A. Manyon, Routledge and Kegan Paul, 1961. [Ed.]

10 Obviously it is not under a threat of mortal danger that anglers form their

association or old ladies set up a system of swopping books: but these groups, which in any case respond to some very real exigencies and whose objective meaning relates to the total situation, are superstructures, or, in other words, groups which are constituted in the general, permanent regroupment activity of collectives (class structures, class against class, national and international organisations, etc.). From the moment that the stage of the dialectical regroupment of dialectics has been reached, totalising activity *itself* becomes a factor, a milieu and a reason for secondary groups. They are its living determination and therefore its negation; but, at the same time, they confine it entirely within itself, and their dialectical conflicts take place through it and by it. In this way, as we saw in *The Problem of Method*, it is possible to study them either horizontally (and empirically) in so far as they determine themselves in a milieu in which the group structure is already objectively given, or vertically in so far as each of them in its concrete richness expresses the whole of human materiality and the whole historical process. Thus I need only concern myself here with the fundamental fact of grouping as the conquest or reconquest of the collective by *praxis*.

Bibliography

Chronological bibliography of the principal works of Sartre

1923
'L'Ange du morbide' *Revue sans titre* (1931)

1931
'Légende de la Vérité' *Bifur* (1931)

1936
L'Imagination (Presses universitaires de France)

1937
'La Transcendance de l'Ego' *Recherches Philosophiques, VI* (1936–7)

1938
La Nausée (Gallimard)
'La Structure intentionnelle de l'image' *Revue de Métaphysique et de Morale* (September, 1938)

1939
Le Mur (*Le mur, La chambre, Erostrate, Intimité, L'enfance d'un chef*)
Esquisse d'une théorie des émotions (Herman et Cie)

1940
L'Imaginaire: psychologie phénoménologique de l'imagination (Gallimard)

1943
L'Etre et le Néant: Essai d'ontologie phénoménologique (Gallimard)
Les Mouches (Gallimard)

1944
Huis Clos (Gallimard)

1945
Les Chemins de la Liberté, I: L'Age de Raison (Gallimard)
Les Chemins de la Liberté, II: Le Sursis (Gallimard)
'Introduction aux Ecrits intimes de Baudelaire' *Confluences* (January–February, 1945)

1946

L'Existentialisme est un Humanisme (Nagel)
Morts sans sépulture (Gallimard)
La Putain respectueuse (Gallimard)
Réflexions sur la question juive (Editions Morihien) (Gallimard, 1954)
Baudelaire (Gallimard)

1947

L'Existentialisme est un humanisme (Nagel)
Situations I (Gallimard)
Les Jeux sont faits (Nagel)
'Présence noire' *Présence Africaine* (November–December, 1947)

1948

Qu'est ce que la littérature? (Gallimard)
Les Mains sales (Gallimard)
L'Engrenage (Nagel)
Situations II (Gallimard)
Visages (Seghers)

1949

Les Chemins de la Liberté, III: La Mort dans Âme (Gallimard)
Situations III (Gallimard)
Entretiens sur la Politique (with David Rousset and Gerard Rosenthal) (Gallimard)
Les Chemins de la Liberté IV: La Dernière Chance (published incomplete as
   'Drôle d'Amitié' in *Les Temps Modernes* November and December)

1951

Le Diable et le Bon Dieu (Gallimard)

1952

Saint Genet, comédien et martyr (Gallimard)
'Les communistes et la paix' I : *Les Temps Modernes* (July 1952)
'Réponse à Albert Camus' *Les Temps Modernes* (August, 1952)
'Les communistes et la paix' II: *Les Temps Modernes* (October–November, 1952)

1953

L'affaire Henri Martin: textes commentés par Jean-Paul Sartre (Gallimard)
'Réponse à Claude Lefort' *Les Temps Modernes* (April, 1953)

1954

Kean, ou Desordre et Genie, adapted from Alexandre Dumas (Gallimard)
'Les communistes et la paix' III: *Les Temps Modernes* (August, 1954)

1955

Nekrassov (Gallimard)

1956

'Le colonialisme est un système' *Les Temps Modernes* (March–April, 1956)
'Sur les événements de Hongrie' *L'Express* (9th November, 1956)

1957
'Le fantôme de Staline' *Les Temps Modernes* (January, 1957)
'Questions de méthode' *Les Temps Modernes* (1957)

1958
'Nous sommes tous des assassins' *Les Temps Modernes* (March, 1958)

1959
Les Séquestrés d'Altona (Gallimard)

1960
Critique de la raison dialectique (précédé de Questions de méthode) Tome I : Théorie des ensembles pratiques (Gallimard)

1962
Marxisme et Existentialisme: Controverse sur la Dialectique (with others) (Plon)

1963
Les Mots (Gallimard)

1964
Situations IV (Gallimard)
Situations V (Gallimard)
Situations VI (Gallimard)

1965
Les Troyennes, d'après Euripide (Gallimard)
Situations VII (Gallimard)

1970
Les Ecrits de Sartre (Michel Contat and Michel Rybalka (eds)) (Gallimard)

1971
L'Idiot de la famille I (Gallimard)
L'Idiot de la famille II (Gallimard)

1972
Situations VIII (Gallimard)
Situations IX (Gallimard)

1973
Un Théâtre de situations (Gallimard)

1974
On a raison de se révolter (with Philippe Gavi and Pierre Victor) (Gallimard)

1976
Situations X

1977
'Sartre par lui-même' (interview with Alexandre Astruc and Michel Rybalka)

1981

Œuvres romanesques, Michel Contat, Michel Rybalka, Genevieve Idt and George H. Bauer (eds) (Bibliothèque de la Pleiade, Gallimard)

1983

Les Carnets de la drôle de guerre (Gallimard)
Cahiers pour une morale (Gallimard)
Lettres au Castor et à quelques autres, I 1926–1939 (Gallimard)
Lettres au Castor et à quelques autres, I 1940–1963 (Gallimard)

1984

Le Scénario Freud, J. B. Pontalis (ed.) (Gallimard)

1986

Critique de la raison dialectique, Tome II : L'intelligibilité de l'Histoire (Gallimard)

1989

Vérité et existence, Texte établi et annoté par Arlette Elkaim-Sartre (Gallimard)

English translations of Sartre's works

Philosophy

Existentialism and Humanism trans. Philip Mairet (London, 1948)
Sketch For a Theory of the Emotions trans. Philip Mairet (London, 1948)
The Psychology of Imagination (London, 1972)
Being and Nothingness trans. Hazel Barnes (New York, 1956 and London, 1957)
The Transcendence of the Ego trans. Forrest Williams and Robert Kirkpatrick (New York, 1958)
Search for a Method trans. Hazel Barnes (New York, 1963)
Critique of Dialectical Reason Volume I : Theory of Practical Ensembles trans. Alan Sheridan Smith (London, 1976)
Notebooks for an Ethics trans. David Pellauer (Chicago, 1992)

Novels

The Age of Reason trans. Eric Sutton (New York and London, 1947; Penguin, Harmondsworth, 1961)
The Reprieve trans. Eric Sutton (New York and London, 1947; Penguin, Harmondsworth, 1963)
Iron in the Soul trans. Gerard Hopkins (London, 1950 and New York, 1951; Penguin, Harmondsworth, 1963)
Nausea trans. Robert Baldick (New York and London, 1949; Penguin, Harmondsworth, 1966)

Collection of short stories

Intimacy trans. Lloyd Alexander (London and New York, 1949)

Plays

The Flies and In Camera (London, 1946)
The Respectful Prostitute (London, 1947; New York, 1949)
Men Without Shadows (London and New York, 1949)
Dirty Hands (London and New York, 1949)
Lucifer and the Lord (London, 1953; New York, 1960)
Kean (London, 1954; New York, 1960)
Nekrassov (London, 1958; New York 1960)
Loser Wins (London, 1960)
The Condemned of Altona (New York, 1961)
The Trojan Women (London and New York, 1967)
No Exit and Three Other Plays: Dirty Hands, The Flies, The Respectful Prostitute (Random House, New York, 1955)
Altona and Other Plays (Penguin, Harmondsworth, 1962)
Three Plays: Kean, Nekrassov, The Trojan Women (Penguin, Harmondsworth, 1969)
In Camera and Other Plays : The Respectable Prostitute, Lucifer and the Lord, In Camera (Penguin, London, 1989)

Politics

Anti-Semite and Jew trans. George J. Becker (New York, 1948)
Sartre on Cuba (New York, 1961)
The Communists and the Peace trans. Irene Clephane (New York, 1968; London, 1969)
The Spectre of Stalin (London, 1969)
Between Existentialism and Marxism trans. John Mathews (London and New York, 1974)

Literary theory and criticism

What is Literature? trans. Bernard Frechtman (London, 1950)

Biography

Baudelaire (New York, 1950)
Saint Genet: Actor and Martyr (New York, 1963)
The Family Idiot trans. Carol Cosman, 5 vols (Chicago and London, 1982)

Autobiography

Words trans. Irene Clephane (London, 1964; Penguin, Harmondsworth, 1967)
Life/Situations: Essays Written and Spoken trans. Paul Auster and Lydia Davis (New York, 1977)
Sartre by Himself (New York, 1978)
War Diaries trans. Quintin Hoare (London, 1984)
Adieux: A Farewell to Sartre by Simone de Beauvoir trans. Patrick O'Brian (London, 1984; Penguin, London, 1985) (Interviews)

Bibliographies

Michel Contat and Michel Rybalka (eds) *Les Ecrits de Sartre* (Paris, 1970)
Michel Contat and Michel Rybalka (eds) *The Writings of Sartre* trans. R. McCleary, 2 vols (Evanston, Illinois, 1974)
Francois and Claire Lapointe *Jean-Paul Sartre and His Critics: An International Bibliography* (1938–75)
Robert Wilcocks *Jean-Paul Sartre: A Bibliography of International Criticism* (Edmonton, Alberta, 1975)

Lightning Source UK Ltd.
Milton Keynes UK
UKHW021553050219
336757UK00016B/219/P

9 780415 213684